PROTEST AND POSSIBILITIES

CIVIL SOCIETY AND COALITIONS

FOR POLITICAL CHANGE IN MALAYSIA

Meredith L. Weiss

STANFORD UNIVERSITY PRESS

STANFORD, CALIFORNIA

2006

Stanford University Press
Stanford, California
© 2006 by the Board of Trustees
of the Leland Stanford Junior University

Printed in the United States of America
on acid-free, archival-quality paper

Library of Congress Cataloging-in-Publication Data

Weiss, Meredith L. (Meredith Leigh).
   Protest and possibilities : civil society and coalitions for political change in Malaysia / Meredith Leigh Weiss.
      p. cm. — (Contemporary issues in Asia and the Pacific)
   Includes bibliographical references and index.
   ISBN 0-8047-5294-X (cloth : alk. paper) —
   ISBN 0-8047-5295-8 (pbk. : alk. paper)
   1. Political culture—Malaysia. 2. Malaysia—Politics and government. 3. Civil society—Malaysia. 4. Political participation—Malaysia. 5. Social movements—Malaysia. 6. Indonesia—Politics and government. 7. Social movements—Indonesia. I. Title. II. Series.

JQ1062.A91W45 2006
306.2'09595—dc22   2005015758

Original Printing 2006
Last figure below indicates year of this printing:
15   14   13   12   11   10   09   08   07   06

Typeset at Stanford University Press in 10/12 Sabon

A Series from
Stanford University Press and the East-West Center

CONTEMPORARY ISSUES IN ASIA
AND THE PACIFIC

Muthiah Alagappa, Editor

A collaborative effort by Stanford University Press and the East-West Center, this series addresses contemporary issues of policy and scholarly concern in Asia and the Pacific. The series focuses on political, social, economic, cultural, demographic, environmental, and technological change and the problems related to such change. A select group of East-West Center senior fellows—representing the fields of political science, economic development, population, and environmental studies—serves as the advisory board for the series. The decision to publish is made by Stanford.

Preference is given to comparative or regional studies that are conceptual in orientation and emphasize underlying processes and to works on a single country that address issues in a comparative or regional context. Although concerned with policy-relevant issues and written to be accessible to a relatively broad audience, books in the series are scholarly in character. We are pleased to offer here the latest book in the series.

The East-West Center is an education and research organization established by the U.S. Congress in 1960 to strengthen relations and understanding among the peoples and nations of Asia, the Pacific, and the United States. The Center contributes to a peaceful, prosperous, and just Asia Pacific community by serving as a vigorous hub for cooperative research, education, and dialogue on critical issues of common concern to the Asia Pacific region and the United States. Funding for the Center comes from the U.S. government, with additional support provided by private agencies, individuals, foundations, and corporations and the governments of the region.

CONTENTS

Acknowledgments

I am indebted to an enormous number of individuals and organizations for their moral and material assistance over the *longue durée* of this project. First, I am grateful to DePaul University for its generous support, including a summer stipend and travel funds to allow me to update my research, and also to Yale University for a graduate fellowship as well as supplementary research funds. My research has also benefited immensely from a Foreign Language and Area Studies grant for language study, from a Social Science Research Council International Predissertation Fellowship, from a National Security Education Program Graduate International Fellowship, and from a Luce Fellowship for Southeast Asian Studies at the Australian National University as well as from a year's attachment at Singapore's Institute of Southeast Asian Studies.

All along, I have been enriched and at times bemused by the interest others have taken in me and my work, and by the tremendous assistance they have graciously proffered. Among the many people I have to thank are Muthiah Alagappa, Winifred Amaturo, David Cameron, Bill Case, Chew Wing Foong, Andrew Chin, John Funston, Terence Gomez, Jomo K. S., Beth Kelly, Ben Kerkvliet, Francis Loh, Kay Mansfield, Anil Netto, Mageswary Ramakrishnan, Saliha Hassan, Jim Scott, Fred von der Mehden, Sek Yong, and, of course, all the many amazing people I have come to know from hanging around Malaysian nongovernmental organizations (NGOs). It goes without saying that I thank my family (especially Dad and Susan) and all those friends who have not just put up with my antics over the course of this seemingly interminable endeavor but have also kept me sane and often even happy throughout. Finally, the mere passage of time has been highly propitious for me. I went to Malaysia expecting to study politics of the radical fringe—then, suddenly, the margins dashed onto center stage. I wish I could say I had planned it that way . . . .

To all the above and more, *terima kasih*!

.

Abbreviations and Shortened Organizational Names

ABIM	Angkatan Belia Islam Malaysia (Malaysian Islamic Youth Movement)
ABRI	Angkatan Bersenjata Republik Indonesia (Armed Forces of the Republic of Indonesia)
Adil	Pergerakan Keadilan Sosial (Movement for Social Justice)
Aliran	Aliran Kesedaran Negara (National Consciousness Movement)
AMCJA	All Malaya Council of Joint Action
APU	Angkatan Perpaduan Ummah (Muslim Unity Front)
AWAM	All Women's Action Society
AWAS	Angkatan Wanita Sedar (Conscious Women's Front)
BA	Barisan Alternatif (Alternative Front)
BN	Barisan Nasional (National Front)
CSA	civil society agent (organization or individual)
DAP	Democratic Action Party
DEMA	Gerakan Demokratik Belia dan Pelajar Malaysia (Malaysian Youth and Students Democratic Movement)
Gagasan	Gagasan Demokrasi Rakyat (Coalition for People's Democracy, est. 1998)
Gagasan	Gagasan Rakyat (People's Might, est. 1990)
Gerak	Majlis Gerakan Keadilan Rakyat Malaysia (Malaysian People's Movement for Justice)
Gerakan	Gerakan Rakyat Malaysia (Malaysian People's Movement Party)
Golkar	Golongan Karya (functional groups)

ICMI	Ikatan Cendekiawan Muslim Indonesia (Indonesian Association of Muslim Intellectuals)
IMP	Independence of Malaya Party
IPF	All Malaysia Indian Progressive Front
ISA	Internal Security Act (1968)
JIM	Pertubuhan Jamaah Islah Malaysia (Malaysian Islamic Reform Society)
Keadilan	Parti Keadilan Nasional (National Justice Party)
KMM	Kesatuan Melayu Muda (Young Malay Union)
KMS	Kesatuan Melayu Singapura (Singapore Malay Union)
LBH	Lembaga Bantuan Hukum (Legal Aid Institute)
LPM	Labour Party of Malaya
MCA	Malay(si)an Chinese Association
MCP	Malayan Communist Party
MIC	Malay(si)an Indian Congress
MPAJA	Malayan Peoples' Anti-Japanese Army
MPR	Majelis Permusyawaratan Rakyat (People's Consultative Assembly)
MSC	Malaysian Solidarity Convention
MTUC	Malaysian Trades Union Congress
NDP	National Development Policy
NEP	New Economic Policy
NU	Nahdlatul Ulama (Renaissance of Islamic Scholars)
ORMAS	Undang-undang Organisasi Kemasyarakatan (Social Organizations Law)
PAN	Partai Amanat Nasional (National Mandate Party)
PAP	People's Action Party
PAS	Parti Islam SeMalaysia (Pan-Malaysian Islamic Party, previously PMIP)
PBS	Parti Bersatu Sabah (Sabah United Party)
PD	Partai Demokrat (Democrat Party)
PDI	Partai Demokrasi Indonesia (Indonesian Democratic Party)
PDI-P	Partai Demokrasi Indonesia—Perjuangan (Indonesian Democratic Party—Struggle)
Pemantau	Pemantau Pilihanraya Rakyat Malaysia (Malaysian Citizens' Election Watch)

PKB	Partai Kebangkitan Baru (New Awakening Party)
PKMM	Partai Kebangsaan Melayu Malaya (Malay Nationalist Party)
PKS	Partai Keadilan Sejahtera (Justice and Prosperity Party)
PMFTU	Pan-Malayan Federation of Trade Unions
PMIP	Pan-Malayan Islamic Party (now PAS)
PPP	Partai Persatuan Pembangunan (United Development Party, Indonesia)
PPP	People's Progressive Party (Malaysia)
PRD	Partai Rakyat Demokrasi (People's Democratic Party)
PRM	Parti Rakyat Malaysia (Malaysian People's Party, formerly PSRM)
PSRM	Parti Sosialis Rakyat Malaysia (Malaysian Socialist People's Party, now PRM)
PUM	Persatuan Ulama Malaysia (Malaysian Islamic Scholars' Association)
PUTERA	Pusat Tenaga Rakyat (Center of People's Power)
S'46	Parti [Melayu] Semangat '46 ([Malay] Spirit of '46 Party, also Semangat)
SABERKAS	Syarikat Bekerjasama Am Saiburi (General Cooperative Society of Saiburi)
SNAP	Sarawak National Party
Suaram	Suara Rakyat Malaysia (Voice of the Malaysian People)
SUPP	Sarawak United People's Party
Suqiu	Malaysian Chinese Organisations' Election Appeals Committee
TNI	Tentara Nasional Indonesia
UDP	United Democratic Party
UMNO	United Malays National Organisation
UUCA	Universities and University Colleges Act (1971)
WCI	Women's Candidacy Initiative

PROTEST AND POSSIBILITIES

INTRODUCTION:
THE ROOTS OF REFORM

It was supposed to be Malaysia's moment of triumph. Despite the trauma of the ongoing Asian financial crisis and the enormous cost of preparations, Malaysia was doing a laudable job of hosting the 16th Commonwealth Games, a major international sporting event. Amid the festivities, on the afternoon of September 20, 1998, Queen Elizabeth II was slated to attend services at a church on one side of Dataran Merdeka (Independence Square) in downtown Kuala Lumpur. Meanwhile, a short walk away, at the Mesjid Negara (National Mosque), recently ousted Deputy Prime Minister Anwar Ibrahim was holding court before a crowd of tens of thousands of *Reformasi* (Reform) supporters. The mass then marched, chanting and singing, to Dataran Merdeka in what was probably the largest demonstration in Malaysia since independence in 1957. Anwar, who had been a student leader and Islamic activist before joining the ruling party in 1982, was arrested at his home later that evening. However, the protests continued into the night and over the next several days. They even reached the grounds of the brand-new Bukit Jalil Sports Complex, primary venue of the games. The ranks of sports photographers, when not covering matches, trained their lenses on protesters fleeing the acid-laced spray of water cannons while foreign journalists, in town for the games, rhapsodized about this latest display of Southeast Asian people power. Though it was Anwar who was beaten shortly after his arrest by the then-inspector general of police, it was Malaysian Prime Minister Mahathir Mohamad who sustained the worse black eye.

The Reformasi movement, launched by Anwar upon his dismissal from the government on September 2, 1998, brought to the fore long-simmering middle-class resentments as well as alternative notions about the nature and goals of governance. The movement spawned its own organizations, including nongovernmental organizations (NGOs) and a new political party as well as several coalitions. For the most part, though, the Reformasi movement drew in long-time activists and brought new urgency and life to perennial concerns of opposition parties as well as portions of civil society, making progress toward these reformist goals seem much more feasible than ever before. The movement was one in a succession of opposition attempts to forge for Malaysia a new political alternative, grounded in the ideology and principles of justice rather than in race and patronage. A communally oriented alliance has held power since independence, legitimating its increasingly firm control in terms of its commendable record of economic performance and maintenance of racial and religious harmony.[1] As the November 1999 elections demonstrated, the opposition's alternative failed to take hold completely—the incumbent government retained power overall. Nonetheless, the Reformasi movement represented a step toward change and serves to highlight the processes involved in protest and reform in an illiberal democracy (see Bell and Jayasuriya 1995) or in a regime that combines democratic institutions with authoritarian constraints.

Why the Reformasi movement developed as it did poses a puzzle. Solving that puzzle requires an exploration of the structural and historical context in which the movement developed, and it means taking seriously the creativity and agency of all sorts of opposition actors. While this discussion cannot hope to yield a deterministic model for political change, it does yield important insights into the how and why of contentious politics, as well as into political dynamics in contemporary Malaysia. In many ways, the Reformasi movement was atypical, from the perspective of studies of social movements. First, so broad a range of groups and individuals from civil society came together that civil society appeared almost to be a unitary actor. Second, the movement drew in opposition parties as well as NGOs and social activists. Those parties, too, set aside significant differences in favor of a common agenda and approach. Third, while street protests, proclamations, candlelight vigils, and so forth, kept things lively, the crux of the Reformasi movement quickly gravitated toward elections rather than more confrontational "informal" tactics. Fourth, the goals of the movement were both institutional and normative: participants aimed for systemic change of state institutions and policies but also for a shift in popular political culture.

Malaysia's experience suggests the importance of taking a broad, context-sensitive lens to contentious politics in order to understand how reformist efforts proceeded, and why. As conceptualized by McAdam, Tarrow, and Tilly (2001), contentious politics involves the making of all sorts of claims on the part of agents of government, members of the polity with routine access to government, challengers lacking such access, politically unorganized subjects, and outside political actors (for instance, other governments). Both contained and transgressive contention consists of "episodic, public collective interaction among makers of claims and their objects," and in both forms, at least one government is directly involved, and the interests of at least one of the claimants would be affected if the claims were realized. Contention is *contained* when "all parties are previously established actors employing well established means of claim making." It is *transgressive* when "at least some parties to the conflict are newly self-identified political actors and/or . . . at least some parties employ innovative collective action" (McAdam, Tarrow, and Tilly 2001: 7–8). At the conjuncture of these two forms of contention is what I term *coalitional capital*, a concept related to social capital, but at the organizational rather than the individual level.

Social capital is the store of interpersonal trust and faith in collective action garnered through associational activity. Collective action both augments and is encouraged by social capital. Abstract as it is, social capital is hard to measure, especially when there are risks to expressing it. The commonly used metric of vibrancy of associational life may be particularly misleading in such environments. The cost-benefit calculus of whether to get involved differs greatly across cases, but that is not to say that citizens in a more repressive setting are any less willing and eager to participate than those who risk much less by speaking out.[2] Even when politicized portions of civil society are relatively weak, however, or when citizens are deterred from activism, the presence of some degree of associational activity makes available the idea of participation, including participation through informal politics. Spurred by some catalyst that makes popular grievances seem especially pressing or the chances for redress unusually high, previously dormant stores of social capital may be relatively easily activated and mobilized. The structural manifestation of this social capital is in organizations that make efficient and effective use of institutional and noninstitutional resources.

Coalitional capital, by contrast, facilitates collaboration across groups. If social capital is related to trust and expectations of reciprocity among individuals, coalitional capital captures the same dimensions at the organizational level. Coalitional capital develops out of the experience of societal organizations' working over time in the same arena and interacting so that the reputations of various organizations are known, groups have some sense of the strategic and ideological orientations of their counterparts, and coordination of efforts is readily conceivable when political opportunity structures are favorable for change. Whereas individuals join groups that represent their interests, coalitional capital may encourage those groups to subordinate their particularistic interests to a broader agenda shared among a range of groups.

Distinguishing between these two concepts helps elucidate how it is that the diversity and internal conflicts of civil society may become manageable as otherwise atomized groups forge a conception of shared goals, in much the same way that individuals in a group both act upon and further elaborate those aspects of their identity they have in common with other group members. In short, social capital bonds individuals; coalitional capital bridges collectivities.

Placed in historical context, recent developments in Malaysia illustrate the activation of latent stores of social and coalitional capital, with institutions developing and coalescing as necessary to further political change. Gradual and even implicit consciousness raising by civil society agents (CSAs)[3] over the long term, which encourages individual citizens to adopt new political priorities or norms, is punctuated by catalysts that galvanize more citizens to reassess prevailing risks and opportunities. CSAs may help convince citizens (for instance, by means of "alternative" media) that the moment seems propitious for change and may help them adjust their cognitive frames and strategies to optimize their influence. At the same time, other oppositional actors, including those in political parties, see the same window of opportunity as well and modify their own frames and strategies accordingly. In sum, CSAs help convince voters and elites that change is necessary and possible, and they suggest alternatives. Opposition parties organize to institutionalize an order in line with these recommendations, an order to be pursued through elections. Finally, activists and organizations from civil and political society pursue a range of strategies both to convince voters to act in accordance with the new norms being promoted and to persuade them that reform really is forthcoming.

The strategies by which CSAs in particular pursue reform are significantly conditioned by the nature of the regime. The context of an illiberal democracy offers an incentive to pursue reform via contained contention—most notably elections—rather than just by transgressive means, even if the latter are not altogether neglected. Where contained contention is not likely to be productive—for instance, in Indonesia, where the incumbent electoral authoritarian regime left very little space for the articulation of competing claims within formal political processes—transgressive contention may seem the only real route to systemic change. These concepts and processes will be explored in depth in chapters to come, and the concrete details of the long-term evolution of reformism in Malaysia (counterpoised against a very different trajectory in Indonesia) will illuminate the underlying dynamics at work. This case study, in turn, suggests a more broadly applicable framework of mobilizing for reform in illiberal polities.

Aims of the Book

This study examines the evolution of a multiethnic coalition for political protest and reform in Malaysia, with particular attention to contributions from CSAs. Malaysia is an illiberal democracy, as described in more detail below. The government is not hegemonic; it leaves at least some space for both CSAs and opposition parties to organize, but it retains a degree of coercive power. Since there is a real chance of political change through contained contention, and since such change may be less destabilizing or likely to be suppressed than change pursued through less institutionalized means, activists have an incentive to pursue reform through lobbying, elections, and the like, rather than just through extra-institutional forms of collective action.

Malaysia's illiberal democracy has proved essentially stable since independence, though control has grown increasingly centralized in the hands of the executive, especially since the 1980s. The departing British colonists ceded power to a tripartite coalition of race-based parties in 1957; that initial coalition, or an expanded version of it, has remained in power ever since. The endurance of the government is not due just to manipulation and coercion, though such factors are not absent. The opposition usually wins 40 to 45 percent of the popular vote in general elections, and often not just "a toehold in parliament" but also control over one or two states' legislatures (Case 2001: 50). Most Malaysians understand and are committed to at least a limited version of democracy (Welsh 1996) and see the ruling coalition both as competent in maintaining racial and religious harmony in addition to economic growth and patronage and as obliged by the certainty of elections to heed its constituents' interests (Crouch 1993). Malaysian political institutions perpetuate "mass complacency," usually forestalling pressure for political change (Case 2001: 47). Furthermore, over time, the development of the regime has nurtured persistent sources of conflict among opposition parties. These sources include communal divisions, even if the parties eschew such principles; ideological divisions, especially regarding Islam and socialism; and particular personalities, especially since many smaller opposition parties have splintered off from larger ones (Barraclough 1985a: 36).

History suggests that systemic reform in Malaysia is highly unlikely to come through political parties and electoral contestation alone, as might be possible were political competition more free. Also, especially since the ruling coalition has co-opted so many challengers over the years, no single party could alone hope to unseat the incumbent government. Other sorts of organizations have greater flexibility and room for ideological and strategic maneuvering than do parties, so informal and formal segments of the opposition complement each other. Hence a coalition for reform benefits from the inclusion, as formal or informal partners, of NGOs, trade unions, public intellectuals, or other groups or activists alongside political parties. It may be that not all these sectors are closely interlinked, but all must be able to locate some common denominator around which to frame their cooperation. CSAs generate ideas and strategies, give credibility to a reformist coalition, draw in additional supporters, help with publicity and consciousness raising, and monitor parties and elections, even if formal politics is not their primary or usual focus. In the process, CSAs help bridge gaps or fortify links between political parties' leaders, members, and perspectives, both by demonstration and by facilitation of changes in popular political attitudes or priorities. The processes of negotiating, building trust, and setting rules among diverse elements of the opposition are helped by the participation of the sort of politically engaged, pro-democracy, ideologically noncommunal CSAs that have been evolving in Malaysia, especially since the 1980s. How these processes unfold is suggestive of important angles and insights that can more broadly inform the analysis of contentious politics.

Overall, this project has four primary analytical aims. First, the work examines the significance of regime type in shaping citizens' engagement. A history of limitations placed by an authoritative state on political parties or social organizations, or of incentives given to play by the rules, goes a long way toward explaining why reformists choose the strategies they do from among a broad repertoire of contained and transgressive options. Second, the study introduces and examines the concept of coalitional capital. While social capital is a necessary ingredient of collective action, coalitional capital tells us more about how groups work together to bridge social cleavages and rally broad-based support for systemic change. Considering both these levels allows the development of a nuanced, process-driven framework of short-term and long-term cultural and institutional change. Third, the cases considered here demonstrate how variations in political opportunity structures—or "collective attribution of threat and opportunity," in McAdam, Tarrow, and Tilly's terms (2001: 95)—yield shifts in reformers' rational calculations about the chances for success as well as in their choices about framing and strategies. Fourth, the study affirms that CSAs and political parties play coordinating and complementary roles in political change processes. Given their different goals and time horizons, CSAs and parties have different comparative advantages in promoting and institutionalizing reform.

Empirically, the project sets out to explore whether and how Malaysian political culture has changed in recent years, what the respective roles of CSAs and political parties are in advancing political (especially noncommunal) alternatives, and how the illiberal democratic regime has affected the structure of its opposition. Comparative reference to Indonesia demonstrates the role of coalitional capital and the importance of political history and regime type in determining how protest proceeds. These questions are significant to the study of Malaysian politics and of civil society more generally. For one thing, overcoming communalism is among the stated objectives of virtually all Malaysian governmental and opposition parties. Exploring and weighing alternative ways to achieve this goal is clearly warranted. For another, most theoretical treatments of civil society are premised on a liberal democratic framework. Even the growing literature on NGOs, and on democratization in the postauthoritarian societies of Latin America, Africa, and central and eastern Europe, presents a very different institutional environment from that of most of Southeast Asia. Finally, in an apparent era of reformist movements, careful examination of how and when these movements arise, of their preconditions, limitations, and departures from the past, and of their likely trajectories or predilections toward or for particular strategies could be enormously revealing and could carry some degree of predictive value.

Not only does this study thus add to the corpus of empirical knowledge about events and trends in Malaysia, it also contributes to a more theoretical conceptualization of how the likelihood of political reform is affected both by institutional development over time within civil society and political society and by an increased political role for CSAs. It is important to note, however, that the focus here is far more on the dynamics than on the outcomes of contention, and more on how participants and mechanisms concatenate than on whether they succeed in their objectives.

Methods, Framework, and Terminology

This work draws on a range of political, historical, and sociological literature. It also combines a range of primarily qualitative approaches, including use of interviews, participant observation, and published and unpublished (including oral) texts. Quantitative resources such as survey data are used when possible, but reliable data are scarce. Contemporary and prior political norms, priorities, and strategies are traced through coalition platforms, press statements, election results, and the like. Complementing the Malaysian case study is a more narrowly focused examination of Indonesia that highlights the importance of regime type to understanding the nature of contention and emphasizes (by its absence) the role of coalitional capital and how it differs from social capital. Any project of this sort is complicated by problems of defining and measuring key concepts, such as norms and civic or political culture, together with the dearth in Malaysia of reliable public opinion surveys to help gauge what people are and were thinking. However, these are not insurmountable hurdles: norms can be extrapolated from behavior, for instance, and surveys of political attitudes must in any case be taken with a healthy dose of skepticism.

It is worth explaining briefly at the outset how this study treats the concept of *civil society* (to be described more fully in the next chapter). Valuable empirical and analytical work is apt, unfortunately, to be downgraded or misconstrued either because its use of such terms as *civil society* and *social movements* does not conform to standard Western practice or because its author tries too hard to make findings fit these definitions. By now it is trite to point out that when we look for civil society in a non-Western state, we are looking for a realm premised on a liberal democratic framework and hence are unlikely to find something that meets all the quibbling conditions of prevailing definitions, particularly in terms of identities activated (ascriptive or voluntaristic) and degree of autonomy from the state. At the same time, if we see a sphere of activity between state and family in which individuals form associations and networks to advocate for certain politically oriented goals—a sphere that perhaps even self-consciously refers to itself as a civil society—then surely we can accept that sphere as a "legitimate" civil society. In other words, in this study I use the terms of the literature as reference points rather than as regulations, and I hope by doing so to develop a more nuanced, context-sensitive vision of what these terms can mean in different places and at different times.

In a stable illiberal democracy, CSAs hobble themselves if they shun involvement in or links with political society. Even though the gamut of social movement organizations is, theoretically, supposed to remain independent and not seek power within the state, those sorts of ideals are less practical outside liberal democracies, especially when there is little or no available middle ground for regularized access and influence in the form of American-style professional lobbies. Interestingly, though, scholarly literature on proper spheres for NGOs and political parties has fostered doubts among some Malaysian organizations and activists. They know that their NGOs are not considered by most academics to be "nongovernmental" if they ally themselves with political parties, but they also know that their struggle is likely to be fruitless and ignored if they do not forge bonds at least with opposition parties. At the same time, the government throws those rather academic definitions back at social activists, declaring that those who wish to influence politics ought to do so through political parties (so they can be trounced, presumably, in elections that are less than fair), not civil society organizations (see Gurmit 1984).

While a broad definition of the term *civil society* is thus useful in capturing the dynamics and diversity of activism in an illiberal democracy, the distinction between civil society and political society still matters. Here, I define a civil society as a realm rather than as a specific set of actors. Malaysian civil society is populated by those groups and individuals who, regardless of their perspectives or organizational bases, debate, evaluate, and challenge or support official discourses, interpretations, structures, or policies. By contrast, Stepan (1988: 4) defines the term *political society* (referring specifically to a "democratizing setting") as "that arena in which the polity specifically arranges itself for political contestation to gain control over public power and the state apparatus"; he explains, "At best, civil society can destroy an authoritarian regime," but actual democratization requires the involvement of political society as well.

What is the shape, then, of civil society in Malaysia? First, visible, coherent associations are only one part of what comprises this realm. Other key components of civil society include networks of public intellectuals or floating activists, trade unions, student groups, and even perennially out-of-power opposition political parties, which tend between elections to function more like NGOs than like parties (for example, by focusing on service delivery and issue advocacy, but without benefit of access to state resources). All these groups and individuals may be referred to as *civil society agents*. Still, it may be helpful to separate opposition parties out from this category, since ultimately their end goals are different from those of groups in civil society, even if most of their means of achieving their objectives and interim aims are the same. Second, while Putnam (1993) excludes Catholic organizations from among the producers of social capital, and Gellner (1994) posits that civil society is qualitatively different from what is found in transnationally oriented Islamic societies, all sorts of groups and perspectives are to be found in Malaysian civil society. To exclude Islamic or other religious groups from a study of civil society and social capital generation in Malaysia would be to seriously distort the picture, particularly when it comes to political activism among the Malay majority. Third, as this diversity suggests, the collective noun *civil society* implies a uniformity of purpose and perspective as well as unflinching civility, both of which are rarely if ever found in the domain in any country. Not all actors and organizations in Malaysian civil society are able even to get along amicably, let alone cooperate closely.

Other terms should be understood in the same way. When this study refers to *nongovernmental organizations* or *social movements*, it refers to groups that would probably label themselves as such, even though they might not be so labeled by others. The average Malaysian NGO, for instance, is small, with meager grassroots links at best, and generally enjoys a rather close working relationship with at least selected (usually opposition) parties or politicians. Such a group hardly fits the official definition of an NGO. Similarly, a network of organizations and activists struggling toward a particular set of goals, whether these goals are related to the environment, to gender, to human rights, or to some other realm, is regarded in Malaysia as a social movement. It may seem retrograde or irresponsible so cavalierly to set aside our carefully crafted official definitions. Doing so, however, places attention on the processes involved, not on the terms used to define them, and contributes, in the end, to a better idea of what these terms really represent outside the liberal democracies in which they were coined. All the same, as will become clear in chapter 2, this work owes much to the ever-growing literature on democracy, civil society, and related institutions and phenomena.

Theoretical Implications

Too often, empirically rich studies are agnostic with regard to theory. At the same time, more theoretically inclined studies tend toward mechanistic accounts, coding of events, or ideologically constrained models that preclude or ignore the very significant intersection and overlap of formal and informal politics. Empirically driven but theory-enhancing studies of civil society hence crave elaboration. The present study thus introduces new data, a new approach, and new analysis.

The chapters to come treat political reform as both a normative and an institutional process. Especially in an illiberal democracy, the government maintains control not just by coercion and other material means but also by approximating ideological hegemony as closely as possible so that alternatives appear less compelling. Without shifts in popular political culture, reformists may be unable to garner and maintain sufficient support for the changes they hope to impose. The normative shifts pursued by reformers in Malaysia have been toward curtailing racialized politics in favor of more class-oriented, Islamist, or liberal democratic perspectives; toward emphasizing moral rather than economic payoffs, whether civil liberties, good governance, or Islam; and toward promoting more consistent political participation. It is quite difficult to assess what individual voters' norms are, and whether and how they might have changed. Nevertheless, a fairly good idea of these norms and changes can be gained from discussions over the Internet; editorials and essays;

speeches; interviews; the platforms or other documents of political parties, NGOs, and coalitions of groups; and the few surveys and other studies that have been done, especially when these sources are supplemented by conventional wisdom, rumor, and the ever-important "coffee-shop talk."[4]

Moreover, the workings of CSAs do not occur in some sort of black box. There are several specific steps through which CSAs promote changes in political norms and culture.[5] Social cleavages—in Malaysia, these are primarily racial and religious differences—play themselves out differently in NGOs and in parties, since the focus in NGOs is on advocating for issues and not on divvying up positions of power. Therefore, as a first step, and given this distinction, compromise solutions may be explored among CSAs to resolve collective action problems that might otherwise stymie coordinated attempts at reform. A history of collaborative campaigns and informal networking helps in this process and in cementing trust. As a second step, CSAs can reinforce the reputation of a reformist coalition and its platform by contributing respected, comparatively selfless leaders to political society, by offering advisors to make sure electoral initiatives stay on track and amicable, by providing grassroots support for mobilization, civic education, and campaigning, and by endorsing a coalition or particular candidates as worthwhile. As a third step, CSAs can enforce reciprocity, to ensure that voters and parties keep their promises to one another. Some sort of monitoring is crucial in order to make sure that if a new coalition comes to power, it will actually implement the platform on which it ran. Insofar as CSAs secure a role for themselves in the coalition, they may have more clout in holding a reformist government to its promises. As a fourth step in promoting change, CSAs can facilitate the institutionalization of new political norms by providing examples of them—for instance, by being noncommunal in membership and focus, if that is what they are advocating.

These factors imply a set of ideal-typical prerequisites that must be fulfilled in order for CSAs to be optimally effective at affecting norms and adherence to norms. CSAs must themselves be credible in living up to the new norms they tout. It helps, too, if CSAs are active before elections, both with election-oriented activities and with other sorts of endeavors, but not so involved in electoral politics that they jeopardize their claim to being disinterested advocates for the public good. CSAs need to have at least some degree of grassroots linkages or media access, or else they will be ill equipped to do more than "preach to the converted." In the same vein, if CSAs have no track record on which to be judged, they may not be taken seriously or trusted by the general populace. It is important to note that even if some activists join political parties or other formal political institutions, CSAs must not lose sight of their own monitoring function and independence. A corollary is that CSAs, just like political parties, cannot be so reliant on a few key leaders as to be hobbled without them.

While parties and NGOs alike may face difficulties in organizing, activists may elect to engage through either sort of body or through both. Which mode they select is based on ideology as well as on strategy. The goals of CSAs relate to issues, whereas the aim of parties is winning elections. Therefore, their methods and definitions of success differ. CSAs may be willing to innovate in order to bring together all who support a given issue, whereas parties are prone to be more risk-averse and to focus more on their specific constituencies unless circumstances compel them to cooperate (see Lumumba-Kasongo 1995: 409). Decisions about strategy also rely on rational calculations: the government may react less harshly to some forms of dissent than to others. In Malaysia, for instance, the regime has stayed as stable as it has through "the practiced calibration of electoral institutions, allowing heightened contestation to take place in one arena, but then containing it in another" (Case 2001: 47). As a result, activists may determine that their best course of action is to engage through organizations in either civil society or political society, and by means of either contained or transgressive forms of contention.

Scope and Background

Chapters 3 through 7 explore in depth, on the basis of a primary case study of Malaysia and a secondary examination of Indonesia, how reform processes play out over time. The story begins at the margins of Malaysian history. It is hardly surprising that, just as the history of Singapore is often presumed to be the history of Lee Kuan Yew, the history of Malaysia is often construed as that of the ruling coalition and its leaders, not least among them Mahathir Mohamad, prime minister from 1981 to 2003. While voices other than theirs have generally been either muted (in view of repression and perhaps apathy) or too cacophonous to present a coherent refrain, those other voices have been there nevertheless and merit attention. Malaysian political development has also been punctuated by a sequence of social movements, opposition party efforts, and attempts at fortifying a noncommunal pattern of political organization, all of which disrupt the official narrative of harmonious consociationalism[6] and benign paternalism.

Ethnicity represents the most prominent and pervasive line of cleavage in Malaysian politics, economics, and society. Of Malaysia's 23 million residents, 65 percent are *bumiputera* ("princes/sons of the soil," or

Malays and smaller indigenous groups), 26 percent are Chinese, and 8 percent are Indian. Racial categories largely mirror and reinforce religious divisions, especially the lines between Muslims and non-Muslims, since Malays are legally required to be Muslim. It is only recently that the correspondence between ethnicity and occupation, which correlates at least loosely with class, has eroded. Malay dominance is constitutionally guaranteed, its justification drawing more on claims to indigeneity than on numerical superiority. This dominance translates not only into political power and preferential economic policies but also into a national character based on Malay culture, religion, and language.

Malaysia's parliamentary order and civil society reflect this ethnicized system. Since independence, the country has been led by a quasi-consociational coalition of race-based parties. Indeed, even though opposition parties in particular stress nonethnic issues, most Malaysian political parties are, by design or default, communal. That is, either they represent the interests of a particular ethnic community (or some subset of one), whether or not membership is restricted to that group, or they focus on nonracialized issues but have trouble attracting supporters of more than one race. Moreover, since the first real flowering of associational life in Malaya, around the 1920s, the bulk of all other sociopolitical groups have likewise been communal in nature. There may be nothing inherently wrong with so racialized an order, and in fact Malaysia has suffered much less violent ethnic unrest than have many other plural societies. Regardless, this system is contrary to what both the government and its opponents claim to want in the long term. Government policies since independence have aimed at integration, particularly through language and education policies, as well as at affirmative action, in order to erase the identification of race with occupation or class. At the same time, historical and recent opposition efforts have highlighted the need for members of all communities to recognize their common interests and work together if systemic change is to be an option.

Key societal groups started to coalesce in political parties as Malaya edged toward independence after the Second World War. Most parties that sought to center on noncommunal issues were and are repressed to at least some extent. Most, although not all, of these initiatives have found support mainly among non-Malays. The end result is that a greater proportion of Malay interests than non-Malay interests has been accommodated by reasonably potent (and legal) political parties. Moreover, a process of ethnic elites' bargaining, on behalf of their communities, in a racialized contest for state largesse has been cemented by the installation, upon independence, of the tripartite Alliance coalition (later reconstituted as the Barisan Nasional, that is, the National Front, or BN), by the suppression of class-based political initiatives, and by the consistent failure of alternative coalitions. This order has fostered the persistent predominance of race-based rather than multicommunal parties and coalitions.

Many of the constituencies or interests excluded from the array of legal political parties (and especially from the governing coalition) were and remain labor-oriented. A substantial proportion of Islamists, too, have been marginalized politically, whether they have chosen to join Islamic parties or to act from outside formal politics. Hence, since independence, Malaysia's two key opposition constituencies, both party-based and otherwise, have represented the far left and the far (religious) right, although the character and specific programs of each constituency have changed over the years. Given how little these groups seem to have in common, aside from the fact of their marginalization, building a coalition with enough clout to unseat the incumbent government has remained problematic for over four decades.

Open advocacy of communalism has diminished over the years, with even parties in the BN now more likely to tout "development" and "harmony" than the rights of their respective racial groups. At the same time, the divide between Muslims and non-Muslims has to some extent supplanted race as the political cleavage of record, though the categories "Muslim" and "Malay" are largely coterminous. For instance, when opposition parties attempted to overcome their legacy of polarization in order to forge an electoral pact in 1990, it was religion that stymied their efforts as the secular, Chinese-based Democratic Action Party (DAP) could not cooperate with the Parti Islam SeMalaysia (the Pan-Malaysian Islamic Party, or PAS). However, toward the end of the decade, as CSAs developed and extended their influence and networks, and as the government found its legitimacy in crisis, the climate for coalition building changed.

By the late 1990s, a range of both religious and secular NGOs had been working singly or jointly for some time. While most of the politicized, pro-democracy NGOs in Malaysia are communal in character, to at least some extent (mostly because of persistent linguistic, residential, and occupational divisions that coincide with racial categories), few if any are so in principle. Islamic organizations are the principal outlet for Malays, while issue-oriented groups focusing on human rights, gender, housing rights, and other concerns tend to attract more non-Malays, though there are exceptions. Most of these secular advocacy groups are quite new. NGOs per se have only really developed in Malaysia since the 1970s, with most growth only since the mid-1980s.

Both Islamic and secular NGOs have generally eschewed formal political involvement (in the sense of nominating office bearers for legislative office, for instance), yet many are highly politically involved or have strong links with political parties. While new secular advocacy organizations are generally not overtly class-oriented, they are for the most part sympathetic to social democratic or socialist-inclined appeals, facilitating cooperation with leftist parties. For their part, mass Islamist organizations have a long history of personal and institutional ties with both Malay and Islamic parties in the government and the opposition. Through the late 1990s, PAS and the Islamic groups affiliated with it reframed their appeals, seeing an opportunity to find allies and cement more broad-based support against the BN. They played down their Malayness and stressed instead a nonracialized, Islamic concept of justice. That stance opened up common ground with non-Islamic NGOs and parties.

Starting in mid-1997, the "Asian flu"—a stunning economic crisis—swept southeast Asia. Malaysia was not immune. The currency, employment, and growth rates plunged. Although the country was less hard-hit than some others in the region (Indonesia, for instance), the crisis severely undercut popular confidence in the government's economic programs and heightened awareness of corruption and "money politics" in the BN. Meanwhile, the same economic crisis had helped to catalyze a massive protest movement in Indonesia, which ultimately toppled Soeharto and demonstrated anew the capacities of "people power." Other coincidental difficulties, from a stifling bout of air pollution to a mysterious swine-borne disease, further stimulated a popular sense of grievance against the government.

Then, in September 1998, United Malays National Organisation (UMNO) Deputy Prime Minster Anwar Ibrahim was ignominiously dismissed from the government and the party and was made to stand trial for alleged sodomy and corruption. His ouster proved a turning point in making the mass public—especially the Malay middle class—perceive a fortuitous change in political opportunities. Popular among many social activists for his at least rhetorical support of Islam and social justice, Anwar launched the massive Reformasi movement, which persisted after he was confined to prison. Islamic and secular NGOs alike, along with trade union activists, students, public intellectuals, and opposition party leaders, formed several coalitions of CSAs and parties over the course of the Reformasi movement. Central to all were questions of good governance, civil liberties, and the perceived predations of the government. All capitalized, too, on intense popular anger over Anwar's treatment: among other things, he was beaten in custody, given a trial of dubious fairness and a harshly punitive sentence, and denied permission to travel overseas for spinal surgery. The theme of *keadilan* (justice) provided a credible basis and message on which Islamic and secular organizations, including CSAs as well as PAS, the DAP, and the newly formed Parti Keadilan Nasional (the National Justice Party, or Keadilan), could cooperate and mobilize the broader public. Perceiving an opportunity for systemic change, the participants in the Reformasi movement thus altered their collective action frames to capture as broad a constituency as possible.

In the same vein, CSAs, having brought critical common issues to the fore over years of advocacy work, changed their strategies to be more effective in capitalizing on political opportunities once elections seemed imminent. CSAs active in Reformasi directed their energies to electoral politics, helping to formulate, reinforce, publicize, and lend credence to the joint message of usually polarized opposition parties. The focus and structure of issue-oriented coalitions in civil society presented a model for cross-party cooperation; moreover, a number of Reformasi activists ran for office, whether or not they were "politicians" in the usual sense. The spate of NGO or "social issue" candidates, representing all three main ethnic groups, helped keep the debate centered on issues, not race or religion, and reasserted to voters the opposition's commitment to these substantive concerns.

The opposition's campaign in 1999 was cast as the logical extension of a social movement rather than "politics as usual." United in the Barisan Alternatif (the Alternative Front, or BA), the opposition made a concerted effort to run an idealistic, nonethnicized campaign. In line with this approach, activists from civil society were deemed equally competent to stand for office (though most joined a party first, if only for convenience in campaigning), and actual party affiliation was downplayed, albeit perhaps more in rhetoric than in reality for most candidates. The parties involved (especially PAS and the DAP) came as far as they did in their negotiations, and in communicating their agreement to the general public, largely by dint of the active cooperation of CSAs, including alternative media.

A large factor in the relative success of the BA in cohering and having a real impact at the polls was that the coalition was not a few parties struggling to suppress their differences in pursuit of a shared foe but was instead rooted in, supported by, and monitored by a wide range of CSAs and could call upon a proactive, normative agenda that evoked a sequence of reform initiatives from the past. Previous coalition-building initiatives from the 1950s through the 1990s had left activists not only with a repertoire of contained and transgressive strategies of contention but also with coalitional capital: the groups involved were familiar with each others' ideologies and goals, had established means of communicating, and had built up at least some degree of mutual trust and expectations of reciprocity at the organizational level.

Communalism and developmentalism have not been expunged as key political priorities. Still, there has been a shift toward these discourses' sharing political space with alternative priorities of good governance, civil liberties, and socioeconomic justice. Individual voters have been urged, through issue-advocacy campaigns and more direct messages, to vote along new lines—in other words, to accept and internalize these new political priorities or norms. These voters have also been urged to reconceptualize political participation more broadly: to understand "democracy" not solely in procedural terms, as voting once every five years, but as staying legitimately and continuously engaged and critical.

Many or most of those who voted for the BA in 1999 might have done so just as a vote against Mahathir or in support of Islam and Anwar rather than as a vote for Keadilan. The fact that the BN fared so much better in the 2004 general elections, after Mahathir had stepped down as prime minister, indicates that the incumbent coalition remains both powerful and popular. Still, that "justice" discourse clearly had at least some sway over voters, especially in 1999, and has pressured UMNO to cultivate a reformist image itself. Also, a preference for multiracialism has clearly already taken root, to some extent, even within government rhetoric, and even if the idea of more equitable development has been less well accepted among those not on the receiving end of proposed redistributive policies. The persistent salience of the *keadilan* theme and its attendant foci seem assured if for no other reason than that these are among the only bridges to unite PAS with the secular left-wing opposition, and to unite all these parties with CSAs' resources and experience in order to challenge the government as effectively as possible.

Caveats

These processes all sound rather inevitable and irreversible. It is worth asking why, if civil society is so potent and promotes such lofty ideals of multiracialism and social justice, it has failed to get the general public to internalize these ideals more fully. Perhaps most important, racial and religious fears are still very significant, though the latter have largely upstaged the former. Thus the BN warns Chinese—non-Muslims—not against supporting Malays but against supporting strident Muslims. CSAs have yet to convince most voters that PAS and its adherents will not press for an Islamic state—not least because it was never absolutely clear that PAS would not in fact do so.[7] Furthermore, although they seem to be growing a bit more bold, secular NGOs have generally been very tentative when it comes to religious issues, with non-Malay/Muslim NGOs hesitant to intervene in anything related to Islam. As a result, these NGOs promote multiracial perspectives but have had rather little to say about multireligious issues, particularly in recent years.

Old-style communalism remains salient, too, aside from its transmutation into religious divisions, primarily because of economic incentives that favor those particular identities. Government policies privilege Malays and their fellow *bumiputera* and make ethnic identity the center of a whole system of economic, social, and political rewards. Contributing to this persistent vertical segmentation are language differences (and hence the media accessible to members of various communities), an ingrained tendency to trust those of one's own group more than others, racially segregated settlement patterns, and a host of other factors. Even the BA parties were not immune in 1999: the leadership of Keadilan, for instance, included only a token sprinkling of non-Malays, and its electoral appeals were sometimes communally tinged. Indeed, as the BN often warns, Malaysia's ethnic balance could break down over time: the country is hardly immune to the centrifugal tendencies endemic to plural societies (for instance, Bosnia and Indonesia). In 1999, opposition actors saw multiethnic cooperation as the most promising avenue for achieving the sort of polity they wanted. If political culture evolves in a different direction, Malaysians' ideas about race and communalism may change again, too. In fact, the same trajectory of coalition building that was followed in the 1990s, in pursuit of multiethnic cooperation, could conceivably be pursued in the future for more particularistic ends, especially given how personalistic the process was, even in 1999. Regardless, the evolution of opposition politics and the progress of the Reformasi movement in Malaysia suggest that this two-level process of reform (in civil society and political society, over both the short and the long term) is most likely to bring both cultural and institutional change—and it is progress toward reform, not the fact of whether reformers actually achieve their goals, that is analytically relevant here.

Shifting our gaze to Indonesia clarifies what this framework can and cannot explain. This comparison is particularly revealing for exploring the importance of coalitional capital in facilitating coordinated, proactive mobilization. Three decades of authoritarian rule had left Indonesian opposition parties debilitated and CSAs mutually wary. The collective realization that threats of repression were comparatively low (given factional splits in the military), while the opportunity for change was high on account of Soeharto's unprecedented weakness in 1998, led CSAs and opposition parties in Indonesia, as in Malaysia, to rework their collective action frames and strategies in pursuit of systemic reform. That mass upsurge brought down the authoritarian order but did so before all involved had established any sort of proactive consensus. While democratization is gradually proceeding, the CSAs most critical at the transgressive stage were largely barred from influence at later stages. As in Malaysia, then, CSAs and political parties alike enjoyed certain advantages and attempted to collaborate in Indonesia's Reformasi movement, but historical and contextual factors rendered those processes significantly different in each country.

Summary of Conclusions

I conclude that CSAs, as one part of the political opposition, broadly defined, help to bridge the gap between disparate political actors by promoting changes in political culture both before and during efforts at further institutional reform. In a political system in which the governing coalition co-opts virtually all but polarized actors and leaves relatively little space for dissent, inventive coalition-building arrangements, premised on prior and ongoing cultural shifts and galvanized by periodic catalysts from within or outside the system, make reform possible. The key contributions of CSAs lie in their helping to change individuals' political norms, opening the range of available strategies to include both institutional and noninstitutional approaches, mobilizing the public to see and act upon changing political opportunities, and helping to validate reformist candidates and parties. The Reformasi movement in Malaysia was different from past movements, not so much because of its noncommunal, *keadilan* frame—since this echoed a sequence of past reform initiatives—as because of the cluster of relatively new (either secular or religious) pro-democracy, ideologically noncommunal organizations that has come to populate Malaysian civil society.

In other words, CSAs may not serve just a minor policy-reform or lobbying function but may actually have an impact on the nature, aims, and shape of the regime as a whole. Therefore, shifts in the shape or orientation of structures within civil society can facilitate political reform, especially given changes in prevailing political opportunities to spark mobilization. This is not to say that *only* CSAs are at work, or that this process is inevitable. Indeed, many of the processes that are probably crucial to the development of politicized, reform-oriented CSAs—such as urbanization, more widespread access to higher education, and the spread of the Internet and other media—no doubt have an independent effect on society that *also* encourages the same normative and strategic trends. Nonetheless, one might then see groups within civil society as the institutional manifestation of, or means of channeling, some of these rather amorphous forces. As these groups persist, they generate coalitional capital, which leaves both CSAs and parties better able to coordinate frames and strategies for taking advantage of moments of weakness within the usually strong government, and to press for reform. Hence the two-track process described here, of long-term cultural shifts punctuated by periods of institutional innovation, proceeds, however gradually, toward the ultimate aim of political change.

Chapter Overview

This study begins in chapter 2 with an introduction to the concepts and theories that frame the work. I describe and evaluate the dominant debates engaged through the study and preview the framework to be filled out by subsequent chapters. Several of the terms central to this study are highly contested. I explain how and why I define and employ those concepts, and how Malaysia's state and civil society correspond or clash with dominant formulations. Chapter 2 makes a case for paying attention to regime type rather than assuming easy comparability of cases; for avoiding essentializing preconceptions about Islamic (or other) societies; and for considering various sorts of political reform as important and valid. In particular, the Malaysian case suggests ways in which CSAs and coalitional capital may help bridge social cleavages that might otherwise cripple opposition coalition-building efforts. The Malaysian case also illustrates the complementarities of CSAs and political parties where both are necessary to reform but are also constrained by a hostile and powerful government.

Once the theoretical context is set, the empirical picture unfolds. Chapter 3 offers an institutional history of early noncommunal political initiatives in Malaysia and of why they failed. The colonial era ended with the purposeful entrenchment of a communal political order that reflected the racialized colonial economy. Those constituencies not absorbed by the coalition that came to power when the British left assumed a position of relatively intractable marginalization, whether represented by opposition political parties, voluntary associations, or both. Moreover, experiences of this period hint at how polarizing, durable, and often debilitating issues of ethnicity, religion, language, class, and education have been to Malaysia's formal and informal opposition.

This narrative continues in chapter 4. The four decades after independence saw the intensification of the racialized order begun earlier and the gradual narrowing of political space. Malay dominance in government, official culture, and patronage structures became more deeply pervasive and unshakable, making noncommunal initiatives seem an even harder sell than before among the Malay majority, the community's internal divisions notwithstanding. Also, the ruling coalition expanded to draw in a host of potential challengers while new and amended laws curtailed informal political participation. Still, moments of economic decline and factionalism within the government revealed how dependent it was on material incentives, and hence how fragile was its hegemony in the face of alternative paradigms. At the same time, demographic and cultural changes, from rising educational and income levels to Islamic revivalism, provided CSAs with new grounds for complaint and mobilization. Over the years, a range of religious and secular associations became stronger, more institutionalized, and more experienced. These groups learned to cooperate across racial and other cleavages around those issues that they had in common, but political parties were hard pressed to do the same. Hence, while citizens became ever more open to the idea of participation, and better educated on a range of sociopolitical issues, institutionalized reform lagged behind normative change.

As described in chapter 5, the situation changed in the late 1990s. Economic and political weaknesses spurred citizens to mobilize against the government. Their protests grew ever more bold as the government failed to respond to popular grievances. CSAs and political parties stepped forward to channel and coordinate this popular frustration. The primary peninsular opposition parties, caught up in the urgency and opportunity of the Reformasi movement and substantially aided by CSAs, found sufficient grounds to cooperate in a plausible coalition, adopting a *keadilan* frame. Meanwhile, CSAs adapted their strategies to take advantage of this window of opportunity, becoming more involved than ever before in electoral politics.

Chapter 6 puts these developments in perspective by exploring how distinctive the Reformasi movement was and what it represented. The BA did not do as well as it had hoped to in the November 1999 elections, yet those electoral data are an imperfect indicator of the depth of change that has occurred, particularly at the level of political culture.

Chapter 7 furthers this discussion by describing the process of reformism in neighboring Indonesia. While, broadly speaking, Reformasi and its catalysts seemed largely comparable in Indonesia and Malaysia, the different long-term evolution of opposition politics in Indonesia, its more authoritarian state and meager stores of cleavage-bridging coalitional capital, and the deeper crisis and faster pace of change there, among other factors, precluded the crystallization of a unified opposition coalition and limited the role of CSAs in institutionalizing a new political order.

Finally, in chapter 8, I sum up these empirical and theoretical findings to consider the implications of the study. Recent developments in Malaysia suggest that political culture and praxis are changing, and the same developments point to the role of coalitional capital in enabling, for instance, Islamist and secular opposition blocs to cooperate. The results of the post-Reformasi elections in March 2004 emphasize the essential stability of BN control, but even this coalition has been forced to adopt a focus on good governance, internal reform, and moderate Islam in order to sustain voters' confidence and obviate support for the opposition. While the specific context of reform initiatives largely determines their shape and focus, the framework developed here suggests important angles for studying reform movements that privilege no sphere unduly and treat both "successes" and "failures" as revealing and significant. Overall, then, this study enhances not only empirical understandings of Malaysian political development but also theoretical conceptions of contentious politics in illiberal democracies more broadly.

CONCEPTUALIZING POLITICAL
OPPOSITION AND REFORM

Achieving superlatives is something of a national pastime in Malaysia—
the tallest building, the highest flagpole, the longest pencil, the biggest
work of bean art. *Malaysia boleh!* (Malaysia can!) is a national slogan.
To what extent is Malaysian politics also exceptional? This study, from
observation of political contention in Malaysia over time, extrapolates
key aspects of mobilization and reform in an illiberal democracy. It is
worth pausing at the outset to set some parameters and to consider where
Malaysia fits in among other polities, and what this case reveals of theoretical value. To do so, I begin in this chapter by defining critical concepts
and considering how these apply to Malaysia. For example, do terms like
civil society mean the same thing in Malaysia as elsewhere? Next, I situ-
ate Malaysia's public sphere: What does it mean to say that the country
is an *illiberal democracy*, and how are the government and opposition
structured? Finally, I preview those aspects of mobilization and reform to
be teased out in later chapters. This last step specifies what the book sets
out to explain, and what is beyond its ambit, and it outlines the angles
that Malaysian experience suggests are particularly critical to understanding political contention and change.

What makes reform plausible in an illiberal democracy such as
Malaysia are long-term political socialization among citizens and networking across sectors, understood in terms of coordination among social groups and across portions of the public sphere. The present analysis
presents a complex perspective that acknowledges the internal diversity
in orientation and function of both civil society and political society. The
focus here is on dynamics and mechanisms as activists and groups collaborate in pursuit of political change. Moreover, in considering the specific context of an illiberal democracy, this study adds to our understanding of regime types and of the nature of the Malaysian state.

Ultimately, the project not only brings events in Malaysia into sharper relief but also suggests a more refined, context-sensitive approach to the study of contentious politics, ranging from the significance of cultural and institutional change to the interplay of individuals and institutions to the factors that favor political change through certain means rather than others.

Concepts and Terms

Concepts central to this study, such as *civil society*, *social capital*, and *NGO*, have very specific connotations in much of the relevant literature. Even though these terms are used relatively freely in the study—taken more as they are understood and applied on the ground than as they are in academe—they warrant clarification. Most important, how do we know if what we see in Malaysia *is* a civil society analogous to civil societies elsewhere? It is not at all obvious that the concept of civil society travels well, and much of the literature on civil society in non-Western contexts is rather atheoretical.[1]

Though modern usage of the term *civil society* dates back to the Enlightenment of eighteenth-century Scotland and continental Europe, attention to civil society was resuscitated through the postwar writings of the Marxist theorist Antonio Gramsci, who portrayed the sphere as a crucial bastion against tyranny. The concept gained renewed salience from the 1970s through the 1990s as activists based in civil society challenged dictators around the globe. Civil society is a sphere, however, not just a weapon against authoritarianism, and it accommodates all sorts of discourses and organizations. It includes all associations outside the state—not just politically engaged groups but also apolitical social welfare, cultural, sports, community, and other associations—and may lack the ability or autonomy to challenge state hegemony (Entelis 1999: 19). Exclusionary militia groups and other sorts of decidedly uncivil organizations are also part of civil society, properly understood (Carothers 1999–2000: 19). Iris Young differentiates civil society from the state and economy in terms of the types of activities found in each: the state coordinates action through the medium of authorized power, the economy through money, and civil society through communicative interaction. Within civil society, citizens may move freely among levels of association concerned mostly with self-organization and networking, with public policies, and with politics, defined as debates about what the social collective ought to do, both normatively and programmatically (Young 1999: 144–48). According to Young (1999: 141), civic associations and public spheres outside state and economy allow self-organization for the purposes of identity support, the invention of new practices, and the provision of some goods and services. Perhaps even more important, public spheres thriving in civil society often limit state and economic power and make their exercise more accountable to citizens.

Indeed, Foley and Edwards (1996: 46) concur that "to the extent that civil associations are strong, they challenge governing institutions to meet particular needs, aspirations, and conceptions of the common good," regardless of regime type. In the process, however, associations may lock up needed resources, polarize society, and battle one another for control of the state. As a result, "there is no reason in principle why the 'counterweight' of civil society should not become a burden to a democratic as well as an authoritarian state" (Foley and Edwards 1996: 39). This insight reveals a central problematic in conceptualizing civil society. Civil society is a neutral concept—it is not inherently good or bad—and "democracy can be decidedly incivil" (Hall 1995: 26–27). Citizens may join associations that strengthen problematic cleavages, foment violence, or ultimately undermine a democratic regime. Sheri Berman (1997) presents the prototypical example of this possibility in her discussion of interwar Germany. There, a flourishing civil society exacerbated the divisions among socialists, Catholics, and Protestants and provided ready-made institutions through which the Nazis could infiltrate and eventually dominate German society. As explained in chapter 1, the present study uses the term *civil society agent* (CSA) to reinforce the fact that civil society is a realm rather than an actor and may include a panoply of organizational forms, strategies, and perspectives. One cannot legitimately speak of civil society as a coherent, solidaristic actor in the same way that one may be able to speak of the state. To say that CSAs play political roles, then, is to say nothing about what those roles may be or how they may advance or disrupt the efforts of the government, economic enterprises, or other CSAs.

Overall, Malaysian civil society is structurally comparable to its counterparts elsewhere, even if its specific makeup is not quite what the literature would predict. The most immediately obvious distinction is the prominent role of religious groups in Malaysian civil society. Suggesting that Islam and civil society are basically incompatible, Ernest Gellner (1994) insists that Islamic societies, which presumably would include Malaysia, are too clientelistic and supranational in orientation (being focused around an *ummah*, an Islamic community based on shared faith rather than on territory) to support a civil society. He says of Muslim communities, "If the ruled judged the rulers, they did so by applying the religious norms of sacred law, rather than the secular principles of a Civil Society. . . . The expectation of some additional Civil Society, which could hold the state to account, on top of the *Umma* defined as a shared commitment to the implementation of the [Islamic] Law, would seem almost impious, but in any case unrealistic" (Gellner 1994: 22, 28).[2]

What Gellner describes appears to be the ideal form of what is termed *masyarakat madani* (a society modeled on that of Madinah in the time of the Prophet Mohammad) in Malaysia and, less consistently, in Indonesia. *Masyarakat madani* refers to a caring society built upon Islamic principles of communal interdependence. Citizens in a *masyarakat madani* are encouraged to be self-sufficient, civically conscious, and engaged in sociopolitical discourse and practices so that they debate such issues as democracy, pluralism, social justice, accountability, and good governance in a free, ethical environment. The concept is clearly akin to that of civil society, but it is less adversarial in approach—more a "civic society," specifically inspired by Islamic history. Moreover, *masyarakat madani* refers to an all-encompassing system of social organization, much as Islamists promote Islam as *ad-deen*, or a complete way of life. In such a society, rulers and the ruled are both to be held to the same moral, value-based (as opposed to performance-based) standard. Moreover, *masyarakat madani* occupies a moral space, meaning that, unlike civil society, it is not dependent upon the goodwill of the government for its perpetuation.[3] The principles at the root of the social order are morality, justice, fairness, civility, and consultation rather than majoritarianism.[4]

In practice, the terms *civil society* and *masyarakat madani* are commonly elided, even by those specifically trying to make a case for the latter.[5] For instance, the chief advocate of the *masyarakat madani* model in Malaysia, former Deputy Prime Minister Anwar Ibrahim, defines *masyarakat madani* as "*civil society* with democratic characteristics" (Anwar 1997: 9; emphasis in original). Similarly, Chandra Muzaffar (1997) tries to differentiate between *masyarakat madani* and civil society but identifies the latter as the Western counterpart of the former—and attributes prominent campaigns of secular Malaysian NGOs to *masyarakat madani*. The same dilemma colors studies of *masyarakat madani* in Indonesia, where that term is sometimes also used. Ahmad Baso (2000), for instance, explains that the term *civil society* is translated either with a cognate or as *masyarakat madani*. All the same, he cites scholars like Azyumardi Azra (2000), who argues that *masyarakat madani* implies cooperation rather than a power struggle between government and social groups, and who presents a more civilized approach to reform than might be found elsewhere. Muhammad Hikam (2000) concurs that *masyarakat madani* is a linguistic device used to stress the exclusivity or distinctiveness of Islam, but he suggests that use of the term constructs a misleading dichotomy and downplays the multiplicity of Indonesian value systems. Indeed, Syamsurizal Panggabean (2002: 92) scoffs that *masyarakat madani* is simply "Arabic for *civil society*" (2000: 92), and Adi Suryadi Culla (1999: 3–9) offers a whole list of synonyms, from *masyarakat kewargaan* (familial society) to *masyarakat beradab* (civilized society) to the English *civil society*, though acknowledging that shades of meaning distinguish these terms.

More broadly, Milner (1991) concludes that Islamists may articulate a genuinely different epistemology from nationalists or royalists, but that all tend to converge on the same common ground of "politics" in terms of how they present and justify their positions. In the same vein, Hefner (2000: 12–13) provocatively but plausibly describes Indonesia as having an emergent discourse of an Islamic state as supporting "democracy, voluntarism, and a balance of countervailing powers in a state and society." This discourse is readily to be found also in Malaysia. In other words, the distinction between civil society in a secular society and its counterpart in Muslim societies should not be overdrawn. Not only are the relevant terms often conflated, both may also be seen at least to approximate a Habermasian public sphere. The teleologies of Islam and secularism are distinct, and there certainly are Islamists who genuinely see power and the state as Gellner suggests they do.[6] However, Islamist and secular activists may allow those lines to blur for strategic purposes. For that reason, I acknowledge the distinctive end goal of Islamists yet still categorize them as part of civil society.

Nongovernmental Organizations and Social Movements

Like *civil society*, the term *nongovernmental organization* (NGO) loses versatility and import if too narrowly defined. An NGO may be defined as a group of citizens engaged in collective action for self-help or issue advocacy outside the aegis of the state. Initially, literature on NGOs in the developing world focused primarily on groups involved with economic development (credit schemes, collectives, skills training, and so on). This focus was in part an artifact of how governments themselves treated NGOs: as "mere subsidiaries of government agencies" (Yamamoto 1995b: 5). Attention has shifted, though, particularly since the 1980s, toward advocacy-oriented NGOs, such as human rights and women's groups, most of which have a distinctly political bent. For instance, the contributions to Yamamoto (1995a) demonstrate this trend among NGOs and scholars throughout the Asia-Pacific region. Most organizations in the region focused initially on charitable work and social services, often oriented toward organized religion, then more on community development, and increasingly on such issues as the environment and civil liberties.

Students of these sorts of associations have resorted to creative nomenclature instead of using the term *NGO*. Most common is the tendency to speak of social movements and constituent social movement organizations (SMOs). The literature on social movements is broad enough that the term is not unduly constraining; all sorts of collective endeavors seem to qualify. Bert Klandermans's vague definition of a social movement is representative: "a set of interacting individuals who attempt to promote, control, or prevent changes in social and cultural arrangements" (Klandermans 1989: 3). Mario Diani, surveying available definitions, identifies what social movements have in common as an emphasis on networks of informal interaction, shared beliefs and solidarity, collective action on conflictual issues at the systemic or nonsystemic level, and action largely outside the usual institutions of social life. What characterizes the subcategory of new social movements (NSMs) is a specific collective identity shared by the actors involved that may endure even beyond particular protest events or campaigns (Diani 1992: 7–16). With their critique of growth and "resistance of tendencies to colonize the life-world," NSMs tend to draw in young, well-educated members of the new middle class (Habermas 1981: 35). NSMs and the SMOs that comprise them might be seen as symptoms of the institutionalization of particular grievances, as resources for goal achievement, as democratic niches for the forging of new identities, or as sponsors of meaning for transforming structural changes into grievances (Klandermans 1989).[7]

As is common among others involved in NSMs (Offe 1985), Malaysian activists challenge efforts to limit the definition of what is "political" (efforts undertaken in order to exclude certain issues from governmental agendas), yet they also accept the premise that certain contradictions of advanced industrial society are better resolved through private action than through government regulation. Still, the "old politics" of struggles over economic growth, distribution, and security remains germane in Malaysia, and social movements continue to target the state rather more than would ideal-typical NSMs. What blurs the distinction is that, as Offe suggests of NSMs, the space of action of Malaysian social movements is at least largely noninstitutional politics, or transgressive rather than contained contention. Participants select these tactics not out of ignorance of conventional means (or contained contention) but on the basis of opportunities and risks associated with various forms of engagement. Furthermore, like NSMs, Malaysian political movements include elements from "peripheral" groups and the old middle class but are rooted in the new middle class and imbued with a sense of the power of human agency to bring about sociopolitical change. The politics of this class fragment "is typically a politics *of* a class but not *on behalf of* a class" (Offe 1985: 833; emphasis in original). While issues of redistribution and economic justice may be significant, the demands expressed are not class-specific, and activism tends to involve broad cross-class alliances.

Other scholars coin neologisms to stress distinctions among associational forms in different contexts. Jeff Haynes (1997), for instance, refers to "non-institutionalized socioeconomic and political bodies in the developing world" as "action groups." Such groups may not be locally or grassroots-based but have some common trait uniting their members, as well as a real sense of agency. Even if they accept aid from domestic and foreign allies, action groups seek to achieve their goals through their own activities. These groups are nearly always defensive in orientation, are generally concerned with the long-term protection of livelihoods or the sociopolitical position of subordinate groups, and are usually prevented from achieving their goals in the short term (Haynes 1997: 4–8). This definition, too, is not quite appropriate for some Malaysian associations. While the yen to find just the right terminology is understandable, speaking in terms of action groups seems unduly constrained—and really rather redundant. The term *NGO* is better-known and more commonly applied by both analysts and self-referencing activists, and hence it is preferred for this study.

Scholarly interest in Malaysian NGOs has germinated only recently and has been catholic in its inclusion of groups.[8] Surveying Malaysian NGOs, Lim Teck Ghee (1995) divides them into five categories: groups related to the environment, consumer issues, human rights, development, and women. Among the organizations Lim discusses are some that work quite closely with the government at times, such as consumers' groups, which might be excluded under a more dogmatic standard. Tan and Bishan (1994) start by distinguishing the relatively small number of issue-oriented NGOs from among the ranks of registered societies (including social clubs, mutual aid associations, credit cooperatives, and more). They distinguish first between government-organized NGOs (GONGOs), of which there are many, and autonomous NGOs. Tan and Bishan then subdivide autonomous NGOs into community-based organizations organized around ascriptive criteria, community service organizations for specific service aims, worker-employer associations, women's organizations, youth organizations, professional organizations, and coalitions and campaign groups. They also offer the simpler dichotomy of community service and welfare NGOs, or development and issue-oriented NGOs.

Many Malaysian associations are far from the sorts of grassroots-based, implicitly democratic groups presumed and privileged by advocates of NGOs.[9] Judith Adler Hellman (1994: 133–35) suggests that this disjuncture is not unusual: "The assumption that movements are automatically more democratic seems as ill-founded as the assumption that they inevitably promote democratization simply because they make demands on the system." All the same, Hellman finds that popular movements may help with formation of new identities, the expansion of civil society, the search for new ways of doing politics, and the mobilization of new sectors of society. Even comparatively hierarchical or authoritarian voluntary associations can foster self-determination and self-development by facilitating identity and voice (especially for usually excluded or marginalized groups), innovation, and provision of goods and services (Young 1999: 149–50). Such empowerment does in fact occur in Malaysia, as constituencies such as urban squatters, indigenous peoples, and women discover strategies for mobilization and locate empathetic communities in civil society to magnify the force of their demands. Such groups thus serve a pro-democratic end, even if they are not themselves paragons of democratic organization.

Malaysian NGOs also diverge from those in many developing countries in that relatively few groups have ever concentrated on alternative development strategies, such as agricultural extension activities, skills development, or credit provision. The Malaysian government has taken the lead itself in rural development, provision of social services, and the like, rather than leaving a vacuum for developmental and politically engaged NGOs to fill. Malaysia's reluctance to accept international development aid even when conditions warrant (which they seldom do anymore) means that pressure from agencies like the International Monetary Fund to involve NGOs in development projects—in the process, legitimating and strengthening such groups—has been scant. Hence most studies on the roles of NGOs as partners in development are not really applicable.

What is important for now is just to emphasize that this study follows the prevailing practice in Malaysian studies of taking an inclusive approach and not being too doctrinaire about what constitutes an NGO, efforts at taxonomy notwithstanding. Such an approach is not merely convenient but also reflects the exigencies of activism in an illiberal democracy. The comparatively restrictive legal environment of such a regime limits the sorts of protest or organizations allowed and may privilege working through or alongside political parties (especially parties in government) rather than through genuinely nongovernmental, fully autonomous associations.

Social Capital and Coalitional Capital

Broadly speaking, it is social capital and coalitional capital that give CSAs their ability to cohere for political import. *Social capital*, popularized as a concept and a term especially by the work of Robert Putnam (1993, 2000), refers both to the resources for collective action accumulated by past experience of engaging in associations (stores of trust and norms of reciprocity, for instance) and to the attributes of people favoring civil engagement (a predilection for trust and reciprocity). For Putnam, the associations that matter in political terms are secular and horizontal. Such associations invigorate democratic participation and bolster democratic institutions by fostering social trust, generated within networks of reciprocity and civic engagement. Putnam's thesis has been praised and castigated with equal fervor, a situation that reflects the vigor of the debate on the nature and value of social capital. His usage raises questions about the ways in which social capital is produced and maintained (Levi 1996), the methods for studying social capital and the causal links imputed to it (Tarrow 1996), and the ways in which associational life—and thus, presumably, social capital—have changed over time, ways that include interaction with political systems (Tarrow 1996; Foley and Edwards 1997; Levi 1996). More broadly, Michael Foley and Bob Edwards (1997) caution that use of the construct of social capital is too often undertheorized and oversimplified. For instance, studies underplay the conflictual character of civil society as well as the roles of the family, the school, and the workplace—not just the role of voluntary associations—in promoting attitudes and habits appropriate to an engaged and "civil" citizenry.

Some types of groups or networks are more effective than others at accomplishing particular political goals. Not all social capital and institutions that generate it are alike. For instance, Putnam (1993) enthuses that participation in secondary associations helps develop dense networks of civic cooperation, generalized trust, and norms of reciprocity. Margaret Levi (1996), however, offers the important caveats that the processes involved are deceptively complex and that collective action is not always a good thing for social cohesion, trust, or democracy. Instead, following on the work of other researchers, Levi suggests that different sorts of popular mobilization may foreground particularistic demands related to such ascriptive criteria as ethnicity or religion, even to the point of undermining democracy. Ashutosh Varshney, too, admonishes that associations organized along the lines of ascriptive identities have only limited power to foster durable identification with the larger whole. Making the case for considering informal activities as well as those oriented toward ascriptive identities as possibly critical elements of civil society and of the production of social capital, he explains that "the *purposes* of activity rather than the *forms* of organization should be the critical test of civic life" (Varshney 2002: 32; emphasis in original). Similarly, Foley and Edwards (1997) propose that superior resources for social capital may be found in highly polarized or fragmented societies (for instance, in Indonesia, as described in chapter 7). Indeed, even a dense civil society may not do much for democracy if too many organizations are apolitical or antidemocratic in character, hierarchical in structure, or insufficiently autonomous and insufficiently empowered to wield real influence vis-à-vis the government or dominant socioeconomic interests (Rueschemeyer 1997: 10–11). Supporting such contentions are empirically grounded studies such as Varshney's (2002), which offers a compelling argument for the greater facility of intercommunal than intracommunal associations in forestalling outbreaks of ethnic violence in India.

Taking these critiques seriously, the present study carries the debate on social capital a step further by acknowledging a distinction between how individuals and groups interact. The counterpart to social capital at the level of collectivities is *coalitional capital*, or the resources and qualities that lead groups to engage with one another for shared ends. Like social capital, coalitional capital is built up over time, through experience of past interaction among groups in civil society or between groups in civil society and political society. Coalitional capital does not "cause" coalitions—to say that groups see some shared purpose or trust each other is not to say that they will see reason or opportunity to mobilize at any given moment. Moreover, just as individuals may trust each other but still have little in common, a history of interaction does not necessarily mean that particular groups will ever recognize a shared end, given the variety of objectives to which groups may aspire. All the same, the concept of coalitional capital is useful in moving the discussion beyond the level of when and why individuals engage and the bonds that form among citizens, to acknowledge the dynamics of cross-group interaction—especially since, in some types of regime, political change may require a broad-based campaign.

It is not enough, however, merely to say that CSAs build and draw upon social and coalitional capital. In the case of Malaysia, for example, culture, language, and dominant institutional arrangements follow ethnic lines, and the weight of tradition tips the scales toward communalism. It is not surprising, then, that citizens and organizations alike gravitate toward alliances based on ascriptive identities. However, if Islamist groups allied only with one another, if Chinese groups did the same, and so forth, then escape from a communal paradigm would remain highly unlikely. If, by contrast, groups perceive an opportunity for political change that would benefit all sorts of organizations, then they may essay to frame their claims differently or to innovate in terms of tactics, in order to coordinate their efforts with those of other groups. Doing so generates new stores of coalitional capital, and it may expose individuals within groups to sets of counterparts outside their usual experience, thus also augmenting social capital. In the process, new possibilities for political change arise. Even if a given venture fails, future reform initiatives may draw upon that venture, and the collective resources it generated, to make collaborative mobilization easier to achieve.

The Public Sphere in Malaysia:
The State and Its Discontents

The nature of CSAs, the sorts of reform they desire, and the means by which they pursue their aims has much to do with the nature of the regime in question. Not all states or economies are alike; there is no reason to assume that all civil societies are alike, either. This study concerns processes of political change in an illiberal democracy and, specifically, one marked by deep social cleavages that significantly shape individuals' and groups' political identities and allegiances. Central tenets of this work are that the nature of the regime substantially conditions the nature of engagement, and that political change in an illiberal democracy includes normative as well as institutional dimensions. First, then, I set the parameters of Malaysia's public sphere; next, I define the term *illiberal democracy* as it is found in Malaysia; and, finally, I consider the structure of the regime in order to understand what changes are pursued by the incumbent government's opponents, and when conditions may seem propitious for achieving those ends.

The Public Sphere

Anthony Milner (1991) suggests that it is only recently that politics, defined as the discursive practices indicative of a public sphere, was "invented" in Malaysia. Drawing on Pocock and Habermas, Milner explains that, prior to about the 1920s, Malayans saw themselves as subjects of a particular sultan, not as citizens with the power and authority to legitimate that sultan's rule. Once Malayans took it upon themselves to suggest policies or comment upon those passed down by sultans (or by colonial or Islamic leaders), those officials found themselves obliged to justify their choices and perspectives in terms designed to appeal to the masses. In other words, a public realm developed where previously there had been none. In this space, citizens could form associations, gripe about their leaders, suggest better policies, and otherwise assert their preferences regarding how society and the state should be ordered.

In contemporary Malaysia, the politically engaged public sphere includes political parties as well as civil society. The latter includes secular and sectarian civic and welfare associations, guilds and unions of workers and employers, student organizations, and individuals who take it upon themselves to serve as public intellectuals.[10] What these actors have in common is that they see and comport themselves as political actors in the public realm. However, Malaysia's strong state has arguably more power than CSAs to regulate what sorts of organization and behavior are to be found in the public sphere.

Illiberal Democracy

Any discussion of political opposition in Malaysia is necessarily premised upon an awareness of the power and scope of the illiberal democratic regime. An understanding of political mobilization and reform in Malaysia must be attentive to context; studies based on other cases—even other non-Western regimes that are also illiberal—may not speak well to the Malaysian case. In brief, the government allows a certain degree of dissent but retains the ability to punish or crush its detractors. Moreover, the government maintains control not just by restrictions on civil liberties and brute force but also by sustaining a degree of ideological hegemony and skillful co-optation of interests. In an illiberal democracy, "the dominant and intrusive role of state power in most aspects of . . . social life channels political change to serve the managerial and technocratic ends of the state" (Bell and Jayasuriya 1995: 15). The system can be understood, therefore, both in terms of institutions and in terms of interests and ideology.

Institutions. By now a veritable litany of characterizations is available for identifying what is distinctive about political arrangements in any given Asian state. Malaysia, for instance, has been labeled quasi-democratic (Zakaria 1989), authoritarian statist (Tan 1990), semidemocratic (Case 1993, 2004), statist democratic (Jesudason 1995), pseudodemocratic (Case 2001), electoral autocratic (Diamond 2002), competitive authoritarian (Levitsky and Way 2002), and more. These distinctions are significant for highlighting how much leeway the government allows for dissent and mobilization (and especially for free and fair elections), but they also carry a normative loading, especially in their characterizations of the regime as either more democratic or more authoritarian.[11] My focus here is on dynamics within the regime rather than on taxonomies across regimes, so I acknowledge the options but leave to others the last word on labels. Given the fungibility of these terms, I choose to refer to Malaysia by the descriptive *illiberal democracy*. The Malaysian polity has procedures and institutions characteristic of a democracy, but it is illiberal in its constraints on popular participation and civil liberties. In such a regime, the government is not neutral but intervenes in most aspects of social life to promote its idea of the good; it tends toward "rationalist and legalistic technocracy" and promotes "a managerial rather than a critical public space and civil society" (Jones et al. 1995: 163–64).

Legitimacy in most "Asian democracies" rests to a significant extent on the maintenance of at least a facade of democracy: rare is the Asian leader with the gumption to forgo elections altogether. New Order Indonesia, best characterized as (hegemonic) electoral authoritarian, is a good example. Soeharto's government was clearly intrusive and coercive, and political competition was tightly regulated, yet Soeharto regularly validated his seemingly unshakable rule through unfree, unfair elections. However, within the region, more substantial liberalization has seldom been aggressively or consistently pursued. As Gordon Means (1996: 103) asks of Malaysia and Singapore, for instance, "Why have basic democratic institutions survived in these countries, while democratic ideals and practices have not?"

Malaysia inherited from its British colonists a constitutional monarchy with the institutions of parliamentary democracy. Elections for state and federal legislatures have been held within five year intervals almost without fail since even before independence in 1957. Elections are called by the incumbent government and are organized by a nominally independent elections commission. Dozens of political parties have competed over the years, and the opposition regularly garners well over one-third of the popular vote. The powers of the monarch (which position rotates among the hereditary sultans of the peninsular states) are limited and were further scaled back in the 1980s. The judiciary was once more free to rule without interference and to exercise judicial review, but these powers, too, have been curtailed over time. A coalition of communal parties, first called the Alliance and then expanded and reconstituted as the Barisan Nasional (the National Front, or BN), has governed since independence. Associational activity outside the state is allowed but is monitored and restricted. Excitement about elections and voter turnout is consistently high, but other forms of political participation are generally discouraged, the means of discouragement including restrictions on civil liberties (speech, association, and so on).[12]

Indeed, the status of elections provides strong support both for and

against Malaysia's democratic credentials. Elections do not simply legitimate the ruling party's continued dominance; it is not unusual for opposition parties to take control of one or two states' legislatures and to secure a fair number of seats in the federal parliament. A more pessimistic
view is that competitive elections have been allowed to continue only because it is so hard to envision the BN's losing at the federal level, so elections "did not threaten the established political order" (Crouch 1993:
137–39). Moreover, emergency provisions have been invoked twice—in
Sarawak in 1966, and in Kelantan in 1977—to overthrow opposition-
controlled state governments (Crouch 1993: 138), and over the years the
electoral system has become increasingly skewed in favor of the BN. For
instance, the comparative ratios of voters to representatives between predominantly non-Malay, urban constituencies and predominantly Malay,
rural constituencies have grown ever more stark, since it is rural Malay
voters who traditionally have been the most consistent supporters of the
BN (Case 2001; Crouch 1993; Ong 2002).[13] Moreover, under Mahathir
Mohamad, prime minister from 1981 to 2003, electoral contestation was
increasingly diverted into party-level elections (Case 2001: 47). This
arrangement granted Mahathir an additional stabilizing safety valve,
since he could prevent challengers from gaining a foothold in the party
before the contest reached the broader electoral arena.

The Malaysian state has drifted far from its foundational framework.
Simon Tan chooses the moniker "authoritarian statism" to capture
Malaysia's incremental fusion of the branches of government, transfer of
power to the executive, decline in rule of law and the functional roles of
political parties, and growth of parallel power networks cross-cutting the
formal organization of the state (Tan 1990: 33–35). Such changes increase the scope for coercion in governance, leading Simon Barraclough
(1985b) to challenge characterizations of Malaysia as democratic at all.
Barraclough describes how Malaysia's highly efficient Special Branch,
state-sponsored citizen volunteer groups, legislation, and other mechanisms discourage dissent so that the government need not resort so often
to actual sanctions. Coercion has been most persistently used in Malaysia
against those seeking to mobilize class-based opposition, especially left-
wing parties, and more recently against Islamist opponents, particularly
those trying to mobilize rural Malays. These devices may further alienate,
aggravate, and make martyrs of particular segments. However, if coercion drives opposition elements underground, the government stands to
gain, since it may portray its challengers as contemptuous of the constitutional process and hence as fundamentally illegitimate. Overall, incidents like the vendetta by Prime Minister Mahathir against judicial independence in the mid-1980s, along with the rising reliance upon repressive

apparatuses and ideologies, reveal the executive's "preference to rule by coercion instead of ruling by manufacturing consent" (Tan 1990: 41–42). These processes engender mutual disrespect between the government and its opponents, rendering constructive engagement less likely (Means 1996: 109).

The level of coercion by the government has not been constant or undifferentiated. Over time, the institutional development of the state and its efforts to preclude dissidence have significantly narrowed the space available for opponents. James Jesudason (1995) traces the institutional development of the Malaysian state back to the colonial era and details the dialectic that developed between state and civil society as both took shape. He suggests that the development of nonparty associations able to mount effective challenges to the incumbent government was stalled by such structural features of the Malaysian state as the external imposition of democracy, the early concession of universal suffrage, and the entrenchment of a strong bureaucracy prior to the expansion of political participation. The need to appeal at regular intervals to an electorate compels the government to perform at a satisfactory level, but the significant overlap between the interests of the government and those of key social groups has reduced incentives for those groups to urge further liberalization. In other words, substantial constituencies have a stake in the prevailing order and an incentive to engage with the government primarily through contained, institutional means. Jesudason concludes, "The result is that statist democracy can never become a target of collective resentment so easily as in nonelectoral authoritarian regimes" (1995: 353–54). Enough of the opposition has gained just enough to accept the rules of the game that these opposition actors confirm Malaysia's democratic credentials—but William Case (1993) specifies that this democracy is comparable to a Latin American *dictablanda* or *democradura*, in which limited avenues for participation maintain a level of popular satisfaction that is minimally sufficient for stability.

Overall, though, the regime *is* stable. Tan (1990) suggests that change is likely only as a result of severe economic failure; Jesudason (1995) posits either severe economic failure or blatant abuse as catalysts for change; and Means (1996) adds globalization and the creeping intrusion of "Western values" to the list of possible triggers for reform. Moreover, although simply unseating one set of elites does create an opportunity for regime change, including an opportunity for democratization, there is no assurance that this will happen (Levitsky and Way 2002: 59).

Interests and Ideology. As these analyses suggest, the Malaysian government sustains itself not just through institutional means but also by careful management of which interests remain outside or are incorporated into the state. James Jesudason characterizes the Malaysian state as "syncretic": mobilizing ethnic sentiment for support, the ruling party has maintained Malay dominance and forestalled non-Malay rebellion through pro-growth policies and selective cooptation. Vertically structured identities, such as religion and ethnicity, "crowd out secular identities and ideologies based on class politics and notions of autonomy from the state, promoting a clientelist consciousness that undercuts the development of effective alliances and ideologies against the regime" (Jesudason 1996: 131–35); moreover, "the state's role in patrolling religious boundaries, particularly by way of rules preventing exit options for Muslims, precludes the free negotiation and blending of ethnic and religious identities" (148). In sum, to forestall the development of a programmatic alternative to the regime, the government does its best to co-opt the middle ground and leave the opposition only narrow, polarized constituencies concerned with communal rights, theocracy, or economic redistribution. Similarly, Crouch argues that rather than just repressive, the government has also been at least somewhat responsive to societal pressure, especially from the Malay community. To maintain Malay support, for instance, the BN has favored Malays in language and cultural policies, rural development schemes, and a comprehensive program of positive discrimination in business, employment, and education (Crouch 1993: 138). He sums up, "A balance was achieved in which democratic institutions forced the government to be responsive to popular demands while authoritarian restrictions ensured that it remained in power" (140).

In line with its absorption of organized interests, the government also preempts the formulation of alternative ideas and demands by sustaining a certain degree of ideological hegemony. Means (1996: 113) notes that Singapore's official national ideology—supposed to encapsulate the very essence of the "Asian values" leaders like Singapore's Lee Kuan Yew and Malaysia's Mahathir extol—"makes no mention of democracy, social justice, human and political rights, cultural pluralism, or religious freedom, except that 'Confucian values' are presumably enshrined in its fundamental assumptions." Sheila Nair (1995) explores the nature and extent of this ideological project in discussing who resists state power, and when and why, in Malaysia and Singapore. She finds that both governments justify strong disciplinary action against critical social forces by construction of internal threats to national unity. However, the government's nationalist ideology may be challenged by other discourses when it reproduces ethnic, class, or other differences, as happens with the Malay-focused Malaysian nationalist ideology. This caveat suggests the need to examine more carefully the ways in which such identities play out in the government and opposition.

The Government and Its Opponents

Social pluralism and Malay dominance are both fundamental to Malaysia's national identity. The ever-increasing Malay proportion is still only two-thirds—and was initially barely one-half—of the population, yet Malay supremacy has been entrenched since the British system of indirect rule and is written into the national constitution. Chinese comprise the largest minority, with around one-quarter of the current population; Indians comprise most of the remainder. Moreover, all Malays are constitutionally bound to practice Islam (and most non-Malays are non-Muslim), so the country's preeminent religious cleavage rather neatly follows the racial divide.[14] Political institutions since independence have been designed for the seemingly inimical purposes of upholding a leading role for Malays and maintaining racial and religious harmony—and the government legitimates its continued dominance largely in terms of meeting these twin goals. Opponents of the regime, by contrast, have suggested that stable accommodation need not require so communal an approach and have offered various alternative frameworks, some in the direction of liberal democracy and full equality, and others not.

Alvin Rabushka and Kenneth Shepsle (1972: 8) assert that "a primary task in plural societies is the subordination of 'primordial sentiments' to the requirements of civil politics" so that satisfaction of the demands of one social group is not to the disadvantage of other groups. The Malaysian government has played up differences across communal groups when cross-group linkages seemed to jeopardize the racially stratified, inegalitarian status quo. Even if such tactics are more discursive than material (though, in fact, the government's rhetoric of Malay dominance is reinforced by racialized economic and other policies), they prevent emergence of a common ideal of the nation, and they privilege a certain set of identities. Malaysian pluralism could take any of several forms, with the population segmented in terms of ethnic, class, religious, regional, or other lines.

Partly as an artifact of economic development, identities aside from race have gained increasing politically salience in Malaysia over time. As Case (1993), Banton and Mansor (1992), Saravanamuttu (1992), and others point out, members of the middle class are especially prone to look beyond the racial lines reinforced by the omnipresent state. Moreover, as Robert Hefner (1999: 7) explains of Singapore, Malaysia, and Indonesia, "the sheer pace and breadth of economic growth have created new linkages among social groupings, and encouraged some in the middle class, the arts, media, and even the business community to promote a new culture of participation, and perhaps even a new partnership with government." The "new and socially restless middle class" in the three countries simultaneously critiques the balance between state and society and edges towards forging transethnic, national cultures (Hefner 1999: 7).

However, particularly when the government can claim responsibility for development policies that benefit (or create) the middle class, and when alternative governments are untested, the bourgeoisie may be loath to overturn the comfortable status quo. David Martin Jones and David Brown (1994) capture this dynamic in Singapore; the gist of their argument clearly applies beyond the island. They assert that Singapore's middle class has not demanded political liberalization for reasons including the culture of *kiasu* (a local term for "afraid to lose" behavior), widespread dependence on the state, the government's manipulation of rhetoric to promote confusion or insecurity, official promotion of so-called Asian values and political institutions, and the government's inclusionary corporatist strategy, which facilitates effective decision making, preempts alienation and opposition, and makes the regime look more democratic. In this environment, middle-class culture is characterized by anxiety, uncertainty, and a preference for conformism (see also Puru-Shotam 1998). Jones and Brown (1994: 87) fault these "neurocratic" tendencies in explaining the persistence of Singapore's "managerial corporatist" framework. In Malaysia, many of the same processes also take place, but the racialized bent of economic policies—which have been consciously tailored, especially since 1970, to speed the development of a Malay middle class—cause middle-class complacence to be as easily equated with acceptance of a communal order as with identification of cross-racial bourgeois interests. These competing tendencies do not preclude mobilization around alternate political priorities, but they make the process more complex.

Consociationalism and Control

Malaysia's ruling coalition approximates a *consociational* model as described by Arend Lijphart (1969: 216): "government by elite cartel designed to turn a democracy with a fragmented political culture into a stable democracy." This sort of democracy is defined "not so much [by] any particular institutional arrangement as [by] the deliberate joint effort by the elites to stabilize the system" (213). Elites representing all core social groups share power in a grand coalition; beyond a fair basis for power sharing, the specific features of consociational government vary by state. In some states, for instance, consociational principles extend to the electoral level.

Musolf and Springer (1977: 116) point out that Malaysia's government is consociational only to a certain extent, and that the success of consociational government in the country "is far from certain." Most important, the Alliance (now the BN) has been challenged from the outset by noncommunal parties: some parties even within the BN (especially in Sabah and Sarawak) cross ethnic lines, and parties or factions compete within as well as across communal groups. Moreover, Malay dominance of the ruling coalition has grown stronger over time, contrary to the basic premises of the consociational model. Lustick (1979: 326) draws this angle out in distinguishing between consociational and control models; the latter "focus on effective group control over rival group(s)." As Lustick explains, both models presume the persistence of deep vertical cleavages, but they attribute causality to different factors in maintaining stability: in the consociational model, stability is attributed to compromise and cooperation; in the control model, stability is attributed to domination by the strongest group (generally via a mix of coercive and noncoercive means). Malaysia's government may still be termed *quasi- consociational*, at least as a matter of convenience, since a basic premise of the BN is that Malays "choose" to share power with non-Malays for the sake of racial harmony, fairness, and stability, but the limits to consociationalism in Malaysia, and the government's closer fit with a control model, should be taken seriously.

While mobilization along class lines has always been a possibility—and one that has particularly worried the government, especially in the 1950s and 1960s—policies to undercut unions, the banning or repression of parties on the far left, and the coincidence of racial and class cleavages have done much, at least until recently, to prevent a class framework from supplanting communalism. Perhaps the most compelling alternative discourse available to reformers in contemporary Malaysia and Indonesia is Islam. The bulk of the transition or democratization literature makes scant reference to religion, aside from recognizing the importance of church-based organizations in mobilization and perhaps in the generation of social capital.[15] In Malaysia, Islam has been used since the 1970s to articulate a pro-poor agenda and a middle-class challenge to corruption and has been spurred to prominence by restrictions on the political arena. Constitutional amendments following racial riots in 1969 removed such issues as Malay special rights from the table but left Islamization still available as a defining agenda. The contradiction between Islam as Malaysia's official religion and the persistence of a largely secular state,[16] as well as concern among some *dakwah* (Islamic revivalist) groups that the rural and non-*bumiputera* poor would be neglected by middle class–oriented pro-Malay economic policies, lent grist to the Islamist challenge (see Lyon 1979, among others). The compelling appeal of this discourse has afforded Islamist NGOs and parties an effective weapon against the government. At times (and increasingly, in recent years, with the spread of "civil Islamic" discourses) this approach is coupled with secular arguments for liberalization, making it all the more fruitful an avenue for protest (see Hefner 2000).

Analytical Overview

With these definitions and conditions in mind, I turn to the questions underlying the chapters to come. It is with the possibility and process of protest and reform that this study is centrally concerned. In many ways, Doug McAdam, Sidney Tarrow, and Charles Tilly's work on "contentious politics" (2001) frames the project. McAdam, Tarrow, and Tilly examine interrelationships between state structures and forms of protest, between "contained" and "transgressive" contention, and among forms of resistance from foot-dragging to revolution. Putting social movements on a continuum with revolutions, they suggest that what distinguishes episodes and forms of contention is just the extent to which the challenge posed puts existing structures of power at risk.

A question immediately raised by observation of contentious politics in Malaysia is why social movements do not evolve into more menacing forms but drift instead toward co-optation or "containment." Jean Cohen (1985: 664) proposes that contemporary social movements embody "self-limiting radicalism," since they represent "a self-understanding that abandons revolutionary dreams in favor of the idea of structural reform, along with a defense of civil society that does not seek to abolish the autonomous functioning of the political and economic systems." The target of such movements is not the state or the economy but civil society, including changes to collective identity and the structures of everyday life. Even so, protest in Malaysia could be more vociferous and has been so in the past. Something about the context in which contention occurs seems to favor contained instead of transgressive strategies; a primary goal of the present study is to identify what these contextual factors are and how they operate.

Analysis of reform processes in Malaysia and Indonesia suggests four angles that are especially helpful to understanding both how and when mobilization occurs in Malaysia, but also the extent to which processes in Malaysia are exceptional or replicable. The framework developed here is limited. A core part of the argument is that regime type matters to the nature of contention, and so, clearly, a universal model of mobilization and political change would hold little validity. All the same, the questions raised by Malaysia's experience, especially as contrasted with that of

Indonesia, are broadly relevant, and the specific conclusions reached here contribute to our understanding not only of Malaysia but also of other, similarly situated regimes. The case studies to come suggest four interlacing dimensions to be considered in studying political reform: that regime type is significant to the nature of mobilization and organization; that not just social capital but also coalitional capital facilitates coalition building; that shifts in structures of political opportunity encourage adaptation of collective action frames as well as of strategies; and that political parties and CSAs play complementary roles in pursuing institutional and normative change.[17] These dimensions are not all new; what makes this discussion relevant is how they intersect, and what the insights gained suggest about how to study processes of political change.

Regime Type and Mobilization

It is not just the outcomes of mobilization but also the way in which protest occurred that distinguish the Reformasi movement in Malaysia from its coeval counterpart in Indonesia. One of the most significant determinants of how protest occurred in each country was the sort of regime in place at the time. Illiberal democracy in Malaysia leaves an incentive for contained contention: the opposition includes functioning political parties, and these parties stand at least some chance of electoral victory. In Indonesia, by contrast, the electoral authoritarian New Order regime could not be effectively challenged at all through established channels of formal politics. Transgressive contention—the use of innovative tactics by both newly and already constituted political actors—was a more promising option. The relative capacity of the government to crack down on certain forms of protest, in addition to the incentives granted for pursuing some strategies as opposed to others, partly explains activists' strategic choices.

Moreover, the nature of the regime helps determine what sort of oppositional institutions are available. Malaysia's government is only moderately coercive by comparison with New Order Indonesia's. In the latter, opposition parties were crippled by constraints on electoral contestation. Malaysian opposition parties may not face a level playing field, but most have long been allowed to operate above ground, to express dissent openly, and to contest elections as legitimately constituted political actors. Furthermore, a wide variety of CSAs has been far more free to operate in Malaysia than was the case in New Order Indonesia, even though NGOs (especially student groups) in Indonesia were allowed somewhat more space and scope than were opposition parties. Hence, even when, in 1998, options for contained contention were thrown open in Indonesia with the resignation of Soeharto, relatively few organizations were prepared to take advantage of that opportunity. Singapore provides a useful contrast to both these cases. Singapore's government maintains "permanently active mobilization" (Jones and Brown 1994: 87), but as part of a carefully cultivated "civic" rather than "civil" society. Citizens are urged to engage energetically with politics and policy, but they are organized and mobilized to work with, rather than independently of or against, the government.

Moreover, Chazan (1992: 298) uncovers a tautology in mechanisms of protest, or at least an institutionalized bias toward contained contention: "Those voluntary associations that are politically effective are also the ones that have already accumulated a fair amount of political capital on the national level," and groups wanting to influence policies "have a vested interest in increasing their involvement on the national level." States, furthermore, realizing that strong NGOs can actually boost the government's effective capacity, may be inclined to work with rather than against such groups, even if the states are unable to control them completely. In other words, both state and society may recognize real advantages to mutual forbearance and even cooperation. Even in cases of regime transition, agitation may readily give way to orderly, moderate electoral politics and to a more cooperative than confrontational style. For instance, Philip Oxhorn (1994) draws on the experience of Chile to propose that new forms of incorporation, including the mechanisms of post-transition electoral politics, may be better than protest for the long-term interests of at least parts of the popular sector. Therefore, the shift to democratic politics includes demobilization of the popular sector and redirection of efforts toward electoral politics—although at that point, those grassroots groups without skills for or access to institutional channels may find themselves ignored.

Coalitional Capital

The type of organization and mobilization found in a given state feeds into the next dimension: coalitional capital. Even authoritarian regimes allow some development of social capital.[18] What they may be more effective at precluding is the development of coalitional capital, or the resources and experience with which groups may formulate broadly appealing alternative ideas about governance and policies and build cross-cutting coalitions with which to pursue those ideas. If it can be presumed that an illiberal state prefers not to change, the impetus for reform must come from below. However, neither social capital nor coalitional capital can be manufactured instantly; both come out of sustained interaction among individuals or groups. Reputations, social trust, and norms of reciprocity need time to percolate. Reform processes are thus best understood in historical context. At what point did groups form in political society and civil society? To what extent have they interacted in the past, and how has the nature of that interaction altered over time? The sort of mobilization one might expect from a consistently democratic state, in which groups have had at least some chance to organize over the years, is thus different from what one might expect in a longtime authoritarian regime, in which groups have had little space and opportunity to engage proactively with one another and to envision and pursue systemic alternatives.

How substantial reformers' impact is against a relatively authoritative state may depend on how coordinated a challenge they present and thus how hard they are to suppress. Popular protest may force a policy response, for instance, but pervasive, long-term change generally requires something more organized and systematic than a spontaneous mass uprising. For instance, Jeffrey Winters (2001: n.p.) bemoans Indonesia's "politicus interruptus" and the fact that "the reform movement in Indonesia both peaked and collapsed on the same day" in 1998 when the masses toppled Soeharto but lacked the coordination to deepen the regime transformation and oppose the installation of former vice president B. J. Habibie as the new head of state. Michael Bratton and Nicolas van de Walle (1992), too, find that African governments introduce reforms in response to protests from loose, multiclass coalitions of groups, protests sparked either by external events or (primarily) by contingent domestic factors, but that these governments are likely to concede only "manageable" reforms or to resort to co-optation or crackdown.

More thoroughgoing reform may require a degree of unity among antiregime activists. Such a coalition requires that opposition groups reach some degree of consensus in terms of agenda, structure, and tactics. In other words, to avoid being silenced by the government, those who enunciate alternatives need a degree of organization and coalitional capital—which is tough in an atmosphere of repression (see Boudreau 1999). Especially where electoral contestation is far from free and fair, a reform coalition is more likely to be successful than are disparate parties struggling alone. In an illiberal democracy, one way in which the incumbent government may increase its chances of being continually reelected is by fragmenting the opposition (as through selective cooptation) or otherwise limiting the options for opposition parties. Examples are the hardly coincidental evolution of divergent opposition clusters (pro-Chinese, Islamic, socialist) in Malaysia, the banning of proletariat-uniting communist parties under so many Cold War governments, and, under Soeharto's New

Order, the forced restriction of Indonesia's political parties to three government-sponsored options. Under such constraints, with at least minimal social pluralism assumed, no one party is likely to be able to muster adequate support to defeat the incumbent government. Indeed, even if a single opposition party could capitalize on resentment against the government to defeat the odds and come to power, chances are slim that its policies and perspectives would carry broad enough appeal to keep it there. While hard to build, an opposition coalition is therefore likely to be necessary.

Attribution of Opportunity and Threat

The question of when mobilization occurs or escalates is less reliant on regime type; in all contexts, circumstances are at times relatively more or less favorable for pressing contentious claims. McAdam, Tarrow, and Tilly retreat from the more common language of "political opportunity structures"—defined as "the configuration of forces in a (potential or actual) group's political environment that influences that group's assertion of its political claims" (Brockett 1991: 254)—in order to emphasize that these shifts cannot be read automatically and invariably by all actors. They speak instead of "attribution of opportunity and threat." They define such attribution as "a crucial mechanism in mobilization" involving "(a) invention or importation and (b) diffusion of a shared definition concerning alterations in the likely consequences of possible actions (or, for that matter, failures to act) taken by some political actor" (McAdam, Tarrow, and Tilly 2001: 95). How a given citizen interprets events—which depends in turn on the media to which she has access, as well as on the persuasiveness of the interpretations provided by CSAs, the government, and competing parties—determines both whether she will see the situation as ripe for change and how she will weigh, at that moment, the apparent benefits and costs of mobilization.

Attribution of opportunity and threat does not necessarily start mobilization so much as redirect it by encouraging reformers to adjust their framing devices and strategies to take advantage of propitious moments.[19] Indeed, attribution processes are one mechanism among many, and they have more to do with timing than with causality. McAdam, Tarrow, and Tilly (1997: 153) warn, "So broad has the concept [of political opportunities] become that there is danger of its confusion with the political environment in general and with post hoc 'explanations' that find opportunities only after movements have had success." The groups involved at moments of mass protest may not be new or previously dormant, especially if the society has and generates enough social capital that citizens are usually involved in various sorts of social networks. Attribution of opportunity or threat instead catalyzes coalitional capital, if available, when what seems possible is systemic change: newly and previously constituted groups collaborate to discover commonly held perspectives and goals and to coordinate their strategies, in hopes of optimizing their combined impact. For example, in Malaysia in 1998, when economic crisis and a crack in the political elite made the opportunity for systemic change seem high, Islamist and secular organizations adopted a common "justice" frame, and CSAs as well as parties made electoral contestation a primary strategy. Clearly, though, attribution of opportunity or threat concatenates with other factors, including the presence of grievances that trigger a sense of relative deprivation; the existence of collective-action traditions, repertoires, and frames from past experience; and the availability of material and organizational resources (Ekiert and Kubik 1998: 549).

Complementary Roles of CSAs and Political Society

Coordination of strategies need not entail duplication of efforts. Theorists are only now beginning to turn their attention to the division of labor between CSAs and political society, including parties as well as state structures. Goldstone (2003: 2) asserts firmly, for instance, that "social movements constitute an essential element of normal politics in modern societies, and that there is only a fuzzy and permeable boundary between institutionalized and noninstitutionalized politics. . . . [S]tate institutions and parties are interpenetrated by social movements, often developing out of movements, in response to movements, or in close association with movements." His essay, along with the volume it introduces, rejects traditional insider-outsider models of politics that frame social movements as marginal to mainstream politics and instead argues for the complementarity of social protest and routine forms of political participation. Boudreau (2001: 165), too, makes the case that "protest movements are not discontinuous from other aspects or periods in . . . people's lives. . . . *Individuals* and *social groups* that join demonstrations . . . do so as part of lifelong struggles, both to satisfy basic human needs and to figure out and act upon more abstract principles of rights and justice" (emphasis in original). The balance between these forms of engagement, though, owes much to the nature of the regime and to the sorts of participation proscribed or permitted. As Boudreau poignantly observes (2002: 165–66), some individuals can meet their material and normative needs "in rather routine manners—by going to work, obeying traffic laws, or voting in elections"; others—for instance, the poor, or those living under repressive regimes—find that "the law offers scant promise of justice" and thus must engage continuously in (presumably transgressive) collective action.

Given the nature of an illiberal democratic regime, if nonviolent social activists remain dogmatically aloof from formal political engagement, they may get nowhere, since an unsympathetic government can suppress them and their ideas. Opposition parties, for their part—divided and weakened by a strong state and a less than fully democratic system—cannot act independently of nonparty activists, or else what sets each party apart from its competitors will keep them all from allying to unseat their larger and stronger common opponent. Moreover, while political parties alone are unlikely to be able to achieve political reforms in an illiberal democracy, civil society can do no better on its own. William Galston (2000: 69), extrapolating from Alexis de Tocqueville, neatly summarizes the interlacing of these loci of activism: "It is a mistake to believe that civil society can remain strong if citizens withdraw from active engagement in political associations. Over time, the devitalization of the public sphere is likely to yield a privatized hyperindividualism that enervates the civil sphere as well." Garner and Zald, however, assert the organic links between venues for activism, implying that withdrawal from parties need not be so detrimental. They argue that activists decide whether to organize in movements or in parties on the basis of ease and of each alternative's predicted payoffs, and they declare, "The politically oriented social movement sector is a continuation of politics by other means" (Garner and Zald 1985: 138). In short, CSAs and parties play complementary roles: "The initial mobilization may be best orchestrated by civil society, but political parties are the only actors who can provide the required institutional framework" (Doherty 2001: 28).

CSAs and political parties have different overarching goals and definitions of success. While CSAs "can promote democracy, social justice, and well-being . . . there are limits to what citizens can accomplish in civil society alone" (Young 1999: 153). It is in addressing the state that political parties find their inviolable niche. Most important, political parties have gaining control of government as their avowed end; CSAs do not. Parties hold greater historical and legal validity than CSAs as "political" actors, and so they need not fight as many battles just to prove their right to participate. Indeed, CSAs lack any mandate for dictating political developments. NGOs, moreover, faced with no sort of electoral imperative encouraging them to maximize their base, are more prone to represent disparate niche communities, regardless of how encompassing the functional networks within civil society may be. Fundamentally, too, even if political parties are organized around such cleavages as class or ethnicity, institutionalized party competition is still the primary force for establishing democratic norms and preventing authoritarian rule (Lipset 2000). Hence political parties cannot be marginalized from a reform movement, even if the features of illiberal democracy require parties to find innovative ways of working with each other and with nonparty organizations in order to press their agenda with any hope of success. Indeed, too strong an emphasis on civil society rather than on partisan politics may undermine representative politics and jeopardize liberalization; a safer option is collaboration between strong, inclusive parties and elements from a vibrant civil society (Doherty 2001).

A coordinated effort at reform may allow CSAs and political parties to pursue their respective comparative advantages, playing complementary rather than identical roles in pursuing reform. Particularly when political reform seeks to change the foundations of the regime—as is likely in either an illiberal democracy or a more authoritarian regime—reform entails both normative and institutional dimensions. CSAs tend to have a comparative advantage in long-term normative change (changing citizens' ideas about criteria for good governance or political participation, for instance), whereas political parties have an advantage in advancing institutional reforms that embody those normative shifts. It makes strategic sense for activists to take an inclusive, normative approach in challenging a regime. As Iris Young explains (1991: 151), such a strategy has greater clout and validity than does advocating for special interests:

When civic movements expose power in public discussion and demand that the powerful give an account of themselves, they sometimes simply assert particular interests against others. Often, however, they make moral appeals about justice, rightness, or the collective good, rather than couching their criticism in self-interested terms. Sometimes the force of public moral appeals made by otherwise powerless people effects a change of policy because the powerful agents have been successfully shamed.

In Malaysia, for example, advocates for greater official support for Chinese education phrase their arguments not just in terms of minority rights but also in terms of these rights' being for the sake of national resilience, which includes promoting an ethic of tolerance and respect for diversity rather than narrow-minded chauvinism (consider Chinese Guilds 1985; Chinese Organisations 1999). Such appeals take advantage of common ground uniting oppositional actors while making reformist demands appear morally irrefutable and universally relevant.

This normative project extends broadly to the acculturation of democratic ideals, which then can be activated in the course of participatory praxis. For instance, Mainwaring and Viola (1984: 17) argue that it is

CSAs in Brazil and Argentina that "question the semi-democratic political culture . . . and bring new values, perspectives, methods, and approaches to the political arena," but that their " 'apolitical' means of doing politics may curtail their ability to transform political regimes" more directly (20). Along these lines, Törnquist (1993) distinguishes between two processes: democratic empowerment and the democratization of politics. He acknowledges the pivotal role of mass protests and demonstrations in bringing down the Marcos government in the Philippines in the 1980s. However, he finds that this largely middle-class movement failed to entrench a real alternative or foundation for democracy, especially at the grassroots. To be meaningful and durable, liberalization must include not only a change of institutions but also empowerment of all citizens and the fostering of alternatives built through "more or less democratic organizing, management and cooperation" (Törnquist 1993: 503). Törnquist's argument therefore suggests that groups with the capacity and potency to force institutional reforms must do so, while others address norms and practices of democratic citizenship.

At the same time, the parties with which CSAs engage are not just those of the opposition. Weighing their options, CSAs may find the pursuit of change from within more likely to be fruitful than a struggle against the institutions of the state[20]—but this path carries a degree of risk. John Dryzek (1996) captures this dynamic in Mexico's democratization. He warns that while different social groups seek inclusion in the government in order to ensure their influence, exclusion may be a better and more pro-democratic strategy for these groups and for civil society as a whole.[21] The inclusion of opposition activists in positions of potential influence within formal politics could drain civil society of the resources it needs to be effective, leaving the government ultimately unchecked, harder to challenge, and more dominant.[22] In much the same way, James Jesudason (1996) describes the balance between benign incorporation and enfeebling co-optation in Malaysia's "syncretic" state. In McAdam, Tarrow, and Tilly's (2001) framework, inclusion shifts the terrain of contentious politics from transgressive to contained, or it may undercut contention by creating an identity of interests and claims between CSAs and the state. The same conclusions should hold for groups that seek inclusion in a potential, as opposed to an incumbent, government. CSAs may see their best chance for efficacy in entering an opposition electoral coalition with a chance of taking over the government. Their entrance grants legitimacy[23] to that opposition coalition but may not guarantee primacy for the activists' demands unless these are also imperatives for the coalition.

A central contribution of the present study is its consideration of the relative contributions of CSAs, political parties, and state institutions to political processes. Bratton (1989: 425) reminds us, "There are many basic political and economic functions which must be performed for which the state is uniquely equipped," even if " 'politics' has not become conterminous with 'the state.' " This lesson is especially pertinent to the present case. CSAs can and do influence the government and its policies, but they cannot and should not replace the government or formal opposition, and, as Dryzek admonishes, they need to be on guard against unsought incorporation or marginalization. Furthermore, collaboration among CSAs and political parties may bring additional individuals and groups into political decision-making processes and may facilitate the sharing of ideas at both formal and informal levels. However, the broader implications of such strategies have not really been examined. For instance, the intervention of CSAs may tilt the balance of power among political parties so that parties adopt particular stances. However, as implied by Levi (1996) and by others in discussing different sorts of social capital, this influence may not be in the direction of inclusiveness. The involvement of Chinese educationist NGOs with the Democratic Action Party (DAP) in Malaysia, for example, has arguably contributed to the party's Chinese-chauvinist image. Under pressure from these groups, the DAP may have adopted more pro-Chinese policies in its platforms over the years than it would otherwise have done. At the same time, greater involvement in formal politics may compromise NGOs' image as self-abnegating or "nongovernmental." Hence a collaborative approach may be a useful strategy in the short term, but in the long term it could diminish the moral authority of the CSAs involved.

Conclusion

In sum, this study conceptualizes the development of contentious politics as occurring over the long term, rather than presenting dramatic events in isolation, and it makes no effort to constrain the object of analysis too tightly. All sorts of oppositional activity, both formal and informal, and targeted at political culture or state institutions, are linked elements of a larger syndrome. A contentious episode or cycle—the protests after Anwar's ouster, or the Reformasi movement more broadly, for instance—can be understood only in the context of local history and the prevailing regime. CSAs and political parties alike contribute to political change, and change may continue even if it is not immediately reflected in votes or institutions. Through a combination of normative and institutional change, based upon activism within and across civil society and political society, viable, entrenched political reform becomes more feasible, if only incrementally achieved. Empirically, the chapters to come trace out how such gradual change has been pursued in Malaysia and compare that experience with Indonesia's. Analytically, the result of this investigation is a framework for understanding protest that is theoretically and empirically revealing, but realistic. This framework specifies angles for investigation, rather than mapping out a deterministic account of when and how political reform will happen in any given case, thus laying the ground more for further research than for pat conclusions.

POLITICAL DEVELOPMENT IN
THE COLONIAL ERA

A study of the ways in which regime type shapes oppositional possibilities, of how changing political opportunities yield shifting trajectories for
activism, and of how coalitional capital develops over time must start at
the beginning of politicized associational life in order to understand how
the polity came to be structured and oriented as it is. By the time Malaysia gained independence, in 1957, the contours of civil society and political life were roughly in place. The colonial period left a legacy of communalism, capitalism, parliamentary democracy, and a relatively high
degree of state surveillance and control. By the time the British departed,
they had done all they could to ensure that a team of race-based, moderate parties was prepared to take over, despite the fact that other alternatives had already presented themselves and continued to press for influence. These early efforts at reform may be seen as the first steps in a
long-term, iterative process of Malaysians' mobilizing around alternative
political norms in hopes of restructuring the polity.

In the two decades before the Second World War—around the time
that Milner (1991) posits "politics" took root in colonial Malaya[1]—modern associational life really began to take shape on the peninsula. Colonial subjects, spurred on by exhortations in the local media, came to act
as "citizens" and coalesced in autonomous groups. A high degree of racial segmentation was common from the outset, given that occupational
patterns, as well as religious and linguistic divisions, primarily followed
ethnic lines, but some noncommunal organizations also formed. While
most of these early groups were initially oriented less toward politics than
toward welfare issues, sports, or just socializing, many soon developed a
more politicized orientation. It was not until after the Second World War,
though, as preparations for independence progressed, that activists began
to have a real option of joining a political party and competing for con-

trol of the government rather than confining their struggle to other types of sociopolitical organizations. The process of state formation, and particularly the centrality of accessible, arguably effective political parties, largely determined the shape—and especially the relative marginalization—of political forces outside the state as well. The relative inclination of members of different ethnic and class groups to engage with the state via political parties or through nonparty organizations presaged still-relevant calculations on how to ensure influence while avoiding unwanted co-optation.

It is with the shape of associational life at the juncture between colonialism and independence, as political agendas crystallized and political institutions began to take shape, that this chapter is primarily concerned. As the development of the first sociopolitical organizations demonstrates, the communalism now so intrinsic to Malaysian political life was and is neither absolute nor inevitable. Rather, promising noncommunal initiatives of that critical era lost out to a quasi-consociational alternative preferred by the departing British and local capitalist elites. Noncommunal political institutions limped on, but without the stature and potential they had before the Alliance coalition came to power in the 1950s.[2] These early contests informed later normative alternatives: the competing "nations of intent" of the 1950s (Shamsul 1996b) are much the same as those striving for ideological and institutional ascendance in the 1990s and beyond.

Colonialism and Communalism

Prior to the coming of the British, what is now Malaysia was a group of independently governed states linked by culture, language, and trade. At the time, except in the entrepôt cities of Malacca, Penang, and Singapore, the peninsular population was almost entirely Malay. Malaya's population became increasingly heterogeneous as the colonial economy developed. The British, requiring a massive labor force to work their rubber plantations and tin mines, imported hundreds of thousands of laborers from southeastern China and southern India between 1870 and 1930. Immigrants outnumbered indigenes in Singapore and Malaya by the eve of the Second World War. By independence, in 1957, the population of the Federation of Malaya was about 50 percent Malay, 37 percent Chinese, and 11 percent Indian (Roff 1994; Andaya and Andaya 1982).

For reasons of efficiency, economy, and moral mission, the British administered Malaya through a system of indirect rule.[3] The colonial authorities maintained the traditional Malay aristocracy as (largely disempowered) rulers and implemented a paternalistic system of Malay special rights with regard to land, education, and positions in the colonial civil service. Beginning around the turn of the twentieth century, British education of select Malays for plum civil service jobs created a new, English-educated, Western-influenced Malay leadership group that derived legitimacy both from inherited social status, since most were drawn from among traditional elites, and from association with the colonial regime. Pro-Malay policies were further enhanced in the early 1920s with the recruitment of more Malays to the lower ranks of the public sector, and with the provision of schools for Malays even in rural areas. Given the status and job security conferred by government service, few English-educated Malays sought employment outside the public sector. Nonetheless, as the British preferred, the vast majority of Malays remained peasant cultivators in rural villages, their lives largely unchanged by colonialism. These sorts of parallel policies nurtured class divisions among Malays, which were later reflected in divergent political allegiances and priorities.

British policy toward the other racial communities was also bifurcated. Chinese and Indian laborers comprised the bulk of the colonial industrial and plantation agricultural workforce. English-educated non-Malays, while largely excluded from positions of political or administrative authority, held the majority of subordinate-level government clerical and technical jobs by 1920, and it was non-Malays, especially Chinese, whom the British entrusted with economic power. Chinese and Indians, more often English-educated and urbanized than were Malays, were stereotyped as more industrious. Regardless, the British categorized all Chinese and Indians as unassimilable, transient immigrants, notwithstanding the increasing number of them domiciled in Malaya; thus did the British avoid responsibility for integrating them into a Malayan whole (Roff 1994).[4]

Intentionally or not, the British presence, aside from cementing a colonial-capitalist economic and political order, fundamentally altered perceptions of ethnicity in Malaya. In particular, it was only in the eighteenth to nineteenth centuries that "Melayu" (Malay) began to be used widely as an ethnic category rather than just as a referent to place of origin within a set of autonomous Malay polities. The influx of immigrants under colonialism, especially Chinese but also Europeans and others, may have encouraged popular expressions of group identity among peasant Malays who shared a common grievance of *kemunduran* (backwardness) by comparison with the Chinese and wealthier non-Malay Muslims. The same process of developing a unified racial consciousness was repeated among Chinese, Indians, and smaller communities.[5] In addition, as in other colonies, the spread of newspapers was closely linked with the emergence of nationalism and the "imagined communities" (Anderson 1983) of Malays, Chinese, and Indians in the Malay peninsula. This trend really began among Malays with the monthly *Al-Imam* in Singapore (1906–1908), and it escalated as nationalist agitation gained steam.

It is unclear to what extent the British actively pursued communalism as a prophylactic against class-based mobilization. Collin Abraham (1997) insists that the British first created an economic order in which occupational categories were segmented by race and then purposely encouraged strong ethnic identification and loyalties to forestall class-based mobilization. He argues that colonial labor-recruitment policies consciously sought to weaken the bargaining power of any one group (for instance, by discouraging the importation of labor from Indonesia because those workers would share ethnic ties with Malays) so that the British could divide and rule. Poor Malays came to identify with other Malays, not with poor Chinese or Indians, and they remained trapped in the politics of a semifeudal peasant economy. The Chinese, left largely to themselves by the British, responded by developing norms that emphasized ethnic solidarity as a means of economic survival and mobility. The smaller Indian population, unable to assert itself politically or economically, basically separated itself out and lived in isolation.

An alternative explanation by Zawawi Ibrahim (1989: 128) suggests that while there is no "inherent logical connection between ethnicity and the imperatives of capital," the former "assumes importance because of its coincidence with factors which are deemed crucial for capital in a given instance; though not necessarily through conscious design or intention." In other words, it was in the interest of British capitalists to keep the mass of Malays tied to their subsistence agrarian base, producing staple foods and being "good peasants," while Chinese and Indian workers staffed plantations and mines. Thus emerged an "articulation between ethnicity and the economic division of labour of the colonial order" (Zawawi Ibrahim 1989: 130) even as class divisions, such as between Malay peasants and landlords, formed within ethnic groups. Hence capital sought just to prevent ethnic groups' uniting along class lines, regardless of the implications for intercommunal relations.

The Japanese occupation during the Second World War played a key role, too, in cementing racial consciousness but also nurtured a sense of entitlement to political engagement across communities. Malay nationalists, armed and empowered by the Japanese, fought a proxy war against the British, represented mainly by British-armed Chinese.[6] With this violent and racially charged preface, the Japanese surrender ushered in a bloody fourteen-day ethnic riot, the biggest in Malaysian postwar history. Communal killings continued for some time even after the reinstatement of British rule (Andaya and Andaya 1982; Shamsul 1996a). Over the course of the war, too, it was through associations established by the Japanese that many in Malaya, especially women, gained their first exposure to mass political activity. Among these associations were the Malayan Reconstruction Co-operative Association and the Malayan Welfare Association (both established in 1944), which took part in rallies and public lectures. Indeed, as early as October 1942, the Japanese encouraged women to increase their involvement in public life and the market economy, ultimately stimulating both rural and urban women to join men in postwar political activism (Manderson 1980). The occupation also fostered politicization among Indians, many of whom were active in the anti-British Indian Independence League and Indian National Army. Many of these activists, though, became disillusioned with these organizations and with Japanese rule, eventually turning against the Japanese and coming to favor the British (Ramasamy 1984).

Nationalist Imaginings

As Tan Liok Ee (1988) convincingly relates, the Malay term *bangsa* refers to a "natural" community, defined by descent and cultural, linguistic, and religious characteristics; the political or territorial nation is the *negara*. Malay nationalism was and is premised on the notion that *bangsa Melayu* (the Malay race) would have become a political nation in its own right, with *tanah Melayu* (land of the Malays) as its territory, if not for colonial arrangements. Even today, Tan insists, the use of a form of *bangsa* instead of *negara* to mean "national" (as in *bahasa kebangsaan* for "national language") implicitly reasserts the primacy of the ethnic group. While *bangsa* is sometimes used to refer to all Malaysians, it is more commonly understood to refer only to *bangsa Melayu*. From the start, Malay nationalism was aimed not so much at the British as at local Chinese. It focused on the economic and political deprivation of Malays in their own land and hence validated the reservation of special rights and status for Malays. Muhammad Ikmal Said (1996: 39) concurs: "Malay nationalism does not attempt to carve out a politically autonomous area for itself. Rather, it is a project that seeks to build a Malay political roof over the structures of the modern state." The role of language symbolized this exclusiveness. In Indonesia, the national language served to unify diverse nationalist groups; in Malaya, by contrast, Bahasa Melayu served as an ethnic rather than a supraethnic means of political communication (Anderson 1998: 325).[7]

Malay nationalists were never a homogeneous group. While all agreed that Bahasa Melayu should be the official and national language in independent Malaya, factions differed regarding the importance of the other key symbols of Malayness: *agama* (religion) and *raja* (rulers). Shamsul (1996b) identifies three different Malay "nations-of-intent," one identified by territory, one by Malay cultural and linguistic characteristics, and one by religion. Moderate "administocrats" (administrators and aristocrats; see Chandra 1979) emphasized the role of the *raja* as custodians of Malay culture and Islam. The Malay left recognized the importance of Islam but rejected the feudal polity dominated by the traditional ruling class. Finally, the Islamist leadership was committed to replacing the secular state with an Islamist one.

The Mandarin term *minzu*, by contrast, as Tan (1988) explains, is a modern concept signifying the community in a general sense. In the Malayan context, *minzu* referred more to the "imagined" moral community linked by Chinese language and culture than to ethnic Han chauvinism. *Minzu* was distinct from *guojia*, the nation in a territorial and political sense. One *guojia* may contain several discrete but equal *minzu*. Under this framework, Malays had no claim to preferred status as indigenes, and more recent migrants did not need to sacrifice their cultures in order to belong to the new nation. In contrast, *bangsa Melayu* could not acknowledge any other group as having an equal claim to membership in the Malayan nation without itself losing status. The rhetoric of *minzu* was essentially confined to the Chinese-educated community. However, by the late 1920s, English-educated Straits Chinese,[8] too, had begun making demands for greater representation and participation. Straits Chinese nationalists called for a nation founded on the will to live together, a common Malayan consciousness, and full equality and democratic participation. Their conception stressed equality among individuals rather than among communities, as implied by *minzu*. Both perspectives, though, opposed the segmentation of Malaya into a Malay core and a non-Malay periphery. Hence many ethnic Chinese, viewing the nation in strictly political terms, thought of themselves as Malayan but not Melayu, and thus deserving of citizenship without needing to become culturally Malay (Tan 1988).

The majority of Chinese in postwar Malaya were not migrants; many of their families had been on the peninsula for generations. Even if their primary attachment was to their ethnic communities, the most important goal of Chinese and other non-Malay nationalists was secure status within a Malayan political community (Tan 1988). In negotiations with the British and Malays, local Chinese and other non-Malays pressed for rights of full citizenship, unrestricted opportunities for economic advancement, and the preservation of vernacular languages and schools as well as outlets for public cultural expression. As citizens, Chinese Malayans increasingly voiced demands, harboring "the unrealistically high assumption that Chinese would be treated as the equals of Malays," with only belated awareness that neither British officials nor Malay elites shared this expectation (Heng 1996: 506). These conflicting perspectives and presumptions colored later debates on the shape of the independent nation in terms of territory, citizenship, and policies and encouraged communal segmentation on philosophical as well as practical grounds.

Prewar and Immediate Postwar Malay Organizations

It was in Malays' prewar sociopolitical organizations that the shift of issues from the sphere of social activism to that of formal politics was most evident, as new political opportunity structures advocated revised strategies for engagement. Divisions between the aristocracy and the agrarian masses, perpetuated by the British despite such innovations as broadly distributed land titles and mass education, meant that cross-cutting Malay social organizations (aside from long-standing, unstructured institutions for cooperative effort and mutual help, known as *gotong-royong* or *tolong menolong*) were slow to emerge. Moreover, both tradition and British policy encouraged Malays to see the government as responsible for protecting their interests. This orientation curtailed the perceived need for autonomous Malay organizations, even well after independence (Tham 1977).

Although the majority of Malays remained in rural areas and occupations throughout the colonial era, economic and social changes under capitalism, including increased urbanization and social differentiation, encouraged a shift in Malay associational life. Among urbanized Malays, as William Roff explains (1994: 178), "The circumstances of urban life—its heterogeneity, competitiveness, and relative freedom from customary sanctions and authority—produced for individuals both an often confusing sense of personal insecurity and a newly defined group awareness." From the advent of colonialism until the late nineteenth century, the need for social identification was largely met in the urban Straits Settlements of Singapore, Penang, and Malacca by the formation of urban *kampung* (villages) of Malays from the same places of origin and, often, the same economic specializations. As urban life grew more complex and intense, however, and as the colonial order matured, these patterns of residence and occupation became less clear-cut, and the significance of traditional structures for prestige and status waned (Roff 1994: 180–81).

New associational forms emerged around the turn of the century—mainly literary, social, religious, and "progress" associations. Initially these associations were led by "Malayo-Muslims" (Arabs, Muslim

Indians, and *peranakan,* or Straits Chinese) rather than by Malays, since the former were more involved in administration and more affected by economic competition from the Chinese. This leadership appealed to solidarity along linguistic and religious rather than purely communal lines. The associations emulated Western organizational forms. In particular, voluntary, membership-based clubs for study, sports and recreation, and cultural activities proliferated in towns and larger *kampung* from at least 1910. However limited their objectives, and despite divisions along economic and educational lines, these associations had some capacity for social integration and improvement of self and society. Still, until the mid-1920s, most Malay and Malayo-Muslim organizations in the Straits Settlements and in the peninsular states remained social, cultural, and economic in orientation and not political, even if some occasionally made representations to the government on relevant matters (Roff 1994: 181–87; Tham 1977).

Gradually, social change encouraged Malays to appeal to their community in recognizing a common future and pursuing economic development and cultural revival. Roff (1994: 185) describes this transition,

perhaps the most notable feature of the cultural welfare and progress associations was the way in which, despite their almost invariably local origins and circumscribed membership and their lack of direct contact with each other, they all practically without exception recognized the larger Malay society of which they were a part and spoke in holistic (if not necessarily nationalistic) terms of the task of improving the educational and economic status of the Malays within the plural society.

It was the self-improving impulse that generated the establishment of early twentieth-century progress associations, institutionalizing the idea of a meaningful Malay community within a multiracial polity. Young, modern, English- or vernacular-educated Malays (teachers, government servants, small-scale businessmen, and journalists) took the lead in these groups, not Malayo-Muslims as before. Among these associations were the Persekutuan Keharapan Belia (New Hope Society, established in Johor Bahru in 1916); the Persekutuan Indra Kayangan (Heavenly Land Society, Alor Star, 1918); the Persekutuan Perbahathan Orang-orang Islam (Muslim Debating Society, Muar, 1919); and the first of the Persekutuan Guru-guru Melayu and Persekutuan Guru-guru Islam (Malay and Islamic Teachers' Associations, established over the course of the early 1920s). These groups discussed the problems of living as Malays in the modern world and developed self-help and educational programs to contribute to Malay advancement (Roff 1994: 184–85; Tham 1977).

These organizations were supplemented by an array of quasi-political and literary associations that developed through the 1930s. The first such group was the nationalistic Kesatuan Melayu Singapura (Singapore Malay Union, or KMS), established in 1926. While fundamentally a politically conservative, welfare-oriented group, the KMS aimed to raise political awareness and promote Malays' economic and educational development (Roff 1994: 188–95). New media also both heightened Malays' identification along racial lines and clearly demarcated other communities as different and threatening, implicitly urging race-based political mobilization. Particularly from the late 1920s through the 1930s, the proliferation of Malay journals, according to Firdaus (1985: 58–59),

assisted the newly emerging elites to educate the masses politically, as well as to challenge, gradually, the traditional social and political structure. At the same time, more forthrightly, they reminded their readers of the increasing economic dominance and demographic growth of the immigrant races.

Bangsawan (Malay opera) and other theatrical performances were also used for political socialization, though "under the guise of promoting Malay language and literature" (Firdaus 1985: 119–20). It is hardly surprising that, aside from stirring up nationalist sentiment through their writings, many among the literary elite—which included journalists, essayists, and writers of political fiction and poetry[9]—were eventually also active in political parties.

Over one hundred Malay nationalist newspapers and journals in existence between 1930 and 1941 offered a forum for members of the new intelligentsia to voice their sociopolitical critiques. Even prenationalist, parochial political organizations led by pro-British aristocrats were largely prompted by newspaper polemics (Firdaus 1985). At least two journals played a special role in forming and sustaining the first pan-peninsular Malay organizations: the Persaudaraan Sahabat Pena Malaya (Malayan Association of Pen Pals), established in 1934 on the initiative of the Penang-based newspaper *Saudara,* and the Kesatuan Melayu Muda (Young Malay Union, or KMM, 1938), which involved the Kuala Lumpur–based *Majlis.* The Persaudaraan Sahabat Pena Malaya, although self-consciously nonpolitical, united a larger number of geographically and socially diverse Malays than any previous organization had done. The KMM constituted "the first organizational embodiment of radical ideas among the Malays" (Firdaus 1985: 63–64; see also Tham 1977; Roff 1994).

Nonetheless, despite congresses on the role of associations in the Malay community in 1939 and 1940, and growing awareness of Malay rights and interests, the impact of prewar radical nationalist associations was limited. They were hindered by relatively low membership, popular uncertainty regarding political inclinations, persistent state (rather than national) parochialism among Malays, limited economic resources, and disagreement over who actually constituted the Malay community.[10] Moreover, thanks largely to British policies favoring the traditional aristocracy in economic and administrative positions, a reform-minded new middle class did not develop outside the urban Straits Settlements until later (Roff 1994; Tham 1977). The immediate postwar period saw significant development in the nature and type of Malay associations, but their basic characteristics persisted. Most groups were still social, recreational, or welfare-oriented, though these were complemented by a significant cohort of literary and (quasi-)political associations that took up nationalist objectives.

By the 1950s, two elite groups had emerged among Malays, one comprising mostly government servants or bureaucrats (many of them also aristocrats) and the other composed of teachers, journalists, and others educated in the native schools.[11] The former group concentrated on political associations and the latter on literary and cultural associations. However, both sets of organizations sought to protect the Malay community against "the encroachment of alien influences, institutions and interests" (Tham 1977: 28–32). As independence drew nearer, most Malay political organizations evolved into political parties, and the community's attention shifted more firmly from self-help to the state.

It was in this era that Malay women, too, began to organize around nationalist aims as well as traditional welfare concerns. Malayan women's groups of the 1940s and 1950s were almost all communal in nature,[12] and only the Malay ones tended to be political. Promotion of female education was one of the key issues for early, formal politicized women's associations. The first of these was the Malay Women Teachers' Union (founded in Johor, 1929), followed by a similar union founded in Malacca in 1938. The KMS had a women's section by 1940. Other groups focusing on both home economics and adult literacy formed at around the same time. Among these groups were numerous associations known as *kumpulan kaum ibu* (mothers' groups). These confederated at the state level in 1947 and then, in line with the broader shift among Malays from associational to party involvement, united in 1949 as Pergerakan Kaum Ibu UMNO (Kaum Ibu, UMNO Mothers' Movement, renamed Wanita UMNO, or UMNO Women, in 1971), the women's wing of the United Malays National Organisation (UMNO). Though it had little real authority within the party, Kaum Ibu took a strong stance on plans for independence and raised political awareness among rural Malay women as well as among the wives of prominent political and community leaders. Other Malay women's groups were also actually the women's sections of new political parties, such as the nationalistic Angkatan Wanita Sedar (Conscious Women's Front, AWAS), which was the women's section of the Partai Kebangsaan Melayu Malaya (PKMM, Malay Nationalist Party, formed 1945 and disbanded in 1950) (Manderson 1980; Lai 2003; Khadijah n.d.).

Prewar and Postwar Chinese Organizations

Although Chinese immigration had begun on a small scale long before the British arrived on the scene, the main influx of ethnic Chinese into Malaya started in the mid-nineteenth century. The British imported Chinese laborers to work mainly in tin mines and plantation agriculture, especially rubber tapping. The community was concentrated in Chinese-majority, culturally distinctive urban settlements, mostly on the west coast. Chinese organizational life reflected these conditions, for instance in the persistent segmentation between the long-resident Straits Chinese and more recent immigrants, and the enduring strength of original village, clan, and dialect ties. In addition, many immigrants retained strong ties to China, even establishing branches of mainland political parties in Malaya.

The British tended toward benign neglect in governing the Chinese. Therefore, the community relied heavily on its own means. Community mobilization spawned a range of cultural and welfare societies, an enormous network of Chinese-medium primary and secondary schools, and eventually labor unions as well as a sort of community policing through secret societies, including those belonging to the Triad Brotherhood, active since the seventeenth century. Especially significant were *shetuan,* or Chinese organizations based on clan, regional, and occupational links. Some *shetuan* existed from the late eighteenth century, though most were twentieth-century creations. In 1949 there were over 1,500 *shetuan* in colonial Malaya. The most important were each state's Chinese chambers of commerce and Chinese assembly halls. Dominated by wealthy businessmen who were expected to be benefactors to their communities, the *shetuan* network represented the real power structure of the Chinese community (Tan 1997).

Starting around the turn of the twentieth century, and initially in response to pre-1949 nationalist and revolutionary movements in China, Malayan Chinese associations gradually grew more political. Both the Kuomintang (KMT) and the Chinese Communist Party (CCP) rallied support in Malaya. Then, beginning in the early 1950s, Chinese education and language, together with the defense of multiculturalism more generally, became key factors in Chinese political mobilization and demands. Even earlier, many Chinese societies, although they were "essentially social and community welfare agencies" (Tan 1983: 113), "bordered on the political even if this political aspect was vague and not so explicitly and systematically laid out" (Lee 1985: 131).[13]

While other communal organizations were probably of more lasting significance to ethnic Chinese, secret societies particularly worried the British. These societies, especially the political Triad Brotherhood, existed both in China and among Chinese communities elsewhere. Brought overseas by early Chinese immigrants, secret societies operated on a range of fronts—political, social, and criminal—and developed a mystique based on secrecy, ceremony, and intimidation. Some societies had eligibility criteria related to dialect group, place of residence, or type of employment, but others were less restrictive, even welcoming non-Chinese (Mak 1981; Blythe 1969). Secret societies claimed enormous influence and membership. As of 1888, Singapore purportedly had eleven secret societies, with 62,376 members; and Penang, five societies, with 92,581 members (Hicks 1996: 91). As Blythe (1969: 1) describes the secret societies, they

provided the individual with a social background, a body politic in miniature, in and through which he found authority, protection, assistance, a sense of kinship, and, through the ritual bond, possibly some measure of spiritual content, in a foreign land where the ruling power was completely alien in race, language, religion, manners, and customs.

This motivation was not so different from the impetus driving Malays to settle in *kampung* and form associations upon their relocation to unfamiliar, largely non-Malay, urban areas, and it proved equally likely to result in communal segregation.

At first, colonial authorities deemed an outright ban on secret societies implausible. They agreed instead to leave it to the societies' leaders to control their own members. Eventually, though, in light of bloody outbreaks sparked by Chinese factional rivalries, the British prohibited and worked to eradicate secret societies. Between 1869 and 1916, the colonial government enacted a series of ordinances requiring registration of societies and forbidding anything having to do with Triad societies. The British also extended throughout Malaya the Chinese Protectorate system, which had first been introduced in Singapore in 1872 to advise the government on Chinese affairs and facilitate communication with the community (Blythe 1969: 2–7). Despite these measures, some secret society personnel were later active in the formation and campaigns of political parties (Blythe 1969).

More overtly political, and hence threatening to colonial authorities, was Chinese nationalism, whether focused on China or on Malaya. This movement emerged at the turn of the twentieth century as an offshoot of nationalist agitation in mainland China. The three chief streams for Chinese nationalism in Malaya were the Kuomintang Malaya (KMTM), formed in 1913 with backing from the conservative merchant leadership of Chinese associations; the Malayan Communist Party (MCP), which won the support of most Chinese schools and labor organizations; and the Straits Chinese British Association (SCBA), formed in 1900 to represent the interests of English-educated, *peranakan* professionals and entrepreneurs. The colonial government attempted—not very successfully—to control the KMTM and the MCP, especially via schools, whose communal parochialism, autonomy, and role in the recruitment of rebels were seen to threaten the federation (Heng 1996; Enloe 1970).

Chinese nationalism in Malaya was linked from the outset with the Chinese education movement. Chinese schools had been at the center of community life since well before the Second World War and were an important site of political socialization of both boys and girls.[14] Schoolteachers played a dominant role in Malayan Chinese political life throughout the 1920s and 1930s, and school management committees included key community leaders. Some schools and teachers supported the KMT; others, the CCP. Chinese teachers were therefore key targets of British colonial surveillance and control before and after the war. During the anticommunist postwar Emergency, the colonial government established a network of informers among teachers and students and conducted raids on schools suspected of supporting the MCP. Those teachers deemed "undesirable" were denied registration—required for their employment as of 1920—and were sometimes deported. Also, Chinese schoolteachers and students were among the thousands killed for anti-Japanese activities during the Japanese occupation (Tan 1997).

As Malaya edged toward independence, both English- and Chinese-educated Chinese presented a view of nationhood colored by experience with Chinese-medium education, favoring a multiethnic, multilingual state, even if they accepted Malay as the primary national language. British and Malay elites, in contrast, advocated a unified, Malay-based national culture, supported by a single language and a monolingual education system (Tan 1988). The Chinese educationist lobby, often disparaged as chauvinist or extremist, has struggled since the 1950s to resist the encroachment of the state into the curriculum and medium of instruction of vernacular schools and to press for public financial support and official recognition of these schools. First at the state level and then at the national level, teachers united, and eventually launched the United Chinese School Teachers' Association (UCSTA), in December 1951. The United Chinese School Committees' Association (UCSCA) followed in 1954.

These organizations were central to the formulation of Chinese responses to colonial and independent governmental reports and policies on education and language. Given their strength, the UCSTA and the UCSCA have also been critical to the fortunes of Chinese political parties (see Tan 1997).

Chinese labor organizations also became a potent political and social force, especially once Chinese guilds and associations had developed into trade unions.[15] Unlike the Chinese education movement, the labor movement as a whole strove from the outset for a noncommunal orientation and involved members of all ethnic groups, especially in the mass trade unions for plantation and other workers. Smaller labor associations developed, though, that were essentially exclusive to Malayan Chinese. For instance, Chinese women in the service sector, including *amah* (domestic servants), laundresses, restaurant workers, and prostitutes, formed associations that, among other functions, bargained with employers for favorable wages and working conditions (Rohana 1988). However, it was the mass trade unions that posed the greatest challenge to the state and illustrated the potential for noncommunal organizing, despite the leading role of Chinese workers in the movement. Chinese workers organized the first strike in Malaya in 1926, and other serious labor actions followed. By 1927, the Nanyang (South Seas) General Labour Union (NGLU) had formed in Malaya on the instructions of the Communist International's trade union organization. The NGLU achieved a membership of 5,000 from over forty unions, though it was nearly eradicated by a police crackdown in 1928–1931.

In 1930, the General Labour Union (GLU) was formed from the remnants of the NGLU. Dominated by ethnic Chinese, the GLU was established by the MCP not just for immediate economic gains but also for the purpose of boosting workers' solidarity and awareness over the long term, especially by means of industrial strikes.[16] A series of strikes among workers from docks and harbors, mines, rubber estates, collieries, and other sectors, spearheaded largely by ethnic Chinese, wracked the economy, especially from 1934 through 1942, and again amidst the poverty, inflation, and food shortages of the final years of the Japanese occupation and postwar period. Women—who, despite their high labor-force participation rate, had been completely excluded from early Chinese guilds and workers' associations—also began to get involved by the 1930s, at least on rubber estates, where they remained most actively involved through the 1960s (Rohana 1988; Lai 2003).

The GLU was renamed the Pan-Malayan Federation of Trade Unions (PMFTU) in 1947. At its height that year, the PMFTU controlled 241 of 277 registered unions and 74 percent of organized labor. While Chinese predominated, the federation represented workers of all races. In fact, an Indian, S. A. Ganapathy, was elected chairman in 1947, heading a central committee composed of four Chinese, two Indians, and two Malays. Then, in 1948, as part of a policy of encouraging only "responsible," pro-British unions, the colonial government amended the Trade Unions Ordinance to allow only unions catering to specific organizations and industries to register. This rule effectively banned any general labor federation, including the PMFTU, a prohibition which made class-based mobilization more difficult than organization along communal lines, given the racially segregated structure of the labor force (Stenson 1980; Dass 1991).

Prewar and Postwar Indian Organizations

Ethnic Indians often formed organizations in colonial Malaya along communal or caste lines, but sometimes more on the basis of class. Malayan Indian groups served religious, cultural, and economic purposes, and to some extent they paralleled movements in India. For instance, in line with a contemporaneous movement in India, a subset of Malayan Indian associations around the 1920s concerned themselves with reforming Hinduism and correcting abuses of the caste system. Others provided support for the independence movement in India. Like Malay and Chinese organizations, Malayan Indian organizations began to take on a more political character over time. However, lack of a shared sense of cultural identity complicated mass associations and allowed disparate Indian organizations to stress in-group identity and highlight differences across subcommunities (so, for instance, Muslim Indians tended to associate more with Malays than with Hindu Indians). Ethnic Indians were divided along urban-rural lines, which tended to follow caste, linguistic, economic, and educational cleavages, particularly in the prewar period. Moreover, foreign-born and local-born Indians tended to disagree on such political issues as the extent to which Malaya belonged to the Malays rather than to all resident communities; since the 1920s, economic and political elites have been drawn from among a Western-educated, professional minority with limited grassroots links (Ampalavanar 1981; Rajoo 1985; Tham 1977).

Still, intracommunal cleavages were not insurmountable. For instance, in the 1930s, the influential *Dravida Kalagam*, a social movement imported from Madras that encouraged self-respect among Tamils, spread in Malaya among educated Indians (schoolteachers, journalists, and others) as well as among estate workers. Also, the first political body claiming to represent all Indians, the Central Indian Association of Malaya

(CIAM), formed after a long struggle, which included a 1937 visit to Malaya by Jawaharlal Nehru, during which he reportedly chided middle-class Indians for their indifference to the community and called for Indian unity. CIAM activists—mainly Western-educated intellectuals and plantation elites—were influenced by and identified with the nationalist movement in India and were supported by the government of India. A few made statements regarding the British treatment of Indians in Malaya, but they had little impact. The CIAM was more effective in mobilizing workers along class and nationalist lines and encouraging them to speak up for their rights, by means that included the militant strikes of the early 1940s (Ramasamy 1984; Rajoo 1985; Dass 1991).

Since so many Indians were employed by large European-owned estates[17] or in government departments, prewar Indian organizations often focused on improving conditions of work for the community. Most notably, ethnic Indians, along with Chinese, were among the first to establish modern, Western-style trade unions in Malaya.[18] Conditions of labor on estates (mostly rubber plantations) were particularly deplorable, with low wages and a miserable quality of life. However, estate owners' cultivation of caste divisions and plentiful provision of toddy, which encouraged alcoholism, made unionization difficult either among Indians or in conjunction with others, especially Malays. Therefore, unionization efforts among estate workers in particular would have been hard to further without additional catalysts. Primary among such stimuli were the quest for independence in India, which spurred concern for the plight of Indian workers in Malaysia, in addition to the efforts of radical journalists, who played a significant role in politicizing Indian workers through their writings and through direct mobilization. Increasing interaction among Indian, Chinese, and Malay workers in cities, sawmills, harbors, railways, and elsewhere, together with the influence of revolutionaries from China, India, and Indonesia, also aroused class consciousness and opposition to colonial capitalists. By 1927, largely Indian social and professional associations had formed among clerical, administrative, and technical workers, as well as among staff on estates. While confined to educated groups, these organizations also encouraged mobilization among the mass of estate workers.

Gradually, as the labor force became more settled and labor shortages rendered the British less able just to ship recalcitrant workers back to India, Indian estate workers became more militant. For instance, by the mid-1940s Indian workers had formed the *Thondar Padai* (Youth Corps), together with a women's wing, as a Gandhian reformist movement. While this movement began in opposition to toddy drinking, it came to address larger issues of economic welfare and trade unionism and to organize workers for militant strikes. Meanwhile, Indian labor unions were formed by district in several states, beginning in 1946, with these efforts usually spearheaded by former Indian National Army members. Increasing numbers of Indian workers also linked forces with the PMFTU and the MCP. The working-class alliance thus forged, and the debilitating strikes waged in 1945–1946, secured immediate, substantial wage increases for Indian workers, though these came together with harsh responses from the government, including the execution of key labor activists.

However, it was the government's long-term policy of fostering more tractable unions—a strategy continued by the postcolonial state—that proved most effective in curbing labor militancy among Indians and others. A case in point was the amalgamation of smaller unions into the National Union of Plantation Workers (NUPW) in 1954, under the aegis of the British high commissioner, and the concomitant proscription of more proactive estate workers' unions.[19] Though the NUPW was the united agent for a huge mass of workers, it has never been very aggressive or effective in securing significant improvements to the dismal conditions of work and low wages of estate laborers.[20] As a result, membership in the NUPW has fallen precipitously over the years. Indeed, whether or not entrenchment of racial cleavages was their goal, the colonial and postcolonial governments' intolerance of a strong trade union movement effectively crippled the potential of labor organizing for at least tempering communalism with class consciousness.

More broadly, a number of hurdles have precluded the formation of stronger organizations among Indians, particularly among women and the mass of Indian poor in estates and factories. These factors include poverty (and the reluctance of the middle class to get involved in the affairs of the poor), residual caste stratification, poor resources, the authoritarian culture prevalent in Tamil schools, and the predominance of paternalistic rather than grassroots-based, cooperative institutions in estates (Institute of Social Analysis 1989). Although some ethnic Indian women were active in the Indian Independence Movement and others were members of voluntary associations (including at least one Indian Women's Association formed by 1946), overall they played a minimal role in early politically oriented associations. For instance, Indian women workers outnumbered their Chinese counterparts in the prewar era and were subjected to social problems, such as sexual molestation on estates, but few if any were involved in the trade union movement at least until the mid-1940s. Even the women's auxiliary of the Malaysian Indian Congress (MIC), the primary political party representing Indians, was established only in 1975, though women had been encouraged to take a more active part in the party from as early as 1946 (Khadijah n.d.; Manderson 1980; Rohana 1988). In short, communal and noncommunal organizations alike faced difficulties in attracting consistent and widespread ethnic Indian support prior to independence, and class-based options were constrained by antagonistic government policies.

Forging a Political Order, 1945–1957

Chaos greeted the British upon their return to Malaya following the Japanese surrender. The MCP's Malayan People's Anti-Japanese Army (MPAJA), supported by the British during the war for its anti-Japanese efforts, had redirected its energies in the interim against those suspected of having collaborated with the Japanese, most of them Malays. The MPAJA had taken over some villages, and radical Sufi Islamic sects sought control of others. The period marked the nadir of ethnic relations on the peninsula. Chronic food shortages, damaged infrastructure, and the devastation of so many lives lost under the Japanese contributed to the extreme tension and uncertainty. Gradually, the British reasserted control, curbed the communists, got the economy working again, and began to prepare Malaya for independence.

It was at this juncture that the first legal, viable political parties formed in Malaya, including the primary parties that have controlled the government from independence until today. Most major sociopolitical groups formed political parties, but only some were condoned by the colonial government. After a brief period of reluctant but unavoidable support for the MCP during the war, for instance, the British quickly banned the party in light of the threat it posed to the dominant order. Those parties the British favored (and which, not surprisingly, soon established their preeminence) were accommodating, race-based parties led by Western-educated elites, capitalist in orientation, and basically accepting of the Malay-centric order the British had sustained. Class-based groupings, or those too insistent on equal rights and standing for non-Malays, were strongly discouraged. These priorities proved persistent and continue to affect activists' options for mobilization.

Plans for Independence and Pressures for Communalism

In 1947, the colonial authorities presented a blueprint for independence, the Malayan Union plan. Its announcement provoked a frenzy of political organizing, including the launching of several political parties, and was a watershed moment in cementing political identities. The

Malayan Union proposal involved transferring the sovereignty of the Malay states from the Malay *raja* to the British, who would establish a centralized polity consisting of the Straits Settlements and the Federated and Unfederated Malay States of the peninsula. The Malay *raja* would retain some authority, but immigrant races—Chinese and Indians—would enjoy equal citizenship with Malays. These liberal citizenship provisions were to reward ethnic Chinese for the service they had rendered to the British during the war (Andaya and Andaya 1982: 245–56). An estimated 83 percent of resident Chinese and 75 percent of resident Indians would have been eligible for citizenship (Tan 1988: 14). Given that the plan failed to acknowledge Malay sovereignty and would have rendered Malays just one *kaum* (social group) within their own native land, a group possibly even outnumbered among citizens by non-Malays, the mass of Malays were incensed by the proposal (Tan 1988: 13–17). Fierce Malay opposition obliged the British to abandon the Malayan Union proposal. While debate over the plan tended to polarize along ethnic lines, the quest for alternatives also gave rise to multiracial initiatives.

It was with the debate over the Malayan Union in the late 1940s that the first significant multiracial political coalition came to prominence. While the United Malays National Organisation (UMNO), formed in 1946, fought to rally all Malays behind its opposition to the Malayan Union plan, a number of Malay, Chinese, and Indian organizations took a different approach. They formed the All Malaya Council of Joint Action (AMCJA) and then also Pusat Tenaga Rakyat (Center of People's Power, PUTERA) to debate and promote an alternative view, crystallized as the People's Constitutional Proposals. The core parties involved were the MCP, the PKMM, and the MIC (which, though composed of ethnic Indians, initially preferred that political parties not represent single ethnic groups). Other societal associations—most notably the potent PMFTU and Chinese chambers of commerce as well as the Malayan Democratic Union, the Malayan Democratic League, the Malayan People's Anti-Japanese Ex-Service Comrades Association, and the All-Malaya Women's Federation—also collaborated. All initially united in the AMCJA, but the PKMM and other Malay groups broke off to form PUTERA, which continued to work in alliance with the AMCJA. The aim of the AMCJA–PUTERA coalition was noncommunal, "Malayan" cooperation. Specifically, the coalition advocated an autonomous Malaya including Singapore,[21] an elected legislature, and citizenship for all residents, though it accepted Malay as the national language and special status for Malays. To press its point, in October 1947 the AMCJA–PUTERA launched a successful *hartal* (complete stoppage of economic activities). However, while the campaign educated people politically, it only made the British more resolute about dealing primarily with the less "extremist" UMNO.

The extent of popular support for this multiracial initiative is hard to gauge, but most Malays probably opposed it. Stenson (1980: 119) insists, "It may be asserted safely that [the AMCJA-PUTERA coalition] represented a wider range of Malayan opinion than the Sultans and the U.M.N.O."; membership in the AMCJA affiliates totaled "a claimed" 400,000, while the PKMM (which spearheaded PUTERA) and its affiliates had an estimated membership of 60,000 to 100,000, comparable to UMNO's. Even Stenson concedes, though, that it was primarily English-speaking urbanites, not the mass of rural Malays or non-Malay workers, who supported the coalition. PUTERA in particular relied mostly on minorities in Malay society, often Indonesians or city dwellers, and its leaders were "tainted" by communism and association with the Chinese. Meanwhile, the non-Malay working class "was probably the least well-informed section of the population with regard to constitutional issues" (Stenson 1980: 125). In the end, the initiative failed, largely because of racial issues. In particular, despite its claims and objectives, the AMCJA remained heavily linked with pro-China and pro-India nationalism rather than with Malayan nationalism, thus antagonizing its Malay supporters. The British exploited these difficulties to woo more conservative Malays and non-Malays away from the coalition. Regardless, the AMCJA–PUTERA alliance was significant, since it reflected "the beginnings of a truly national consciousness embracing Malays and non-Malays on the peninsula" (Tan 1988: 18).[22]

After much debate, and upon consultation with the administocrats in UMNO, the Malay *raja* finally proposed the Federation of Malaya Agreement (FMA) to replace the Malayan Union proposal.[23] The FMA plan recognized the sovereignty of each *raja* in his state, granted Malays special rights, restricted citizenship for non-Malays, and excluded Singapore. (Later, in 1963, Singapore was brought into the reconstituted Federation of Malaysia along with the Borneo states of Sabah and Sarawak but was forced to secede two years later.) Implemented on February 1, 1948, the arrangement ensured that most Malayan Federation citizens—78 percent of eligible applicants—were Malay (Heng 1996: 504–5). With independence in 1957, Malay became the sole official and national language, Islam the official religion, and the Malay *raja* the constitutional monarchs of Malaya. In addition, the system of Malay special rights, begun by the British in the early 1950s, was continued. The Malays maintained their "protected" status in the polity, encapsulated in article 153 of the federal constitution, a status that included preferential quotas in the civil service, the judicial service, the customs service, the police force, the armed forces, institutions of higher learning, the awarding of licenses and land, and access to credit and other facilities (Andaya and Andaya 1982: 256–57; Funston 1980: 4–11).[24] Now, though, the *raja* rather than the British served as guarantor of Malays' *kedudukan istimewa* (special position).

Despite the restrictions placed on their citizenship and status in the new federation, non-Malay elites agreed to the FMA, albeit with reservations.[25] Three factors facilitated compromise. First, the elites of the various communities had in common an English-language education, a Western-oriented outlook, and economic interest in cooperating with fellow members of the commercial bourgeoisie and aristocracy (Brown 1994). Second, as James Scott (1968) suggests, the Chinese and Malay elites were both spurred by fear—the Chinese feared submersion in a Greater Indonesia, the Malays in a Greater China—and so the FMA did not look so bad by comparison. Third, a key part of these founding agreements was the implicit "bargain" between Malays and Chinese: the Malays would dominate politics, but the Chinese would remain largely unhindered in their business pursuits and economic dominance. Moreover, consociational institutions would facilitate negotiations among the elites of all the major communities so that each group could extract concessions through compromise solutions. UMNO represented Malay interests in negotiations, and the Malayan Chinese Association (MCA), formed in 1949, represented the Chinese. In bargaining for independence and for the shape of the subsequent Alliance government, the MCA had little choice but to accommodate UMNO, and so it focused primarily on establishing citizenship on the basis of place of birth (*jus soli*). However, according to Heng (1996: 505), "In conceding [the] special position of the Malay rulers, Islam as the state religion, Malay as the sole national language, and special rights treatment for Malays—the MCA had, in fact, acquiesced to Malay hegemonic status in the new nation state."

Entrenching a Consociational Framework

The departing British preferred to hand power over to a set of moderate parties that were led by Western-educated elites and that were able to rally their respective communities away from communism, radical Islam, and other problematic alternatives. The British favored UMNO for Malays, the MCA for Chinese, and the MIC for Indians. All three parties attracted a mass base but were firmly led by generally wealthy, well-educated, and well-entrenched elites. UMNO joined first with the MCA and then also with the MIC in the Alliance, a multiethnic coalition for consociational governance. In its first polls, the inaugural Federal Legislative Council elections in 1955, the Alliance won 81 percent of the popular vote and 51 of 52 seats, divided up mainly by race of the majority of voters in each constituency. However, UMNO grew increasingly dominant over time, and even as the three core parties, for the sake of cooperation, played down racial appeals, the fundamental structure and focus of each party remained communal.

Interestingly, though, all three of these parties at least flirted with the notion of *not* becoming communal bodies.[26] Dato Onn bin Jaafar,[27] founder of UMNO and "the foremost leader of the Malays" (Vasil 1971: 37), suggested as early as 1949 that UMNO needed to evolve into a Malayan, rather than just Malay, party. Under pressure from Onn, UMNO decided at its May 1949 general assembly to allow non-Malays to become associate members. Onn also tried to force the party to accept a single nationality, which would include people of other races. However, UMNO refused to be renamed the United *Malayan* National Organisation in 1951, opposing the change on the grounds that Onn's plan to speed up independence would expose Malays prematurely to Chinese and Indian economic power.[28] Branded a traitor to the race for his efforts, Onn resigned from UMNO and launched the Independence of Malaya Party (IMP) in 1951. Onn had not thought he was severing all ties with UMNO, assuming it would eventually ally with the IMP. Instead, Tunku Abdul Rahman, Onn's successor as president of UMNO, declared that any party member who joined the IMP would be expelled from UMNO (Vasil 1971: 41–52).

The IMP was significant not so much for the seats it won—never very many—as for the ideology it represented. According to Vasil (1971: 37),

this was the first major attempt to bring together the people of different racial origins into one non-communal political organization. For the first time it was acknowledged by a prominent Malay [Onn] that the non-Malay communities too had a legitimate and rightful part to play in the political evolution and development of Malaya.

Along with other individuals later important to the IMP, Onn belonged to the Communities Liaison Committee (CLC) established by the British in January 1949 to foster better cross-racial relations. While the CLC was not directly linked with the IMP, the motivations behind the two organizations were broadly similar, and both organizations drew in leading lights from all communities. Onn saw the primary aims of society as intercommunal harmony, racial integration, and eventual independence (Vasil 1971: 41–42).[29]

The IMP's mission was to establish a sovereign state with equal opportunities and rights for all, although it paid special attention to workers.[30] The party began with the endorsement of sections of organized labor, particularly the powerful Plantation Workers' Union of South Malaya and the Malayan Trades Union Congress (MTUC, formed in 1950), whose president was on the IMP's organizing committee. However, lack of agreement at early MTUC meetings, and the contemporaneous formation of labor parties in some states (especially the Selangor Labor Party, in December 1951) suggest that labor was not fully united behind the IMP (Jomo and Todd 1994: 98–101; Vasil 1971: 49). Despite its founders' initial high hopes that the IMP would become the preeminent representative of the Malayan nation, the party failed to attract substantial Malay or Chinese support; only the Indian community gave it a strong endorsement. Onn had expected Malay support to be slow in coming, but Chinese leaders, including several MCA officeholders, had pledged their full backing but then disassociated themselves gradually from the IMP following the formation and success of the UMNO–MCA Alliance in the 1952 Kuala Lumpur municipal elections (Vasil 1971: 37–39; Snider 1977).

Indeed, it was to oppose the IMP that the Alliance first formed. As late as June 1952, UMNO seemed unlikely ever to agree to a power-sharing agreement, as its official line was that Malaya was for the Malays only.[31] However, the participation of the IMP turned the municipal polls into a test of strength of national consequence among political groupings (Vasil 1971: 54, 80). While MCA representatives purportedly had approached the IMP prior to the elections about a possible coalition, the IMP declined, since it was not only confident of a win on its own but also deemed it inappropriate to ally with a communal party. Instead, the local branches of the MCA and UMNO reached an agreement. Ultimately, all the IMP's Malay and Chinese candidates were defeated. The party won only two seats, both of them in wards with large numbers of Indian voters. Conversely, the victorious UMNO–MCA coalition garnered little if any support among Indians (Vasil 1971: 56–58). Vasil explains that the IMP, which ran a campaign centered on noncommunalism and popular sovereignty, fared so poorly not only because it had yet to consolidate itself fully as a party but also because it "had to contest elections before it had the opportunity to change the communal orientation of the people" (Vasil 1971: 59–60). Even so, the party could not completely avoid communal considerations, particularly in assigning candidates to contest in different wards. Also, although the IMP forbade its members to campaign for communal representation, members who did so (most on behalf of the MCA) suffered no penalties. The IMP concluded that Chinese voters did not support the party, since the party could not offer them any special inducements, and since it lacked strong ties with the community. Chinese voters therefore reverted to their traditional loyalty to a communal organization (Vasil 1971: 55–61).

This betrayal by the Chinese so angered Onn that in 1954, after some tinkering with the policies and platforms of the IMP—in an effort to expand its appeal to Chinese and Malays, and after a Malayan National Conference, in April 1953, to discuss plans for self-government[32]—Onn launched the Party Negara (National Party) as the IMP's successor. Calling itself "an all-community party," and starting with a framework similar to that of the IMP, Party Negara soon developed into virtually a Malay communal party. It favored Malay as the sole national language, acknowledged the status of the Malay *raja*, and urged quotas on further immigration of non-Malays. The party attracted little new support and lost the backing of the MIC. Insisting he was not anti-Chinese, Onn declared nonetheless that he would not accept Malays' being controlled by non-Malays. By 1960, he advocated Islam as the state religion and Melayu as the sole nationality. Party Negara only ever won seats in 1959, in the predominantly Malay state of Terengganu, and grew dormant after Onn's death, in 1962 (Vasil 1971: 82–92).

Non-Malays obviously had more to fear than Malays from communal politics, as Malays constituted a clear majority of Federation citizens. Hence it is not surprising that both the MCA and the MIC hesitated before accepting a distinctly communal framework. When formed, the MCA united Chinese-educated merchant-entrepreneurs, representatives of Chinese associations, Chinese educationists, and English-educated Straits Chinese. Its founding father, Dato Tan Cheng Lock, was a great supporter of Onn and also helped form the IMP. Initially a social organization, the MCA quickly developed into a strong pressure group for the Chinese. Concerned that it could not go very far in protecting Chinese interests on its own, the MCA sought a partner. Rebuffed by the IMP, the party chose to join forces with UMNO in 1952. Tan campaigned for neither the MCA nor the IMP, excusing himself after the fact with the ambiguous statement "Principles are more important than people. I support the principles of the IMP, UMNO–MCA co-operation and Sino-Malay cooperation" (quoted in Vasil 1971: 64). Though the elections marked the start of a rift between Tan and Onn, for the MCA successful cooperation with UMNO offered access to power without sacrifice of its independent identity as a party (Vasil 1971).

In the early days of the Alliance, the Chinese had more power in the coalition, not least because the British were still there to protect Malay interests, reducing the risks associated with granting concessions to non-Malays. Also, the MCA was able to assert its equality with UMNO when elections were still held just at the municipal level, since so much of the urban population was Chinese. Even in the first national elections, in 1955, the Malays conceded—albeit not without protest—about 30 percent of seats to the Chinese, who constituted only a little over 11 percent of the electorate. Soon, however, Malays came clearly to dominate decision making, especially in negotiating with the British for independence and in drafting the constitution in 1956–1957 (Vasil 1971: 10–20). After independence, UMNO grew much stingier in allocating seats to the MCA. Vasil (1971: 15) explains that

the MCA got caught in a vicious circle, since the more it gave in to the UMNO the more it lost support among the Chinese; and the smaller its base in the Chinese community the less significant became its bargaining power with the UMNO in the Alliance. . . . It now became an important feature of UMNO strategy to keep the MCA weak enough (in terms of popular Chinese support) so as to make it dependent on the UMNO and not enable it to make excessive demands on behalf of the Chinese community and at the same time popular enough among the Chinese to deliver the necessary votes, in addition to the larger UMNO vote, to retain the Alliance in power.

As UMNO asserted its ascendancy, the MCA became more overtly communal. Tan Siew Sin, later president of the MCA, explained in 1956 that, given Malay rhetoric about being the "master race" of Malaya, "the non-Malays . . . have to be communal merely to ensure their survival" (quoted in Vasil 1971: 16). Nonetheless, forced to give in to UMNO as the constitution was drafted, the MCA found that the Alliance framework limited its space for maneuvering: the party could not respond to Chinese associations' demands that Chinese be accorded the status of an official national language, that Malay special privileges be phased out, or that citizenship rights be liberalized. Over time, as the MCA failed to stand up to UMNO in support of key Chinese demands, many of its supporters grew disillusioned. At the same time, the MCA consciously distanced itself from more radical Chinese associations, claiming, for instance, that they were guided by KMT elements. Led then by English-educated, business-oriented leaders, the MCA came to appeal primarily to moderate middle- and upper-class Chinese voters. The party faced strong challenges, not only from opposition parties but also from insurgent alternative leadership groups that sought to take the MCA in new directions. Even when new leaders won, however, UMNO still did what it could (such as controlling the selection of candidates for elections) to promote more accommodating, less assertive leadership in its coalition partner (Vasil 1971).[33]

Similarly, the MIC balked at accepting a communal political framework but eventually had little choice. The Malayan Indian Association (MIA), predecessor to the MIC, was formed in 1936 among local-born Indians. It was never very influential, since its Western-trained elitist urban leadership failed to penetrate the Indian masses in estates and rural areas. When formed, the MIC was intended more as a pressure group than a communal party. The then-president of the MIC even contested as a noncommunal IMP candidate in the 1952 Kuala Lumpur elections (Vasil 1971: 56). In October 1954, though, after much debate, the MIC opted to join the UMNO–MCA Alliance as its only way of holding at least some power. The MIC has never been fully representative, monolithic, or highly potent as a partner in the governing coalition. Still, its presence helps validate the governing coalition's claims to representativeness, guarantees that Indians get some level of representation in government and some concessions, and undercuts claims that non-Malays would be better off with a noncommunal basis for governance.[34]

Genesis of the Leftist and Islamist Alternatives

While UMNO, the MCA, and the MIC could claim the support of most Malayans by the time of independence, they did face challengers. Strongest among these opponents were the Pan-Malayan Islamic Party (PMIP, later called by its Malay name, Parti Islam SeMalaysia, or PAS) and parties organized around class and economic issues (some of them also with a specifically communal flavor). The PMIP, which developed out of the religious wing of UMNO in the 1950s, came to pose a threat to UMNO in the fight for Malay votes, particularly on the east coast, but really only after independence. The fact that, ever since the colonial era, there have been parties and other political organizations with a left-wing premise suggests that it is not just race per se that is so central to Malaysian politics; rather, it is the intersection of race with class.[35] The heyday of the labor-oriented alternative was shortly after independence, but its roots had developed long before the British departed. Prior to independence, the most prominent such parties were the MCP and various groups within the Malay left.

For a short time, at least, beginning with the MCP during the depression of the early 1930s, class became a key organizing principle for political mobilization in Malaysia, particularly among non-Malays. The colonial government allowed labor union registration in 1940—a reluctant and delayed response to the formation of the illegal MCP in 1931.[36] The MCP, according to Khong (1987: 11–20), aimed "to carry on the struggle for national liberation, formulate a military programme for the overthrow of imperialism and feudal aristocracy and to establish the Soviet Republic of Malaya by the coordinated efforts of the proletariat and peasantry," and it sought the inclusion of Singapore in Malaya; universal suffrage; equality regardless of race, class, religion, or sex; linguistic freedom; and a mixed economy under control of the state, all run by a joint dictatorship of the revolutionary classes. The MCP remained mostly Chinese in composition, largely because the plantation and mining labor force among which the party recruited was heavily Chinese, but also because of the party's rather indiscriminate attacks on Malays in the immediate postwar period and its Sinocentric bent, such as in its support for allowing dual Malayan and Chinese citizenship. However, the MCP did not consider itself an ethnic party, and for ideological as well as strategic reasons made serious, persistent efforts to enlist Malay peasants and teachers, Indian workers, and indigenous Orang Asli (indigenous peoples of the peninsula).[37]

By 1941, the MCP was the strongest political force in the country, leading the British to work with the party in the guise of the MPAJA during the war. In late 1945, after the Japanese surrender, the party operated as an alternative government to the British Military Administration in about 70 percent of small towns and villages with a predominantly Chinese population, the start of an insurgency that trickled on for three decades after having been substantially subdued by the early 1950s.[38] Particularly with the onset of the Emergency in 1948, the British worked to quash the MCP. They promoted the formation of the MCA in 1949 to mobilize an effective alternative Chinese leadership that could assist in counterinsurgency, and they cracked down on the labor movement as a whole in the 1940s. According to Benedict Anderson (1998: 325), "The British branded the insurrectionaries as above all ethnics, and in fighting them played ethnic politics to the limit, most significantly disfranchising a large part of the Chinese community and enhancing the position of the conservative, collaborationist Malay leadership." The last holdouts from the MCP finally surrendered in the 1970s, but the communist bogey remains a pet government scapegoat.

Concurrent with the rise of the MCP was the formulation of a class-based, left-wing Malay challenge to the British, although the Malays' aim in general was specifically Malay nationalism. This movement, led by Malay-educated intellectuals influenced by Indonesian nationalism, promoted the concept of *Malaysia Raya* (Greater Malaysia). The majority of Malays distrusted the movement, finding its views too radical. Among the organizations of the Malay left were the PKMM, the KMM, Angkatan Pemuda Insaf (Movement of Aware Youth, API), AWAS, and

Syarikat Bekerjasama Am Saiburi (General Cooperative Society of Saiburi, SABERKAS). Some of these groups were prime movers in the AMCJA–PUTERA initiative.[39]

However, aside from that somewhat fractured and clearly unsuccessful coalition attempt, Malay and non-Malay left-wing parties failed to unite prior to independence. This segmentation was partly due to a lack of constructive interaction between representatives of the two movements and, indeed, among ethnic groups as a whole outside a narrow stratum of elites. Furthermore, the discourse of ethnicity was accentuated by the politics of decolonization and nationalism, with the economic plight of the *bumiputera* pitted against that of the Chinese as the British departed. What these parties had in common was more their condition of marginalization than any actual ideology or substantive goals. The further entrenchment of the dominant order of race-based parties has served over time to augment the polarization of the opposition, leaving elusive the sort of noncommunal unity that Dato Onn tried to forge in the 1950s, and frustrating attempts to shift political norms and remake political institutions.

The fact remains, though, that noncommunal parties and associations have a long legacy in Malaysia. The Alliance—"a freak of history," in Vasil's words (1971: 10)—was not the first and will not be the last effort to forge a coherent, cross-racial platform and political order. To some extent, Malaysia's quasi-consociational order is an accident of history and capitalism, since the British promoted the arrangement most clearly conducive to their own interests and did their best to stamp out vestiges of communism and other sorts of radicalism. As the story continues, it will become clear that these efforts to quell alternatives were never fully victorious. The successors to early class-based and Islamist opposition groups, however polarized, remained active in the years to come, cultivating their respective bases and capitalizing on the government's moments of weakness.

EXPANSION AND MATURATION OF CIVIL
AND POLITICAL SOCIETY, 1957-1997

Over the course of four decades after independence, the Malaysian polity developed as a stable, illiberal democracy. The array of political parties continued to expand, although opposition parties grew ever more polarized and marginalized. At the same time, civil society broadened and deepened, though it was still marked by persistent communalism. There were a few key attempts—echoes of the AMCJA, Dato Onn bin Jaafar, and the IMP—to bring to fruition an alternative vision of noncommunal electoral politics. These efforts were largely unsuccessful. Especially with the introduction of strong new race-based policies in the 1970s, communalism came to seem ever more invincible in the public sphere. Moreover, with the BN's expansion into a behemoth of over a dozen parties, in addition to increasing executive centralization in the 1980s, the space for contained contention narrowed. Gradually the locus for envisioning alternatives shifted from political society to civil society, as the changing political order—the concatenation of the narrowing of space in electoral politics with the expansion of outlets in informal politics—encouraged increasing political activism outside the ambit of formal politics.

From 1957 through the mid-1990s, neither the development of political society nor that of civil society was without pitfalls. Punctuating the evolution of the polity was not just the violent upheaval of race riots in the late 1960s but also intermittent, sometimes serious, factional squabbles within and among government as well as within and among opposition parties. As for the growth of civil society organizations, it was obstructed most significantly by periodic harsh crackdowns on the part of the government against activists and their organizations, to reinforce the veneer of broad societal consensus. With more or less the same coalition in power all along, opposition parties developed in a rather ambiguous space between government and civil society, and portions of civil society grew increasingly politicized. Engaging with some of the same issues, and faced with similar constraints, over time CSAs and opposition political parties edged toward closer cooperation. By the mid-1990s, their combined efforts had achieved some impact on the political perspectives of the mass of voters, but the gaps dividing sections of the opposition, both formal and informal, proved too significant to bridge under prevailing political and economic conditions.

The persistent marginalization of noncommunal alternatives to the Malay-dominated, quasi-consociational regime remained entrenched from 1957 through 1997. Opposition parties and CSAs pressed singly or in coalition over the years for a range of alternatives, from class-based frameworks to noncommunal Islamism. However, while the discourse of developmentalism supplanted, to some extent, that of communalism over this period, government institutions and policies remained highly racialized. It is hardly surprising, then, that ethnic identities continued to upstage a shared Malaysian identity.[1] Mahathir Mohamad (1970: 4–5), then recently expelled from UMNO, concluded of the period before a cataclysmic episode of racial violence in 1969:

There was a lack of inter-racial strife. There was tolerance. There was accommodation. There was a certain amount of give and take. But there was no harmony. . . . The Malays and Chinese may live as neighbours. They may meet each other in their daily business and even socially. But when they retire, they retire into their respective ethnic and cultural sanctum, neither of which has ever been truly breached by the other. And in their own world their values are not merely different, but are often conflicting.

So persistently communal an order is inherently tense. As von Vorys says (1975: 7), "It is easy to see that as long as ascriptive criteria are preeminent, majority rule is tantamount to condemning some individuals and groups to the position of permanent minority."

Later, as prime minister, Mahathir set a goal of overcoming communalism by the year 2020, with all groups incorporated into a unified *bangsa Malaysia* (Malaysian nation). In this ideal future state, Malaysians "of all colours and creeds" would be free to practice their own customs, cultures, and religion, and there would be no identification of race with economic function or "backwardness" (Mahathir 1991: 2–4). This official preference helped to shift Malaysian political culture by legitimating a noncommunal orientation. The state's doing so allowed opposition parties and CSAs to seize the opportunity to emphasize a noncommunal frame, one in terms of which the racially organized regime could readily be challenged.

All the same, achievement of this multicultural vision was thwarted by the conflicting political aspirations of each ethnic group. Cynthia Enloe warned in 1970 that the greater participation of all the races in the political process had, paradoxically, rendered Malaysia's national unity more fragile than before. The Alliance formula depended on lower levels of political participation: each ethnic group was "expected to demonstrate its national allegiance by trusting its respective elite to bargain on the community's behalf," and Chinese were supposed to remain satisfied with economic rather than political power. Instead, "mobilized and assertive ethnic interest groups" imperiled peaceful accommodation (Enloe 1970: vii). The situation arguably grew less volatile after the time of Enloe's writing. Still, the racialized structure of political and economic rewards, the communal implications of both economic restructuring and religious revival, and continued state repression of alternative avenues for political expression and organization made significant systemic reform unlikely through the late 1990s, despite rising popular frustration with key aspects of the sociopolitical order.

From Alliance to Barisan Nasional Rule

Malaysia's basic political parameters have changed little since independence. Having swept the polls in the federal elections of July 1955, the Alliance coalition of UMNO, the MCA, and the MIC took over from the British upon independence, in 1957. With UMNO always at the fore, the Alliance ruled through 1969. Malaysia's first prime minister, Tunku Abdul Rahman, was instrumental in getting the coalition off the ground. Relatively nonpartisan and tolerant of some noncommunal initiatives, the *tunku* mixed well with the various communities, protected the interests of the wealthy regardless of race, and tried to work around contentious issues. It helped, too, that, before 1969, UMNO was less aggressive than it later became in its regulation of non-Malays' educational, political, and cultural interests, and so the MCA and the MIC were keen to cooperate. As ethnic mobilization intensified, however, this accommodation cost the *tunku* Malay support. He was eventually forced to retire by a "palace coup" of "young Turks" who ushered in a new regime under Tun Abdul Razak, following ethnic riots in 1969 and the subsequent imposition of emergency rule (Chandra 1984).

Remaking the Alliance Order

The first decade after independence was far from placid for the Alliance, but it was in 1969 that the fragile communal balance shattered. Mahathir (1970: 15) suggests that the assumptions underlying the Alliance framework were fundamentally misguided:

In the first place the Government started off on the wrong premise. It believed that there had been racial harmony in the past and that the Sino-Malay cooperation to achieve Independence was an example of racial harmony. It believed that the Chinese were only interested in business and acquisition of wealth, and that the Malays wished only to become Government servants. These ridiculous assumptions led to policies that undermined whatever superficial understanding there was between Malays and non-Malays.

By the time of the May 1969 elections, popular disenchantment with the government was high among all groups. Incidents of racial violence had been mounting over the preceding several years. The most significant recent outbreaks had been a series of communal clashes beginning in Penang in November 1967.[2] In political terms, Malays felt that UMNO leaders had amassed too much power for themselves, disproportionately favored a few close supporters, did not do enough to redress the imbalance of wealth between themselves and the Chinese, had done too little of substance to further rural development, and had grown resistant to criticism. At the same time, ethnic Chinese both within and outside the MCA were becoming increasingly forthright in their demands. Better-off Chinese criticized the MCA for not checking growing government regulation of and intervention in the economy, and lower-income Chinese protested that the MCA was only protecting Chinese business interests. The government could not stem a "worsening racialist trend" as pent-up grievances came to the fore in response to "the violently communal appeal of the opposition parties" (Mahathir 1970: 14).

Popular disaffection resulted in a much-reduced margin of victory in the elections for the Alliance. The MCA fared especially poorly. Perhaps most importantly, the Selangor state government was evenly divided between Alliance and opposition parties, and it was unclear who would form the state government. On the eve of the election, the mostly non-Malay Labour Party of Malaya (LPM) had staged a massive, racially incendiary funeral march for a party activist slain by police. That provocation was compounded by exuberant postelection rallies by the Chinese-majority Democratic Action Party (DAP) and Gerakan Rakyat Malaysia (Malaysian People's Movement, Gerakan) on May 11–12. In response, the Selangor state branch of UMNO organized its own victory demonstration for the evening of May 13. With rumors flying of attacks on Malays in other parts of town, some participants brought weapons in case of trouble. Angry Malays began to strike out against Chinese people and property in Kuala Lumpur. The police, initially absent, were not readily able to restore order. Official statistics counted 196 deaths, mostly of non-Malays, and 439 people injured. The government declared a state of emergency, imposed a curfew in the capital, and suspended parliamentary democracy for twenty-one months, with rule by the National Operations Council (NOC), headed by Tun Abdul Razak, in the interim. Allegations have floated about ever since that the government planned either a pogrom or at least a show of force, but there is no hard evidence of such a plan, and critical discussion of the incident has been suppressed.[3]

Although communal tensions were at the root of the riots and the preceding LPM march, both events actually dramatized growing intracommunal divisions based on economic and career opportunities, urbanization, and facility with English (Enloe 1970). The probably misguided insistence of the government—especially on the part of Tunku Abdul Rahman—that the riots were part of a communist plot to destabilize the state and take over power only highlights the extent to which class or economic factors were at play, rather than just communalism. In his personal account of events, the *tunku* explained, for instance, that communists used racialism to win the hearts and minds of Chinese voters, a tactic that would not have worked had the people been prosperous and happy, but that was very effective after twelve years of the anticommunist Emergency and its attendant uncertainty and misery (Abdul Rahman 1969: 18–20).[4] Nonetheless, young Malay and Chinese have-nots remained mutually hostile rather than allies, and PMIP campaign rhetoric lambasted UMNO for having sold out to Chinese interests.[5] Still, as Enloe (1970) points out, many of the Malay youths, in particular, who participated in the postelection riots did not seem specifically motivated by party allegiance or political anxieties.

With the resumption of parliamentary government, the Alliance was recreated as the Barisan Nasional (BN, National Front). Though similar to its predecessor in framework and approach, the BN co-opted several former opposition parties with the argument that all parties needed to stop politicking and work together for the good of a nation torn by racial strife.[6] Gerakan and the People's Progressive Party (PPP) joined the BN in 1972. At the cost of an internal split, PAS (formerly called the PMIP) joined in 1973, though it retreated to the opposition in 1977. Also, in 1970, at Tun Razak's urging, the Sarawak United People's Party (SUPP) opted to ally with the Sarawak Alliance to head that state's government (Chin U.-H. 1996). The remaining opposition came together in an informal parliamentary opposition bloc comprising the DAP, Sarawak National Party (SNAP), United Sabah Action Party (USAP), and smaller partners (though plans for an opposition secretariat and joint manifesto came to naught).

The BN is farther removed from a consociational ideal than the Alliance was. While Arend Lijphart's model presumes some degree of formal equality among members of the various communities, Malaysian politics is premised at least as much upon Malay dominance as upon multiracial power sharing. Under the Alliance, ethnic Chinese had more political bargaining power, given their geographical concentration and dominant economic position as well as elite-level friendships and understanding. The community's relative potency declined after 1969: neither the MCA nor the DAP could seriously challenge UMNO and check the erosion of Chinese rights (Yeoh 1988; Chin 2001). Ethnic Indians have never been in a particularly good bargaining position, given their smaller numbers. Moreover, Malays and other *bumiputera* have come to represent a clearer majority of the population, thanks to comparatively high birth rates and the inclusion of Sabah and Sarawak, but no longer Singapore, in the federation.[7] This demographic shift has been compounded by successive electoral redistricting exercises to render *bumiputera* votes, especially those from rural areas, increasingly potent in elections.[8]

Besides co-opting potential challengers, the BN passed new legislation prohibiting debate on "ethnically sensitive" issues, even in Parliament. These matters included any reference to Malay special rights, non-Malay citizenship, Islam, the status of the national language, and constitutional provisions regarding the *raja*. In addition, the government set up the multiethnic National Consultative Council in 1969 to prepare a national ideology, the *Rukunegara* (Basic Principles of the State), and laid a "consensual" framework for a new economic strategy. Shortly afterward, with the Local Government Act of 1976, the federal government restricted the number of municipal and district councils and abolished elections for them in light of opposition parties' success in those polls, especially in heavily non-Malay towns and cities.[9] Opposition parties and activists have since consistently demanded the reinstatement of local-level elections, to no avail (see Saravanamuttu 2000). These efforts to sweep communal tensions under the rug have been a qualified success. Ethnic violence has clearly diminished since the 1950s and 1960s, but communal sentiments are arguably more keen now than before 1969.

Given the nexus between racial and economic grievances, the New Economic Policy (NEP, 1971–1990) and subsequent National Development Policy (NDP, 1991–2000) were particularly critical to the government's efforts at preventing further communal violence. The NEP aimed to reduce poverty overall, increase Malays' share of equity and decrease that of foreigners, and reduce the identification of race with occupation. It transformed the state's economic role from laissez-faire to interventionist and pro-Malay, though the program was premised more on growth with equity than on actual redistribution. While still targeted mostly at Malays, the NDP was seen as less ethnically divisive and more pro-growth than the NEP. It eschewed numerical targets for equity ownership and focused instead on strengthening *bumiputera* business competence and capacity. While the NEP and the NDP were effective in reducing poverty and developing a Malay middle class, they disproportionately benefited certain sectors. Still, some benefits were quite broadly distributed, especially opportunities for Malays in tertiary education and the urbanized workforce. These advantages have been charged, however, with contributing to the development of a "subsidy mentality," including the belief that Malays require assistance for survival.[10]

The fact that UMNO was able to formulate and implement so discriminatory a set of policies as the NEP and the NDP reaffirms the scope and potency of Malay political power. Nevertheless, UMNO's broad political base is prone to destabilizing factional divisions (Means 1991). Leadership crises, although they are regular features of the political landscape within UMNO, have been associated with periods of significant unrest, as in 1969, 1987, and 1998. Moreover, as Malay demographics have changed—not least as a consequence of the NEP and the NDP—so have those of UMNO. The party was initially dominated by rural interests, especially schoolteachers. As late as 1981, teachers still constituted the largest group within UMNO, representing about 40 percent of members. By 1987, they were only 19 percent, surpassed by businesspeople and professionals (Funston 1988: 365). These trends have continued since then. With such changes have come new demands from an increasingly assertive new Malay middle class as well as heightened internal competition, given the ever more lucrative rewards to be won through political office (see Gomez and Jomo 1997; Gomez 1991).

Non-Malays in the BN

Despite complaints that the government is too staunchly pro-Malay, to the detriment of other ethnic groups, non-Malay parties, particularly the MCA, have retained a substantial degree of clout in the BN. The size, importance, and international connections of the Chinese community protect it from serious assault. The BN has addressed some Chinese grievances, though generally in a low-key way; the MCA even released a supplement to its election manifesto in 1986, to remind voters of the concessions it had received. It is largely because of such concessions, from patronage in the form of sharing government contracts to tolerance for at least privately funded vernacular education, as well as because of non-Malays' fears that any alternative government could be less adept in maintaining racial and religious harmony, that non-Malay parties in the

BN maintain their support (see Ng 2003). Policies such as the Malay-centric National Culture Policy of 1971 have withstood even strong and sustained protests from non-Malays (Kua 1985), but the BN relies on more than just Malay support. The government, forced to woo Chinese voters as Malay support dipped in the 1990s, proved more willing then than previously to accommodate Chinese demands. Furthermore, in line with the principles of Mahathir's *Vision 2020* (Mahathir 1991), there has been an attempt since the mid-1990s to encourage dialogue and to move toward multiculturalism, a change welcomed by non-Malays (Milne and Mauzy 1999). This shift, though, has been coincident with Islamization and the continuation of Malay special privileges, as UMNO has had to fight ever harder to maintain Malay support—which is, at the end of the day, more important to UMNO than that of non-Malays. Hence the MCA and Gerakan have come to gain political legitimacy "by providing 'service' to the community coupled with not-too-subtle reminders that the community would face political and social catastrophe if their 'moderating' voice were no longer in government or if PAS came into power" (Chin 2001: n.p.). Such appeals imply acceptance of a high degree of marginalization.

Even the MCA has been forced to remain circumspect in criticizing UMNO's policies, and in its own appeals to the Chinese community. For instance, the government objected to the success of the MCA's Chinese Unity Movement in the early 1970s, a campaign backed by a wide range of groups, including English-educated professionals, Chinese educationists, merchants, and youths from New Villages.[11] UMNO wanted a coalition partner with credibility among the Chinese, but not one to rally what it saw as inflammatory, chauvinist sentiments. The government imposed a newspaper blackout on the campaign in June 1973, and several of the movement's advocates were expelled from the MCA soon after (Heng 1996). Though still calling for Chinese unity, so that the community will not lose its bargaining power vis-à-vis UMNO, the MCA has tried to tone down its communal focus in recent years. For example, in 1993, the party launched its "One Heart, One Vision" campaign to encourage a more multicultural "Malaysian," rather than communal, orientation. The following year, the MCA amended its membership rules to allow individuals with just one Chinese parent to join (Heng 1996; Milne and Mauzy 1999; Yeoh 1988).

The Chinese-majority, former opposition parties in the BN still carry less clout than the core members, although Gerakan maintains a significant presence in particular regions, especially Penang. Gerakan was formed in 1968 by notables from the LPM and the United Democratic Party (UDP) and several prominent individuals. Established in opposition to Chinese chauvinists' increasing control over the LPM and the UDP, Malays' domination of the Alliance, and increasing authoritarianism and constraints on civil liberties, Gerakan styled itself as a noncommunal, moderately socialist, pro-democratic party. Though it strove to attract Malays as well as non-Malays, the party has always mainly drawn Chinese members (Vasil 1971; Snider 1968; Snider 1977). The PPP, which joined the BN with Gerakan, occupied a comparable niche for a time among Chinese voters in Perak on account of its championing of minority rights, including Chinese education and multilingualism, but it had lost momentum by the early 1960s (Vasil 1971).

As for ethnic Indians, they have been represented in the government from the outset primarily by the faction-ridden, Tamil-dominated[12] MIC, the smallest of the Alliance/BN linchpins but Malaysia's largest Indian party. Indians, the poorest of Malaysia's three main ethnic groups, have realized the least progress toward the government's targets for economic development, despite a succession of MIC-led schemes to help Indians prosper in business. Since Indian Malaysians do not constitute a majority in any parliamentary constituency (although they are significantly concentrated in several), they lobbied in the early 1950s for a certain number of seats to be reserved for the community, fearing that their "political oblivion" would otherwise ensue (Ampalavanar 1981: 119–21; Jayasooriya 2004). While Indians wield less influence as a community than do the more numerous Chinese and Malays, the MIC has contested with consistent success for the seats allotted the party by the Alliance/BN.

Particularly outside peninsular Malaysia, the term *non Malay* takes on a very different connotation, representing far more than just ethnic Chinese and Indians. The BN has taken a different approach to incorporating denizens of the East Malaysian states of Sabah and Sarawak. The two states together control one-third of parliamentary seats, including a substantial number of non-Malay majority ones. Politics in East Malaysia has long followed its own patterns, though recent trends indicate that Malay-Muslim dominance and the standard BN formula are becoming increasingly entrenched. Sabah and Sarawak, having been brought late and somewhat half-heartedly into British Malaya, and then joining Malaysia only in 1963, retained greater autonomy than did their peninsular counterparts. In fact, Sabah joined the federation only upon acceptance of "twenty points" guaranteeing particular rights and prerogatives, the erosion of which had fostered mounting disenchantment with the federal government by the 1970s. When political parties first formed in Sabah and Sarawak, in the late 1950s, many were multiethnic, such as the original SUPP and SNAP as well as Sabah's Parti Berjaya (Success Party) and Parti Bersatu Sabah (PBS, Sabah United Party). From the

1970s on, however, the de facto organization of political parties along ethnic lines became more common, despite the persistence of strong internal divisions within ethnic groups.

Sabah and Sarawak had experienced periods of local nationalist agitation, and then, by the 1980s, rising resentment against Muslim *bumiputera* domination. Representing these nationalist movements in the 1980s were Parti Bansa Dayak Sarawak (PBDS, Dayak Race Party of Sarawak), founded in 1983, and the Kadazan-majority PBS (Roff 1969). With the rise of Dayak and Kadazan nationalism came a worsening of ethnic relations in Sabah and Sarawak, but both movements had lost ground by the mid-1990s. Dayak and Kadazan voters never fully united in the PBDS or the PBS, especially since ethnic boundaries are more fluid in Sabah and Sarawak than in peninsular Malaysia, and no single ethnic group constitutes a majority in either state.[13] Moreover, BN-led developmentalism and federalization (including the selection of leaders according to the federal government's preferences, and gerrymandering to render non-Muslim *bumiputera*-majority constituencies a minority of total seats) have taken firm hold over political life. After the PBS's midcampaign desertion of the BN, in 1990, UMNO entered Sabah itself to contest the 1994 state elections. UMNO and its partners have controlled Sabah ever since, either by winning outright at the polls (often by threatening loss of development funds if they were not elected) or by convincing opposition legislators to "hop" over to the BN. Similarly, a Muslim-dominated coalition has governed Sarawak since 1970, when the federal government declared a state of emergency and removed the Iban chief minister. Ultimately, the increasing entrenchment of Muslim *bumiputera* rule in both states means that non-Muslim *bumiputera* will find it ever harder to assert themselves politically, particularly from outside the BN, despite perennial protests over Islamization and Malayization, interference and control by peninsular Malays, and official neglect of local cultures.[14]

Frustration with state predation on their lands, together with the slow pace of development, has also fostered a rise in ethnic consciousness and political agitation among another subset of non-Malays: the Orang Asli, or indigenous peoples of the peninsula. Orang Asli voters have been especially provoked by forced resettlement schemes, which began with anticommunist measures in the 1950s and have continued since with the reclassification of gazetted lands for development. Moreover, as among non-Muslim *bumiputera* in Sabah and Sarawak, Orang Asli political awareness has been nurtured by policies designed to encourage their assimilation into Malay society and Islam as well as by increased (though still comparatively slim) educational opportunities since the 1970s, by the formation of the Persatuan Orang Asli Semenanjung Malaysia (Peninsular Malaysia Association of Orang Asli, POASM) in 1977, and by the efforts of vocal political leaders.[15] Orang Asli activism has become increasingly proactive and varied since the mid 1990s (see Nicholas 2000). Even so, the Orang Asli are too few in number and too politically disorganized to be a significant political force, and they typically see little alternative to the BN. Hence, when the Parti Orang Asli (POA) formed in 1999, it hoped to affiliate with the BN to represent the community's interests.

Challenges to the System

For the first forty years after independence, although the Alliance/BN government remained firmly entrenched, it faced periodic challenges. The most obvious lapses in the prevailing stability were in the mid-1960s (culminating in the violence of May 1969) and the mid-1980s. Fear of a challenge to Malay supremacy—branded Chinese chauvinism by the government—led to the forced secession of Chinese-majority Singapore from Malaysia in 1965. Then the simmering frustrations of young Malay havenots, amid the concomitant rising political fortunes of urban non-Malays, spilled over into a series of violent outbreaks, culminating in the bloody riots after the 1969 general elections. Some time later, as the economy faltered in the mid-1980s, factionalism within UMNO festered until the party split in two. One faction continued on as before, as UMNO Baru (New UMNO). The other tried to develop a new premise and a new coalition as Parti Semangat '46 (Spirit of '46 Party, S'46), with only limited success. Throughout, UMNO also faced an Islamist challenge, represented primarily by PAS. In these contests, opposition parties provided institutionalized channels for alternative views. These parties drew their core support from among the ranks of frustrated leftists, non-Malays irritated by their politically and culturally disadvantaged status, and Islamists dissatisfied with UMNO's moderate stance on Islam.

While most opposition parties are at least officially noncommunal, most attract members primarily from one ethnic or religious group and rely to at least some extent on communal appeals. The primary peninsular opposition parties have long recognized the limitations of communalism, especially since these parties have been contesting against a communally organized regime. Therefore, since the Alliance years, they have advocated political cooperation grounded in something other than ethnic loyalty—for instance, class status and economic condition rather than ethnicity per se. However, as Enloe (1970: 132) concedes:

the difficulty of presenting such an argument in contemporary Malaysia is that all too often occupation, status, urbanism, are all dictated by ethnicity; therefore, what in a more ethnically homogeneous society would appear as a socio-economic class demand takes the form in Malaysia of a communal demand and often becomes inextricably wound up in ethnic sentiments.

While the identification of race with socioeconomic characteristics has diminished since the 1970s, opposition parties are still hard pressed to convince the public not only that their parties are noncommunal but also that the major issues of the day are, too. The left-wing opposition, for instance, has been hindered historically not only by state repression and conflicts among parties but also by its inability to garner Malay support and thus expand its base.

Still, Malaysia's opposition political parties boast a colorful history and have made concerted efforts at political change over the years, however limited or uneven their success. Between independence and 1997, the primary peninsular opposition parties were the Labour Party (LPM), Parti Rakyat Malaysia (Malaysian People's Party, PRM), the People's Action Party (PAP) and its successor, the Democratic Action Party (DAP), Parti Islam SeMalaysia (Pan-Malaysian Islamic Party, PMIP or PAS), and S'46. These parties, along with various smaller ones, can be loosely grouped into two clusters, one socialist (primarily, though not exclusively, supported by non-Malays) and the other Islamist and Malay. As described later, parties within and across these two clusters did interact over the years but were too polarized to sustain deep cooperation, especially given the increasing strength and centralization of the government.

The Socialist Cluster

The constituency and aims of the socialist or left-wing cluster of parties have fluctuated dramatically over time. This cluster's primary progenitor was the Malayan Communist Party (MCP) and the radical trade unions of the 1930s and 1940s. As these organizations were harassed into oblivion, a shifting array of socialist parties took their place, most of them officially noncommunal but dominated by non-Malays. The first significant labor-oriented initiative was the Socialist Front of 1957–1966 and its component parties, the LPM and PRM. Within that period, Singapore's PAP entered Malaysia and spearheaded the Malaysian Solidarity Convention. After the departure of Singapore from Malaysia, several opposition parties united in what was basically a non-Malay front for the 1969 elections, but the debacle of the subsequent riots ended this initiative. By the 1970s, with the ouster of the *tunku* and the debut of a more Malay-centric order in UMNO and the BN, the onus had shifted largely to the DAP and to a rather cowed, less racially provocative vision of democratic socialism.

The Socialist Front. The formation of the Socialist Front, in 1955, marked the first institutionalized effort to build a noncommunal opposition coalition to challenge the Alliance. Composed of the LPM, PRM, and minor partners, the front linked disparate marginalized constituencies through the common denominator of democratic socialism. What made such an initiative possible at that time, but not later, were both a less rigid and powerful regime than subsequently and a still significant labor movement.[16] By the mid-1960s, however, the front had collapsed, having succumbed to intractable communalism and power struggles as well as to government repression.

As of the late 1960s, Vasil (1971: 93) labeled the LPM "the main ideologically orientated noncommunal political party in Malaysia," even though the party had drifted into an increasingly communal niche by then. The LPM's roots lay in a group of state-based labor parties that formed upon the British announcement of municipal elections in the early 1950s. In June 1952, representatives of several state labor parties, twenty-one trade unions, and the Malay socialist organization SABER-KAS met in Kuala Lumpur and established the Pan-Malayan Labour Party (PMLP). This loose-knit confederation denounced communism but not colonialism and sought mutual prosperity for Malaya and Britain. With the rise of a more anticolonial, radically socialist leadership, the PMLP was renamed the Labour Party of Malaya in June 1954. The LPM's constitution demanded immediate self-government, liberal citizenship laws, Malayanization of the public service, a planned economy, greater democratic justice, and agrarian reform. The party proposed, too, that no one race owned Malaya or deserved special privileges; other proposals were federal rather than state-level nationality, Malay as the national language and English as the second language (though the party also proposed strong support for multilingualism), merger with Singapore, only limited powers for the Malay *raja*, an elected president, and a secular state. The LPM was routed in the 1955 general elections, but it did much better in municipal elections in Penang in December 1956, thanks to organizational improvements, a swing to the left in the party, and Chinese disenchantment with the MCA (Vasil 1971).

The character of regional labor parties and the LPM changed over time. The initial labor parties' leaders were almost all English-educated representatives of "responsible" unions allowed by the British and associated with the moderate Malayan Trades Union Congress (MTUC).[17] Membership was low and composed mostly of ethnic Indian or Chinese ordinary workers and English-educated white-collar workers, including a large number of government servants—many of whom had instead supported the Radical Party of Penang in the early 1950s. After independence, a high proportion of new members were Chinese-educated, generally from the working class, and often more radical.[18] Given the dearth of Malays involved in the more organized sector of the Malayan economy, the LPM never attracted a mass following among Malays, especially after its denunciation of Malay special rights. Though the LPM made no communal appeals in its early years, the coming of independence honed communal antipathies until the party found itself increasingly championing non-Malays, especially Chinese. The pull of communalism grew particularly potent as the MCA and the MIC lost ground to UMNO within the Alliance, and after the LPM joined with PRM in the Socialist Front in mid-1957. At the same time, the party also drifted left until, by 1966, it had assumed a blatantly pro-Peking (that is, pro-communist) and Chinese-chauvinist character and leadership (Vasil 1971; Snider 1977). Indians remained involved, however. In fact, as Ampalavanar explains (1981: 137–38), "Indian involvement in left-wing parties, particularly the Malayan Labour Party, was responsible for the emergence of an Indian élite which was truly non-communal and commanded a very considerable allegiance among working class communities."

The LPM's eventual partner in the Socialist Front, PRM, was formed in 1955 as a nonracial socialist party. The party's roots lay in Second World War–era radical Malay organizations, such as the PKMM, and in the efforts of their anticolonial leaders, most notably Ahmad Boestamam (PRM's president from 1956 to 1966), Burhanuddin Helmy (who joined the PMIP), and Ishak Hj. Muhammad (who became head of the LPM). PRM sought immediate independence for Malaya, wider political rights, and the release of all political detainees. Its grounding philosophy was the Soekarnoist *Marhaenisma,* a form of nationalistic social democracy focusing on the poor. The party's aims were more radical than those of the LPM. PRM advocated a much larger role for the state, with large-scale nationalization of the means of production and distribution as well as a *Melayu Raya* to include Malaya, Singapore, Sarawak, North Borneo, and Brunei, and with strong links to Indonesia (Vasil 1971; Sanusi and Ang 1998).

From the start, PRM appealed only to a small section of mostly lower- and middle-class young Malays, primarily on the west coast. Older Malays and strongly devout Muslims generally supported the PMIP, and the middle and upper classes favored UMNO. PRM was attacked by both these opponents on the grounds that communism and left-wing ideas were anti-Islam, foreign, and anti-Malay (since such ideas were so closely identified with the Chinese in Malaya). In a bid to bolster support, PRM later gave more attention to Malays' special position but still fared poorly. While some Chinese-educated Chinese joined the party for tactical reasons in the late 1950s, they were never really courted or integrated into it (Vasil 1971; Sanusi and Ang 1998).[19]

The LPM's and PRM's decision to collaborate in the Socialist Front was partly an admission of the intractability of racial politics: the LPM could not attract Malay votes, and PRM attracted very little else. At first it had not mattered to the stronger LPM that Malays found little appeal in democratic socialist ideas, since the support of any particular community was ideologically insignificant, and in any case non-Malays made up a good part of the electorate of towns and cities (the only places polls were held before 1955). However, independence brought the possibility of actually establishing a socialist federal government, which required winning broader support, particularly among Malays. As for PRM, it sought to augment its 5,000-strong membership and improve its organizational structure and funding (Snider 1977). It was by then clear that opposition parties had to unite if they were to pose a viable challenge to the Alliance. Negotiations between PRM and the LPM began in September 1956 and dragged on until shortly after independence. Initially, the Socialist Front intended just to contest the 1959 general elections. Its aims were to forge a democratic socialist united front to form the government, cooperating also with counterparts in other nations; to merge Singapore with Malaya; and to promote the political, social, and economic emancipation of the people, especially workers. The front was loosely organized, and the two parties campaigned largely separately.[20]

Although both parties in the Socialist Front tried somewhat superficially to combat communalism and expand into new areas, the LPM focused primarily on garnering support among non-Malays and PRM among Malays. This division of labor accentuated the parties' communal character. According to Snider (1977: 13),

it is clear that the general commitment to socialism which linked the Labour Party and the People's Party [PRM] had a mitigating effect on these two parties when they were tempted to make overtly communal voter appeals commonly made by most other Malaysian parties. However, neither of the Socialist Front partners were able to free themselves completely from the magnetic pull of communal polarization so prevalent in Malaysian politics.

This "magnetic pull" was the result of linguistic, occupational, cultural, and ideological differences across the nonelite segments of each community, which even a shared attachment to socialism could not overcome. Unlike the leaders of the Alliance, those of the Socialist Front had little in common. The LPM was then still led by English-educated moderate professionals; later it was led mainly by Chinese-educated Chinese, and PRM was headed by extreme left-wing, pro-Indonesia Malays. With its larger middle-class base and nonreliance on full-time politicians, the LPM also had more funds at its disposal. Apart from such issues as the position of the *raja* and special privileges of the Malays (on which the LPM was willing to compromise), as well as language and education policies (which proved as difficult to settle for the Socialist Front as for the Alliance), the objects of the two parties were broadly similar. Still, PRM flatly rejected an LPM proposal that the two parties merge to form the Socialist Party of Malaya, citing the wide gap between them. The contrast between the "Socialist Front Manifesto" issued for the 1959 elections and the two parties' previous statements revealed how much the LPM and PRM had needed to compromise on issues including citizenship; language and education policies; the status of Malay special rights and the *raja*; and nationalization of economic enterprises (Snider 1977; Vasil 1971).

Meanwhile, the fortunes of the MCP, which had been defeated in armed struggle, were on the decline. The colonial government had pronounced in 1955 that the LPM and PRM were the pawns (willing or not) of the MCP, which planned to seize state power upon the victory of the United People's Democratic Front in the polls (Government of Malaya 1959). Also, the mid-1955 "Amended Programme of the Malayan People's Liberation Movement" and the MCP's December 1955 "Peace Manifesto" proposed that the movement broaden its base—for instance, drawing in Malay peasants by showing greater respect for Islam and Malay customs. The colonial and postcolonial governments clearly saw the MCP's attempts to lure rural Malays and Orang Asli to its cause as a genuine threat (see Government of Malaysia 1971; Snider 1977). Then, in the early 1960s, the PRM-linked Partai Komunis Indonesia (Indonesian Communist Party) and its Indonesian Chinese counterpart developed more of a rapport, further intimating the compatibility of PRM with the LPM and perhaps strengthening the bond between them (Snider 1977). Large numbers of MCP workers emerged to join the LPM in 1958–1959 (though others purportedly stayed underground to prepare for armed insurgency), joined by MCA supporters searching for a more effective party (Vasil 1971; Government of Malaysia 1971).[21]

In the 1959 elections, the Socialist Front won 10 percent of the vote at the state level and 13 percent at the federal level, coming in third nationally behind the Alliance and the PMIP. However, LPM candidates fared much better than those from PRM. The Socialist Front won seats only in largely non-Malay states. Moreover, PRM succeeded only in urban areas—Kuala Lumpur and Johor Bahru—and not among Malay peasants or fishermen, a result suggesting that its success was largely due to the support of Chinese and Indians from the LPM. PRM's failure to secure Malay support caused serious strains in its relationship with the LPM.

Much of the support for the LPM, however, especially of its Chinese-educated candidates, was due less to ideology than to quiet campaigning on communal issues, especially multilingualism and support for Chinese education, to capitalize on the MCA's weakness. In subsequent local and town council elections in 1960 and 1961, the Socialist Front found cooperation difficult, bickering first over the nomination of candidates and again after the polls (Snider 1977; Vasil 1971).

Soon after independence, education and language policies became increasingly salient and divisive for both the government and the Socialist Front. Central to the debate were the recommendations of a committee headed by Abdul Rahman bin Talib, then the minister of education. The recommendations, submitted in mid-1960, put Chinese and Tamil schools at apparent risk of closure or reorganization and required that all public examinations be conducted in Malay or English. The LPM, particularly the Chinese-educated in the party, wanted protections for vernacular education and for each community's language, literature, and culture in addition to the abolition of English's official status. These positions were unacceptable to PRM, which considered the recommendations of the Rahman Talib committee fair and necessary for the creation of a united Malayan nation. The LPM and PRM reached only a shaky compromise of convenience that more or less reflected PRM's position. These differences were temporarily submerged after Tunku Abdul Rahman announced plans in May 1961 for the expansion of Malaya into Malaysia, though the differences resurfaced before the 1964 general elections (Vasil 1971).

The one point upon which all opposition parties—not just the Socialist Front but also Party Negara, the PPP, the UDP, and the PMIP—could at least temporarily agree in 1962–1963 was condemnation of the merger of Malaya with Singapore, Sabah, and Sarawak (see Vasil 1966). All agreed that the federation was being constituted by the Alliance without the free consent of the people of those territories. In addition, the PPP, the UDP, and the LPM opposed the unequal treatment accorded the different territories, and PRM opposed the merger, since Indonesia disapproved. The parties formed a joint opposition group in Parliament under Abdul Aziz Ishak of the National Convention Party (NCP, Parti Perhimpunan Kebangsaan)[22] to express their dissatisfaction. However, with the start of Konfrontasi (Confrontation) with Indonesia in 1962—Indonesia had attacked Malaysia in response to the latter's territorial expansion—opposing Malaysia came to seem pro-Indonesia and antinational. Protest was also fruitless, since federation was a fait accompli, so the PPP and the UDP dropped their opposition.

The LPM, particularly its English-educated leaders, tried to shore up a united opposition front in early 1964. The PPP declined to join because it did not want to work with parties still so staunchly anti-Malaysia, and the PMIP would not deal with predominantly Chinese parties. Also, the Chinese-educated wing of the LPM would not cooperate with the too-bourgeois UDP (which PRM considered too much a Chinese communal party anyway) or Malay Party Negara. In short, the plan collapsed. Even the LPM and PRM campaigned basically independently of one another and on a communal basis, though each made the issue of Konfrontasi and Malaysia—styled as a neocolonial plot to push the country into war—its core issue. The Socialist Front's unyielding stance on the formation of Malaysia cost that party much support in the 1964 elections. The LPM won fewer seats; PRM and the NCP, none at all (Vasil 1971).

The Alliance government did not take kindly to the Socialist Front. Starting at the outset of Konfrontasi and continuing beyond the crisis, the government had hundreds of leaders and members of opposition parties, including those of the Socialist Front, arrested under the Internal Security Act (ISA), a law allowing detention without trial in the interest of national security. Next, in late 1964, to stem the influence of the Socialist Front, the PPP, and the UDP in New Villages and urban centers, the government suspended all local council elections indefinitely, instituting appointed local and municipal councils instead (see note 9, above). Furthermore, in July 1973, the constitution was amended to make Kuala Lumpur a federal territory, governed by appointees rather than elected officials. This change disenfranchised around a million voters, most of them non-Malay. Finally, the government declared a number of LPM and PRM branches illegal, which put pressure on the already strained Socialist Front relationship (Vasil 1971; Saravanamuttu 2000).

Pressure also came from inside the front. Aside from the old conflicts over integration and language, as well as personality clashes and disputes between English- and Chinese-speaking Chinese, LPM moderates blamed the Indonesia-influenced PRM for forcing the Malaysia issue—a lost cause—to be the central election issue. By early 1966, PRM had refused to cooperate further with the LPM, and the LPM had lost faith in the utility of a coalition with the electorally weak PRM. In late 1965, PRM withdrew itself from the Socialist Front, followed by the LPM. By that time, the LPM's membership was almost entirely Chinese-educated Chinese, mostly from New Villages and urban areas in Selangor, Penang, and Johor, and the party's orientation was increasingly Chinese-chauvinist. The party opted out of constitutional politics, seeking power through "mass struggle" instead (Vasil 1971). The LPM was later banned, in the wake of the 1969 elections and violence in which the party's supporters had played a key role.

PRM, however weak, proved more enduring. When, in 1965, a group of young intellectuals led by Kassim Ahmad came to power in the party, PRM underwent a radical change. It changed its name to Parti Sosialis Rakyat Malaya (Malayan People's Socialist Party, PSRM), with scientific socialism as its ideology. The government, charging that the party was communist and atheistic, cracked down on the PSRM and arrested more leaders, leaving the party frail but still viable (Sanusi and Ang 1998).

The Malaysian Solidarity Convention. Despite the protestations of opposition parties in Malaya and the annexed territories, Malaysia was formed in 1963. At the time, the People's Action Party (PAP), led by the charismatic lawyer Lee Kuan Yew, controlled Singapore's government, as the party does to this day. Before Singapore's merger with Malaya, the PAP had relied solely on a noncommunal, socialist appeal, but it realized that this approach was inadequate in Malaysia. For the 1964 elections, the PAP advocated an order in which all people, regardless of race, religion, and culture, could get a just share as equal citizens. UMNO equated this message with the Chinese chauvinism of parties like the PPP, the UDP, and the LPM. Tunku Abdul Rahman feared that Lee would eventually rally most Chinese to his side, both posing a threat to Malay dominance and spurring Malay extremists within and outside UMNO to become more aggressive in response (Vasil 1971).

The *tunku's* fears were not entirely unfounded. Lee had been working to forge a pact with other opposition parties and politicians, the Malaysian Solidarity Convention (MSC). The MSC was a loose alliance of the PAP, the UDP, the PPP, the SUPP, and the Machinda Party of Sarawak. It was formalized in May 1965 with the signing of a joint declaration calling for a "Malaysian Malaysia" in which the legitimate interests of different communities would be more secure than in a Malay Malaysia (Lee 1998: 17). This concept, set forth in a series of speeches (see Lee 1965a; Lee 1965b), proposed that as long as all citizens remained loyal to the nation, Malaysia should be democratic, tolerate legitimate differences of opinion, respect diversity, and belong to Malaysians as a whole rather than to any one race.

Lee argued against the Malay press and critics among the Malay leadership—who denounced him as "an enemy of the people of Malaysia" (Lee 1965a: 8)—that his was not a communal endeavor but an attempt to surmount communalism. He insisted that Malaysian demographics mandated against exclusiveness or intolerance, especially for the Chinese and Indian minorities, and that Malay chauvinists threatened political harmony and stability while stifling opponents. As PAP chairman Toh Chin Chye expounded at a June 1965 MSC rally in Singapore, "Experience has shown that in similar countries, a united nation can arise only if one race does not aspire to be the master race but instead all citizens are equal irrespective of . . . race" (Lee 1998: 616). In contrast, the *tunku* set forth UMNO position in an August 1964 interview (Vasil 1966: 51):

It is understood by all that this country by its very name, its traditions and character is Malay. . . . In any other country where aliens try to dominate economic and other fields, eventually there is bitter opposition from the indigenous people. But not with the Malays. Therefore, in return, they must appreciate the position of the Malays.

While the PAP was in fact working more to unseat the MCA in the Alliance than to challenge UMNO, the party's outspoken presence alarmed Malays and incited a communal propaganda campaign by UMNO. Eventually Singapore was obliged to leave the federation, becoming an independent republic on August 9, 1965.[23]

While the rest of the PAP was forced out of Malaysia with Singapore's secession, the party's sole Malayan representative in Parliament, C. V. Devan Nair, remained. He first led a Malaysian PAP, but the government would not allow the Singapore-based party to continue. Nair then launched the Democratic Action Party (DAP) in 1966. The DAP maintained the slogan "Malaysian Malaysia"[24] and worked to build up a mass base among non-Malays, hoping Malay support would follow in time. As articulated in the party's 1967 "Setapak Declaration," the DAP favored racial equality, opposed the division of the population into *bumiputera* and non-*bumiputera*, and attacked Malays' constitutionally guaranteed special position (which the PAP had never dared do) but also proposed land reform and other strategies to boost the income of rural Malays. The party declared that while it supported Bahasa Malaysia as the national language, it could not "accept a language and education policy based on the erroneous premise that the propagation and permanence of the national language can only be finally secured on the basis of the eventual deculturation of two major communities in Malaysia—the Chinese and Indians" (Democratic Action Party 1991: 6). For the 1969 general elections, the DAP endorsed political, socioeconomic, and (especially) cultural democracy. The party tried to project itself as the chief defender of non-Malays' rights and interests, with particular attention to the residents of New Villages (Democratic Action Party 1991; Vasil 1971).

The DAP worked to develop its image and scope, despite constant harassment. The party launched a newsletter, *The Rocket* (published in Malay, English, Chinese, and Tamil), in August 1966. In April 1968, the DAP started its Labour Bureau—with fully one-quarter of the party's

Central Executive Committee members from trade unions, an emphasis on labor issues was hardly surprising—followed by women's and youth wings in the early 1970s. Throughout, party leaders—from Secretary-General Goh Hock Guan and his successor, Lim Kit Siang, to *Rocket* editor and member of Parliament Fan Yew Teng—were threatened, detained, or co-opted as part of the government's persistent efforts at undermining the party. Between 1971 and 1974, for instance, the DAP lost four of thirteen members of Parliament (MPs) and eleven of thirty-one state assemblymen to the BN (Democratic Action Party 1991: 21). Also, on grounds of security, the BN banned public rallies after the 1974 elections, making it ever harder for the DAP and its fellow opposition parties to reach voters.

The 1969 Elections and their Aftermath. Opposition parties tried to build a coalition for the 1969 elections, but the resulting pact was less inclusive or formal than the Socialist Front had been. There were no fundamental ideological or programmatic differences separating the DAP, the PPP, and Gerakan. What set them apart was degree of commitment to particular aims, the emphasis each placed on attracting Malays as well as non-Malays, and the personalities involved. The three parties' shared support of mild socialism and representative government, in addition to their fear of the growing authoritarianism of the Alliance government and their awareness that without some way of working together they would split the opposition vote, led them to cooperate with one another, their past disagreements notwithstanding.[25] They divided state and parliamentary seats on the basis of each party's organization and expected level of support in each constituency (Democratic Action Party 1991; Vasil 1971). The Alliance's strategy, by contrast, was premised on UMNO's expectation that it faced its greatest threat in the PMIP. Malays in the northern and eastern states, no longer confident that the Alliance could protect them, had turned to the PMIP. In consequence, the Alliance focused on appealing to Malays, making little effort to woo non-Malay voters on behalf of the MCA and the MIC. Non-Malays consequently grew ever more dubious of the Alliance's concern for other communities, despite the fact that Malaysian demographics mandated that the BN should pursue both Malay and non-Malay votes in order to retain its standing.

The elections showed that the MCA and the MIC could no longer claim to be the preeminent representatives of their respective communities, thus signaling the possible end of the Alliance system. The Alliance as a whole suffered, winning only 48 percent of the total vote, but the MCA fared particularly poorly. Conversely, all the opposition parties did better than before, especially the DAP, which emerged as the largest opposition party in Parliament. Gerakan also did very well, its support based mainly on the popularity of several party leaders and the backing of trade unions. The party took control of the Penang government, the first time a party representing non-Malays had captured a state legislature (Vasil 1971). Despite the progress of these supposedly noncommunal parties, the events surrounding the 1969 elections represented a grave setback to race relations and to the cause of noncommunal politics. Indeed, the *tunku* emphasized communalism in castigating the opposition. The DAP and the PPP clearly represented different communities from those represented by the PMIP, but the *tunku* complained: "The DAP, PPP, and PMIP have joined hands against the Alliance. This communal trend is very disturbing because it cuts across the very policy we all cherish" (quoted in Barraclough 1985a: 37–38). Racial outbursts both represented and stimulated general tension, and the violence and resultant government crackdown seriously impaired public confidence in the democratic order.

The Post-1969 Era. The DAP remained the single most successful opposition party at the federal level from the resumption of parliamentary democracy in 1971 through the late 1990s. PRM also remained active, although with virtually no success in elections, and a fluctuating array of opposition parties continued to post some gains in Sabah and Sarawak. Other than these parties, the primary opposition to the BN came from Islamist and Malay-centric parties rather than from those oriented around a labor or socialist ideology. It is notable that the main opposition parties have all remained at least officially noncommunal, although none has managed entirely to surmount racialism.

For instance, patterns of support for the DAP suggest that in the 1970s to the 1990s voters saw the DAP as a party of and for non-Malays. Indeed, in most recent general elections, the DAP has garnered a greater share of the Chinese vote than has the MCA, peaking at 20.3 percent of the popular vote in 1986 (Heng 1996). It may be that Chinese voters recognize that the MCA is better positioned to obtain federal funds for development projects, but that they support the opposition for more narrow ethnic issues, such as Chinese educational and cultural interests (see Lai 1997). Although not above manipulating ethnic issues at times, since the mid-1980s the DAP has tried harder to present itself as a social-democratic alternative organized around class rather than race. The party has made an effort to recruit Malays into its leadership and has focused on exposing scandals and corruption, advocating political accountability and liberalization and pressing for economic justice and racial equality.

Its noncommunal social justice identity has made the party acceptable to some urban Malays, though most "prefer to see the DAP as a watchdog rather than as a power broker" (Jesudason 1996: 139–40).[26]

The PSRM also remained active after 1969. The party reinvented itself in 1990 in a bid to gain more support. Renamed Parti Rakyat Malaysia (PRM), the party still calls for progressive social change but no longer espouses socialism. Even so, given its socialist legacy (a turnoff for many voters), harassment of the party, and the general prevalence of racial politics, all of which make it difficult for a party not oriented around race to find a niche, PRM has remained small and persistently weak. The party boasts long-standing, close ties with issue-oriented NGOs as well as with class-oriented groups, such as those dealing with labor or land rights, particularly in the Klang Valley (Kuala Lumpur and vicinity), Johor, and Penang. Especially in the mid- to late 1990s, PRM grew in size and impact. Applications for membership increased, mostly from among the middle class and the urban NGOs. Nonetheless, electoral success has remained elusive.[27]

The Islamist and pro-Malay Cluster

Parti Islam SeMalaysia (PAS, the Pan-Malaysian Islamic Party, initially referred to as the PMIP) has been at the center of a cluster of Islamist parties since the party's formation in 1951; most of the others are small offshoots of PAS. While these parties focus on Islam rather than on race per se, they are in practice almost exclusively Malay. Moreover, PAS gained momentum at the start from touting a Malay-chauvinist line and has carped consistently that UMNO, in not supporting Islam more wholeheartedly, is betraying the race.[28] This dual stance has made cross-party opposition collaboration difficult. While socialist parties have been the primary opposition alternatives for non-Malay voters (far less so for Malays), Islamist parties have maintained a strong position among Malays but hold limited appeal for non-Malays, few of whom are Muslim.

Rooted in the Malay nationalism of the late 1940s, PAS initially opposed both colonial rule and the conservative UMNO leadership, including UMNO's concessions to and electoral alliance with non-Malays. The party attracted disenchanted UMNO members, radical Malay nationalists (some of them from the PKMM), and Islamist reformists. PAS was long the only communal alternative to UMNO for Malays and the only peninsular party not led by Anglophone politicians. Until the formation of S'46, in 1987, and aside from a short stint in the BN from 1973 to 1977, PAS remained UMNO's main rival, especially in northeast

Malaysia. The party attacked UMNO on matters of Malay rights and Islam (Y. Mansoor 1976; Enloe 1970; Jesudason 1996).

The Islamic resurgence that has swept Malaysia since the 1970s has changed the character of PAS as well as that of UMNO. The *dakwah* movement has been particularly powerful among university students. John Funston (1985: 171) explains, "Although 'dakwah' (literally, to call or invite) is loosely translated as missionary activities, in the Malaysian context this refers more to the task of making Muslims better Muslims than converting the non-believer." *Dakwah* activism is also motivated partly by the desire to strengthen Malay identity while "cleansing" it of residual Hindu and animist elements. A common tenet of the different strands of the movement is that Islam should be not only a religion but also a guide to the organization of politics, the economy, and society as a whole.[29] The resurgence and the organizations it has spawned, such as Angkatan Belia Islam Malaysia (Malaysian Islamic Youth Movement, ABIM, founded in 1971), have brought a new influx of members to PAS because of its commitment to instituting Islamic laws and governance. The rising popularity of PAS and the Islamic resurgence itself forced a response from UMNO. In the past, UMNO had seen Islam as a source of stability, not trouble. In the 1950s and 1960s, for instance, Islam served as a bulwark against the spread of communism. As PAS and "fundamentalist" Islam came to pose more of a challenge, however, the government responded through a combination of co-opting *dakwah* activists (most notably former UMNO deputy prime minister Anwar Ibrahim), building Islamic institutions (the Islamic Bank, the International Islamic University, a government-supported *dakwah* group, and so on) to prove its Islamist credentials, and using force (calling a state of emergency in Kelantan in the late 1970s,[30] and cracking down on worrisome sects or leaders[31]).

Even though PAS has always supported the establishment of an Islamic state in Malaysia, initially the party was not so far removed in its policies from UMNO; hence its willingness to join the BN in the 1970s, in the interests of Malay unity. It was not until a change of leadership in 1982 brought to prominence a younger, more radical cohort that the Islamist component of PAS ideology really superseded the Malay nationalist strand. These new leaders, many of them educated in Saudi Arabia or Egypt, were inspired by the Iranian revolution to pursue Islamist governance, under which Islam would no longer be "subordinated to Malay culture and nationalism" (Alias 1994: 182). At that point, UMNO and PAS diverged. PAS pressed for socioeconomic justice, condemned the NEP as ethnically based, and espoused noncommunal Muslim brotherhood. By the 1990s, PAS had acknowledged that a unified opposition—crucial to posing a credible challenge to the BN—would require the downplaying of Islamism. This framing significantly benefited the party.[32]

In the late 1980s, another prominent opposition party formed that, while not explicitly an Islamist party like PAS, cast itself as particularly sensitive to Malay interests, not least Islam. Parti Semangat '46 (Spirit of '46 Party, or S'46), renamed Parti Melayu Semangat '46 in 1994, was a short-lived but influential splinter party of UMNO. The party formed in the wake of a severe economic recession in 1985–1986. Cutbacks in government expenditures had limited patronage resources. These constraints especially affected smaller-scale Malay businessmen and led them to believe that the government catered only to well-connected Malay tycoons. Moreover, a series of serious financial scandals, some of them involving government-linked firms and banks, had shed doubt on the aptitude of Mahathir's economic management. Mahathir's only partly successful attempts to take for himself some of the powers of the *raja* and to counter Islamic extremism further eroded his credibility and support (Funston 1988).

Under pressure, UMNO split into two teams: team A, led by Mahathir and Ghafar Baba, and team B, led by Tengku Razaleigh Hamzah and Musa Hitam. This split was not only the first serious challenge to the party's president and its unity, with the UMNO cabinet divided almost in half, but also the first time that "criticisms against UMNO leaders were as strong from within the party as from opposition groups outside" (Funston 1988: 366; see also Khoo 1995: chap. 7). Having narrowly lost the 1987 UMNO party elections, Razaleigh and Musa, with their followers, left the party to form S'46 while Mahathir stayed with UMNO, renamed UMNO Baru, since UMNO had been declared illegal in a high-profile court case.[33] S'46 courted support from trade unions and civil rights groups and forged alliances with both Malay and non-Malay opposition parties. While some who had joined S'46 did so both because of their failure within Mahathir's UMNO and because of personal ties to Razaleigh, they were amenable to developing new policies. S'46 benefited in that regard from being able to distance itself from less popular government policies, including aspects of the NEP (though the party still supported the continuation of preferential policies in some form; see Jomo 1996).

However, as the economy picked up in the late 1980s, S'46's fortunes began to wane. Many members defected back to UMNO. James Jesudason explains that the party was stymied by a fundamental dilemma facing Malay opposition parties. S'46, he says,

was courting the same constituency as the UMNO but did not have the resources to offer a better economic deal. The party's platform was a laudable one which promised the independence of the judiciary, the repeal of unjust and repressive laws, the elimination of business investments by political parties, and the restoration of workers' rights. . . . While these issues attracted some Malay middle-class support, much of the Malay population, from the middle classes to the villagers, did not regard Semangat as better placed to channel benefits to them than the UMNO [Jesudason 1996: 138].

Eventually the leaders of S'46 decided to pursue a specifically Malay constituency, discarding the party's original multiethnic, social democratic platform. The party argued that UMNO's diminution of the powers of the sultans had jeopardized the position of the Malays by weakening an essential constitutional guarantee for Malay special privileges. This strategy may have won S'46 some support among rural Malays, but it cost it the backing of non-Malays. Tengku Razaleigh dissolved the party in 1996. He and many other former S'46 members were subsequently reabsorbed into UMNO, though others were denied readmission or entered PAS instead (Jesudason 1996; Case 1993).

Attempts at a Merger between the Socialist and Islamist Clusters

The 1990s saw leftist and Islamist opposition parties striving more sincerely than in the past to collaborate. By that time, Mahathir had extended executive power and consolidated control in the BN to such an extent that state and party institutions were nearly synonymous. Both clusters of opposition parties acknowledged that some degree of cooperation would be necessary if the BN were to be ousted. Nevertheless, the resulting coalitions were basically just unsteady electoral pacts, cemented more by necessity and determined leaders than by substantive agreement or sympathy on the ground. The fundamental premises of the leftist and Islamist contingents remained too divergent for common ground to be obvious or compelling. The push for unity began with the run-up to the general elections of 1990, when a range of opposition parties mobilized what coalitional capital they had to unite in a pair of interlinked coalitions. By 1995, the camps had more or less split apart, although various segments of the opposition still cooperated to some extent.

In 1990, S'46 anchored two coalitions, the Angkatan Perpaduan Ummah (APU, Muslim Unity Front) and Gagasan Rakyat (Gagasan, People's Might). While some of the parties involved had worked together before,[34] this alliance was more formal and far-reaching. S'46 was critical to both groupings, although less dominant in either than UMNO is in the BN. The APU was an Islamist coalition including S'46, PAS, and two smaller Islamist parties, Parti Hisbul Muslimin Malaysia (HAMIM) and

Barisan Jama'ah Islamiah Se Malaysia (BERJASA, Malaysian Islamic People's Front), both of them splinter parties of PAS.[35] The APU was strongest on the heavily Malay east coast. Gagasan included S'46, the DAP, PRM, the All Malaysia Indian Progressive Front (IPF),[36] the small Malaysian Solidarity Party (MSP), and Parti Bersatu Sabah (PBS) as a last-minute addition.[37] It contested primarily on the west coast and in the south, promising a more democratic and less corrupt two-coalition system, protection of human rights, greater attention to lower-income groups, states' rights for Sabah and Sarawak, and an end to ethnic and religious politicking (Khong 1991b). The dual coalitions of the APU and Gagasan represented "a tortuous way for Semangat 46 to span the deep ideological chasm between the DAP (and, later, the PBS) and PAS" (Khoo 1995: 323–24). The arrangement allowed the DAP to cooperate with PAS, despite the latter's Islamization program, without sacrificing the urban Chinese vote; it downplayed PAS's extremist image and emphasized S'46's Malay roots (Jomo 1996; Jesudason 1996).

S'46 and its partners tested their wings with a series of state and parliamentary by-elections. By the time of the general elections, they were confident that they could at least deny the BN its two-thirds majority (enough to allow passage even of constitutional amendments) in Parliament. In the end, PAS took control of the state government in Kelantan and gained a number of seats in Parliament and in other states' legislatures, but S'46 did much worse than expected, and the DAP did no better than previously. This disappointing result was due to several factors. For one thing, the strong economic recovery of 1988–1990 had muted dissent against Mahathir, especially since the opposition lacked funds for patronage. For another, UMNO's control of the timing of the elections and of media resources hampered the opposition in explaining its ideology and programs. Moreover, UMNO's recourse to ethnic scare tactics dissuaded Malay as well as Chinese voters from supporting the opposition; most notably, Mahathir and other UMNO leaders questioned the nature of the DAP's collaboration with PAS, cautioning non-Malays that supporting PAS even indirectly might open the door to an Islamic state, and warning that Chinese and Christian elements from the DAP and PBS planned to attack Malay rights and to Christianize Malaysia, starting with Sabah. In addition, despite their claims to multiracialism, opposition politicians failed to maintain ideological and programmatic unity, and they resorted in the end to particularistic appeals. Finally, party activists and voters suffered from insufficient coalitional capital: they found it difficult to overcome ingrained suspicions and to cooperate with one another, having little in common aside from a shared foe. In fact, S'46's subsequent remake of its image, undertaken to appeal specifically to Malays, called into question how sincere its earlier espousal of noncommunalism had been, and PAS's pursuit of Islamist reforms in Kelantan proved UMNO's warnings to be not without substance.[38]

By the time of the 1995 general elections, Gagasan was in disarray. By pursuing an aggressive Islamization program in Kelantan, PAS had dissuaded the DAP from even indirect cooperation. After long debate, the DAP withdrew from Gagasan in January 1995. Meanwhile, the IPF had joined the BN, S'46 had given up on multiracialism, and a number of key PBS leaders had defected to the BN after the 1994 Sabah state elections. The APU remained intact. It formed a loose electoral pact with other opposition parties—just close enough to avoid having too many three-cornered fights, but without a declaration of unity. Despite the opposition parties' cautious optimism going into the polls, the BN, with a well-organized campaign and lots of money to spend, trounced them (see, for instance, Netto 1994). Both the healthy economy and the redelineation of electoral constituencies in 1993 worked to the advantage of the incumbent government. Opposition parties drew large crowds for campaign functions but fewer votes than in 1990, particularly among non-Malays. The DAP was especially disappointed with the result in Penang, where the party had expected to ally with S'46 after the polls to form the state government. Fearing that a vote for S'46 would benefit the DAP, Malay voters chose UMNO instead, while Chinese voters were scared off by the BN's insinuations that the DAP's cooperation with S'46 would ultimately help PAS and its Islamist agenda. The opposition lacked both a coherent, unified program and the means by which to convey such an agenda to the public, and so it was at a loss to counter the BN's splintering attacks. The mass of voters therefore defaulted to a communal political orientation in practice, even if normatively they were supportive of noncommunalism.[39]

Through the mid-1990s, then, the polarized, communal structure institutionalized by the British and postcolonial government in politics, the economy, and society continued to stymie party-based attempts to reorient politics. According to Barraclough (1985a: 41), "the imperatives for unity . . . invariably proved weaker than the divisions caused by communal sentiment, ideology, and the desire for an individual identity," since the core opposition parties had "almost nothing in common other than their opposition to the *Barisan.*" In the meantime, the BN consolidated its control through a combination of effective policymaking, patronage, and coercive efforts to undercut challengers and limit the space for dissent. If not inevitable, communalism and the BN came to seem largely inescapable, at least on the federal level, since the political opposition lacked the coalitional capital and normative support among voters to develop and sustain so convincing and coherent an alternative.

The Growth of Nonparty Political Organizations

Political parties have remained the primary institutionalized channel for political participation in Malaysia since independence. However, particularly since the 1970s, a range of other public interest associations have developed alongside state institutions and political parties to advocate for specific interests or issues. These nongovernmental organizations (NGOs) are the progeny of the quasi-political associations of the pre-independence, pre-electoral era. NGOs differ most fundamentally from opposition parties in that success for the former is defined in terms of issues, not legislative seats as for parties. However, the growth of nonparty associations has had a dramatic impact upon the fortunes and tactics of opposition parties, and vice versa. NGOs advocate for many of the same issues as do opposition parties, and so they help reinforce or even shape parties' messages while fostering a general culture of critical and continuous political engagement. By the late 1990s, "the opposition" in Malaysia had clearly come to include more than just political parties, although the links between parties and NGOs remained relatively hazy and inconsistent.

NGOs, negotiating a restrictive legal environment (described in detail below), champion a host of issues, such as environmentally sustainable development, prevention of violence against women, attention to the plight of urban squatters, improvement of working conditions for local and migrant labor, and prevention and redress of the abuse of power by government and the police. In addition, various politicized associations espouse an Islamist perspective on society and government. Foreign NGOs do not have a significant presence in Malaysia, although foreign funding agencies support certain local organizations,[40] and Malaysian civil society groups engage with a variety of international causes. Among these have been self-determination in East Timor and Aceh, democracy in Burma, Muslim rights in Kosovo and Palestine, and an end to trafficking in women and children. Partly because of the legal risks of involvement with critical advocacy organizations, many committed civil society activists pursue similar aims either independently or through trade unions, opposition parties, or religious institutions. The full array of these activists and organizations may be considered civil society agents (CSAs). A central contribution of CSAs to Malaysian politics is in helping to formulate alternatives to the ethnicized status quo. However, CSAs are not themselves immune to ethnic, religious, and personalistic divisions, nor are they all ideologically compatible.

Despite their weaknesses, organizations in civil society may encourage a more thoroughgoing issues orientation, help erode communalism, and offer an alternative form of engagement for those who feel disempowered or disadvantaged by the state. The advocacy NGOs that have developed in Malaysia since the 1970s are usually open, in principle, to members of all races, as are mass religious organizations, labor and professional associations, and other bodies. In practice, however, most are segregated because communalism is so deeply ingrained in Malaysian life, religious cleavages tend to follow communal lines (and religious revival has exacerbated some cleavages), and language barriers complicate interracial communications (Chandra 1984). The organization of civil societal organizations along lines of ascriptive criteria may serve to cement these identities further and may fail to generate the sort of social capital most useful for precluding ethnic conflict, even if these effects are unintended, (see Varshney 2002). In general, English-speaking, middle-class, urban non-Malays predominate in secular advocacy groups, most of which are small and concentrated in Kuala Lumpur, Penang, and a few other cities.[41] Given these demographic traits, such NGOs may seem elitist or may be out of touch with the mass of the population, although certain groups (for instance, women's groups) may be relatively more diverse. The organizations with a large rural presence tend less to be issues-based advocacy groups than to be youth, welfare, religious, and agricultural or labor-related associations or else government-organized NGOs (GONGOs). Politicized Islamist groups are, not surprisingly, dominated by Malays. Groups linked with other religions (Christianity, for instance) are composed primarily of Chinese and Indians, though the barriers between subgroups of non-Malays may erode in such groups.

These cleavages notwithstanding, advocacy organizations can articulate issues "without the slightest tinge of ethnicity," and at least sections of each community can identify with issues raised by various groups (Chandra 1984: 368–69). For instance, religious NGOs, especially Islamist ones, foreground the loss of religiosity and spiritual values among state actors in critiquing the government. Still, some, such as ABIM, Jemaah Islah Malaysia (JIM, Malaysian Islamic Reform Society), and Persatuan Ulama Malaysia (PUM, Malaysian Islamic Scholars' Association), have at times also been as critical and outspoken as predominantly non-Malay, secular NGOs on broader issues of human rights, social justice, and democracy (see, for instance, Jomo and Ahmad Shabery 1992; Saliha 2003). Table 1 offers a rough typology of Malaysian associations.

By the late 1990s, the actual practice of civil society organizations had changed only slightly since the 1970s, although the activities of some groups, like student organizations, had been significantly curbed by government crackdowns. The rhetoric of communalism seemed to carry less legitimacy than previously; as Enloe (1970: 142–44) stated of occupational, religious, and recreational associations through the 1960s, "Unlike political parties, non-party associations are legitimately able to pursue expressly communal ends [and] make the most explicitly ethnic demands on the political system." But today that characterization fits only a subset of NGOs. Even now, however, among the most broad-based and potent associations still active are Chinese associations highlighting issues related to vernacular education, language, and culture.[42] Some of these groups' demands appear noncommunal but take the form of initiatives by and for non-Malays. For instance, over two dozen Chinese guilds and associations issued a joint declaration in 1985 against racial polarization and discrimination, Malay-centric policies, the growing rich-poor gap, human rights violations, antidemocratic practices, religious fanaticism, and the like (Chinese Guilds 1985). Certain of these demands were clearly more in the interests of non-Malays than Malays, but others could conceivably have been considered multiracial. In fact, more recently, Chinese and non-Chinese organizations alike went to great lengths to convince the government and the public that a similar list of seventeen demands presented in 1999 was not a communal or anti-Malay initiative.[43] Certain inherently racialized debates, however, such as over the Malay-centric National Culture Policy conceived in 1971, are particularly divisive, since they aggravate the communal tendencies in civil society.[44]

On the other end of the spectrum, though the array of *dakwah* organizations may decry racialism, it is not surprising that, in a polity in which Islam is a constitutionally defined key component of Malay identity, defense of Islam often takes the form of defense of Malay interests or of attacks on other cultures and religions.[45] The fervor of Islamic revival owes much to the same realization of continuing Malay "backwardness" that led to the 1969 riots and to the reassertion of Malay ethnic identity, typified by the *bumiputera*-oriented policies of the 1970s and 1980s. The *dakwah* movement in particular appealed primarily to young Malays, who had flooded local and foreign universities from the 1970s on, thanks in part to quotas and scholarships introduced under the NEP, only to find themselves out of their element and eager to find a community with which they could relate (Zainah 1987; Chandra 1987).

The flagship *dakwah* organization of the early 1970s was ABIM, founded in 1971 and still Malaysia's largest NGO.[46] ABIM was formed to enable Muslims who had been active, while in school, in Pertubuhan Kebangsaan Pelajar Islam Malaysia (PKPIM, the National Muslim Students' Association) to continue their *dakwah* activities after graduation. From 1972 through 1982 the group prospered under the charismatic leadership of Anwar Ibrahim—the "one person who could be cred-

TABLE I
Typology of Malaysian NGOs

	Issue advocacy	Islamist (including dakwah)
Examples	Suaram, AWAM, Aliran, Consumers' Association of Penang, Tenaganita, POASM	ABIM, JIM, Pertubuhan Kebangsaan Pelajar Islam Malaysia, Sisters in Islam
Membership	Chinese and Indian, middle class	Malay
Constituency	Undefined, varies by issue	Muslims (some students)
Location	Urban	Nationwide (some based on campuses)
Size	Small core, broader base of sympathizers	Mass membership
Language	English	Malay
Resources	International links, links with government and grassroots (varies with group), publications, research capabilities, limited funds	Regular meetings, moral authority, international links, publications, funds
Issue areas	Gender, environment, consumers, human rights, urban poor, Orang Asli, migrant workers, HIV/AIDS, and so on	Islam, social justice, ummah beyond Malaysia
Activities	Seminars, workshops, petitions, legal aid, reports, public education, service provision, advising government	Sermons, workshops, education (including schools), petitions, service provision
Links	Substantial ties among local groups and with international secular advocacy organizations	Substantial ties among local groups and with international Islamist organizations
Political bias	Left wing; ties to DAP, PRM, Parti Sosialis Malaysia	Varies with organization; ties to PAS, UMNO, Keadilan
Selected leaders	Irene Fernandez, Gurmit Singh, Tian Chua, S. Arutchelvan, Zaitun Kasim	Anwar Ibrahim, Siddique Fadzil, Zainah Anwar

NOTE: This matrix describes ideal types of organizations. Exceptions to each category are plentiful. Not included here are trade unions, ad hoc campaign-specific initiatives or coordinating bodies, GONGOs,

Professional	Chinese	Religious (non-Muslim)
Bar Council, Malaysian Medical Association, Association of Women Lawyers, Malaysian Islamic Medical Association	Chinese chambers of commerce, Dong Jiao Zong, Selangor Chinese assembly hall	Society for Christian Reflection; Consultative Committee of Buddhist, Christian, Hindu and Sikh Religions of Malaysia; Christians for Adil
Middle-class professionals, some exclusively Muslim	Chinese, some primarily Chinese-educated	Chinese and Indians of that religion
Professionals	Chinese	Christians, Buddhists, and so on
Urban-based but nationwide	Towns and cities	Mainly urban
Large	Large	Varies with religion
English, Malay	Mandarin	Varies with organization
Funds, expertise, authority	Funds, expertise, experience, community support, links with political parties and media	Regular meetings, moral authority, expertise, international links
Varies with profession, policy-focused	Chinese education, language, and culture; civil liberties	Social justice, civil liberties
Seminars, letters, service provision, advising government	Schools, seminars, petitions, service provision	Prayer meetings, workshops, petitions, service provision
Coordination with advocacy groups, links with international professional bodies	Substantial ties among local groups, with advocacy groups, and with Chinese organizations in Asia	Substantial ties among local groups and with international religious organizations
Varies with organization (some lean to left)	Ties with MCA, Gerakan, DAP	Varies with organization
Raja Aziz Adruse, Tun Suffian, Ramdas Tikamdas	Kua Kia Soong, Wong Chin Huat, Ouak Suak Hing	Goh Keat Ping, Jojo Fung, Rajen Devaraj

international NGOs with a local presence (such as the World Wide Fund for Nature, Amnesty International, or Consumers International), and social organizations having no obvious political bent.

ited with founding the Islamic revival movement in Malaysia" (Zainah 1987: 11). While PKPIM and ABIM are motivated by a commitment to *dakwah*, Anwar also encouraged the organizations to address issues of socioeconomic justice, linking these with Islamist ideals. ABIM espouses the principle of *kesederhanaan* (moderation) and advocates an incremental approach to social and political change. Other *dakwah* organizations, particularly the Islamic Republic (IR), were more radical and political in approach. IR eventually nudged PKPIM and ABIM from their preeminent position on university campuses (Zainah 1987). Two other main groups in the *dakwah* movement are Darul Arqam (House of Arqam), which promoted an austere, self-sufficient communal lifestyle, guided by Islam and with total gender segregation, and the less influential Jamaat Tabligh, a mission-oriented, all-male organization (Zainah 1987).

The progress of ABIM presents an apt case study of the links between Malay civil society and political party–based activism. Though officially nonpartisan, ABIM was initially closely associated with PAS; many ABIM members are in PAS, and among PAS leaders are several former ABIM stalwarts.[47] Particularly in the 1970s and early 1980s, in line with PAS's struggle, ABIM vociferously attacked UMNO's hesitant Islamization, criticizing un-Islamic practices, challenging the state to develop Islamic leadership and policies locally and internationally, and implying the ultimate aim of establishing an Islamic state. Nonetheless, when Anwar was brought into UMNO, shortly before the April 1982 elections, avowing that he sought change from within, many of his ABIM supporters followed. Several rose to high positions in the government and the bureaucracy along with Anwar, who became deputy prime minister in December 1993 after having held several ministerial portfolios. ABIM's denunciation of the government thereafter become more muted, although the NGO still offered critiques of various policies and projects.

By then, however, the government's trajectory was no longer so far removed from ABIM's preference for development along Islamist lines. During Anwar's tenure in government, and under his influence—and in response to the challenge of PAS and *dakwah* groups—the government officially launched a program of gradual Islamicization. Accompanying a program of *penyerapan nilai-nilai Islam,* the assimilation of Islamic values in government administration, the BN government introduced Islamic reforms into the banking and financial sectors, strengthened Islamic education programs in schools and the observance of Islamic rituals in official settings, and enhanced Islam-related programming and coverage in the state-controlled media. Moreover, as championed by Anwar since his ABIM days, the government further emphasized the Malay character of the state through language and education policies, even as it stressed power sharing and *muhibbah,* or cultural and religious tolerance and accommodation (Zainah 1987; Saliha 1997; Saliha 2003; Weiss 2004a). Anwar's fall from grace in 1998, and the implications for ABIM and its fellow Islamist associations, are discussed in the next chapter.

Other institutions within civil society also remain highly ethnicized and often notably depoliticized. For instance, the racial and religious structures of the state have deeply penetrated the trade union movement, fostering a "high degree of ethnic suspicion and stereotyping" among workers (Chandra 1984: 363–64). Though recent development policies have eroded the ethnic division of labor that crystallized in the colonial era, ethnic consciousness remains strong among workers, and government policies clearly privilege ethnic over class identities. The creation of a Malay industrial labor force could conceivably spur identification more along class or even gender lines than racial lines. However, as Ackerman posits (1986: 164), "The rank-and-file members tend to perceive their unions as appendages of the national political arena where competition for resources is pursued through mobilization of ethnic voting blocs." Moreover, although more Malays have become employees[48] since the advent of the NEP, many join Muslim workers' societies rather than trade unions. Indeed, even if union leaders try to avoid communalism, multi-ethnic unions are vulnerable to racialized demands and preferences, from requests for days off for ethnically specific holidays to links with communal welfare and youth associations, including those tied to communal political parties.

The demographic shift in trade unions has been echoed in other sorts of employment-oriented organizations since the 1970s. Professional bodies were dominated by non-Malays until 1969, after which time the ethnic composition of the professions began to change more rapidly. Nonetheless, since Malays are more likely than non-Malays to enter the public sector, and since professional associations generally draw from the less restrictive private sector, Malay participation in professional associations remains comparatively low. In the professions, too, Malays may join separate Islamist societies. Malay economic associations, including provident associations, chambers of commerce, and guilds for various trades and professions, some with an Islamist perspective, have been gaining strength since the 1960s. These organizations have come to rival long-influential non-Malay commercial associations, such as Chinese chambers of commerce, which have been potent since before independence. At the same time, social, youth, and farmers' associations declined in the early 1970s, their activities largely supplanted by government programs and projects (Tham 1977; Chandra 1984).

While professional associations, especially for the legal and medical professions, have taken the government to task on occasion, trade unions worry the state more. The government, echoing colonial-era efforts, has taken strong steps to keep unions from assuming a more political role or from fostering a more inclusive class consciousness. The state's heavy involvement in business and industry means that its interests tend to coincide with those of capital. The anti-unionism of multinational firms, especially American firms, has reinforced the state's stance. Trade unions are constrained by a series of restrictions. The 1959 Trade Union Ordinance, for instance, prohibits large general unions,[49] excludes political party officials from unions (though some unionists have joined parties and successfully contested elections),[50] and limits the range of issues on which workers are allowed to negotiate or strike. The Industrial Relations Act sets additional restrictions on collective agreements in pioneer industries. Public sector unions have been denied even the fundamental right of collective bargaining since the late 1970s,[51] and the policy of voluntary recognition of unions lets private sector employers prolong the process of recognition or induce workers to resign from a union. More general legislation has also been used against trade unionists, including the suppression of strike activity through the declaration of states of emergency in the 1960s and the detention of hundreds of unionists under the ISA. The state has also promoted in-house unions rather than broader national-level ones, to keep workers from identifying an opponent higher than the firm's management or uniting too broadly (Grace 1990; see also Jomo and Todd 1994; Dass 1991). As a result of these measures, the number of strikes has declined precipitously over time.

Female workers have always been at a particular disadvantage in terms of labor and unionization. Even today, women workers are erroneously viewed as temporary or reserve participants in the labor force and, at best, as secondary earners whose real sphere is the household.[52] This presumption is used to justify much lower pay for female workers than for men—despite campaigns since the mid-1940s for equal pay— and to deny women the protection of unions. Some progress has been made, but women still face not only discrimination in wages, promotion, and employers' willingness to hire them but also sexual harassment. Moreover, in all sectors except among unions for almost exclusively female occupations (such as nursing or domestic work), unions that are therefore predominantly female in membership, union leadership has been male-dominated from the outset.[53] Many female workers, such as those involved in small-scale agriculture or business, unpaid family work, or irregular textile and garment work, cannot even join unions. The situation in the electronics industry is illustrative. In 1988, women composed as much as 80 percent of the 85,000 workers in the industry. Late that year the government, having blocked earlier efforts by the (male-dominated) labor movement to organize this sector, announced that electronics workers would be allowed to join or form unions, but only in-house unions.[54]

While a unified, multiethnic labor movement is unlikely to develop under these conditions, there have been cases of strong, united action—though not always with positive results. For instance, thousands of retrenched electronics workers, mostly women, from two Penang factories launched a campaign in 1985–1986. The workers united across racial lines for picketing, a sit-in, and meetings with government leaders (Grace 1990). The watershed moment in contemporary labor history, though, was the Malaysian Airline System (MAS) strike in 1978–1979, involving workers from the Airlines Employees Union (AEU). This action is widely held to have ushered in a new antilabor era in Malaysia, and it "showed the extent to which the government was willing to act in order to suppress industrial action, as well as the labour movement's inability to resist government repression and the lack of significant public support for labour actions in the 1970s" (Jomo and Todd 1994: 142). In late 1978, MAS employees, negotiating a new collective agreement with their management through the AEU, instituted a work-to-rule, refusing to work overtime. The situation quickly escalated. Over two hundred employees were suspended, eleven were dismissed, and twenty-three were detained under the ISA. The AEU was deregistered in April 1979, and labor laws were toughened in 1980 to preclude comparable industrial actions in the future. Unions have largely been reduced to such limited measures as "unofficial withdrawal of cooperation," and even these remedies may be considered illegal if too well coordinated (Jomo and Todd 1994; Dass 1991). Labor-related NGOs have tried at times to organize and provide for workers in lieu of trade unions, but these bodies lack collective bargaining powers, may raise workers' expectations without being able to satisfy those hopes, and are themselves subject to repression.[55]

Student activism has to some extent followed a course similar to that of labor activism. Like workplace-based movements, student movements were significantly affected by the influx of Malay students into universities with the start of the NEP, especially given religious revivalism. Prior to 1969, student initiatives generally reflected a nonethnic perspective. By 1975, Malays were in the majority among tertiary students, and the most significant societies, in terms of their influence on students' values and attitudes, were (clearly communal) religious ones. Among students, as among workers, moments of mobilization have been met with harsh repression and with the reinforcement of legal constraints. Malaysian students have a tradition of activism dating back to Chinese secondary school students' demonstrations against what they saw as the government's stifling of Chinese culture and education in the late colonial period. In the 1960s and early 1970s, Malaysian student groups joined their counterparts elsewhere in protesting American aggression in Indochina and were active in welfare and community projects. The University of Malaya Students' Union (UMSU) even issued a manifesto and staged nonpartisan public rallies around the country during the 1969 general elections, to inform voters about important issues facing the country.

As student bodies and university political clubs grew more aggressive in critiquing government policies in the 1960s, the state began to fight back. In 1964, the government required that all applicants for admission to universities and colleges obtain a "suitability certificate," a ploy for weeding out suspected communists and otherwise subversive or "undesirable" elements. Then the Universities and University Colleges Act (UUCA, passed in 1971), was introduced during the state of emergency following the 1969 elections. The act prohibits all student and faculty organizations from affiliation with, support for, or opposition to any political party, trade union, or unlawful group, and it bars students from holding office in any trade union or political party. Regardless, students still protested against the demolition of squatter houses near Johor Bahru in September 1974, and then, two months later, they demonstrated in support of a peasant movement in Baling, Kedah. The authorities cracked down on these protests, detaining scores of students, lecturers, and youth and religious leaders under the ISA and other laws. Soon after, the government claimed that the Malay-dominated UMSU was being used by an allegedly pro-communist Chinese Language Society member to spur campus unrest. All student publications in the universities were suspended or banned, and the UUCA was amended to set new restrictions and tougher penalties. Supplementary regulations further restricted university lecturers and staff. Some degree of campus activism persisted, resurfacing especially in times of political unrest or around particularly contentious issues. This activism is on a lesser scale than previously, and it is debilitatingly fragmented along racial and religious lines.[56]

The Potential and Limitations of Political Opposition

Through the late 1990s, CSAs were no more capable than opposition political parties of mustering sufficient coalitional capital to cement a broad coalition and articulate a coherent platform to challenge the government, its communal structure, and its policies. As the ethnic and other gaps dividing NGOs, trade unions, and student groups suggest, associations were more likely to tout multiracialism than to practice it. Just as important, the state hardly hesitated to use its power to cut short threatening campaigns, making further mobilization ever more difficult. The most infamous incident involving the governmental exercise of repressive power was Operation Lalang, in 1987 (see below), when over one hundred activists were detained under the ISA; but the ISA and related acts were also used on a smaller scale and on a number of other occasions as well.

James Jesudason (1995: 345) sums up the limitations of CSAs in pursuing broad political change (with reference specifically to ABIM's attempts at horizontal networking): "Groups have allied on the basis of specific grievances against the state, but are not able to go further to formulate an alternative ideological program for the society. Once the state responds to particular grievances or co-opts the leadership of oppositional groups, these temporary alliances tend to dissipate." The institutional development of the polity, overlap between the interests of the state and those of key social groups, and zero-sum ethnic and religious identities that have come to the fore have discouraged democratic participation and allowed the state to incorporate and control significant constituencies. As a result, it remains hard for larger groupings—groupings that cut across ethnicity, or that could challenge the state—even to emerge, especially since Malays' political concerns tend to be channeled through governmental, party, and Islamist organizations rather than through the secular middle-class civic organizations frequented by non-Malays (Jesudason 1995). The fact that CSAs were even able, in the late 1990s, to think in terms of an "alternative ideological program" and to ally across these cleavages (as discussed in chapter 5) suggests how changes in political opportunity structures encourage innovation in collective-action frames and strategies.

The relative benefits of cross-racial organization are generally higher for non-Malays than for Malays. Malays constitute a demographic majority, Malay-based parties dominate the political order, and UMNO has generally done a better job of representing the Malay community than have its partners for their communities (Enloe 1970; Jesudason 1996). Not only are non-Malay communal parties comparatively weak, their communities are also more internally divided (and initially were composed mostly of uprooted immigrants); their gripes against the government are also frequently ethnic concerns to which the government is not sympathetic. Faced with less encouraging prospects, non-Malays may find more room to maneuver in civil society than in formal politics, where an unequal alliance with a Malay party may be politically expedient (as exemplified in the BN). The relative strength or potency of these spheres thus helps channel activism. Tham (1977) traces this situation to the evolution of prewar, quasi-political Malay associations into political parties. Even prior to the NEP, Tham suggests, Malay economic and other organizations tended to put pressure on the government in order to obtain privileges and assistance, whereas non-Malay organizations feared governmental encroachment on their affairs and interests. Reform groups today that attract substantial Malay support still often work closely with the government.

Even when nonracialized support would have seemed easy to muster, it remained elusive through the 1990s. Muhammad Ikmal Said (1992) explains that Malay and non-Malay leftists both tend to be communal, even when their programs are fairly "universal," and despite the fact that their distance from one another deflects mass support. He attributes this entrenched racialism to characteristics of colonialism, immigration, and the contemporary state as well as to the different market positions of Chinese and Malays. Moreover, CSAs may help educate the public and highlight weaknesses of the regime, but they are unable to articulate an alternative institutional framework. As Jomo argues, it is not only that most NGOs have tended to eschew engagement in politics and political analysis; given the "political manipulation" of "ethnic, religious, language and other differences," individuals also lack a coherent sense of belonging within the polity, and, he suggests, "it is difficult to advance a greater sense of civic rights and responsibilities in a polity to which one has an ambiguous relationship" (Jomo 1996: 89–91; see also Jesudason 1996).

This ambiguity extends beyond the individual level to the position of politicized civil society vis-à-vis the state. The relationship between these two realms is decidedly ambivalent. On the one hand, even associations usually focused on social welfare, rather than issue advocacy, have periodically mobilized in contention with the state for political aims over the years. On the other, NGOs willingly accept the burden of providing certain social services, and they collaborate with the government in formulating and implementing policies on environmental, consumers', women's, and other issues when their expertise is needed.[57] Still, while CSAs (usually "moderate" ones) may be given a hearing, the state retains the final say over policies. As the activist Zaitun Kasim describes the usual process, "They call it a dialogue; we call it a briefing."[58]

The government's periodic attacks on civil society are generally directed specifically at what may be termed *political NGOs*, or NGOs "that engage in public debates and dissemination of information relating to civil liberties, democratic rights, good governance, accountability of the government to the people, people oriented leadership—all of which relate to the central issue of democratic participation" (Saliha 1998:

17–18). Malaysia has no shortage of organizations; as of December 1998, there were 29,574 societies registered under the Registrar of Societies (Government of Malaysia n.d.). The majority of these organizations are recreational, religious, or otherwise apolitical. Probably only about one hundred of them might be classified as political NGOs (Tan and Bishan 1994: 7). Realistically, though, only a few dozen such groups at most are really active, as reflected in campaigns on various environmental and human rights issues. In light of such disparities, Garry Rodan (1997: 162) proposes that only groups "involving regular attempts to advance the interests of members through overt political action" constitute civil society, and that all other groups belong to civic society. This dichotomy may introduce some terminological confusion, but is useful in capturing the distinction between political associations and all others. Of notable importance is the fact, discussed below, that it is among political NGOs that cross-cutting coalitions have been most common since the 1980s, with large numbers of diverse NGOs collaborating on environmental conservation, domestic violence, repeal of the ISA, and other issues. Issues, not racial or other characteristics of the groups' constituencies, are of primary significance for most political NGOs.

The most significant factor inhibiting individuals from getting involved with political associations, and associations from becoming more political, is Malaysia's regulatory environment. Article 10 of the federal constitution guarantees freedom of speech, freedom of expression, and the rights of peaceful assembly and association. However, a range of laws, some of them dating back to colonial and postcolonial campaigns against secret societies and communists, curtail CSAs and discourage would-be activists. All associations[59] must register under the Societies Act of 1966 and must conform to its stipulations on funding, membership, and so forth. Spontaneous protest is largely precluded by the Police Act of 1967 (amended in 1988), which mandates a police permit for any public meeting of more than five people. The police have frequently refused permits for assemblies organized by NGOs and opposition political parties. To reach the public and policymakers, CSAs are thus forced to rely primarily on seminars, symposia, and their own publications as well as on representations to government officials and the media. However, these initiatives, too, are limited by the Printing Presses and Publications Act of 1984 (amended in 1987), under which all publications require a yearly permit,[60] along with stiff legislation on libel, contempt of court, and official secrets. Taken together, these and other laws determine not only which NGOs may exist as legal entities, what funding or members they may seek and accept, and what they may do but also how a CSA may make its case to the public (M. Weiss 2003).

It was in opposition to these regulations that some of the most impressive coalitions among CSAs developed in the 1980s and 1990s. For instance, a set of amendments to the Societies Act, passed rapidly and with little consultation in 1981, sparked a mass movement for their repeal. The amendments defined a political society as any society that issued public statements, and they required all such societies to register accordingly within three months. Political societies were subject to special constraints on office bearers, members, and foreign affiliation or sponsorship. After an energetic campaign by a coalition of over one hundred NGOs, the 1981 amendments were modified (Gurmit 1984). As Barraclough (1984: 460) explains, this campaign was particularly significant in showing "the increased political role of interest groups . . . [despite] the narrowing of channels for political participation in the 1970s, the growing irrelevancy of electoral competition, a parliament that has little deliberative function, and the stifling of attempts to create a more critical press." A comparable campaign several years later, however, was less successful. In 1986, a set of proposed amendments to the Official Secrets Act sparked one of the most massive campaigns ever mounted against a government policy in Malaysia. The amendments strengthened a law that already denied public information to public interest societies, journalists, and others, complicating discussion and debate. This time the government was less yielding, and it passed the amendments anyway (Gurmit 1987; Means 1991: 196–98).

The deterrent effect of these laws is underlined by their enforcement, however sporadic. For example, both the sociopolitical reform group Aliran Kesedaran Negara (Aliran, National Consciousness Movement) and the *dakwah* organization ABIM were threatened with deregistration in the early 1980s, though both were ultimately allowed to persist. Darul Arqam was less fortunate. It was banned in 1994 for its allegedly deviationist Islamic teachings and practices. Likewise, Institut Pengajaran Komuniti (IPK, Institute for Community Education), a Sarawak-based group involved with an NGO coalition against the massive Bakun Dam project, was deregistered in early 1996.[61] The government frowns particularly upon challenges to economic development—for instance, protests against such megaprojects as dams—as well as on groups that advocate for human rights or political reform. Actual crackdowns are seldom required, though. The political culture encouraged by the government discourages debate or even critical thinking on "sensitive" topics, and the presence of laws such as the ISA keeps the public fearful of being too openly supportive of antigovernment initiatives.[62]

Nonetheless, the creation of martyrs also sparks some degree of indignant protest and encourages CSAs (and often opposition parties) to recognize a common enemy. For example, the human rights group Suara

Rakyat Malaysia (Suaram, Voice of the Malaysian People), one of Malaysia's most vocal advocacy organizations and a linchpin of several NGO coalitions, was established in 1987 to support ISA detainees. The state may actually have encouraged otherwise independent and self-absorbed NGOs in the direction of collaboration, since

the state's many reactive attempts to encapsulate and force the NGOs into the confines of its own corporatist politics provided the NGOs with the experience of working together, organizing national campaigns and forming solidarity networks, as well as generating unwanted international publicity for the state. With each successive campaign, NGO links grew stronger (Tan and Bishan 1994: 24).

The formation of campaign networks not only spreads work and costs over a larger base—a crucial benefit, given CSAs' scarce human and financial resources—but also reduces risk. A few lone activists are easier targets for the government than a broad coalition.[63] As will become clear in the next chapter, such networks may lay the groundwork for more formal political coalitions, too.

Favorable coverage of CSAs is scant in the government-controlled mass media, aside from occasional features on environmental conservation, domestic violence, or other social issues. Some independent journals arose to redress this lack as early as the late 1960s—for instance, *Opinion* and *Pemerhati* (Funston 1980). These were gradually supplemented by NGO-published journals and newsletters, opposition party newsletters, and a few more liberal periodicals. Also, the Internet had become integral to civil society's communications by the mid-1990s, with the typical NGO supporting e-mail and, often, a Web site. Nonetheless, the media available to CSAs are more conducive to "preaching to the choir" than to winning new converts.

Ubiquitous government rhetoric, emphasizing that NGOs represent antinational "special interests" and are out of touch with the masses, works subtly but persistently to sway public opinion. Central to this argument is the insistence that Malaysian democracy is not like Western liberal democracy; rather, the local variant accepts some controls as needed for safeguarding ethnic harmony, majority rights, and the political stability necessary to development. This discourse highlights the substantial successes of the government in meeting people's needs—painting critics as "ungrateful"—and challenges those who would oppose government policies to do so through political parties (which can be discredited at the polls) rather than through civil society. Such remarks represent citizens' primary exposure to civil society activism, since CSAs enjoy nowhere near the media access and grassroots reach of the government.

The 1980s saw some colorful outbursts by the government against NGOs. In late 1986, the government launched an attack against critical interest groups, challenging them to register as political parties in order to prove that they had public support, and branding several NGOs and opposition parties "thorns in the flesh."[64] Prime Minister Mahathir lambasted these "intellectual elites" as "tools of foreign powers" and saboteurs of democracy (Means 1991: 194; see also Gurmit 1990). In the same vein, after a 1987 NGO conference on the Malaysian constitution, Mahathir "depicted the participants as a small group of frustrated, elite intellectuals attempting to seize power and presuming 'to make policies for the government' "; Anwar, then deputy prime minister, called the organizers "arrogant intellectuals" who wanted to "force their views down the government's throat" (Means 1991: 198–9; see also Khoo 1995).

This sort of bombast signaled the start of the major crackdown known as Operation Lalang, which was carried out against party- and civil society–based opposition and was followed by a sharp attack on judicial independence. The preceding six months, in particular, had seen spiraling championship of ethnic interests, especially with respect to perceived assaults on Chinese education and culture and rumors of forced conversions to or from Islam. The menace felt on each side was reinforced by grandstanding displays of both Chinese and Malay communal unity. The BN government feared not only a breakdown of its own famed harmony (to compound UMNO's internal factionalism at the time) but also racial violence, which seemed a real possibility. Thus, in late 1987, 119 activists and politicians were detained under the ISA and were charged with incitement of racial sentiments and with showing Marxist tendencies.[65] Three periodicals—*The Star, Watan,* and *Sin Chew Jit Poh*—were suspended indefinitely.[66] Then, in 1988, the lord president and five justices of the Malaysian High Court were sacked after interpreting the law in ways not favorable to the government.[67] The powers of the judiciary were also curtailed by the addition of "finality clauses" to legislation, a way of precluding recourse to the courts and removing the courts' power of judicial review.[68] As a result, "virtually overnight, the modified separation of powers was terminated and the judiciary was stripped of much of its independence and power" (Milne and Mauzy 1999: 47). These crackdowns reaffirmed both the authority of Mahathir and his government and the hazards of voicing a challenge.

All the same, and however haltingly, public support for such civil society–endorsed issues as environmentalism and human rights did increase among all ethnic groups from the 1970s through the 1990s, and it was bolstered by a few high-profile cases. Environmentalism, for instance, was of concern to few Malaysians prior to the mid-1980s Asian Rare Earth debacle. In that case, the improper dumping of radioactive waste products spurred both the formation of activist support groups and a series of high-profile court cases, and this activism drew wide public sympathy (see Consumers' Association of Penang 1993). Similarly, in the late 1980s, increased attention to logging and development in Sarawak, including both environmental and native land-rights issues, heightened public awareness (Means 1991). The ranks of committed civil society activists remain thin, however. Only a small core of individuals sustain their movements between surges of wider public support.[69]

In general, then, from independence through the late 1990s, Malaysian CSAs were hard pressed to define their positions as political actors, negotiating between autonomy and co-optation and between civil society and formal politics. The political process was officially reserved for political parties, with limited scope for traditional lobbying activities. Even so, NGOs' supposedly nonpolitical status empowered them in specific ways. As Nair says, "When these groups speak critically on issues of public policy, they can claim that they do so not as party or politically motivated agents exploiting an issue for electoral gain, but as nonpartisan groups voicing the concerns of all citizens" (Nair 1999: 97–98).

Many CSAs developed links with political parties over the years, nurturing coalitional capital in the process. Such ties came at a cost, however. Gordon Means, referring to NGOs' campaigns on human rights and democracy, points out that "the fact that the DAP usually played a highly visible role in the various seminars and conferences considering such issues only served to identify these interest groups with what the government considered to be implacable hard-line critics of the regime" (Means 1991: 198–99). Some NGOs, aware of such risks, voluntarily limited the role of politicians, or even of members of political parties, in their organizations. It was not uncommon, however, for activists from NGOs, trade unions, or other civil society associations to join political parties when they felt that their aims might be more easily achieved through formal political channels. A good example is the exodus, over the years, of large numbers of *dakwah* activists from ABIM, JIM, and their ilk and their migration to UMNO, PAS, and other Islamist or Malay-oriented parties. Likewise, the DAP enjoyed a boost when a clutch of seasoned civil rights activists joined the party in August 1990 "in order to strengthen the emergent Opposition Front" (Kua 1996: 3). CSAs generally enjoy less cordial relations with component parties of the BN. Cooperation is complicated by the non-negotiability of CSAs' demands and by a history of mutual mistrust. Still, selective accommodation to the government grants CSAs a degree of recognition and legitimacy and ensures that their voices are not completely marginalized or ignored. Communal Chinese organizations, for instance, have cast their lot with either the opposition (generally the DAP since the 1970s) or the government (the MCA or Gerakan), depending on which side promises more and seems better able to meet the organizations' demands.

An unsympathetic government, relatively low popular commitment to voluntarism and political activism, persistent racial and religious cleavages, and stifling regulations curtailed the development of an effective or united opposition sphere in Malaysia in the decades after independence. Indeed, the factors that catalyzed protest most effectively were the very ones that signaled the difficulty and danger of speaking out: increased executive centralization and stronger government, lack of judicial independence, a litany of repressive laws, and the increasing prevalence of corrupt practices and "money politics."[70] Moreover, while unsatisfactory economic growth spurred widespread discontent, such as among Malay youth in the late 1960s, among peasants in the early 1970s, and among small businessmen during the recession of the mid-1980s, these moments of protest ultimately resulted in crackdowns, as in 1969, 1974, and 1987, not least to divert attention from the government's too-evident failings. Regardless, opposition parties and CSAs persisted throughout the period. Sustained by a nucleus of committed activists, these bodies explored and espoused political, social, and economic reforms and did their best to communicate their ideas and orientations to one another and to the broader public. Most important, neither opposition parties nor CSAs remained ideologically or strategically moribund. Both changed their collective-action frames and strategies as circumstances warranted, particularly in order to ally across ethnic, religious, or sectoral lines. Toward the end of the 1990s, as described in the next chapter, this process was stepped up and extended in light of changing economic conditions and political opportunities.

THE REFORMASI MOVEMENT AND THE 1999 ELECTIONS

Malaysia's political opposition entered a new phase with the Reformasi movement that began in 1998. By late that year, a combination of economic crisis, the sensational fall of a popular leader, mounting awareness of the government's authoritarian tendencies, increasing support for Islamism in the face of apparent moral degeneration and Western dominance, and demonstration effects from Malaysia's neighbors had restructured political opportunities and catalyzed disparate frustrated elements to form a more united, powerful force. Deputy Prime Minister Anwar Ibrahim was charged with sodomy and corruption and was purged from his government and party posts in September. The former student activist returned to his *dakwah* movement roots. He captured the imagination of Malay youth in particular as he rallied the public to demand *reformasi*, or wide-ranging political and economic reforms. Having coherent issues and compelling martyrs around which to organize, CSAs and opposition parties joined forces to challenge Prime Minister Mahathir Mohamad's government and induce a political transformation. Even with the opposition mobilized and united as never before, however, the BN still managed to wrestle its way back into power with the November 1999 general elections, albeit with a much reduced margin of victory.

Since then, Reformasi activism has petered out, and the BN has consolidated its grip anew. While not an example of transformative change, this movement still reveals the ways in which variations in structures of political opportunity translate into new strategies and framing devices for reformers, and the ways in which the nature of the regime shapes the style and substance of reformist initiatives. The Barisan Alternatif (BA, Alternative Front), formed in 1999, seemed poised to endure well beyond the polls, though initial glowing assessments proved overly optimistic. Islamist and secular partners in the coalition both centered their appeals on social justice issues, particularly good governance and civil liberties.

The BA gave institutional form to a normative shift encouraged by CSAs, which advocated not just for particular policy changes but also for a more open, less communally oriented political environment and for acceptance of sustained, widespread political engagement. In the Reformasi era, CSAs accepted a far more significant role than previously, both in mass political consciousness raising and in building an opposition electoral coalition. Political parties remained the prime arbiters of institutionalized politics, but CSAs established themselves as vital to the process of political reform.

Stimuli for Reformism

Against a backdrop of decades of percolating discontent, especially among the urban middle class, several triggers escalated calls for change. The so-called Asian flu of 1997–1999 really set things off. Amid a regional economic crisis of staggering dimensions, Malaysia's currency, the ringgit, collapsed to about one-half its former value. The Kuala Lumpur Stock Exchange plunged, the property market buckled, bad loans surged, and the government struggled to find the political will and expertise to set things right again. The difficulty of doing so, particularly without recourse to the International Monetary Fund (IMF)—Mahathir's nationalism forbade such an abnegation of sovereignty—led to debates on proper policy approaches and increased awareness of the country's vulnerability to outside economic forces. At the same time, selective government-led bailouts and the slow pace of financial and corporate restructuring increased frustration with the government. Instances of apparent cronyism and corruption appeared in sharp relief, even if such practices were less rampant than elsewhere in the region. Anwar Ibrahim, as finance minister, advocated IMF-style, free market–oriented corrective measures. Mahathir preferred more innovative measures to stabilize the currency and cushion the economy from further speculative pressures. Mahathir fired Anwar and implemented the latter set of policies. The economy improved, but Anwar went down fighting, accelerating a political crisis.

The Anwar Factor

Anwar Ibrahim provided a focal point and charismatic leadership that helped turn amorphous discontent with the economy and the government into an organized reform movement. He had been an activist for Malay-language education, social justice, and Islam and was the leader of ABIM in the 1970s. After two years' detention under the ISA for his support of a peasant uprising, Anwar joined UMNO in 1982. He rose quickly in the government to become Mahathir's heir apparent. Less radical by that time than in his student days, Anwar remained popular both locally and abroad. Well-spoken, intelligent, and politically savvy, Anwar embodied the *orang Melayu baru,* or "new Malay," as a devout Muslim who embraced economic and social modernization. Moreover, in a party increasingly plagued by money politics, Anwar maintained an image as comparatively clean and uncorrupt, even though he was in fact imbricated in these practices (Gomez and Jomo 1997). In early September 1998, Anwar was unceremoniously removed from his positions in the government and UMNO. Though his ouster coincided precisely with the sudden imposition of the stringent currency and capital controls favored by Mahathir, Anwar was ostensibly fired for sexual misconduct. Before charges were even laid, Mahathir explained in graphic detail—repeated in stunningly explicit lead articles and banner headlines in the press—that his erstwhile deputy was guilty of adultery, sodomy, and trying to cover up evidence of his trysts.

Anwar's fall was sudden but not unexpected. For some time, Mahathir had been checking Anwar's power by giving more and more responsibility for economic policymaking to Daim Zainuddin, later Anwar's replacement as finance minister. Moreover, in June 1999, the muckraking book *50 Dalil Mengapa Anwar Tidak Boleh Jadi PM* (50 Reasons Why Anwar Cannot Be Prime Minister; see Khalid 1998) mysteriously found its way into the delegate bags of attendees at UMNO's general assembly. Though Anwar insisted that the claims in the book were defamatory, some of them resurfaced among the legal charges levied against him. Speculation was rife that Anwar had been planning a coup at that assembly instead of waiting for Mahathir to follow through on his promise to hand over power. However, Mahathir outwitted Anwar. For instance, he undercut Anwar's charges of cronyism by revealing how many of Anwar's friends and relatives had benefited from government largesse (see Funston 1999).

Anwar was not immediately detained. For eighteen days he toured the country, giving extremely well-attended public lectures on justice, the purported evils of Mahathirism, the prevalence of cronyism and corruption, the need for social safety nets, and the urgency of reform. Anwar averred that he had been pressing for change from within, and he stressed his role in developing low-cost housing and other people-friendly policies while in government. He was warmly reclaimed by ABIM and other Islamic NGOs, and then gradually by a wide array of other groups as well.[1] Islamist groups in particular command an immense grassroots network. They were able to rouse tens of thousands of mostly Malay youths to espouse Anwar's cause and his calls for Reformasi. Opposition parties, such as the DAP and PAS, also proclaimed their support.

After leading an enormous rally in Kuala Lumpur on September 20,

1998, Anwar was finally arrested, together with a number of his followers. In addition, hundreds of demonstrators were eventually charged with illegal assembly and related offenses. Anwar was initially held under the ISA before other charges were specified. Opposition to the ISA became the central issue of the nascent Reformasi movement. The popular furor mounted when, nine days after his arrest, Anwar appeared in court with serious head and neck injuries. As the Royal Commission of Inquiry concluded in March 1999, Anwar had been beaten in custody by Rahim Noor, then inspector general of police, and had then been confined under the ISA so that his injuries could be concealed. Anwar first went on trial for abuse of power in November 1998. He was found guilty on all four charges on April 14, 1999, and was sentenced to concurrent six-year terms for each count—a severe sentence by Malaysian standards. His trial for sodomy began the following month. On August 8, 2000, Anwar and his adoptive brother, Sukma Dermawan Sasmitaat Madja, were both found guilty. Anwar was sentenced to a nine-year term, to run consecutively with his previous sentence, and Sukma to six years and four strokes of the cane. The unfairness and sensationalism of both trials were widely criticized by domestic and external observers.[2]

Once Anwar had been detained, the Reformasi movement continued to develop, though "Justice for Anwar" remained a potent rallying call. Before his arrest, Anwar had designated his wife, the ophthalmologist and political neophyte Wan Azizah Wan Ismail, his successor as head of the movement. Wan Azizah developed an enormous following, attracting thousands to her emotional but rather banal speeches. For a time, these followers held massive weekend street demonstrations, mostly in Kuala Lumpur but also occasionally in Penang and other cities, for *keadilan* (justice) and against Mahathir.[3] Reformasi protesters demanded protection for civil liberties and repeal of the ISA. They decried constraints on the media and the judiciary and lambasted what was called *KKN* (an Indonesian acronym for *korupsi, kolusi, dan nepotisme,* usually translated in Malaysia as "corruption, cronyism, and nepotism"). At least as prevalent as these demands were calls for Islamization as the solution to the perceived moral decay of the government and society. Shouts of *Allahu akhbar* (God is great) and *takbir* (a call to praise God) peppered demonstrations, many of which took place around mosques and at prayer times. The demonstrations met with increasingly harsh crackdowns by the police. These street protests had largely tapered out by mid-November, but they resumed at key moments, such as at the announcement and anniversaries of the verdicts on Anwar's cases.

Additional Factors

Other key events spurred additional communities, besides Anwar's supporters, to perceive an opportunity for reform. These events served as barometers of popular support for the government and for alternatives, and they helped indicate which issues were of key concern to various constituencies. The August 1998 sentencing of opposition parliamentarian Lim Guan Eng to two concurrent eighteen-month prison terms was particularly important in generating popular indignation. Lim, deputy secretary-general of the mostly Chinese DAP, and son of party leader Lim Kit Siang, was charged with sedition and publishing false news. He had published a statement on behalf of a Malay woman whose granddaughter had charged then-Melaka chief minister Rahim Thamby Chik with statutory rape. While the charges against Rahim, a stalwart supporter of Mahathir, were dropped for lack of evidence, the girl was sent to a reform institution (Democratic Action Party 1998; "A Shameful Episode" 1998). Lim attracted wide sympathy among Chinese as well as Malays for having put himself on the line for a Malay—a rare occurrence in racially divided Malaysia.

Rahim Thamby Chik's case was only one of several instances of purported or admitted bad conduct among UMNO politicians during this period. For instance, in December 1996, Selangor *menteri besar* (chief minister, or MB) Muhammad Muhammad Taib was caught by immigration authorities in Australia with $768,000 in undeclared currency in his luggage. His successful defense earned him added derision at home: the politician blamed his poor English for his failure to follow regulations and declare the cash. Back in Malaysia, the Anti-Corruption Agency investigated Muhammad but acquitted him of wrongdoing. He resigned anyway from his government posts in the wake of the controversy, but the UMNO General Assembly voted him back into a party vice presidency in 2000. Then, in August 2000, Muhammad's successor as Selangor MB, Abu Hassan Omar, resigned suddenly, ostensibly for reasons of health and family but in a hail of rumors over an alleged sex scandal.[4] Mahathir was at pains to select a "clean" replacement for that ill-fated post.[5]

Meanwhile, around the same time as Lim Guan Eng's trial, a crisis was brewing in Indonesia, and it peaked with horrific riots in mid-May 1998. Malaysians, especially Chinese, feared that the ethnic violence there might spread. Amid these concerns, in late August a false rumor was spread via the Internet and was swiftly disseminated via e-mail, cell phones, and word of mouth: Indonesians or Malays (versions varied) were reported to be buying *parang* (knives) in an area of downtown

Kuala Lumpur that had been the scene of racial rioting in 1969 and were attacking Chinese. The government arrested four Malaysians and charged them under the ISA with rumormongering for spreading this story over the Internet, and their arrest sparked a round of protest against this use of the law. Nevertheless, the rumors of violence lent fodder to fears that overly strong pressures for reform might put the country's stability at stake.[6]

Several months later, the March 1999 Sabah state elections were commonly if not quite accurately perceived as a bellwether of what was to come in the next general elections. Peninsular opposition parties saw the elections as a chance to discredit Mahathir's government, while their local counterparts saw the polls as a last stand against money politics and the racialization of politics in their state under the BN. In the end, the BN retained firm control of the legislature, despite a strong effort by opposition parties. However, analysts charged that the BN's win was thanks in large part to gerrymandering, vote buying, enfranchisement of large numbers of foreign migrant workers, glowing promises of development projects, and frightening threats about what would happen if the opposition won (Loh 1999a; Suaram 1999).[7]

Concurrently, a viral epidemic that crested in March–April 1999 incensed Chinese Malaysians. They claimed that the government had been dilatory in dealing with the crisis and had not fairly compensated the affected parties. The outbreak of the newly discovered Nipah virus, initially diagnosed as Japanese encephalitis (some cases of which were also present), was traced to pigs, which were anathema to Malay Muslims, but which also constituted a roughly $400 million industry in Malaysia. It was only after dozens of deaths that the government took action with mass vaccinations and culling of livestock. The government had no plans to compensate the owners of the hundreds of thousands of pigs to be culled. Private sector contributions funded a lottery and compensation scheme for pig farmers and their families, but this effort did little to alleviate feelings of neglect and unfair treatment among the Chinese. For many, in fact, the lottery scheme was a bitter reminder of a similar initiative that had been undertaken during the anticommunist forced resettlement schemes of the 1950s.[8] Only grudgingly did the government offer a nominal payment to supplement these volunteer efforts.

Both the government and its opponents, meanwhile, were at pains to make their cases directly to the public regarding the culpability of Anwar and the implications of Reformasi. For instance, a UMNO Supreme Council member formed the short-lived People's Anti-Homosexual Volunteer Movement in response to the suddenly heightened awareness of things like sodomy in Malaysian society. The government also issued a series of unsubtle threats to the effect that if Malaysians—especially Chinese—supported the opposition, Malaysia would become as riot-torn and bloody as Indonesia. At the same time, the proliferation of thriving alternative media, including webzines, listservs, news magazines, and political party newsletters, allowed the airing of diverse viewpoints. Among those making their views known were foreign observers, including Al Gore, the American vice president, who extolled the "brave Malaysians" of the Reformasi movement in a speech during 1998's Asia Pacific Economic Cooperation (APEC) forum in Kuala Lumpur. Such proclamations lent ammunition to the government's increasingly shrill condemnation of nefarious foreign influences and conniving Westerners.

In a time of such widespread ferment and diverse complaints, it is likely that even without the Anwar factor, substantially more Malaysians than usual would still have manifested their disappointment with Mahathir's government. However, the Islamist wing in particular would probably not have gathered so much steam, nor would the various critical camps have had an easy time finding common symbols around which to rally. In the same vein, had Anwar not known that he had substantial backing in civil society, it is unlikely that he would have acted so rashly after his ouster. However, Anwar could be reasonably confident that ABIM and other organizations, as well as a raft of clientelistic followers, would rally to his side. In other words, the scope and scale of the Reformasi movement would have been less if not for Anwar, and Anwar's strong activist credentials and political capital were crucial to his successful launch of the movement.

The What, Who, and How of Reformasi

The Reformasi movement linked a wide array of protesters who had divergent aims and concerns under a commodious if amorphous umbrella. Reformasi constituted a broad-based popular movement for social, political, and economic change. It was represented politically by the BA coalition and in civil society by conglomerations of NGOs, trade unions, and other activists cooperating across sectors and issue areas. The groundswell of opposition to Mahathir, the BN, and specific government laws and policies conveyed in opposition-oriented media (especially on the Internet) was also tied to the Reformasi movement. As Farish Noor explains (1999a: 6, 13–14),

it is precisely because of its lack of exhaustive content that the concept of *reformasi* has become so effective as a tool for political and ideological confrontation. . . . [The project's] openness and unfixity prevents any attempt to foreclose or fulfil its promise in narrow and exclusivist terms that would spell an end to its pluralistic and democratic potential.

However, as Farish went on to predict, the movement and its leaders were forced to specify precisely what they meant by "reform" and to articulate concrete, pragmatic objectives once the political crisis matured. Particularly as elections approached, the aims of Reformasi had to be somehow encapsulated in a broadly appealing electoral platform.

Over the course of events, the Reformasi movement attracted an unprecedented range of active and passive supporters. Most Malaysians seemed to agree that at least some degree of change was warranted. For instance, 85 percent of respondents to a mid-1999 survey agreed with the statement "Malaysia needs a political, economic and social re-assessment" (Weiss 2000b: 8).[9] However, the bulk of Reformasi activists were young, middle-class Malay men—the movement was not nearly so multiracial and egalitarian as its leaders proclaimed. The prototypical Reformasi activist appeared to be a Malay male in his twenties, educated locally (probably through the tertiary level), employed (quite possibly in the public sector), a devout Muslim, based in a city (probably Kuala Lumpur) even if not originally from there, and a fan of Anwar. Still, a significant number of non-Malays, mostly Chinese and Indian, as well as women of all races were also involved in the movement. Many were Western-educated NGO activists, Chinese educationists, labor activists, students, or professionals. Specific constituencies, such as the Kadazan opposition in Sabah, also piggybacked to some extent on the fervor of the movement, although their specific demands reflected local priorities.[10]

It is notable that among the more comprehensive documents detailing specific reforms demanded were two that originated with Chinese activists: the "People Are the Boss" declaration and that of the Malaysian Chinese Organisations' Election Appeals Committee (also known as Suqiu),[11] both of them promulgated in mid-August 1999. (The comparable "Group of Concerned Indian Citizens' Demands," a list of fifty-one demands for the abolition of communal politics and more, received less attention.) The online "People Are the Boss" campaign was started by an informal group of ethnic-Chinese journalists as a noncommunal citizens' awareness campaign. The list of signatories included not only Chinese Malaysians but also a number of Malays and Indians. The project's "Declaration on the People's Awareness"[12] explains that the government is appointed by and empowered by the people; the people thus have the right and responsibility to monitor their "employees" and hold them accountable.

Suqiu proved more controversial. At the forefront was the Suqiu Committee, a lobbying and monitoring group composed of thirteen national-level Chinese guilds and associations. In addition, over 2,000 Chinese organizations nationwide endorsed a list of seventeen core demands that was drafted as a wish list, submitted to all political parties, and accepted at least in principle by the BN's Malaysian Chinese Association (MCA) and Gerakan, the SUPP, and the BA. Some of the demands, such as those for promoting democracy, human rights, justice, women's rights, and national unity, are nonethnic. Others are considered communal, such as demands for modernizing New Villages and encouraging more egalitarian multiculturalism.[13] The MCA presented the demands to the cabinet, but UMNO condemned them as inappropriately communal and threatening.[14] Fiery debate on Suqiu extended well beyond the elections. UMNO swore that it would uphold the position of the Malays, and UMNO Youth staged an aggressive demonstration outside the Selangor Chinese Assembly Hall in August 2000. Others were more supportive of the initiative, particularly those from the BA and civil society, a cohort that included a multiracial array of student and youth organizations.[15] Suqiu's defenders urged that the debate not be rendered so racially incendiary, advising that affirmative action policies be made more need-based, pointing out that the constitution guarantees Malays a special position (*kedudukan istimewa*) but not special rights (*hak istimewa*), and asserting that Islam denies any racial group specific privileges.[16] Eventually, under intense pressure, Suqiu backed down in January 2001.[17]

Aside from these high-profile campaigns, there were NGOs, students, workers, women, and others who produced statements regarding their hopes for reform. These pronouncements articulated such aspirations as competitive and clean elections, decentralized decision making, safeguards against abuse of power by officials, increased popular participation in public life, elements of direct democracy, and a noncommunal political framework (Santiago and Nadarajah 1999). One group of NGOs, for instance, formed the People's Manifesto Initiative to press for more democratic elections. The group remained active and critical after the polls, raising such issues as the lack of democratic space in Malaysia. Less heavily publicized wish lists included the election manifesto of the student group Gerakan Demokratik Belia dan Pelajar Malaysia (Malaysian Youth and Students Democratic Movement, DEMA), the Citizens' Health Initiative (which had developed long before the elections and continued long afterward), and the Trade Union Initiative. In addition, women united for a particularly momentous campaign.

While women of all races were involved in the Reformasi movement, and the women's vote was fiercely courted in the elections, few women played leading roles.[18] The exceptions were people like Wan Azizah and the longtime NGO activist Irene Fernandez. However, in May 1999, an array of women's groups and activists launched the comparatively radical Women's Agenda for Change (WAC). The group produced an eponymous document listing specific action steps to be taken to address gender inequalities and general problems in eleven areas, such as labor, religion and culture, sexuality, and domestic violence (Women's Agenda for Change 1999; Xavier and Chin 1999). Despite the WAC's pioneering nature, the agenda's launch drew surprisingly scant attention aside from several articles in the press on women's engagement in contemporary politics. Supplementing the WAC was the Women's Candidacy Initiative (WCI), a campaign begun in September 1999 to boost women's political involvement, encourage women and men to support female candidates, and get a women's candidate elected to Parliament. The WCI's candidate was the NGO activist Zaitun Kasim, who ran for Parliament as an independent under the banner of the DAP. With the support of the other BA parties, Zaitun presented herself as a nonpolitician and a women's activist. Her campaign, however, focused at least as much on other social issues (the environment, uneven development, and so on) as on gender themes. Zaitun lost, but she made a very respectable showing. Virtually alone among opposition candidates, she received regular and favorable coverage in the English, Chinese, Tamil, and Malay mainstream media, largely because of the novelty of her being a "women's candidate."[19]

The Reformasi movement evolved in a somewhat ad hoc fashion, relying on volunteers for organization (especially prior to the formation of the BA) and drawing upon various collective-action frames, from civil liberties to Islam, to mobilize supporters, especially from outside the ranks of traditional activists. The street protests at the heart of the movement were essentially spontaneous, and not all participants agreed about the ultimate ends of the movement, especially the place of Anwar and Islam among movement goals. Nonetheless, a slate of leading figures soon emerged, among them Mohd. Ezam Mohd. Nor, Chandra Muzaffar, Tian Chua, Sabri Zain, and the 1970s student activist Hishamuddin Rais. These individuals and others, often anonymous or known primarily by Internet aliases, set up Web sites, printed posters and flyers, produced and marketed Reformasi videos and cassettes, advertised demonstrations and workshops, and kept the media (especially foreign journalists and those from the nonmainstream domestic media) informed. Images of, for instance, Anwar as a martyred hero, and Mahathir as a *mahafiraun* (great Pharaoh), were emphasized because they played upon moral shock (Jasper 1997: 106) and made Reformasi accessible to anyone. What made the average *makcik* or *pakcik* ("aunty" or "uncle") in the *kampung* (village) angry with Mahathir was not so much the finer points of economic policy and democratic praxis as the nasty, humiliating way he had treated Anwar.

Participation in the Reformasi movement was not risk-free, although relatively few individuals suffered any penalties. Aside from voting against the BN in elections, the key act of resistance urged was joining urban street demonstrations. Because these are illegal, they are uncommon and frequently have met with violent responses from police. Some elderly citizens, children, and families were to be found at demonstrations.[20] However, the demonstrations tended to attract a more youthful crowd, complemented by gaggles of journalists and photographers and battalions of police and Federal Reserve Unit (FRU) forces. The single most important tactic for educating and mobilizing new audiences nationwide, though, as well as for sustaining momentum among existing supporters, was *ceramah,* or public lectures. *Ceramah* were held all over the country, often as part of "road shows." These Reformasi tours often featured a multiracial cast—for instance, prominent representatives from PAS, the DAP, and PRM speaking in sequence, often along with one or more well-known activists (some of whom eventually joined one of the parties).

The efficacy and popularity of *ceramah* indicates the importance to their organizers and audiences of in-person communication. For attendees, *ceramah* offer the visual effect of seeing prominent leaders close up, as well as the chance to find out who else is supportive of the campaign in question and why. With election rallies prohibited since 1978[21] and media coverage minimal, opposition parties have relied heavily on *ceramah* to bring potential supporters face to face with candidates or party representatives, expound upon party platforms, distribute party literature, and gauge the extent and strength of popular support.[22] *Ceramah* generally require little investment of time or effort for attendees, and they incur relatively low costs for organizers. If the organizers can offer gifts, refreshments, or entertainment, so much the better—but opposition *ceramah* tend to be low-budget affairs. An important feature of Reformasi movement *ceramah,* whether organized by CSAs or political parties, is that they often featured speakers who were Malay and non-Malay, male and female. It has not been uncommon for Malays to be told one thing and Chinese another so that each racial group would believe that its own specific rights and interests were to be upheld. Presenting a mixed slate of speakers reinforces the notion that all communities are being given the same message, regardless of language. Realizing the importance of this "one nation" message, the BA (especially the DAP and Keadilan) held multilingual, multiracial *ceramah* during the 1999 election campaign. Not only could one *ceramah* thus reach out to several language groups, but, as Keadilan candidate Tian Chua explained, while the BN gave one story to the Malays and another to the Chinese, the BA also avoided subterfuge and spoke to all races at once.[23] However, while these events consistently drew large crowds—quite often larger than those attending comparable BN events—it is not clear to what extent the attendees were convinced by the messages presented, or how many of them ultimately voted for the BA, even if they were sympathetic to the movement or antipathetic to Mahathir.

A BA *ceramah* in Bukit Damansara (a posh suburb of Kuala Lumpur) on November 27, 1999, is illustrative. The event featured a mix of party and nonparty activists of varying racial and religious backgrounds, speaking in both English and Malay to a packed crowd willing to brave the rain for hours in order to hear about the worth and integrity of the BA and the ills of the BN. A well-known academic was the first featured speaker, though he was not a member of any party and was only newly registered to vote. He focused on irregularities in the electoral rolls, the comparative cleanliness and issue orientation of the opposition's campaign and record, the BN's more massive economic scandals and other mistakes, and the need for racial and religious tolerance (which, he argued, is in accordance with PAS and DAP traditions). He also vouched for the competence of the relative unknowns in the BA and for the opposition's intent to incorporate experts from varied backgrounds into policymaking. Next up was a BA candidate from a neighboring constituency, who was a human rights lawyer. He addressed the BN's corruption, condescension, and intolerance of dissent; the need for an independent judiciary and police force; the fact that what had happened to Anwar (especially his assault in detention) was wrong, regardless of what one thought of the man; the integrity and responsibility of the opposition; the fact that PAS would not foist Islam upon anyone; and the likelihood of a "Malaysian Malaysia" in the future, even if the BA could not erase all traces of communalism. The speaker also promised that if voters gave the BA a chance to prove itself, the BA MPs would make sure that the prime minister stayed in line, and that he and others who had long been working for the same issues in NGOs would remain committed, win or lose. Then another human rights lawyer and activist gave an impromptu comment. She insisted that what was moving people was that those who spoke out were being silenced by the government, and she echoed an appeal by the previous speaker for those in attendance to canvas on behalf of the BA. As the crowd waited for other speakers to arrive, the master of ceremonies then told his own story, explaining that he had joined Keadilan only one week previously. Finally, the candidate for the local state seat, Mano Haran, offered a spirited harangue, mocking Malaysian Indian Congress (MIC) leader Samy Vellu's extravagant lifestyle and lack of fluency in Malay, and imploring voters to support the four parties of the BA and end Mahathir's regime.

Coalition Building for Reform

The Reformasi movement united a disparate array of organizations from both civil society and political society. Among the groups involved were political parties, advocacy-oriented NGOs, religious organizations, trade unions, and professional associations. These groups were joined by organized and unorganized students,[24] individual activists (particularly professionals and academics), and alternative media. Collaboration across these categories was not always deep, but it appeared sincere. Groups motivated by different underlying philosophies and representing different constituencies have learned, through practice of advocacy in the face of an increasingly consolidated and strong regime, to trust each other and to focus on what they have in common; that is, they have built up coalitional capital. For instance, the underlying motivation for Islamic organizations is religion. Their focus is on moral accountability and, often, pro-Malay policies. Their membership is almost exclusively Muslim Malay, they may prefer some degree of gender segregation, and most communication is in Malay. Issue-oriented advocacy groups are mostly Chinese and Indian in membership; they are usually gender-neutral, operate mostly in English, and phrase many demands in universalistic terms. Still, all these groups espouse *keadilan*, albeit with differing rationales, making collaboration feasible. Identifying such points of convergence among groups and sectors greatly expands the scope, space, and resources for engagement and reform.

Two main coalitions of CSAs and political parties were launched in September 1998 to agitate for Reformasi: Gagasan Demokrasi Rakyat (Coalition for People's Democracy, Gagasan), and Majlis Gerakan Keadilan Rakyat Malaysia (Malaysian People's Movement for Justice, Gerak). The two coalitions included an overlapping range of organizations, including the DAP, PAS, and PRM. Gerak, however, initiated and headed by PAS, included more Islamist groups and maintained a more Islamist orientation than did NGO-led Gagasan. No real attempt was made to segregate political parties and NGOs in these bodies, although, as is clear from the structure of Gagasan (most notably, its being chaired by an NGO activist to deter partisanship), the comparative advantages of both were acknowledged. NGOs in particular are often concerned not to align themselves too closely with political parties. Under the circumstances, all involved seemed to realize that broad-based cooperation on common aims was the best available strategy. Both coalitions focused on human rights and good governance, including repeal of unjust laws, expunging of corruption, freedom of the press, judicial independence, and social justice, although Anwar and the ISA dominated Gerak's agenda.

Over the course of about six months' energetic activity, as the initiative shifted toward parties, Gerak attained a much higher profile than did Gagasan.

By mid-1999, however, both Gagasan and Gerak had been superseded by the BA electoral coalition and were largely defunct. Philippe Schmitter (1992: 431) suggests that this dynamic is not uncommon, since "interest associations tend to be displaced from the center of political life and public visibility by political parties once elections have been announced, if their outcome appears to be uncertain and it seems safe to run for office." Reformasi seemed sure to shake up the polls. Many activists shifted their attention from lobbying the BN for change to contesting elections; some joined or endorsed specific political parties, while others focused more on the conduct of the elections than on their results. With speculation rife that elections were nigh, over forty NGOs, including many from Gerak and Gagasan, formed Pemantau Pilihanraya Rakyat Malaysia (Malaysian Citizens' Election Watch, Pemantau).[25] This new coalition focused specifically on voter education and election monitoring. Pemantau was adamantly nonpartisan, even though most of the activists and organizations involved with it were known to be sympathetic to the BA.

While most of the organizations in Gerak, Gagasan, and Pemantau had been around for some time, the movement for *keadilan* bred new NGOs, too, signaling new levels and varieties of engagement. Among these innovative new groups were the multiracial student organization DEMA; the nonreligious, largely Malay civic education association Bersatu Untuk Demokrasi dan Insaniah (United for Democracy and Humanity, BUDI); the multiracial online network for good governance known as People Are the Boss; and the ambitious, noncommunal Women's Agenda for Change. Most prominent among these new bodies, though, was Pergerakan Keadilan Sosial (Movement for Social Justice, Adil), launched by Wan Azizah to provide an outlet for grassroots supporters of Reformasi. Adil's aims were basically the same as those of Gagasan and Gerak, but individuals could join Adil, whereas Gerak and Gagasan were coalitions of groups. Adil claimed 60,000 to 70,000 "endorsers," but its bid for registration was never approved,[26] and it soon metamorphosed into the Parti Keadilan Nasional (National Justice Party, Keadilan).

These coalitions were significant more for the collaborative approach they embodied than for what they accomplished. Gagasan, Gerak, Pemantau, and the BA shared a noncommunal approach to such issues as human rights and economic justice. All strove for substantive, creative, egalitarian, and sincere collaboration between a range of Islamist (Malay) and secularly oriented, primarily non-Malay organizations. Moreover, the coalitions revealed the interpermeability and adaptability of forces arrayed for *keadilan* and against the government. Challenging the premises of illiberal democracy, the coalitions asserted the legitimacy of CSAs' engaging alongside political parties, at the same time devaluing academic arguments against such involvement. On a practical level, the experience of organizing for Reformasi demonstrated that, however few, small, or scattered Malaysia's politicized NGOs may be, when these groups form activist webs with other sorts of organizations, concerned individuals, and perhaps political parties, they can be highly effective at public education and mobilization. Such networks may successfully pressure government and opposition parties into acknowledging and acting upon demands. Indeed, the high profile and perceived integrity of these Reformasi coalitions seemed to boost the image of CSAs and to call the government's credibility further into question, adding fuel to reformist fires.

From Social Movement to Campaign Trail

What most distinguished the pro-justice agitation of Malaysia in the late 1990s from the prototypical mobilization of civil society–based pressure groups or prior coalition-building ventures of Malaysian political parties was the depth of interaction between political parties and CSAs. Reformasi was never confined just to NGOs and other nonpartisan organizations. Opposition political parties were energetically engaged from the outset, first individually and then in such coalitions as Gagasan and Gerak. However, as elections drew nearer, the fulcrum of the movement clearly shifted from the nongovernmental to the electoral sphere. Once the BA became the preeminent Reformasi coalition, CSAs lost the institutionalized input they had enjoyed as more nearly equal partners in Gagasan and Gerak. Even at the height of the election campaign, though, CSAs retained enormous clout, gaining legitimacy from their moral authority, experience, diligence, and articulate, well-liked leaders.

Reformasi's transition from social movement to electoral campaign began with the NGO Adil, which was superseded as of April 1999 by the political party Keadilan. Both Adil and Keadilan were led by Anwar's wife, Wan Azizah, and were initially meant to coexist. Keadilan's launch, though, put to rest months of speculation about whether Wan Azizah (and Anwar) would merely remain in Adil, join PAS, take over PRM, or try to stage a coup in UMNO. Although Keadilan was multiracial, its primary target was middle-class, middle-of-the-road Malays, particularly from UMNO—people who supported the Reformasi movement and the call for justice, democracy, and an end to BN dominance but did not feel comfortable voting for PAS (Saliha and Weiss 1999). As Wan Azizah later described both Keadilan and PRM, both parties "are Malay-based and multi-racial and represent a new kind of politics, a politics where racial sentiments will be minimised" ("Anwar's Party" 2001). Anwar represented both a symbol and a focal point for Keadilan, although he waited several months before joining the party, stalling purportedly so he could better forge cooperation among parties without being linked to any particular one. Shortly before the general elections, Keadilan had attracted approximately 200,000 members, mostly Malay and including many young voters.[27]

Next, after much deliberation, in June 1999 PAS, Keadilan, the DAP, and PRM announced their plans to contest as the Barisan Alternatif (BA); the coalition and its manifesto were officially launched in late October. The BA was also endorsed by parties in Sabah and Sarawak[28] and by the unregistered Parti Sosialis Malaysia (Socialist Party of Malaysia, PSM). The BA's appeal centered on *keadilan* and the specific demands of the Reformasi movement. The principal opposition leaders formulated a list of ten common issues in June 1999: constitutional monarchy; parliamentary democracy; human rights; rule of law; independence of the judiciary; the rights and responsibilities of citizens; Islam as the official religion, and freedom of religion; Malay as the national language, and the right to use other languages; the special position of *bumiputera*, and rights of other groups; and federalism (Hari 2000). The incarcerated Anwar remained the BA's iconic leader; many of his supporters from UMNO joined PAS or Keadilan.[29] Mahathir, chief target of the BA's barbs, posed synecdochically for all that was wrong with the regime.

Many of the same people were involved at all stages of the Reformasi movement, regardless of whether they hailed from established political parties or civil society. As the BA took shape, it benefited from the participation of CSAs—many of them political neophytes—as candidates as well as advisors and supporters. These activists came both from advocacy groups, such as Aliran, Suaram, and the All Women's Action Society (AWAM), and from mass Islamic organizations, such as ABIM and JIM. Quite a number of Malay as well as non-Malay university students also worked on opposition campaigns. In addition, respected academics and professionals (some also involved with NGOs) helped formulate BA policies and testified to the worth of the cause. For example, three top leaders of Keadilan—Chandra Muzaffar of the International Movement for a Just World, Irene Fernandez of Tenaganita (Women's Force), and Tian Chua of Suaram and the Labour Resource Centre—were longtime NGO activists who felt sufficiently frustrated with the government and hopeful about the BA's chances of success to shift strategies and contest for office.

Their campaigns tended to focus on the same issues these activists had championed before: clean and accountable governance, social justice, multiracialism, enhanced democratic freedoms, and economic redistribution.[30]

Results of the 1999 Elections

Malaysia's tenth general elections were held on November 29, 1999, following a frenetic nine-day campaign.[31] At stake were all parliamentary seats in the thirteen states and two federal territories, plus the state legislatures in the eleven peninsular states. The BN went into the polls with 166 of 193 seats, 162 of which had been won in 1995, with a net of 4 more gained in the interim. With over 71 percent turnout, the BN garnered 56.5 percent of the popular vote, substantially less than the 65 percent it had won in 1995, but comparable to its level of support in prior elections. It easily retained its two-thirds majority in Parliament, with 148 seats (about 77 percent), and kept control of all but two state legislatures. The BN's majorities were sharply reduced in many constituencies, most obviously in the region where calls for reform had been strongest over the previous sixteen months, a result that suggested a substantial shift, especially among urban voters. Moreover, the BN's proportion of the vote was much lower in peninsular Malaysia (with the exception of Johor[32]) than in Sabah and Sarawak.

The BA, especially PAS, made significant inroads into the northern states of Kedah, Perlis, Pahang, and Selangor in addition to posting a near-complete sweep of federal and state seats in Kelantan and Terengganu, on the east coast.[33] The opposition did not fare so well elsewhere, despite having kept most contests as one-to-one fights. The results in Penang, a state known for its tradition of strong support for opposition parties, were especially disappointing. The BA won less than half of Penang's parliamentary seats and just 3 of 33 state seats. Two of the DAP's key leaders, Lim Kit Siang and Karpal Singh, were voted out entirely there. Likewise, in Sabah, another state known for its oppositional leanings, Parti Bersatu Sabah (Sabah United Party, PBS) lost both Kadazan and Chinese votes, winning just 3 of 20 seats. Opposition parties in Sabah and Sarawak face serious handicaps, since the BN has made a concerted effort to counter long-standing oppositional tendencies and to cement its rule in both states; moreover, Reformasi and the "Anwar factor" indisputably had much less resonance there than on the peninsula. Interestingly, although the BA groused about gerrymandering and constituency malapportionment, the opposition clearly benefited at least from the latter in 1999. Malaysian electoral boundaries are skewed to over-

TABLE 2

State and Federal Seats Won by BN and Opposition, 1999

State	State legislatures (Dewan Undangan Negeri)		Federal legislature (Dewan Rakyat)	
	BN	Opposition	BN	Opposition
Johor	40	0	20	0
Kedah	24	12	7	8
Kelantan	2	41	1	13
Kuala Lumpur	–	–	6	4
Malacca	21	4	4	1
Negeri Sembilan	32	0	7	0
Pahang	30	8	11	0
Perak	44	8	20	3
Perlis	12	3	3	0
Penang	30	3	6	5
Sabah	–	–	18	3
Sarawak	–	–	28	0
Selangor	42	6	17	0
Terengganu	4	28	0	8

SOURCE: Suruhanjaya Pilihan Raya Malaysia/Election Commission Malaysia, <http://www.spr.gov.my> (accessed Apr. 3, 2005).

represent the rural Malay vote—votes that PAS avidly poached. Creative electoral districting and the first-past-the-post system helped the BN in Negeri Sembilan, Pahang, and Perak but aided the BA in Terengganu and Kelantan (see Table 2).[34]

The results were not fully satisfying to either side. Among the parties contesting, UMNO suffered the greatest losses and PAS made the greatest gains (see Table 3). Keadilan made a decent showing, too, securing about 11 percent of the vote.[35] For the first time, UMNO secured only a minority of the BN's seats (72 of 148). UMNO found itself beholden to Chinese voters and to the BN as a whole as well as to Sabah and Sarawak. Moreover, many of UMNO's key leaders lost or just barely kept their seats.[36] Support for UMNO had been declining since the late 1980s, as represented most cataclysmically by the split between UMNO Baru and S'46, but the decline continued beyond that period. Moreover, the party had been aware for some time that popular sentiment for Anwar and against Mahathir,[37] as well as real grievances concerning the direction of the party and the extent of money politics, posed serious risks. The elections confirmed these suspicions and indicated which sectors were the hardest hit. Furthermore, while conventional wisdom after the polls suggested that the Chinese vote had swung toward or stayed with the BN, Gerakan did no better than it had done in 1995, and the MCA lost 2 parliamentary seats. The opposition received "considerable support" from Chinese voters in 1999 (especially in the most heavily Chinese

TABLE 3

Seats Won by Party, 1999

Government (BN)			Opposition (BA and PBS)		
Party	Parliament	State	Party	Parliament	State
UMNO	72	175	PAS	27	98
MCA	28	70	DAP	10	11
PBB (Sabah)	10		Keadilan	5	4
MIC	7	15	PRM		
Gerakan	7	21	BA total	42	113
SUPP (Sarawak)	7				
PBDS (Sarawak)	6		PBS	3	
SNAP (Sarawak)	4				
UPKO (Sabah)	3		*Opposition total*	45	113
SAPP (Sabah)	2		*Opposition total 1995*	30	56
LDP (Sabah)	1				
BN direct	1				
BN total	*148*	*281*			
BN total 1995	*162*	*338*			

SOURCE: Suruhanjaya Pilihan Raya Malaysia/Election Commission Malaysia, <http://www.spr.gov.my> (accessed Apr. 3, 2005); Manirajan and Zarina 1999.

constituencies), but the Chinese had been turning increasingly toward the BN over the past few elections (Ng 2003: 88–90). PAS received a far higher proportion of opposition votes than in 1995—probably around half the Malay vote overall—and the DAP received a significantly smaller share, so a Malay became leader of the parliamentary opposition for the first time in thirty years.

All four BA parties did better than before, at least in terms of votes, even if the coalition was unable to achieve its goal of unseating the BN. The BA's failure to win a majority of seats, despite the unprecedented extent and duration of popular mobilization, was partly because its coherence remained uncertain. Participating in the BA seemed to help PAS and Keadilan, but the DAP was left firmly on the defensive regarding its association with the Islamist PAS, suggesting that the mass of DAP supporters were less convinced by CSAs or others of the benefits of coalition and were still more tied to racial or religious allegiances than were the elites actually involved in negotiations.[38] Regardless, the experience of contesting in the BA was a useful one, both for the opposition parties and for the CSAs backing them, and was achieved with a bare minimum of resources and preparation time. Moreover, Pemantau's documentation of electoral fraud and the efforts of sympathetic media to publicize these abuses[39] increased pressure on the Election Commission to become more proactive.

The impact of the Reformasi movement on the polls is hard to gauge. What complicates assessment is that one of the movement's main accomplishments was mobilizing thousands of young or previously apathetic citizens. Many of these people could not vote—either they were not old enough or they were among the 680,000 citizens who had registered to vote earlier in 1999 but whose names did not yet appear on the electoral rolls as of November.[40] With three times the usual number of new registrants, the Election Commission claimed it could not process their names until February 2000, thus shutting the lot out of the 1999 polls. Many of the new registrants were probably motivated by the Reformasi movement and likely to support the opposition. Had those 680,000 new registrants been allowed to vote, they could have made a big difference, given the number of close margins. Many speculated that Mahathir had held the snap elections when he did, rather than waiting for the updated electoral rolls, for just that reason.

The effect of the Anwar factor is similarly ambiguous. A substantial number of voters supported the BA, and particularly Wan Azizah, on account of the way Anwar had been treated and what he symbolized in terms of the injustice of the government and the need for change. Ubiquitous posters showing a battered Anwar played up those sentiments. For many others, though, especially non-Malays, Anwar was probably not a big draw and, as the BA's choice for prime minister, perhaps even detracted from their confidence in the coalition. Many Malays and non-Malays were skeptical of Anwar, seeing him as just another opportunistic BN politician who had been thwarted in his quest for power. Anwar's multiracial rhetoric may have rung a bit hollow to some, given his close association with the pro-Malay, pro-Islam policies of the 1980s and 1990s.

In a broader sense, voters may have remained unsure about just what the BA planned to do if elected. The BA released a proposed budget and engaged vociferously with some of the government's more controversial economic plans[41] but otherwise kept its aims and promises rather abstract. One common theme was that cronyism, corruption, and nepotism jeopardize economic efficiency by allocating too great a proportion of public funds to megaprojects that benefit a narrow elite (dubbed the *UMNOputera*) at the expense of the masses. The candidates said less, though, about the specific remedies they would implement. The BA was clearer in its appeal to certain categories of lower-income voters, promising a monthly wage for workers on agricultural estates, more merit-based affirmative action programs, the awarding of taxi licenses to individuals rather than companies, and the like. Ultimately, though, the focus of the BA's campaign was justice, democracy, and good governance (transparency, accountability, separation of powers, individual freedoms, and lack of corruption) rather than economic development. Their *ceramah* also focused on spanning racial divisions, both from an ideological perspective and as a practical matter: Muslim supporters of PAS, for instance, had to be convinced that it would be "safe" to vote for DAP candidates. Having held power only in Kelantan and, from 1959 to 1961, in Terengganu (both states poor, rural, and overwhelmingly Malay), the parties in the BA could show little evidence of their ability to govern or to achieve their lofty goals.

The BN, by contrast, made much more concrete and persuasive promises. Mahathir could claim with some credibility to have steered Malaysia out of the economic crisis by the time he called elections. As proof, the BN marshaled an array of cheery economic statistics, from stock market growth to the midcampaign announcement that the country's third-quarter growth rate had topped 8 percent. The incumbent government also claimed credit for basically all national development since UMNO and its partners had first come to power, in 1957. Mahathir counterpoised his unorthodox but effective recovery strategies, including capital controls, low interest rates, and a currency peg, against the more free market–oriented measures pursued while Anwar was finance minister, and he highlighted the relative economic deprivation of PAS-governed Kelantan. Bolstered by a host of development grants and promises made during the campaign, the BN strove to convince voters that only its governance could ensure continued economic growth and prosperity. Helping this effort were the BN's enjoyment of the "three Ms": money, media, and machinery. The BN benefits immensely during elections from its access to government machinery and from its perennial control of federal funds to supplement its own coffers. (Mahathir used to be considered a fourth "M" but seemed more of a liability in 1999.) The BN also stressed the inexperience and disorganization of the BA, suggesting (presciently, it turned out) that cooperation between PAS and the DAP could not be sustained, that Anwar was unreliable as a leader, and that racial harmony and stability were at stake.

Without reliable public opinion and exit polls, it is impossible to say precisely how persuasive the BA's social issues–based campaign was among voters, or how much impact CSAs' involvement had upon their decisions. However, the success of NGO activists and others who stood for election on a *keadilan* platform suggests that social issues and "justice" were critical for many voters, particularly in the Kuala Lumpur area. Reinforcing that impression is the fact that Anwar's wife was elected, and that the DAP secured one of its highest margins of victory in the seat formerly held by Lim Guan Eng, the DAP politician jailed in

1998.[42] Moreover, these candidates could rely only upon limited resources and, often, inexperienced volunteers for support. At the same time, the rather dismal performance of the opposition in Sarawak and Sabah—where the BN had long lured support by contrasting the low growth rates of opposition-led Sabah with those of BN-led Sarawak—hints at the allure of the BN's economic promises. The BN compounded its advantage with promises of specific benefits for constituencies and through plentiful, unfailingly favorable media coverage.

Analyses of the results and their import are clouded by the level of mudslinging in the campaign and by purported widespread fraud. The campaign remained basically peaceful, with only minor incidents of violence. However, harsh verbal attacks and "dirty tricks" distracted voters from the issues at hand. The BN launched a media barrage to suggest that only its leadership could ensure stability and growth and preclude riots, that the BA was made up of a bunch of hoodlums and vandals, that foreign powers were funding the BA campaign, that Anwar was not really a good Muslim, that even Anwar's wife did not trust him, and that Chinese support for the DAP would usher in PAS rule and the erosion of Chinese cultural rights (Mustafa 2003). The BN further played up racial fears in several ways, harping on PAS's promotion of *hudud* (the Islamic criminal code) and on PAS leader Nik Aziz Nik Mat's statement that PAS could allow a Chinese prime minister, suggesting that the DAP would end the system of *ketuanan Melayu* (constitutionally guaranteed Malay sovereignty), and insinuating that the DAP, by dint of its involvement alongside Israelis in Socialist International, was a tool of Zionist Jews. The media also reported a string of defections by Keadilan members to UMNO, many of whom Keadilan claimed had never been members. Supplementing this attack were risqué videos of Anwar that were mysteriously distributed to bus stops and elsewhere, and a fake issue of *Harakah*, PAS's newsletter. For its part, the BA and its supporters disseminated photos of Mahathir's wife being kissed on the cheek by another man (an event presented as inappropriate for a Muslim woman), allegations of womanizing by various UMNO candidates, and a patently forged friendly letter from Mahathir to Israeli Prime Minister Ehud Barak. BA supporters also warned repeatedly and without substantiation that BN youth would wreak havoc while sporting BA T-shirts.

The results may have been skewed, too. Many constituencies reported curiously high numbers of spoiled ballots, prompting cries of malfeasance from both sides, but especially from the BA.[43] The BA also protested a range of irregularities in the electoral rolls, declaring that the BN was padding its support with "phantom voters." Furthermore, the BN was alleged to have exceeded campaign spending limits,[44] and a number of candidates and voters complained of vote buying or other forms of coercion by the BN. It was the alternative, pro-BA media as well as the generally anti-BN NGOs, including Pemantau, that publicized the allegations and evidence of electoral misconduct. These sources primarily reach voters already cynical enough to look outside government-controlled channels for information. As a result, the charges may have heightened popular disillusionment regarding the electoral system and the government's legitimacy, but the voters most aware of them were probably already opposition supporters anyway.

Overall, the opposition emerged from the elections stronger than in the preceding parliamentary session and, at least initially, seemed able to work through tense moments in order to cohere. Moreover, the coalition was able to rout spoiler parties, such as the Malaysian Democratic Party (MDP), established in early May 1999 by several former DAP stalwarts,[45] in its pursuit of a two-coalition system. The BA failed to demonstrate convincingly, even in its own rhetoric, that the mass of Malaysians were prepared to vote for issues above and beyond communalism and patronage. Still, candidates such as PRM's Syed Husin Ali and the WCI's Zaitun Kasim made it clear that winning a seat was never really their chief or only aim and that they would continue their advocacy efforts regardless. Zaitun, for instance, explained of her campaign, "It's a consolidation and an expansion of what we were doing all along. . . . Good government should be participatory, so we are seeking NGO representation."[46] Moreover, the parties that fared poorly, especially UMNO, were encouraged to reform. Taking its paltry performance as a "wake-up call," UMNO promptly announced new initiatives to reach out more to the grassroots and to woo women, youth, and intellectuals by means including promotion of younger, "clean" leaders ("Election a 'Wake-up Call'" 1999; Maznah 2002; Abdullah 2003). Such top-down reforms, even if they were only intended to keep the government in power, still signaled progress toward Reformasi goals.

The Changing Place of Ethnicity

Throughout its campaign, the BA, encouraged by CSAs committed to noncommunal politics, made a concerted effort to downplay ethnicity. Still, communalism surfaced at times, particularly when it came to enunciating concrete policy preferences. For instance, BA leaders declared that the coalition, if in power, would not repeal (only reform) the Malay-centric National Development Policy (NDP, successor to the NEP) and that, given Malaysia's culture and history, only a Malay could be prime minister.[47] Residual communalism also colored party rhetoric. One speaker at a campaign *ceramah*, for example, explained that Malays could comfortably support the DAP, since the party's vice chairman, Ahmad Nor, was a Malay, meaning that the party could potentially be led by a Malay one day.[48]

Clearly, though, the tendency to harp on race was much stronger with the BN. Most tellingly, the BN ran a series of campaign advertisements warning Chinese voters not to give up their religious and cultural freedom by voting for the BA. The advertisements implied that if the BA won, PAS would make Malaysia an Islamic state, with no tolerance for other cultures and religions. Before and after the polls, the BN also lambasted the BA for having splintered Malay unity. Members of the opposition coalition would have been hard pressed to respond to such attacks without some reference to what they themselves promised for each community individually; thus at least some substantial part of the BA's racialist rhetoric was in response to the BN's jousts. Significantly, though, while PAS agreed not to press for an Islamic state, and while the BA's common manifesto, *Ke Arah Malaysia Yang Adil* (Toward a Just Malaysia),[49] calls only for a secular state with Islam as a way of life (*ad-deen*) and as the official religion of Malaysia, skeptics questioned all along whether long-term cooperation between PAS and secular opposition parties was really feasible. Still, because the various parties had worked with groups from across the opposition spectrum, in coalitions such as Gerak and Gagasan, their credibility was enhanced in their attempt at cooperation in the BA.

Fundamentally, ethnicity is eroding as the key determinant of political behavior. The Malay and Chinese communities alike are now split, the former primarily between PAS and UMNO and the latter among the MCA, Gerakan, and the DAP. As the priority accorded to communal solidarity slips, other issues come into focus, particularly Islam, corruption, privatization policies, environmental security, judicial independence, individual freedoms, and the decline in Mahathir's personal charismatic appeal. (Since Mahathir stepped down, in October 2003, this last factor is now moot.) The shift toward judging UMNO and other parties on their performance, rather than just on their ideological stances as communal champions, represents a revolutionary if slow change. Hari Singh (2000) suggests that Malay tradition is in the midst of transition. He credits modernization (which obstructs clientelism), cross-ethnic acculturation in cities, the declining stature of the *raja*, and the rise of the "new Malay," able to compete on his or her own merits, for the change. Moreover, with the rationalization that the failure of the government to deliver on its promises justifies a breach of loyalty, the option of "opposition" is now becoming as institutionalized for Malays as for non-Malays. Similarly,

Clive Kessler (2000) compellingly argues that UMNO can never reconstruct the conformist Malay unity of the past, and that the party's messages do not resonate with younger Malays—products of the NEP and of urban life—or with the rural Malays who have been left out of economic development.

At the same time, Francis Loh argues, the diminution of ethnic politics has occurred in tandem with an increase in participatory democracy and a rise in developmentalism and BN policies designed to attract non-Malay support (cultural liberalization, local-level service delivery by BN parties, and so on). These contemporaneous trends have left the political order fragmented and riven by ongoing contests among "competing discourses and practices . . . of ethnicism, developmentalism, and participatory democracy" (Loh 2003: 276–77). Loh terms the "politics of fragmentation and contestation"—evident in both formal and informal politics in 1999, though more clearly institutionalized in the latter— "new politics" (278–80), and he concludes that "the democratic impulse has not yet prevailed in Malaysia" on account of coercive laws and repression, the disorganization of advocates of participatory democracy, and the strong pull of developmentalism and the "political stability" that growth and development seem to require. Loh predicts small swings in voting behavior as this "new politics" becomes more entrenched in formal electoral politics (278–80).

Islam and PAS

Given the significance of Islam to Reformasi rhetoric and goals, no party benefited more from the movement than PAS. As the Reformasi movement gained steam in late 1998, PAS carefully cultivated an image of moderation and tractability and played up its record of comparatively clean, efficient, tolerant governance in Kelantan. The party drew in Malays who might not endorse the creation of an Islamic state but who would vote for whichever opposition party pledged to uphold the cause of justice and govern competently without endangering Malay communal interests. Given the Islamic bent of Anwar's politics and the ABIM ties linking PAS, Anwar, and many other Reformasi leaders, PAS also became a haven for "Anwaristas." In fact, it is impossible to separate out the extent to which Islam per se was what drew voters to PAS, as opposed to the party's support of *keadilan* or just voters' disaffection with UMNO. As the academic and activist Farish Noor suggests (1999b: n.p.),

this vote of frustration against UMNO is not necessarily a vote of endorsement for the Islamist agenda of PAS. PAS should not be led into thinking that the massive show of support it has received is in any way an indication that the Malaysian public endorses its controversial and problematic project of creating an Islamic state in Malaysia.

Maznah Mohamad (2003: 76) concurs: "PAS's platform of Islamization and its purported intention of setting up the Islamic state did not help the party in winning new supporters either, especially outside the Malay heartland. The party . . . merely received an electoral boost out of the Anwar factor." Whatever the inspiration, party membership jumped from 500,000 in September 1998 to about 700,000 by June 1999. While still tiny compared with UMNO's approximately 2.7 million members, PAS posed a potent challenge for Malay votes (Pereira 1999).

Over the course of the Reformasi movement, PAS continued to downplay more exclusive, specifically religious issues for the sake of forging a coalition around a common agenda. Recognizing that its insistence on an Islamist order had precluded the sort of cooperation with other primary opposition parties necessary for political change, PAS had adopted a more moderate frame through the 1990s. Hence, for instance, PAS's very successful 1990 campaign advocated governance based on Islamic values, but with a focus on development and full protection for the civil, political, cultural, and religious rights of non-Muslims.[50] Again in 1999, party leaders affirmed that the creation of an Islamic state could be put on hold in the interest of multiparty cooperation to defeat the BN.[51] PAS strategically made *keadilan* its chief message. As a result, the BA's common manifesto makes no mention of an Islamic state, simply endorsing the official status quo of a society premised upon Islamic values.[52] To complement this more secularized image, some PAS leaders opted for Western-style clothing, and the English language rather than Malay. Seeking a broader base, the party even considered opening associate membership to non-Muslims and reiterated its message of democracy and complete tolerance for non-Muslims. PAS maintained this rhetoric beyond the polls. In November 2003, the party published a much anticipated document explaining its vision of an Islamic state. Party president Abdul Hadi Awang insisted that such a state would be democratic, would ensure non-Muslims' rights, and would be less abusive and more meritocratic than the current regime (Arfa'eza 2003).

PAS styled itself throughout its campaign as a model of clean, transparent, broadminded policymaking and administration. The party was at pains to enumerate its concessions to non-Muslims in Kelantan, from sanctioning the construction of statues of Buddha to removing obstructions hindering Chinese schools (Barisan Alternatif 1999; Weiss 1999; Gomez 1996). When PAS took over the Terengganu state government, in

1999, one of its first acts was to fulfill a campaign promise by curtailing road tolls in the state. Protest against high tolls had been a significant Reformasi issue, especially among non-Malays, who earlier in the year had held vehement protests against the tolls. The PAS government also lifted a ban on pig raising that had been imposed by the BN state government a decade ago, a concession with symbolic value in light of 1999's Nipah virus epidemic and the resultant debate over whether pig farming should be allowed at all in a Muslim-majority country. Still, many within or sympathetic to PAS suggested that the real reason why PAS had no problem working with the DAP or other parties was that cooperation is all part of the *dakwah* project. According to this argument, PAS hopes, in the process of collaborating with non-Muslims, to impress them with the rightness of Islam until enough convert to make an Islamic state easier to achieve. Fadzil Noor, president of PAS in 1999, was unequivocal: "An Islamic State cannot be created overnight. People will first have to understand and accept the idea. If they understand what is involved in an Islamic State, they will know it will be fair to everyone. But yes, an Islamic State is our objective" (quoted in "Fadzil: An Islamic State" 1999).

But strategic backpedaling on the Islamic-state issue may have alienated some of the more radical PAS supporters while failing to capture nervous Malay (and, of course, non-Malay) votes. Saravanamuttu (2003a: 11) explains that while some within PAS "believe Islam to be fully compatible with democracy" and have helped steer the party toward the BA, "many in PAS continue to maintain a literalist-fundamentalist notion of Islam and understand the party's goals in terms of furthering Islamic laws, ultimately an Islamic state. This same constituency within PAS would likely reject democracy as a Western imperialist legacy and as an extension of secularism." It is PAS's strong Islamic appeal that distinguishes the party and commands such staunch loyalty at the grassroots. Indeed, PAS seemed to reassert its Islamist image upon the formation of Keadilan, as if to differentiate itself from the new party. Moreover, despite the party's embrace of Anwar and his cause, PAS leaders initially indicated that PAS's president—rather than Anwar, as proposed by Keadilan—would become prime minister if the BA formed the government.[53] It is unclear how deeply into the rank and file of PAS the party's less Islamist, more justice-based rhetoric penetrated before or after the polls.

For instance, PAS tends toward a hard line on social policies, especially those related to gender. PAS had long excluded women from contesting in elections (a position reversed in 2004), since campaigning was thought to jeopardize women's dignity, involve physical contact with men, and take too much time away from home and family duties.[54] Nik Aziz, PAS spiritual leader and Kelantan MB, was unwilling to make an exception even for Wan Azizah prior to Keadilan's formation.[55] Stirring things up even more, Nik Aziz raised the hackles of Malays and non-Malays alike in March 1999 by questioning whether women should work outside the home if their husbands can provide for them. Then, shortly before the elections, PAS representative Hadi Awang introduced a controversial apostasy bill in Parliament. Nik Aziz has also repeatedly justified not only tight social control but also provisions for *hudud* punishments, even though they contravene the federal constitution. He explains, for instance, that allowing stoning would eradicate many social ills. PAS has also sparked antagonism inside and outside Kelantan since 1995 by banning "un-Islamic" performances (including performances of traditional Malay dances), linking excessive lipstick with illicit sex, proposing a separate hospital at which only female physicians would treat only female patients, banning video-game arcades, snooker outlets, and carnival rides, and suggesting that Chinese would be better off if they converted to Islam (for instance, Hari 2000: 56; Weiss 2004a). Such statements and actions feed both Muslim and non-Muslim Malaysians' fears about the security of their rights and freedoms. While non-Muslims would have full civil rights in an Islamic state, including freedom of religion, their political rights would be curtailed. Not surprisingly, during the campaign the BN played up PAS's remarks and policies, to dissuade voters from supporting the party, and insisted that PAS's *keadilan* approach was an electoral ruse.

Islam was a key voting issue, for UMNO and Keadilan as well as for PAS. The 1999 survey mentioned above, for example, found that nearly half of the approximately 2,200 respondents nationwide (92 percent of them Malay) indicated religion as among the primary characteristics to look for in a candidate or party, whether religion was defined in terms of following Islamic principles, devotion and religious knowledge, or government based on Islamic texts. A much lower proportion of respondents (9 percent, almost all of them Malay) indicated a preference for candidates, parties, and policies supportive of their racial group (Weiss 2000b: 9–11). Accordingly, UMNO stressed its Islamic credentials and programs in certain areas, and Keadilan grew increasingly Islamist in image in the months after its formation—for instance, separating women and men at *ceramah*—perhaps at the cost of alienating some of the more secular-minded supporters. All of Keadilan's successful candidates were Muslim Malays, and at least some of them probably were supported on religious grounds. Clearly, though, an Islamist appeal still seems to win more votes in the eastern and northern states than in consistent UMNO strongholds such as Johor.

In power in Terengganu and Kelantan, PAS soon strained the bonds of the BA by implementing several decidedly Islamist policies and pushed UMNO toward a more Islamist stance as well.[56] PAS insists, however—drawing on contemporaneous dialogue in the Middle East, North Africa, and elsewhere—that Islam is compatible with democracy, including critical discourse and transparent, accountable leadership. After the polls, PAS promptly banned gambling and restricted the sale of alcohol in the state. The party also announced plans—from which it quickly backtracked—for a land tax levied against non-Muslims (*kharaj*). Then, in March 2000, PAS mandated that Muslim women in the two states must cover their *aurat* (parts of the body deemed alluring under Islam—for women, all but the face and hands) and that they must wear *tudung* (headscarves). It is now up to employers of Muslims—even if they themselves are not Muslim—to enforce compliance with this dress code (Ng 2000). A few months later, to the consternation of women's groups, such as Sisters in Islam, and to the scorn of federal religious authorities, the Terengganu state government declared women's voices also to belong to their *aurat*, thus barring women from public speaking and specifically from participating in Quran-reading competitions (Stewart 2000). Offended by these innovations and by PAS's domination of the BA, the DAP threatened on several occasions to withdraw from the BA.[57] It eventually did so in September 2001.

Moreover, while UMNO denied after the elections that it would challenge PAS by stepping up its own Islamization programs, it had been doing so since the early 1980s in order to maintain Malay support. Also, aside from the symbolic blow of having lost a second Malay state to the opposition, UMNO was keen to recapture Terengganu, given that state's enormous oil and gas resources. The federal government tried to undercut the PAS government by refusing to pay oil royalties due to Terengganu in September 2000.[58] These financial inducements had been insufficient to lure voters on the east coast in 1999,[59] but—combined with Mahathir's resignation and other factors—they did enable UMNO's win in the state in 2004.

The Internet and Other Alternative Media

The Reformasi movement thrived not just because of its programmatic content but also because activists had new means of conveying their ideas and plans to a broad audience. The mainstream Malaysian print and electronic media are cowed both by links with government parties and by the

Printing Presses and Publications Act and related legislation. Further-more, licensing requirements and the threat or imposition of censorship encourage self-censorship and "responsible" journalism.[60] Print as well as online alternative news sources have gained increasing circulation and clout in recent years, and both were critical to the progress of the Reformasi movement and to the BA campaign. The availability of these media resources facilitated public education, mobilization, and opposi-tion coalition building.

Both the government and the opposition rely upon the media to pro-pound their own positions and denigrate alternatives. However, the BN has long had the upper hand in media matters. The mainstream media serve more or less as a government mouthpiece, generally ignoring or at-tacking opposition politicians and other critics, and slavishly commend-ing government leaders and policies. This tendency is particularly evident during elections. As Mustafa Anuar describes the situation (1998: 12), "The depiction of political parties in the Opposition coalition as ones that were disparate, and lacking compatibility and direction only strengthens the stereotype of the Opposition as being unreliable, unqual-ified to govern the country. This, in turn, implied that only the BN party can provide the much needed moral and intellectual leadership." During the 1999 campaign, the BN used its privileged media position to describe what it promised the electorate, to highlight real or supposed rifts in the opposition, and—most controversially—to deluge the public with graphic, anti-BA advertisements (Mustafa 2003). However, this election was not the first in which the BN had aggressively pressed its media ad-vantage. For instance, in a particularly significant incident toward the end of the 1990 campaign, the mainstream media published a photo-graph of S'46 leader Tengku Razaleigh Hamzah wearing a Kadazan hat (*sigah*) with a crosslike design. The press deliberately distorted this image to suggest that Razaleigh was a tool of Christians in PBS.

Still, the opposition did and still does have at least some recourse. For one thing, even the mainstream media are not all alike. Several Chinese newspapers and the English-language *Star* and *Sun* were known to be somewhat more generous than others in their coverage of CSAs and op-position parties.[61] This stance, though, got the *Star* in trouble in 1987, when the government suspended the paper for purportedly fomenting racial antagonism. The paper has been less critical since its rebirth. Independent media—including opposition party newsletters, NGO pub-lications, and critical magazines—while subject to the same legal restric-tions as other media, have been known to take more risks, sometimes in-curring penalties. The publications of opposition parties and NGOs basically reverse the biases of the government-controlled media. The most significant of these publications in 1998–1999 was PAS's newsletter, *Harakah,* which became one of Malaysia's most widely read papers. Its circulation reputedly reached 380,000 at the height of Reformasi, though it subsequently declined, whereas mainstream media (sales of which had dropped precipitously during Reformasi) rebounded once "normal politics" returned (Elliott 1999; Pereira 2003). Recognizing the increasing diversity of its readers, *Harakah* augmented its English-language coverage[62] and added attention-grabbing color photos. Legally, only PAS members may purchase *Harakah.* This rule was openly flouted, however. In retaliation, when *Harakah*'s yearly publication permit came up for review, the newsletter's frequency was reduced from biweekly to fortnightly as of March 2000, diminishing the flow of both information and revenue. (Its Internet edition, *HarakahDaily.net,* is still updated daily.) Other opposition parties also have publications—*The Rocket* for the DAP, and *Suara PRM* (Voice of PRM)—but their impact has been much less than *Harakah*'s.

Several NGOs also publish magazines and newsletters that circulate beyond their own membership. The most significant NGO publication is probably the *Aliran Monthly,* published by the Penang-based Aliran. Established in 1977, Aliran is known for its trenchant and relatively unbiased views of both the government and the opposition. However, as of late 1998, the *Aliran Monthly* appeared less critical of opposition leaders like Lim Kit Siang, taking a more partisan stance than previously in supporting the Reformasi movement and the BA. Other NGO sources include ABIM's *Berita ABIM* and *Islamic Review,* the International Movement for a Just World's *Commentary,* the Consumers' Association of Penang's *Utusan Konsumer,* and Suaram's *Suaram Update* and, previously, *Hak.* In addition, a few independent local magazines have styled themselves as Reformasi media. *Detik* and *Eksklusif,* for instance, carried outspoken coverage of the movement but were both suspended, the former in March 2000 and the latter the following month.

Finally, as in so many other places, the Internet has profoundly changed the nature of political communications in Malaysia. The Internet has remained largely free of government control so far and has become a significant venue for critical discourse. The government has critiqued antigovernment Web sites and threatened tighter controls but has been reluctant to tarnish its information technology–friendly image by attempting to censor Web sites.[63] A plethora of pro-Reformasi Web sites sprang up in the months after Anwar's sacking, several of them enduring even well beyond the subsequent elections, complemented by electronic discussion fora, mailing lists, and foreign news sites. For instance, among the highest-circulation news sources in Malaysia today is the Web-based daily *Malaysiakini* (www.malaysiakini.com), launched at the start of the 1999 election campaign. The site includes not only current and critical news but also columns by prominent activists and commentators, significant interviews and question-and-answer sessions, and a lively "letters to the editor" section. Also influential in Reformasi activism were the Web site *Free Malaysia* (no longer active), which published anonymous, distinctly well-informed analyses especially of business and economic affairs; *Reformasi Nasional*; *Laman Reformasi*; the *Free Anwar Campaign*; and other publications. The Web sites of foreign media—often sympathetic to reform efforts—were heavily exploited as well. Among these sites were those of newswires (Agence France–Presse, the Associated Press, the BBC, and the like); news magazines (*Far Eastern Economic Review*, the *Economist*, the now-defunct *Asiaweek*, and others); and a slew of foreign newspapers (especially Australian, American, Asian, and British media). Articles from these sources were frequently posted to discussion groups and Reformasi Web sites.

Online discussion lists likewise played a key role in enabling popular discussion and the dissemination of information. Some of these lists had been operational since long before Reformasi, such as Sangkancil and the newsgroup soc.culture.malaysia. Others, such as ADIL-net and a slew of BA- or Anwar-specific lists, sprang up in the context of Reformasi. These lists featured articles culled from local and foreign media on current events in Malaysia and elsewhere (related developments in Indonesia, for instance, were of particular interest), comments by the lists' owners and subscribers, announcements of upcoming events, and more. Discussion on some lists was mostly in Malay; on others, it was mostly English. While the debates were generally civil, a number of posters were barred for posting inflammatory comments.

Not surprisingly, the touchiest issues tended to be race and religion. Advocates of Islamization and Islamic governance, many of them apparently PAS members or supporters, peppered Reformasi Web sites and e-mail discussion lists, for instance, with passages from the Quran and tracts on the compatibility of Islamic governance with democracy, the sufficiency of women's rights under Islam, the irrefutable responsibility of Muslims to prefer Islamic governance to constitutionalism, and the like. These postings on broad-based, reform-oriented lists sometimes antagonized other subscribers. In the same vein, breaking ranks among Muslims was discouraged even over the Internet. Muslim posters to online discussions who suggested that *hudud* penalties are inappropriate, that women should have the same sociopolitical rights as men, or that Islamic states tend in practice to be undemocratic and repressive were verbally attacked for being worse than *kafir* (infidels),[64] while non-Muslims were told they just did not understand and hence had no right to comment if they posted such critical perspectives. More scholarly rebuttals of dominant interpretations of Islam, most notably from the small but vocal NGO Sisters in Islam[65] or from academics such as Farish Noor, were similarly rebuffed as ill informed or anti-PAS and, by extension, pro-BN.[66] Discussions of race also proved sensitive, whether they involved Malay special rights, the politically correct way to refer to ethnic Indians, the relative lack of Chinese support for the BA in the elections, or other issues.

The role of the Internet in Reformasi conscientization and mobilization helps explain why the movement was predominantly an urban phenomenon, popular especially among youth (including students) and the middle class, not least civil servants. These were the constituencies with the readiest access to the Internet, though cybercafes had been proliferating even in rural areas, and many Web-posted materials were downloaded, printed out, and distributed as flyers. In fact, a common and rather plausible explanation for why Mahathir had to call the 1999 elections when he did was that if he had waited any longer, Net-savvy, antigovernment urbanites would have returned to their families' villages for the Aidilfitri holiday (the celebration at the close of the fasting month, Ramadan) and influenced the less aware villagers to oppose the BN.

While this apparent urban-rural dichotomy is revealing, it was not absolute. For one thing, many of the Malay students or recent graduates active in Reformasi were themselves only recently arrived in the cities from rural areas, often thanks in part to NDP-based scholarships or quota schemes. These young people were presumably already in relatively regular contact with their home villages, no doubt to the extent of sharing the information they had gleaned from the Internet or from their participation in street demonstrations. In fact, Muslim student groups organized trips to *kampung* (villages) beginning in early 1999, purportedly for survey research but more to persuade rural voters to support Reformasi and the opposition.[67] In addition, it was not only the Internet that spread information. Mass-based NGOs such as ABIM as well as the ranks of sympathetic civil servants may also have used their influence in rural areas to sway popular opinion against the BN. Recognizing the threat posed by reformist bureaucrats, including teachers, the government levied a series of threats, to dissuade civil servants from antigovernment activities, mobilization, or even affiliation. Most significantly, though, the fact that PAS and hence the BA proved strongest in the poorest, least urbanized states in Malaysia suggests that factors other than Internet access and urbanization were at least as significant to oppositional consciousness.

Beyond the Polls

The results of the 1999 elections, the anticipated long duration of Anwar's incarceration, something of an economic rebound, the dimming of street protests and of discussion about many of the issues previously deemed so riveting—all signaled that Reformasi had passed its peak by 2000, its goals mostly unachieved. However, outright dismissal of the movement would be facile and unfair. The Reformasi movement marked a change in Malaysian politics both at the level of organization and strategizing and at the level of popular priorities and participation. As one PAS leader explained, Malaysians have now matured politically and opened up to new perspectives.[68] Moreover, given that the movement galvanized young people above all others, including many not yet old enough or registered to vote, the impacts of this long period of mobilization and disillusionment with the BN regime and its leaders may be felt only in years to come. Finally, politicized activism remained at a somewhat heightened level even after Reformasi died out as a movement. The ISA detention of ten Reformasi activists in April 2001, and of two student activists three months later, implied that the government still saw the movement—and specifically Keadilan, from which most of the detainees hailed—as a threat.

Reformasi ushered in a certain degree of reform, but subsequent events shifted political opportunity structures again in such a way as to shut out strong challenges to the basically stable and predictable BN. The BA now includes only two parties: PAS and Parti Keadilan Rakyat, formed from the merger in August 2003 of Keadilan and PRM (Muzaffar 2003). As was clear in the 2004 elections, PAS, now led by Abdul Hadi Awang (generally considered less moderate than his late predecessor, Fadzil Noor), has lost support even among its Islamist base, not to mention among more secular voters, thanks to controversial Islamization efforts in Kelantan and Terengganu, concerns over Islamic statehood, and hype about Islamic terrorism (see Ibrahim 2004; Weiss 2004a). The BN, by contrast, has nursed Malaysia back to economic health, shown it is prepared to counter any threat of Islamist extremism or terrorism, and can rely on a degree of political inertia and on a popular sense of investment in the BN. Finally, Mahathir himself has exited the scene, handing power to his final deputy, Abdullah Ahmad Badawi, as of October 31, 2003. Overall, while PAS remains a threat to UMNO, especially in its traditional strongholds, the rest of the opposition is less so, since discourses of democracy and reform have cooled to their usual low simmer and show little sign of boiling over without the sort of catalysts (economic crisis, a split in the government) that signaled a window of opportunity in 1998–1999.

As for CSAs, they now face the challenges of establishing a balance between activities based in civil society and those oriented toward formal politics, and of leveraging the coalitional capital and changes in political culture built up since late 1998. Elections represent the ultimate test only for political parties, which base their legitimacy on whether they can win seats. For CSAs, the test of legitimacy is whether they can be sure that a critical mass of people support their programs or goals, and whether their advocacy for particular issues produces results. In 1998–1999, CSAs helped to tip the balance in making Reformasi significant and the BA so unusually potent, election results notwithstanding. The next chapter explores the dynamics of this project, to determine what the CSAs did and why, how the nexus between civil society and political society can now be characterized, and whether Reformasi was a singular movement or represents the shape of things to come.

THE SIGNIFICANCE OF THE
REFORMASI MOVEMENT

Given the level of institutional and ideological control in an illiberal democracy, the involvement of CSAs alongside political parties may profoundly alter the strategies, discourses, and ultimate effectiveness of a movement for political reform. The Malaysian Reformasi movement offers a compelling example of these dynamics. As the nature of civil society in Malaysia has changed—its organizational manifestations, its issues and constituencies, its ability to think beyond ethnicity, and its popular legitimacy—so have the options available to opposition parties, even as the increasing consolidation of the BN has seemingly shrunk the space available for parties' articulation of political alternatives. Shifts in the nature and foci of popular political engagement have thus changed the possibilities for reform initiatives. Several factors made Reformasi different from comparable ventures in the past: its relatively coherent aims, and their acceptance by so broad an array of Malaysians; its innovative tactics for mobilization and organization; and its substantive significance. Although the coalition forged by the movement has not persisted in its original form, its progress convincingly demonstrated the limits of the BN's hegemony. In any democracy, significant political reform comes not just from CSAs but also from political parties. In an illiberal democracy, however, reform involves both ideological and institutional shifts, leaving added scope for CSAs' involvement. Malaysia's Reformasi movement demonstrates how that involvement may play out—not to reify the role of CSAs or suggest that a transformational project is anywhere near complete, but to understand how collective attribution of political opportunities encourages CSAs to mobilize and frame messages differently, to forge bonds within and across civil society and political society, making change in political culture and institutions more likely.

The development of an issues-oriented civil society over the past three decades has helped make Malaysians aware of nonethnic issues and their common relevance. In the process, government and opposition parties alike have been encouraged to embrace these issues, albeit with sometimes incompatible justifications, in their quest to expand their support. It is hardly surprising, then, that when an economic downturn left even the primary beneficiaries of thirty years of communally oriented development policies dissatisfied with the results and future prospects of ethnic parties and politics, they saw "NGO issues" as compelling alternate grounds for political action and allegiance. Such a shift is not a rapid process. Transferring one's loyalty from communal politics (quintessentially represented by the BN, despite its recent downplaying of communal rhetoric) for more than short-term or opportunistic reasons—in other words, out of ideological agreement with a different order—requires that alternatives be available and known.

CSAs and some opposition parties had been organizing around these issues for decades, particularly with the development of advocacy-oriented NGOs since the mid-1970s. Their incubation in civil society gave such issues as judicial independence and government accountability a tinge of being for the greater good rather than being the political ends of any one faction. Moreover, as described in chapter 4, the two main segments of civil society—advocacy organizations and Islamic groups—had cooperated on a range of issues over the years, from massive coalitions against repressive legislative amendments to workshops on police brutality. Barriers to cooperation between Islamist and secular groups were lower in civil society than among political parties, since establishing the formal institutions of an Islamic state is not really an issue for Islamist associations, however much they might support such initiatives by an Islamist party.[1]

Opposition parties did sign on to some of these campaigns in the past, but such issues formed only part of any party's electoral platform. In 1999, in contrast, the BA's joint manifesto was an articulation of the objectives of the Reformasi movement. The document set forth a plan for government as CSAs would want it: largely free from communalism and corruption; progressive; democratic; and blithely oblivious to the challenge of agreeing how far political Islam should advance. The component parties of the BA did not reach this level of consensus alone. They were indebted both to civil society's long-term agitation on the coalition's issues, which had built up coalitional capital and primed the public for adoption of new political priorities, and to the initial NGO–party coalitions that gave Reformasi shape and confirmed that the movement could inform a platform broadly acceptable across the opposition, even if ultimately garnering insufficient public support. Political reform in Malaysia—as in other states with only partial assimilation of democratic structures and practices—most probably requires an alliance between civil society and political society and a mix of contained and transgressive forms of contention.

How Reformasi Was Distinctive

The Reformasi movement represents a departure from past Malaysian experience in terms of its aims, scope, and institutions. Still, the movement reflected long-term demographic and ideational shifts, including the development of a multiracial "new" middle class and gradually rising support for social issues. The movement urged Malaysians not just to vote differently but actually to think differently about politics. They were asked to accept and internalize new political priorities or norms, contra the prevailing structure of political incentives and goals. In encouraging genuinely multiracial, issues-based cooperation, Reformasi leaders advocated adoption of a unified political culture, in which all subsets of citizens in a *bangsa Malaysia* (Malaysian nation) would pursue the same broad, nonexclusive goals, preferably more for idealistic than for selfish reasons. Such a shift would require critical reevaluation of the politics of race as well as of the state's developmental vision, fostered by acceptance of a larger role for citizens in ensuring democratic governance. While the momentum for change proved inadequate in 1999, continuing interest in these broad goals holds possibly serious, albeit gradual, implications for the nature of patron-client ties, the continuance of crony capitalism, and the bases of popular evaluation of politicians.

Crucial to the Reformasi movement's progress was the scope of its support. Few of the issues pressed by the movement were new, but the battle previously had been confined mostly to a narrow band of middle-class, Western-educated, and especially non-Malay Malaysians—too small a constituency to force a change. By 1999, reformist discourses were being touted by a broad swath of the population. More Malays, including middle-class Malays and those associated with Islamist organizations, got involved than in campaigns on similar issues in the past. Also, as Saravanamuttu explains (2003a: 14), "because these Malays had contact with the grassroots through their organizations such as [ABIM and JIM], this movement drew in considerable support from lower-class Malays in the rural as well as urban areas." Women, students, "greens," antipoverty activists, and other specific constituencies also joined the collective effort. They apparently deemed systemic change more conducive to achieving their particular ends than just continued lobbying on any single issue. It is worth exploring why Reformasi attracted so broad a following.

Much has been made of the supposed incongruence of Malay political culture with civil society or mass protest. Malay political culture is often described as neofeudal, most famously by the scholar and activist Chandra Muzaffar (1979). According to this model, constructed along guidelines set forth in the sixteenth-century court chronicles *Sejarah Melayu* (History of the Malays), a Malay leader, in exchange for un-flinching loyalty even in the face of blatant immorality or wrongdoing, will not shame his subjects. For their part, those subjects will remain blindly loyal unless and until this pact is violated. The fact that Maha-thir's "shaming" of Anwar was raised so frequently to validate calls for change indicates that at least some aspects of the neofeudal outlook re-main strong; otherwise, such justification would hardly be necessary. So simplistic a characterization of Malay political culture is clearly inade-quate, though, in light both of increasing internal differentiation among the Malay community and of the observable fact that Malays *are* in-volved in civil society, even if they are concentrated in its politicized Islamist wing. Furthermore, Malays have been enthusiastic participants in very "un-Malay" demonstrations and related protest activities, espe-cially during Reformasi, but also at times before and since then.

Overall, Malaysians' and especially Malays' political norms have been shifting.[2] This shift has a generational dimension as younger citizens have come to identify and react differently as political actors from their elders, who tend to retain a more consistent sense of realpolitik.[3] At least among the youth and the middle-class Malay progeny of the NEP, reformist norms of practicing noncommunal politics—preference for moral re-wards over economic payoffs, the expectation of substantial civil liber-ties, and engagement on a continuing basis with political processes—have been gaining currency. Thus, for instance, in the context of Reformasi, at least ten student groups with "antigovernment leanings" (in addition to other groups that supported this cluster) were active on Malaysian cam-puses, not all of these groups registered, formally constituted, or even linked directly with a particular university.[4] Some of these groups, such as the Gerakan Mahasiswa Islam Semenanjung (Peninsular Islamic Students' Coalition, GAMIS), Barisan Bertindak Mahasiswa Negara (National Students' Action Front, BBMN), and the umbrella organiza-tion Gerakan Mahasiswa Mansuhkan ISA (Abolish ISA Student Move-ment, GMMI) openly pursued Reformasi aims (as enumerated in Malay-sian Students 1999). Furthermore, while student groups remained polarized along ethnic and religious lines, they were more willing than previously to cooperate across racial lines. Recognizing that universities were at risk of becoming politicized as in the 1970s, and that student ac-tivism could pose a significant challenge to the state, the government sporadically cracked down with stern warnings, arrests, and expulsions of students throughout the Reformasi period, and particularly harshly afterward. In June 2001, seven students were arrested for illegal assembly (and reportedly were beaten in custody) for joining an anti-ISA demonstration. Two student activists were then detained under the ISA the following month.[5]

Even among older Malaysians, new preferences or perspectives are at least sharing political space with old ones. Concrete evidence of this change is apparent:

- In the 1999 general elections, the opposition won over 40 percent of the vote, and candidates who ran specifically on a social justice platform did remarkably well.
- About three times the usual number of people registered to vote in the registration period that coincided with the height of Reformasi. The government acknowledged that the upsurge was likely due to the mobilization of Reformasi sympathizers.
- Opposition-supporting alternative media matched or outstripped mainstream mass media in circulation during the Reformasi period, and at least some of these (for instance, *Malaysiakini*, the Web-based daily) have retained a significant readership.
- UMNO has made a concerted effort to change and to win back youth, women, and others who, the party admits, have lost faith in the organization.
- Students have continued their efforts at mobilization, in such a way that the government's crackdown has extended well beyond the Reformasi period.
- Terms such as *transparency, accountability*, and *cronyism* have entered common discourse. Government leaders have been forced to respond and reform, by means ranging from admitting that corruption is a problem to setting up the (rather weak) National Human Rights Commission to holding interparty debates and feedback sessions with constituents.

The contributions to Loh and Saravanamuttu (2003) elucidate aspects of these trends. The volume overall agrees with the general conclusions here: that CSAs played more of a role in 1999 than previously, that Reformasi marked a shift in Malaysian politics, and that Malays have been more critical of the BN and willing to seek out alternatives than before. Whatever degree of institutional change has so far occurred, Malaysian political culture now leans more toward "new politics"— characterized by fragmentation of ethnic communities and contesting discourses of ethnicism, participatory democracy,[6] and developmentalism

(Loh 2003: 278–79)—than toward the overwhelming communalism and BN dominance of the past. These conclusions still beg the question of why Reformasi was so distinctive, a response to which requires an understanding of how Malaysian society and politics had changed over the years and given rise to such a movement.

Shifting Cleavages

Contemporary Malaysian society is probably divided more deeply by class than by ethnicity. Economic growth and affirmative action policies aimed at fostering a Malay professional and business community have accentuated intraethnic socioeconomic and cultural divisions and brought class interests to the fore. In particular, while there was a "new" Malay middle class before, composed primarily of administrators, clerks, technicians, teachers, and physicians, this white-collar stratum has expanded dramatically since 1970. The "old" middle class—the petty bourgeoisie—has not diminished, though, but has been sustained by the government's agricultural development programs (Shamsul 1999). At opposite ends of the spectrum there remain the agrarian masses and the political and economic elite. However, despite its efforts, UMNO can no longer claim to be the sole economic mentor for the Malays. The community's economic progress is increasingly predicated on general economic growth rather than on state largesse. The Malay corporate and middle classes are therefore showing less attachment to UMNO—as indicated, for instance, by the number of Malays now willing to vote for parties devoid of patronage resources. Even prior to the Reformasi movement, as many as one-fifth of UMNO members, many of them rich or middle class, had failed even to register to vote (Jesudason 1996). Possibly, then, far from becoming more politically progressive, a portion of the new Malay middle class (with livelihoods independent of the party and the state) may simply disengage from formal politics.

Still, many analysts assert a link between middle-class status and support for democracy, thus predicting a political shift as more Malays enter the middle class. For instance, Johan Saravanamuttu (1992) posits that resistance to the state's increasing surveillance and domination of civil society has led middle-class political actors to develop a multiethnic political framework, prioritizing noncommunal goals of democracy and individual freedoms. Saravanamuttu (1992: 54–59), surveying peninsular Malaysian opinion leaders (mostly officers in voluntary organizations and trade unions), infers that "all ethnic communities have self-consciously avoided giving importance to the issue of communalism even though they exhibit the well-known polarization on political issues."[7]

The breadth of Reformasi support seemed to validate his findings and indicate that discourses of democracy, equality, human rights, and good governance—including the disavowal of communalism, however sticky its residue—had spread beyond middle-class, Western-educated, non-Malay activists to a much wider base.

While Reformasi relied upon the middle class, that support could not be taken for granted. In Malaysia, middle-class individuals, especially Malays, are particularly dependent upon and expected to be grateful to the state for their development and survival.[8] Means (1991: 310–15) explains that "it is a paradox and a matter of irony that the very policy [the NEP/NDP] that was designed to reduce the salience of ethnicity and create a harmonious and integrated society in the future appears to have as its major consequence the perpetuation of ethnic divisions in law, in institutions, and in public policy." While positive discrimination has lessened the significance of racial ties, relative to class or other alignments, it has also generated anxiety, alienation, and low levels of social trust among non-Malays, who fear the expansion of ethnic preference policies.

Patricia Sloane (1996) goes further, suggesting that newly minted Malay entrepreneurs can be expected to retain a racialized outlook because UMNO's communal rhetoric has shaped their ideological perspective. In particular, this rhetoric entrenches the idea that Malay development is for the moral good of the community, not just in the pecuniary interest of the individual. Sloane attributes strongly held sentiments of ethnic solidarity among Malays to a deep-seated sense of victimization, including an urge to close Chinese Malaysians out of Malay business networks as payback for Malays' exclusion over generations by Chinese.[9] In other words, despite the apparent similitude among businesspeople from various communities, economic advancement among Malays may further intracommunal solidarity—at least to the extent of "ethno-class consciousness," as described by Brown (1994)—if only to provide moral justification for capitalist pursuits. Sloane's conclusions are bolstered by Banton and Mansor (1992), who also discern strong adherence to communal rather than universalist norms among urban Malays—more so than non-Malays expect. Still, Banton and Mansor highlight the important finding that bonds of personal obligation may override ethnic preference at the workplace, implying that building a multiracial middle class will eventually erode communalism.

Overall, then, ethnic antagonism could as easily be strong as weak among the Malay middle class. Members of this group may whip up ethnic issues to explain their failure to break into the multiracial top echelon of political and economic power. Furthermore, even if members of the

Malay middle class do identify more along class than racial lines or are concerned about such noncommunal issues as corruption or cronyism in government, they still may be loath to seek reform, since they themselves stand to benefit from state policies and patronage. Communalism is more to the advantage of Malays than of non-Malays; multiracial politics is more in the interests of members of ethnic minority groups than of those in the privileged majority. Given these opposing trends, Abdul Rahman Embong identifies two distinct tendencies. There has been a homogenizing process among the upper middle class—the "new rich" of high-income, cosmopolitan, Western-educated managers and professionals. Concurrently, rather than assimilate along class lines, most middle-class Malays still try to reconstruct the *kampung* in the city and "operate within the domain of Malay cultural values and religious practices" (Abdul Rahman 1999: 120–21).[10] Hence it is unrealistic to expect communalism to die out among Malays anytime soon, even if it is recast in terms of religion or diminishes in the course of economic and social transformation.

As for non-Malays, Chinese and Indians alike have long been active supporters of opposition parties (including multiracial parties) and communal as well as noncommunal NGOs. Therefore, their engagement in Reformasi activism was less surprising. Even if much Reformasi rhetoric seemed basically Malay-centric (particularly as concerned the prominence of Anwar and Islam), the issues were consonant with those commonly pressed by non-Malay activists. Mobilizing non-Malays, especially Chinese, against the government is facilitated by two factors. First, neither the government nor the opposition can survive without the Chinese vote, and so non-Malays know they will be assured at least some concessions from either side if they articulate demands, whether via "a more conciliatory 'politics of internal negotiation' approach," through the MCA or Gerakan, or via "a more confrontational 'politics of pressure' approach," through the DAP or other opposition parties (Ng 2003: 93). Second, the Chinese media have always been less closely censored than the Malay- and English-language media, enhancing a culture of reasonably free criticism and debate within the community.[11] Chinese involvement in Reformasi and in electoral support for the BA was not as strong as it could have been, however. The community's political engagement had declined in the previous decade. Economic growth had encouraged support for consistency and stability, meaning the BN,[12] even if many Chinese Malaysians felt that the government was largely by and for Malays and thus expected relatively little from it. Ultimately, the governing coalition (BN or otherwise) is likely always to be Malay-dominated, and so electoral politics may never carry quite the same weight and urgency for non-Malays as for Malays, and non-Malays' preference for a less communal order may not translate directly into votes.

Ethnicity aside, the Reformasi movement seems to have rekindled a generally long-latent political awareness among women, especially those from the middle class. Women's political activism has long been commonly assumed to be constrained by housewifely worries—which leave little time for dabbling in politics, at least outside parties' women's wings—coupled with a lack of interest in political affairs. Countering those stereotypes, Malay women in particular seemed to have been spurred to political activism by Reformasi, not just the wives of suppressed male leaders (though they were involved, too) or members of women's advocacy NGOs, but also women from *dakwah* groups, professional associations, and more. Significantly, though, the highest-profile of these women, Wan Azizah Wan Ismail, leader of Keadilan, opted not really to style herself as a new model for women's political participation, justifying her leadership instead in terms of being a mother to her people and a good wife who was standing in for her husband in his absence.[13] Moreover, while substantial numbers of women got involved in Reformasi activities, men remained in charge at most movement events, in political parties, and in civil society organizations, women's groups excepted. Regardless, the WAC and the WCI indicate Malaysian women's potential for substantive, well-organized mobilization and lobbying. Poised strategically between civil and political society, these campaigns fluidly traversed communal boundaries and capitalized as far as possible on their links with the broader Reformasi movement.

Meanwhile, religion has emerged as a more salient line of cleavage over the past few decades than at any time previously, precluding any purely class-based explanation of recent political developments. Most obviously, the Islamic resurgence has heightened the divide between Malays and non-Malays. At the same time, fear of constraints upon personal freedoms under an Islamic state has encouraged more "secular" Malays to consider noncommunal political alternatives, in an effort to stem pro-Malay spiraling Islamization, which is the usual result of encroachments by PAS on UMNO's dominant position. Also significant for multiracialism is the progress of the charismatic Christian movement in eroding ethnic walls among non-Malays, particularly within the English-speaking, Western-influenced middle class (see Ackerman and Lee 1988; Kahn 1996).

The Institutional Development of Reformasi and
Opposition Politics

Like most other social movements, Reformasi began as something of an inchoate and reactive surge, focused more on dismantling the existing order than on determining what should replace it. As the movement developed, it took on a more defined shape and agenda. Reformasi transformed itself from a collection of largely unorganized protesters into the broad-based Gerak and Gagasan coalitions, then into the BA. In the process, the movement became increasingly proactive and constructive in approach. Once the BA came to appear more solid—as though it really could cohere and govern—and specific opposition parties to seem legitimate options, the coalition became more attractive to fence-sitters. The BA's appeal strengthened as the BN ignored the issues at the root of all the foment, particularly Anwar and the ISA. Reformasi cannot be dismissed as the vehicle of one irritated ex-leader, the clamoring of unaccountable and unrepresentative NGOs, or the usual carping of frustrated opposition parties. Anwar's case was an important catalyst, but there were larger processes at work.

Indeed, the spate of negotiations that metamorphosed into Reformasi and the BA began well before the Anwar issue took shape.[14] Gagasan started when leaders of human rights, workers', and other NGOs, together with opposition party figures, saw a need to develop a common platform in response to the BN's handling of the economic crisis. PRM called a meeting of parties and NGOs in November 1997; most attendees then and at subsequent meetings were from NGOs and PRM, not from the DAP or PAS, though an April 1998 forum was better attended. The resulting platform, which eventually informed the BA's common manifesto, echoed a human rights manifesto developed by a range of NGOs over the 1990s (Malaysian NGOs 1999) and thus built on previous negotiations. Gerak, more closely tied to support for Anwar, was not intended as an electoral platform, either, but as a single-issue lobby group on the ISA. Neither coalition initially planned to contest jointly, and Suaram advised Tian Chua (proposed by PAS, and accepted unanimously both as head of Gagasan and as chair of the first Gerak meeting before he passed the torch to Fadzil Noor of PAS) not to run for legislative office. The CSAs involved in these efforts saw their electoral function as serving as a mediating force among parties, though convincing NGOs to speak with opposition parties proved more challenging than getting the parties to collaborate. For its part, PRM was to be a bridge between PAS and the DAP. Gerak and Gagasan organized *ceramah* and other mass activities— not least as a display of unity—but substantive meetings generally involved only representatives of constituent organizations. Members of the public were encouraged to participate more through such symbolic means as turning their cars' headlights on at designated times. Reformasi as a whole, though, was essentially leaderless: each group met independently to set its own agenda, and then individuals from different organizations congregated to protest, whereas Gerak and Gagasan were loose coalitions without enforcement power.

Some of the most delicate negotiations came as Reformasi activists had to decide both whether to join a party and which one. The Registrar of Societies' inquiry as to whether Adil wished to register as an NGO or as a party also impelled deliberations. Representatives of ABIM and ex-UMNO members asked PRM whether such new members could join; party leaders responded positively, but PRM's socialist legacy made some of these CSAs uncomfortable. Similarly, PAS's Islamist orientation put off many potential new members, and PAS was not keen to allow Anwar or other Reformasi figures to supplant its own leadership. The idea of forming two or three new parties was broached as well, but registration was too unlikely. Taking over a splinter party from PAS, renaming it, and restyling it as multiracial seemed the most expedient way to channel the passion of Reformasi for elections—though Anwar remained apart as a supreme leader to unite the BA. As a sign of support, the BA's coalition partners (parties as well as NGOs) not only attended Keadilan's launch but also proffered some of their own leaders; Tian Chua, for instance, by then active in PRM, became a key figure in the new party, though Sivarasa Rasiah declined to leave PRM. For the most part, these deliberations remained at the level of leadership, even as individuals joined whichever party or NGO suited them best—and, of course, the level of popular comprehension and endorsement of the BA and its platform varied.

It is important to note that Barraclough (1985a: 36) implies that ideological barriers to opposition collaboration, however debilitating, have always been more significant to party leaders than to ordinary members; these negotiations in 1999, too, seem to have been largely an elite phenomenon. While the challenge of crossing communal borders in the BA took center stage, the coalition faced other hurdles as well. The BA had to cope with all the generic imperatives of coalition building, including negotiating power-sharing arrangements, working out ideological differences, and settling details of leadership and organization. Many of those involved were new to electoral politics—or, if previously involved, were new to the specific tribulations of being in the opposition rather than in the BN. Moreover, amid the predations of an antagonistic government, the coalition had to construct an institutional basis out of four disparate parties.

Khoo Boo Teik offers three reasons why the parties of the BA felt so compelled to unite and install a two-coalition system in 1999 rather than settle for less formalized collaboration, as they had done previously. First, no opposition party had been able to challenge UMNO or the BN on its own. Second, these parties realized that years of "executive aggrandizement" had so weakened public institutions and branches of government that "erecting a bulwark against the further erosion of constitutional government" was vital. Third, Malaysian CSAs discovered "a cultural imperative of coalition building," or "confluence between recent injustice . . . [and] the half-forgotten resistance of the 1980s." Reformasi's metamorphosis into Gerak, then into the BA, Khoo argues, "connected current developments to a long history of coalition building in Malaysian politics" (Khoo 2000: 6). Thus Reformasi drew upon both the expertise of CSAs and the experience of past attempts at coalition building among parties, which nurtured coalitional capital.[15] Never before had parties and CSAs worked in such close concert, especially for actual electoral contestation, nor had any other opposition coalition posed so broad-based and coordinated a challenge.

The Reformasi movement and the BA were to some extent the logical extension of past reform and coalition-building efforts. Nonetheless, their progress demonstrated four key institutional developments in opposition politics. First, the BA's organization demonstrated the coalition's commitment to displacing race as the central organizing principle of political contestation, testing the extent to which the general public had accepted the idea of noncommunal, issues-based politics. Many of the principles and perspectives of the BA were not so far divergent from those of the BN, or they targeted only marginal weaknesses in the regime. Regardless, the basis of cooperation under the two coalitions differed. The BN is officially premised upon a power-sharing agreement among communal parties. That is, while Malays dominate the coalition through UMNO, Chinese can protect their interests through the MCA, Indians through the MIC, and so on. There is little space for noncommunal parties in the BN, although some of its component parties are at least nominally multiracial. The BA, by contrast, included no race-based parties, even if certain of its partners were generally associated with a particular community. At the same time, it would be disingenuous to say that the BA completely shook off the mantle of communalism. With economic, social, and political life so clearly stratified by race, even as cross-cutting class ties become ever more salient, linguistic differences, religious revivals specific to particular ethnic communities, ignorance of other cultures, ingrained habits, and the fact that the BN remains in power ensure the continuing significance of race in politics. All the same, it seems likely that the opposition to the BN will remain ideologically noncommunal for future elections. If nothing else, as Malays and non-Malays increasingly share the same economic space, and hence many of the same concerns, and as PAS finds success in an Islamist rather than an openly Malay-centric appeal, opposition parties stand to benefit more from a class-oriented or Islamist appeal.

The second development relates to the BA's need to run a race without patronage or much promise of it. A guiding principle of Reformasi and the BA was opposition to corruption, cronyism, and nepotism, from wasteful megaprojects to questionable corporate bailouts and misuse of public coffers. Moreover, the BA did not have sufficient resources at its disposal for the type of on-the-spot development grants that the BN could make throughout its campaign.[16] Strapped for cash (despite rumored gifts from Anwar's corporate allies), the BA parties resorted to public appeals for donations before and after the elections. The fact that these parties garnered so many votes without having dispensed any money suggests that patronage politics may be on the wane or may at least represent a less integral part of the future political landscape. As a "UMNO veteran" grumbled of the election outcome in Kelantan, "It is difficult to reason why, despite the people in the state thirsting for development in the 10 years under PAS, they decided to reject the chance to get their needs fulfilled. . . . [It is] as though the roads and poverty eradication projects are of no consequence to them" ("Unanswered Questions" 1999).

Third, the BA's campaign demonstrated a rather startling degree of contempt for "politics as usual." With old-style politics presumed corrupted and corrupting, practiced politicians were less revered than reviled. After months of Malaysians' mocking their leaders and challenging them to resign, by the time of the elections, even opposition politicians seemed to require outside support for legitimation. Affirming that politics was no longer to be left up to politicians alone, campaign *ceramah* were marked by speakers who announced that they were not even party members and yet felt moved to speak by the significance of the issues, the candidates, and the campaign. This development suggests a trend toward a more participatory model of politics than previously, colored by the deeper institutionalization of pro-democratic perspectives in society. An increasingly wide range of individuals seems to feel more empowered and encouraged to express demands directly.

Fourth, CSAs have clearly laid claim to a niche in opposition politics, whether they are working directly with political parties and candidates or endorsing policy positions. CSAs had taken part in previous elections, but they had never played so formal and wide-ranging a role as in 1999. Of particular note was the number of NGO activists who stood for office under the banners of the DAP, Keadilan, and PAS or who managed and staffed campaigns. These individuals enjoy credibility as social activists and were able to help build trust among the various opposition parties. Moreover, they command specific expertise and resources for civic education. For instance, Pemantau strategized not only for more effective election monitoring but also to educate the public on tenets of participatory democracy.[17] Similarly, the fifty-NGO People's Manifesto Initiative, formalizing its role as overseer, set up a parliamentary watch committee to monitor the performance of legislators. Like lobbies, each of these broad-based citizens' groups launched a manifesto before the elections and followed up afterward with legislators. The activist Martin Khor explains that their focus on direct action distinguishes these recent initiatives. While NGOs typically educate the public about their rights and submit proposals to the government, "taking an agenda to Parliament and linking it to the general elections is something new" (Martin Khor, quoted in Oorjitham 2000: 32).[18]

Still, the role of CSAs more generally remained unsettled. Candidates touted the BA's openness to participation by NGOs and the general public as a sign of its flexibility and antielitism. They insisted that if the BA came to power, CSAs would retain a niche and wield real influence on politics and policy. However, influential though they may have been, CSAs had no official standing in the BA except in their alternate roles as party members or leaders. Aware of the contributions of CSAs to the rise of the BA, though, even UMNO seems inclined to offer them more of a role. The new prime minister, Abdullah Badawi, has "made peace" with groups such as the Bar Council and plans to grant NGOs (those dealing with, for instance, women's, consumers', and environmental issues, but probably not human rights) a greater say in policymaking. NGOs see Abdullah "as at least a guy who listens," even if others in his party do not.[19] Regardless, the trend toward greater and more institutionalized involvement of CSAs in formal politics, especially (but not necessarily exclusively) via opposition parties, is likely to persist.

Indeed, the structural distinctions between political parties and other types of associations seem to be blurring. Most notably, Keadilan, which provided a crucial institutionalized bridge between PAS and the DAP in 1999, was helped by its roots as an NGO and by the support of opinion leaders in civil society (many of whom joined the party, rendering it literally a site of overlap between civil society and political society).[20] Keadilan maintained a determined focus on a combination of Anwar and issues that were basically acceptable to anyone seeking at least a modicum of reform. Party rhetoric sidestepped race, religion, and other problematic concerns as much as possible. Still, while its newness ensured that Keadilan, like S'46, could not be blamed for any unpopular policies—since it had not yet had a chance to do anything—novelty was not entirely an asset. Keadilan's leaders were untested, and several were inexperienced or accustomed only to the different stakes and strategies of civil society. Its organizational basis had to be built largely from scratch and in a hurry, its resources were meager compared to UMNO's, and the party could not be judged on its record in government, even if some of its candidates could be evaluated on the basis of prior experience in civil society or in UMNO.

Given its handicaps, the BA could not rely only upon what its component parties had to offer but cobbled together resources, information, and experience from diverse sources. Part of what rendered CSAs such potent political organizers was their role as storehouses of alternative political memory, and hence their ability to recall and build upon successful and unsuccessful past campaigns for reform. Political parties might be expected primarily to recall the votes and seats they have won, using that knowledge to plan more strategically for successive elections. Their overriding goal is to gain enough power in government to pass and implement legislation. CSAs, by contrast, seldom realize such concrete results. Rather, their aims of public education and policy advocacy require ongoing effort, punctuated but not transformed by the progress of elections. The human rights group Aliran offers a clear example. The pages of the *Aliran Monthly* revisit past events of significance to progressive politics and relate them to current developments, offering a broader view than is available in the mainstream media. Moreover, because the magazine treated the BA as part of Reformasi and as one of several paths to reform (see Khoo 2002), the coalition's electoral loss was deemed a setback but not necessarily the end of the campaign. Thus CSAs offered the BA abstract resources, in the form of perspective and direction for informing either lobbying or mass action, as well as more concrete assistance. Moreover, CSAs' civic resources accumulate over time, regardless of electoral outcomes, and may provide ballast to ease opposition coalition building in the future.

The value of such a repository of experience and knowledge also helps explain the significance of independent media. The history of Malaysia as taught in schools or in the mainstream media is the "official" history. In that version, the glorious BN trumps antinational, self-interested challengers, and civil society is a Western invention with little relevance to Malaysia.[21] The publications and libraries of civil society organizations offer alternative readings that are less (or differently) biased than the versions propounded by the government or even by opposition parties. Comparatively free media are fast expanding, thanks in no small part to the Internet.[22] The ready availability of alternative interpretations allows citizens to evaluate competing parties' claims for themselves.[23] However, the sudden appearance of new sources of information, much of it with an aura of veracity just by dint of its being in print (even if such print is online), is not an unmitigated advantage for reformists.

While the cultivation of informed, engaged "Netizens" has prompted encomiums for the capacity of new technology to facilitate civic education and mass mobilization, the effects of the Internet on the development of social capital may in fact be mixed.[24] "Virtual" communications may reach only certain constituencies and be less effective in establishing trust and reciprocity among NGOs, parties, and citizens than their "live" counterparts,[25] particularly as the novelty of Web sites and online discussions wears off. Relying on these channels, younger voters may develop political priorities or attitudes without the benefit of nonverbal cues from or real-time interaction with leaders and fellow citizens. They may also be subject to a barrage of unfiltered information from uncertain sources, making critical evaluation of the perspectives and data presented difficult. Moreover, in choosing chat rooms, Web sites, or discussion lists, voters select a "virtual community" in which they feel comfortable and accepted rather than being forced to find ways of interacting in the more complex "real" (sociopolitically defined) community. While Internet communication may facilitate cross-racial communications and anonymous venting, encouraging individuals to communicate more freely than previously, Malay-dominated forums tend to use Malay language, while non-Malay-dominated ones (also frequented by some Malays) are in English, Chinese, or other languages. Despite their importance in raising political awareness and socialization, particularly among young, urban, middle-class citizens, Internet-based communications can supplement but not replace the more traditional *ceramah*, workshops, house calls, and poster and flag campaigns.

Ideological Continuity and Change

Innovations and rhetoric notwithstanding, the BA remained significantly entangled in the communal order. Most important, the fact that its non-Islamist components won as few seats as they did (though more than in 1995) indicated that its noncommunal, anticlientelistic campaign had not been enough to win over the mass of voters, especially non-Malays. Despite the discourse of Reformasi, most voters were probably still not prepared to vote for social, economic, and political justice (and Islam) over the BN's promises of development projects and at least some assured role in decision making for non-Malays and non-Muslims. Indeed, the BN could still depend upon ethnic scare tactics to convince voters not to reject their communal protectors—although Khoo (2002: 6) argues that PAS and Keadilan successfully resisted UMNO's calls for "Malay unity," especially as shown by Keadilan's victory in the 2001 by-election in Lunas.[26] Even voters attracted to Reformasi and all it promised did not necessarily believe (and rightly so, it turns out) that PAS and the DAP had struck a stable balance, or that it was "safe" for Chinese to vote for the BA. Statements at *ceramah*, and publications' attempts to convince non-Malays that an Islamic state would not be so bad (and that, regardless, PAS could not possibly muster the two-thirds of parliamentary votes needed to change the Constitution accordingly), probably helped demonstrate not that PAS *would* not pursue an Islamic state but only that it *could* not (Social Owl 1999; Wong 2001).

Moreover, to a certain extent, Reformasi represented more the deepening and broadening of prior efforts than the debut of a new sort of politics or leaders. Although the BA tried to stress principles, personalities were still critical and did not represent a dramatic break with the past. Anwar was the quintessential example: he remade his image from that of an advocate for Malay rights and Islam, initially as a social activist and then within UMNO, to that of a noncommunal campaigner for social justice and political reform. Likewise, along with some new faces, the BA included many figures who had been in the component parties (or UMNO) all along, touting many of the same issues as previously, though perhaps with a different overarching perspective. These leaders' legacies and their change in approach may have made some of them appear mercurial or opportunistic. Moreover, their support may have been based at least as much on preexisting personal or other ties as on their new stance. In the same vein, the identities of specific opposition parties were hardly submerged under that of the BA. For instance, in 1999 some candidates campaigned as "BA," some as from one of the parties, and some as from one party but giving prominence also to the logo of a second (generally to stress the link between Keadilan and PAS). Likewise, while commentators spoke of the BA's contest to take over the federal government, popular parlance tended to leave states in the hands of specific parties so that PAS—not the BA—was expected to gain control of more eastern and northern states. This uncertainty persisted after the elections. PAS even set up its own shadow cabinet apart from that of the DAP, and questions of power sharing among parties were among the coalition's most divisive.

Examining the government's response sheds further light on the BA's development. The nature of the regime against which reformers are struggling, including its anticipated or actual reaction to their efforts, helps shape reformers' strategies. Moreover, in an illiberal democracy, the state's coercive power and high degree of control may enable it to forestall or co-opt reform efforts. Expectations about the chances for top-down reforms or the risks of speaking out (for example, attribution of opportunity or threat) factor into protesters' tactics and goals along with ideological or programmatic considerations. Variations in these expectations help explain differences in levels of mobilization, framing devices, and strategies of different sectors across the country. Ng's (2003) discussion of Chinese voters' calculations regarding when negotiation or pressure is likely to be more productive effectively captures this dynamic. These distinctions may be especially pronounced if potential activists see joining an opposition party or supporting an NGO as mutually exclusive routes to reform. Anticipated government responses to each sort of body can have a dramatic effect on the shape and likely impact of reformist efforts, and especially on whether an electoral loss is seen as a temporary setback or a fatal blow.

The Malaysian state has been quick to take umbrage at reform initiatives, however they are organized. Previously, the most plausible route to political reform was presumed to be forming a new political party or negotiating an electoral pact among several parties. Dato Onn's IMP in the 1950s, the Socialist Front in the 1960s, Tengku Razaleigh's S'46 in the late 1980s, and the APU and Gagasan in 1990 are examples of this approach. In 1998, reformists directed their energies toward a social movement instead, mobilizing around issues before shifting their attention to the elections. The government drew on a similar repertoire of responses in each instance. Its most obvious approach has been marginalization and repression of challengers. The state may deny state funds and media support to its opponents, crack down with ISA arrests, or manipulate electoral rules and practices to ensure that BN incumbents keep their seats. Co-optation is also common. Anwar's dramatic move from outspoken ABIM activist to mainstream UMNO politician is a case in point but hardly the sole such instance. The reassimilation of Tengku Razaleigh and much of S'46 into UMNO represents another remarkable coup. Convinced that struggle from the outside was pointless, even S'46 stalwarts were lured back into the fold. Similarly, the BN was at pains to advertise its successful co-optation of BA supporters, especially from Keadilan. Publicizing these defections not only "confirmed" the BN's superiority but also demoralized those still in the BA.

Regardless, however fiercely it has fought proponents of reform, UMNO seems aware of the need to change its tactics, both for rallying support and for assailing opponents. Thanks especially to rising education levels, Malay voters increasingly have new priorities, including concern for human rights and democracy. Rustam Sani (1999) suggests that Mahathir remained unattuned to an emergent new political culture in the late 1990s. Instead, he persisted in a 1960s-style political framework in which feudal conventions and patronage ensured that the party leader's abrupt sidelining of someone like Anwar would not precipitate a crisis. Back then, Rustam argues, the leader was presumed to be right, or he could avail himself, if he had to, of state institutions, such as the police, mass media, and the judiciary, to quell dissent. As society has changed, with demographic shifts reinforced by new information technologies and globalization processes, political culture has changed, too, particularly among the younger generation. Now, sustained not by any one individual or party, the movement must draw its strength "from a popular rejection of—a refusal to remain satisfied any longer with and accept—the political approach and styles of communication of recent, but still residually feudal, times" (Rustam 1999: 6–9).

These 1960s-era tactics are not entirely obsolete, but the culture of UMNO has been changing. Mahathir's resignation and the accession of Abdullah Badawi are likely to speed this trend. The new prime minister has less of a clientelistic network than many others in UMNO. While Abdullah's lack of business links may facilitate a change in UMNO's culture under his leadership, it also weakens him, since his base within the party is less clear, and those with vested interests in the old system may be averse to change. Abdullah has asserted his commitment to cleaning up the feudal, patrimonial image of UMNO. He insists that he aims to promote democracy, by means that include strengthening the separation of powers and the system of checks and balances among government branches and being open to criticism and contrary views—as long as national security and racial and religious harmony are not compromised.[27]

It is evident that the BN has been revamping its message for some time, moving away from specifically communal politics and instead articulating a persuasive but still illiberal and state-directed alternative. Francis Loh (1999b; 2003) proposes that through the 1990s the BN came to sideline ethnicity in favor of a sort of "cultural liberalization" and a politics of developmentalism. The latter really began to take root among Malays with the launch of the NEP, in 1971. It gained ground among non-Malays later, especially with the rapid economic growth of the late 1980s and early 1990s. Voters of all races now seek material advancement and "development," even at the cost of a strong state for policy continuity. Since only the BN has been in power at the national level and hence has both a record of developing the nation and a clientelist network, a developmental framework privileges the BN. Furthermore, development planning has been increasingly concentrated in the hands of a few leaders. Hence, Loh concludes, the BN, like the opposition, is downplaying ethnicism in politics. However, the BN alternative relies upon a set of material rather than ideological incentives and devalues the opposition's counterdiscourse of democracy.

All these processes point to a gradual shift in electoral politics. Both the BN and the opposition have been toning down racial rhetoric in favor of more universal messages, even if progress toward solidification of a broader Malaysian identity has been halting at best. To some extent, these messages are just posturing. However much the BN obscures its communalism, for instance, the whole framework of the coalition is fundamentally based on race. Moreover, nonracialized definitions of the polity could either adopt the contours of a "Malaysian Malaysia," as initially outlined by the PAP in the 1960s, or the religious boundaries of Islam—that is, a political community of the *ummah* (an Islamic community based on shared faith rather than territory), excluding non-Muslims from full citizenship. What forced the secular perspective of unity to the fore for the BA, despite the coalition's strong Islamist current, was a combination of, on the one hand, PAS's ideological commitment to tolerant accommodation and democracy and, on the other, brute demographics: PAS alone cannot command the support needed to unseat the multiracial BN. Political parties are not the sole opinion leaders in Malaysia, however, and this shift in their rhetoric and approach may reflect prior, more meaningful changes on the ground.

It must be asked, therefore, whether Malaysian voters demand a new coalition or framework, or whether the BN's communal formula remains basically satisfactory. The extent and fervor of support for Reformasi, and its concentration in the newest generation of voters, both hint that a large and growing proportion of people do want change.[28] The BN won handily in the 2004 general election, but with Abdullah Badawi proclaiming a new timbre for his coalition, including respect for good governance and Islam. Also, the efforts by both the BN and the BA to tone down racialism in their appeals, however inconsistently, indicate that communalism has lost legitimacy as an organizing principle of politics. Even if middle-class status is not antithetical to communalism, economic change has left Malays and non-Malays with far more common interests and interdependencies than previously, narrowing the possible scope for racially specific policies. At the same time, the fact that the BN could incite racial fears among non-Malays and thereby retain votes suggests that the BA was not altogether convincing in its multiracialism and that CSAs failed to socialize all voters toward reformist preferences.

The Incomplete Internalization of
New Political Priorities

While opposition parties made substantial inroads in the 1999 elections, reform of the political system in line with the demands of the Reformasi movement remains uncertain. The new political priorities that CSAs have tried to institutionalize over the years—adopted by the BA for a combination of ideological and opportunistic reasons—have yet to be internalized fully among the general public. Most important, the overriding concern of these CSAs (and sometimes of opposition parties) to delegitimize communalism as a guiding political principle, substituting a new set of political norms in its place, has only been partly realized. Racial and (just as important) religious identities and interests are still highly significant to most Malaysian voters. Nonetheless, a combination of middle-class homogenization and growing intracommunal divisions, due to economic modernization as well as to uneven religious revival, is eroding the explanatory power of race, especially in mixed urban areas. These changes to the political environment are making voters more receptive to reformers' suggestions for new ways to conceptualize politics.

Communalism will remain salient as long as Malaysia's system of economic and other rewards is largely structured along racial lines. Government policies crystallize and reinforce racial identifications. Particularly thanks to the NEP, the NDP, and now New Vision Policy (NVP), economic incentives favor *bumiputera* identity, and rewards are structured in such a way that Malays may have something to lose in rejecting communalism.[29] For Malays, the whittling away of communal political identities would subordinate Malay dominance, in practice and in principle, to the nonmaterial aim of a more encompassing and egalitarian nationalism, centered on *bangsa Malaysia* rather than on *bangsa Melayu*. This interpretation is offered despite the fact that constitutional provisions, such as the greater weight given rural, mostly Malay constituencies compared with urban, more heavily non-Malay ones, as well as decades of pro-Malay gerrymandering, already guarantee that Malays—whether from UMNO or the opposition—will predominate in Parliament. UMNO has maintained support over the years by convincing Malays that only loyalty to the party can protect their position vis-à-vis the Chinese. Even today, according to Chandra (1979: 115–17), "equating the UMNO position with the Malay position and then using that equation as the basis for validating the leadership's role as the protector to whom the protected should demonstrate their loyalty has undeniably developed into a political habit." Furthermore, language differences, along with concomitant choices of media, race-based settlement patterns, and greater readiness to trust members of the same racial group, continue to compound communal segmentation and make ethnicity the most obvious organizational rubric for all communities.

For these reasons, communal appeals have never been far below the surface in an election, including the elections of 1999, and not just for UMNO and its partners. Jomo explains that as soon as one politician delivers an ethnicized polemic, the race is on to see which side can more adeptly champion the community's cause, even when the issues involved are really more economic than communal. He suggests that,

> most ominously, these rival communal trends actually justify each other's existence, by claiming to defend and protect the communal interests they purport to represent, against allegedly aggressive encroachments and threats by other ethnic communities, and thus willy nilly serve each other's interests. This spiraling antagonism . . . can ultimately only lead to greater ethnic conflict since the interests involved are fundamentally irreconcilable [Jomo 1988: 302].

Even barring another 1969-style conflagration, this "cold war" is unstable, since "a single spark can be enough to set off an explosion" (Jomo 1988: 302). The persistence of communalism was confirmed in 1999 by the BA's reassurances on the perpetuation of Malay rights and by the BN's vividly menacing campaign advertisements directed at Chinese voters, as well as by the fact that in 1999 the main opposition parties still mostly attracted, as they do now, members from one or another racial group. In other words, opposition party rhetoric and CSAs' proselytizing notwithstanding, outright communalism may diminish, but it will not disappear as long as the prevailing structure of incentives favors its maintenance. Moreover, these selective incentives will still be demanded by their beneficiaries. If UMNO were to make affirmative action policies more merit-based, it would challenge its own raison d'être as a champion of Malay rights. The mass of Malays have little reason to pass up these benefits, even if they agree in principle (as not all do) with egalitarian norms.

Furthermore, even if uplifting the racial group per se is not the primary message of any party, improving the lot of the *ummah* may still be. A pro-Islamic message may be seen as basically just another approach to Malay rights. Even if the appeal applies to all Muslims and appears race-blind, the vast majority of Muslims in Malaysia are Malay. Moreover, non-Malay Muslims (of Indian, Arab, Indonesian, Filipino, or Thai descent) historically have not been well accommodated in Malay-based Islamic movements or organizations.[30] Hence, while some proponents of Islam as a nonracial alternative are surely sincere in their protestations, for others religious labels are unsubtle codes for racial categories, with

"Muslim" intended and understood to mean "Malay." PAS's adoption of a noncommunal, issues-based platform is thus not necessarily a sign that communalism is really on the wane. Rather, this agenda signifies that openly racialized discourse is fading (a development that eventually will further the internalization of less segregated attitudes) and that the most salient basis for Malay nationalism may have shifted from a focus on Malay descent to a focus on Malays' shared religion.

Religious cleavages remain so potent, despite the diminution of avowedly racial appeals, partly because CSAs have generally been very tentative at challenging them. Non-Malay/Muslim NGOs, for instance, have been hesitant to speak out on Islamic issues, knowing that any criticism they offer is likely to be disparaged as uninformed and inappropriate. With some exceptions,[31] these groups have therefore promoted multiracial perspectives far more than multireligious ones, leaving the latter for political parties to work out in their negotiations. However, the cooperation of Islamic and secular CSAs on issues, especially those related to "justice" and "democracy," has encouraged the public and political parties to focus on issues that transcend religious lines. For instance, the gamut of CSAs have joined in campaigns against the ISA even when their justifications for participating have differed. Islamic groups condemn the ISA, since it violates Quranic standards for determining guilt and rendering judgment, while secular groups highlight its incompatibility with the Malaysian constitution and international human rights standards. When it comes to voting, however, these points of agreement are overshadowed by (fear of) exclusionary religious programs that have a more substantial impact on most people's daily lives. Regardless, the experience of opposition parties' determined cooperation across religious lines, coupled with the increasing readiness of non-Malay–dominated parties and CSAs to comment on the relative desirability of Islamization, may empower non-Malays and more secularly oriented Malays to be less cowed by fear of Islamist politics in the future.

Furthermore, if voters become more familiar with the specific aims and capabilities of the opposition and confident that reform will not jeopardize economic growth, they may grow more forthcoming in their support. Reform movements face inherent difficulties when their aim is the institution of an untried alternative. Malaysia has had the same basic political order since independence. The most substantial electoral shift was in 1969, when riots and emergency rule forced the restoration of a version of the status quo ante. It is hardly surprising, then, that voters in 1999 doubted the competence of an alternative government or feared that an electoral upset for the BN would bring riots, whether spontaneous or (as the rumors went) instigated by the BN and its supporters.

On a deeper level, too, most Malaysians have been largely content with the country's economic progress under the BN. This satisfaction explains why an economic downturn seems necessary in order to catalyze mobilization. Mahathir went particularly far to make economic development the basis of the government's claim to legitimacy. Therefore, a combination of fear that the economy might not do so well under another government (especially if a change of leaders or policies would be perceived as political "instability," as the BN suggests) and the recognition that economic growth represents the government's fulfillment of its promises discourages advocacy of political change.

Civil societal institutions face the same sorts of ethnic and religious divisions, and these are compounded by questions of these institutions' proper place in the polity. For instance, while they espouse multiracial issues on the whole, Malaysian NGOs are hardly exemplars of noncommunal praxis. Most Malaysians still seem to feel most comfortable in groups of which the majority of members are their coethnics. What nevertheless gives advocacy-oriented NGOs the moral authority to demand multiracialism of opposition parties is that the civil societal groups making these demands are ideologically noncommunal. That is, there is nothing inherent in the group that limits who joins (aside, perhaps, from religion, which may be more or less coterminous with race), and they are defined in terms of issues rather than of race. The nonracialized advocacy efforts of CSAs have kept alternative issues and ideologies at the forefront, easing the task of opposition coalition building.

Still, another roadblock hindering CSAs that advocate noncommunalism and issues common to all is the persistence of racial cleavages within other societal institutions. Though the government has tried since the 1950s to build national unity through language and education policies, these initiatives have not been very effective in forging a common national identity. For instance, Sanusi Osman (1989) characterizes tertiary students as sustaining only limited interethnic interaction, discussion, or understanding, despite ample opportunities to develop cross-racial ties. He explains that students develop a higher awareness of their own identity while attending universities, especially because of the efforts of some campus groups to emphasize ethnic identity and prevent linkages across communities. The entrenchment of stereotypes among students may be expected to have strong repercussions, including the fostering of perceptions of communal biases in government, or notions that not all citizens have an equal right to govern.

One might extrapolate from Sanusi's argument that, with the growth of self-consciously noncommunal or even anticommunal associations on and off campus (a development that has occurred, to at least some extent), these trends might change, yet his findings are consistent with more recent data. Surveying Universiti Malaya students, Sheela Abraham (1999) found that only about 10 percent of her sample self-identified as Malaysians rather than as members of an ethnic group. The sense of ethnic identity was strongest among Chinese students. Likewise, although Bahasa Malaysia was the language spoken most fluently by 87 percent of the sample outside classes and other academic situations, students interacted mostly with members of their own ethnic groups. Abraham concludes that, despite a shared language and policies aimed at fostering unity, polarization along ethnic lines remains a significant problem.

In a slightly later survey, Heng Pek Koon also identified racially specific trends, though of a different sort. Her 1999–2000 study found that about 70 percent of the students surveyed considered a common Malaysian national identity at least as important as their own parochial identities, and Chinese students generally accepted not only the NEP but also Malay as the national language. While most students displayed a high degree of patriotism, they adhered to different "nations of intent": most Malay students named Islam and the Malay language as the most important markers of Malaysian identity, while most Chinese students specified cultural and religious diversity. Heng concludes that the majority of Malay young adults aspire to a more Islamist Malaysia, whereas non-Malay young adults seek a secular, democratic, multicultural Malaysia (Heng 2004: 373–75).

Furthermore, while CSAs provide a key impetus to greater public awareness of and concern with nonethnic issues, CSAs alone cannot transform the political system. They may have a plethora of ideas to communicate to political parties and politicians, but, because of the nature of the organizations involved, their limited constituencies, and government regulations, CSAs' role must be limited to issue advocacy, popular mobilization, and assistance to institutionalized actors in developing, articulating, and pursuing alternative platforms. Even if those parties win election, especially since economic benefits are distributed partially along racial lines in Malaysia, the imperative of the "rice bowl," and suspicions within each group that other groups are getting ahead at their expense, may provoke the renewal of a communal outlook.

However incomplete the normative project of Reformasi remains, the evolution of coalition building over the years, the delegitimation of communal discourse, and the continuing availability of the sort of CSAs active in the movement signify that popular attitudes have changed and will continue to do so. That subgroup affinities are to some extent yielding to other priorities and allegiances will allow more meaningful and sustainable cooperation than previously for elections or other campaigns.

Focusing on the process rather than on current manifestations of change allows generation of hypotheses, however tentative, concerning future trajectories for electoral outcomes, the development of civil society, and popular political culture(s).

Abstracting from Reformasi to a Broader Framework

A fundamental aim of Reformasi was to make voters think differently about politics: to make them prefer different political norms, see themselves as an integral part of the democratic process, and transfer their support from the BN to a new political force. The first of these dimensions underlies the others. Support for a framework of how popular political norms are shifted to encourage political participation along new lines can be found in Elinor Ostrom's (1998) behavioral approach to the rational choice theory of collective action.[32] Ostrom explains that conditions of trust, reputation, and reciprocity can help individuals overcome the temptations of short-run interest and improve results in collective action trials. The long-term, iterative nature of the pursuit of political reform by CSAs and political parties, an endeavor that includes sequential efforts at coalition building, helps to develop reformists' reputations among the general public and their trust in each other so that partnerships become ever more feasible. In fact, trust, reputation, and reciprocity at the organizational level might be considered an operationalization of coalitional capital—the glue that makes collaboration possible and can make a coalition strong enough to garner popular support.

Particularly in Malaysia—where the extent of democracy is limited but not nil, civil society and local government are both comparatively weak, and coalition partners are usually determined before rather than after elections—protest or reformist movements rapidly gravitate toward election-minded bargaining. In an illiberal democracy, there is an incentive to play by the rules, even if the playing field is not level. Change can come through elections (and opposition parties have gained control of several states' legislatures), but the BN regime is powerful enough to have fragmented portions of the opposition and to pose limitations on activities in both political society and civil society. The building of electoral coalitions occurs at several levels, not just among parties or their leaders. As exemplified in the progress of the Reformasi movement, while opposition parties negotiate among themselves concerning the allocation of benefits (primarily parliamentary seats for which each will contest) and standards for coalition rhetoric, individual voters evaluate parties to see if they can trust a new leadership to deliver desired abstract and material goods. At the same time, CSAs negotiate both with political parties and with voters, facilitating communication between them. CSAs also encourage voters to adopt new sets of political values (whether premised, in Malaysia, upon an Islamist or a secular order) by educating them about the requirements of democracy and the failings of the current regime.

Building trust among more or less race-based parties, and among citizens of different races and religions, CSAs have played a central role in explicating noncommunal alternatives. However race-based in practice, many Malaysian NGOs over the years have come to organize more often around issues or on ideological grounds rather than around ethnicity per se. Moreover, they have proved their ability to work together, regardless of ethnic makeup, on advocacy-oriented campaigns, particularly around such Reformasi standards as human rights and constitutional liberalism. CSAs have thus both demonstrated the possibility of focusing on nonracialized issues and spearheaded broad-based coalitions, such as Reformasi's Gagasan, to advocate for such issues. Finally, a number of CSAs have shifted their efforts to political parties. These transplanted organizations and individuals strive for change from within government parties, or they give credence to opposition parties' promises to deliver clean, efficient, more participatory government.[33] When political opportunities seem right for a challenge, as occurred with the Asian financial crisis and the ouster of Anwar, CSAs may shift their collective action frames and strategies in an attempt to institutionalize these normative changes.

Part of the reason why CSAs are so useful to reform efforts in the Malaysian polity as it stands today is that social cleavages may play themselves out differently in civil society than in political society. Ethnic barriers may at times be ignored in negotiations within civil society. For instance, the Reformasi movement saw close, generally unproblematic cooperation among Malay and non-Malay NGOs, particularly on issues of civil liberties and human rights, without nearly the degree of tension endemic to cross-cutting alliances among political parties. Instead, class tends to be a more salient factor than race in defining constituencies and issues in civil society, primarily because of the urban, middle-class, often professional background of so many contemporary activists. Indeed, the "us versus them" rhetoric dominating oppositional politics in 1999 was not so much racialist as classist: poor and middle class people versus the wealthy (presumed to be cronies), with the multiracial middle class dominating opposition parties as well as NGOs.

Translation of CSAs' multiethnic experience is not a simple process, though, given that the aims of CSAs and parties are different. CSAs in the Reformasi movement were fighting for such public goods as accountability and transparency, women's rights, and equitable economic development. The salience of these issues is not confined to any one ethnic, class, or gender group, although religious considerations may temper their relevance for some individuals. By contrast, negotiations among political parties ultimately devolve to seat allocations (which were still made largely on the basis of race in 1999) and to policy statements on such concrete issues as whether to continue pro-Malay affirmative action policies, whether the state should support vernacular education, or—most problematically—to what extent Islamization should be pursued at the state and federal level. Also, the development of more unifying norms could be forestalled if a more explicitly class-based order coalesces.

As the BA took shape, its debt to politicized CSAs became clear in its structure and orientation. The BA maintained a strong ideological emphasis on multiracialism, downplaying debates over Islam as much as possible (though, granted, parties like the DAP had done this all along, too). Public intellectuals with roots in civil societal activism played prominent roles in the coalition, however limited their actual experience in party politics. The NGOs (ABIM, Suaram, and others) that had been networking around relevant issues continued to do so. CSAs also advised parties directly, though their clout varied. For instance, academic and activist advisors largely wrote the BA's proposed budget in 1999, but Suaram was unsuccessful in pressing the BA to divide seats equitably among its component parties (that is, without granting any special premium to PAS). Terms popularized in civil society became buzzwords of opposition parties as well: *accountability, nepotism, draconian, kezaliman* (tyranny). Furthering this adaptation was the fact that civil society–based media (including ABIM's *khuthah,* or sermons, and other oral channels) were so critical to the BA. Perhaps most important, the idea that winning elections is not the only goal, so that conscientization was seen to require more than just a persuasive election campaign, came from CSAs and represented a departure from the philosophy underlying previous electoral pacts.

Like political parties, CSAs face a range of strategic options and must decide how best to direct their energies. For instance, not all the CSAs that were active in Reformasi joined Gagasan or Gerak. Most of the more than 2,000 Chinese organizations (themselves representative of a larger mass of guilds, education-related associations, and other community groups) that signed on to Suqiu did not elect to join those broader coalitions, although certain key groups, such as the Selangor Chinese Assembly Hall, supported such joint efforts as Pemantau. Their reluctance to join particular coalitions did not necessarily mean that those groups did not support the movement. In fact, Suqiu was ideologically consistent with Reformasi, and the rhetoric of the movement was used to vindicate the collective's demands. Moreover, after long deliberation, a few dozen Chinese-speaking community leaders and professionals, believed to have the backing of as much as 70 percent of the resources and networks of Chinese associations nationwide,[34] entered Keadilan en masse in May 1999, joining about 3,000 other Chinese members in the party. Much as had been the case with the twenty-seven Chinese civil rights activists who joined the DAP in 1990, these individuals seemed to view joining Keadilan as extending the locus of struggle, not turning their backs on civil society. Chinese organizations were already extremely strong, especially within the community, and they also wielded some bargaining power in government by dint of their massive membership. Therefore, joining a Reformasi party not only would strengthen that party, signaling to the community that the party was worth supporting, but also would ensure a say for the constituency in question, should Keadilan and the BA come to power.[35]

Aside from Chinese associations, other NGOs chose not to join Gerak and Gagasan. Some may have been deterred by reluctance to belong to something so overtly political and confrontational. For instance, Goh Keat Peng, a Christian activist and Keadilan member, urged fellow Christians, in an interview, to "understand that to participate in a political programme through properly registered political parties is a legitimate exercise within the legal framework of the country" and not to "eschew party politics" or just be quiet "spectators."[36] Others lacked resources to devote to aims aside from the particularistic goals of the organization, shared their more enthusiastic members with groups that were already part of the coalitions, were hesitant to work so closely with PAS or other parties, or had other reasons for remaining apart. Nevertheless, many of these groups or activists were involved to some extent in linked initiatives, such as Pemantau, People Are the Boss, or campaigns for candidates. Their engagement helped to cement CSAs' informal but strong influence on reformist politics. CSAs and opposition parties also pursued monitoring efforts after the elections. Moreover, the simultaneous efforts of opposition parties to maintain shadow cabinets and monitor political developments encouraged parties to follow the example of CSAs by keeping a longer time horizon and looking well beyond elections.

In short, then, the nature of Malaysia's illiberal democratic regime has pushed opposition politics increasingly to assume the timbre of social movement activism (including substantial involvement by CSAs) rather than that of straightforward contests between adversarial political parties and their policy platforms. This process neither began nor ended with Reformasi, though the movement exemplified the dynamics involved. Frustrated with the failure of coalition-building efforts in the past, but cognizant of a rare window for change, political agents of all stripes mobilized for reform in the late 1990s. This movement built upon decades of prior efforts at normative and institutional change that had built up stores of coalitional capital, but the strategies involved reflected changes over time in the nature of the regime, which made certain forms of contention more or less promising, as well as changes in the structures for opposition, most notably the relatively recent development of an array of political NGOs. The normative project of developing a noncommunal, less clientelistic political culture remains incomplete, and the Reformasi movement failed to institutionalize a new regime. However, the process by which these efforts proceeded remains important to our understanding of the dynamics of contention in Malaysia. A brief overview of the contemporaneous, but very different, Reformasi movement in Indonesia will more clearly illumine how the type of regime being contested shapes the nature and scope of protest, the importance of coalitional capital, and the ways in which changing attributions of opportunity and threat foster alterations in reformists' strategies and demands. It is to Indonesia, therefore, that the next chapter turns.

THE OTHER REFORMASI: MALAYSIA AND INDONESIA COMPARED

Some of the same processes and patterns characterizing reform initiatives in Malaysia are to be found elsewhere. CSAs, for instance, play important roles in political socialization, bridging social cleavages, and lobbying for change in many countries. However, the specific contours of reform in Malaysia are relevant principally where other trajectories of protest, whether straightforward electoral contestation, on the one hand, or a mass uprising, on the other, are discouraged by the weak institutionalization of democratic structures and rules so that opponents of the government see a possibility of change through contained contention but are not fully free to pursue such a course. In such a context, long-term consciousness raising and lobbying may ignite more concerted activism. The question of *when* that happens has to do with opportunities. Reformasi in Malaysia, for instance, took shape when the government was vulnerable and significant change seemed truly feasible, leading activists to redirect and intensify their efforts and more of the public to get involved. A comparison of the contemporaneous Malaysian and Indonesian Reformasi movements helps specify which Malaysian processes are generic or distinctive, how the nature of the incumbent regime shapes trajectories of protest, how the availability of stores of coalitional capital influences collaboration, and how critical are changing attributions of opportunity and threat to the search, within both civil society and political society, for new collective action frames and strategies.

In the late 1990s, Indonesia faced a set of conditions broadly comparable to those in Malaysia, ranging from experience of the Asian financial crisis to a degree of support for political Islam to a government largely intolerant of civil societal agitation and a despotic long-term ruler. In Indonesia, though, unlike in Malaysia, these features were coupled with a distinctive military role in government, ingrained suspicions separating sectors of civil society, regional secessionist movements, a history of violent unrest, and a far more ruthless and authoritarian regime that curtailed formal and informal political activity alike. While Malaysian reformists formed a coalition for reform but achieved little by way of regime change, Indonesian reformists toppled President Soeharto and his New Order (*Orde Baru*) regime before reaching substantial agreement on proactive aims. Among the key causes for this disparity are the nature of civil society and political society and the interaction between them in Indonesia. In Indonesia, unlike in Malaysia, activists had little space or incentive to pursue contained contention, though they recognized the unique opportunity for change available in 1998–1999 and saw the benefit of coordinated mobilization for systemic change. The history of government repression of opposition parties and its stifling of civil societal activism, and the resultant lack of coalitional capital, precluded the development and articulation of shared goals across the political opposition, effective bridging of potent societal cleavages even in the short term, and the sort of incremental rather than cataclysmic change found in illiberal democratic Malaysia. Vincent Boudreau explains this distinction (in contrasting "people power" in the Philippines and Indonesia): having "eliminated the possibility of any organized or coordinated social challenge," Soeharto's state never needed to accommodate dissent to bolster its position. Hence, even disruptive and troublesome protest "could not attain the kind of coordination or longevity necessary to contend for state power—or even frame itself as poised for such a contest" (Boudreau 1999: 6).

Placing Indonesia's Reformasi Movement in Context

An overview of the major currents and actors in Indonesia's political opposition through the late 1990s illustrates the complexity and variability of reformist appeals in the country's modern history. Indonesia's New Order regime is best characterized as hegemonic electoral authoritarian, as described in chapter 2: regular elections added a facade of democracy but were not competitive, and scope for opposition parties and CSAs was strictly delimited and enforced by the powerful dominant party. Regime type is thus a key variable in understanding the failure of Indonesian CSAs to build up coalitional capital over the years as in Malaysia. The narrowing of formal political space in Indonesia was not mitigated (as it was in Malaysia) by the availability of space for above-ground, informal political engagement. Students, labor, middle-class professionals, Islamists, the urban poor, NGOs, military officers, and political parties have mobilized and have forged shifting, transient alliances for an array of reformist or reactionary goals but have had to negotiate mutual suspicions and debilitating regulations. The startling and apparently chaotic events of the late 1990s need to be seen in this context.

Indonesia's Reformasi movement built up to its tumultuous climax after a long period of lower-level agitation that gradually gained steam through the latter half of the 1990s. President Soeharto's fall, in May 1998, was precipitated by the regional economic crisis that began in 1997 and by a resulting series of mostly student-based protests. However, by then he was already suffering a crisis of political legitimacy that had been percolating for years. The confluence of economic meltdown, opposition party enthusiasm, student activism, and factionalism made Soeharto and his government ever less popular without clearly indicating what should supplant the status quo.

The precursor to Indonesia's Reformasi movement was an increase in oppositional agitation through the 1980s and the policy of *keterbukaan* (openness) in the first half of the 1990s as Soeharto and portions of the Angkatan Bersenjata Republik Indonesia (ABRI, Armed Forces of the Republic of Indonesia) courted rival institutions for support.[1] Heryanto (1996: 245) explains that mounting "internal friction within the ruling elite" combined with international pressures to provide more room for the consolidation of existing opposition." These developments permitted relatively greater freedom of expression and open debate than previously. The main points of contention were mounting infringements on ABRI's autonomy and political influence along with increasingly blatant state favoritism toward Soeharto's family members and business elites. The latter issue caused widespread discontent. These economic irrationalities became a rallying cry of Reformasi activists as the Asian economic crisis made corruption more obvious and deleterious (Eklöf 1999; Budiman, Hatley, and Kingsbury 1999: sec. 1). Concomitant with these tensions in the government was the invigoration of a growing pro-democracy movement—linked with similar movements in other countries—composed of elite dissidents, activists from new and old NGOs, and students. What eventually provided common ground for a *gerakan Reformasi* (reform movement) were goals that included respecting human rights, enforcing the rule of law, holding fair elections, and reducing the power of the military. Islam was also key for many activists, whether as a motivating force or as the provider of an intellectual premise for democratic reforms (Uhlin 1997). Tracing the development of opposition in Indonesia since the 1960s helps explain the genesis of the groups and issues that eventually brought down the New Order regime.

The Development of Opposition to the New Order

Soeharto's New Order coalition developed in the mid-1960s in reaction to the flourishing of left-wing politics. Facing a rapidly growing communist movement and rural class struggle, President Soekarno had grown increasingly dependent on the left for support. Forces eager to halt this slide found few legal alternatives. The military seemed their only choice. The Islamist community and urban middle classes allied with the army in "Action Fronts" against Soekarno and the rest of the left. Among the middle-class groups were students, journalists, lawyers, intellectuals, and economists, many of them associated with the banned Partai Sosialis Indonesia, the moderate Islamic Masjumi, or the Catholic Party. All the same, the New Order state that ultimately coalesced by the late 1960s was oriented firmly toward capitalist development and political order, anchored by a military base, and sustained by the hegemonic *Pancasila* (five principles) ideology.[2] Its establishment followed a devastating purge of supposed communists in the mid-1960s in which perhaps half a million Indonesians were killed and untold others were intimidated into silence. As the regime took shape, "state and society were portrayed as an integrated and organic whole, where deliberation and consensus replaced the divisive and conflictual politics of the past" (Aspinall 1996: 217).[3]

In line with this image, the government sought to depoliticize society, especially the lower classes, and to control key social sectors through state-founded corporatist groups. Still, two sets of issues remained around which opposition formed over the years. The first set included democracy, the rule of law, human rights, and the like, which sparked protests especially by students in the 1970s. The second set consisted of economic and social issues, especially calls for social justice and a more fair distribution of wealth (Aspinall 1996: 217–21). In the 1970s, it was the forces that had been part of the anti-Soekarno effort in the 1960s that were best able to articulate dissent. Students, secular intellectuals, former Action Front participants, and retired military and civilian officials formed something of a dissident niche, operating primarily out of universities, the media, and a few NGOs. They were based primarily in cities, especially Jakarta and Bandung, and worked with the more liberal sections of the government. These critics shared with the government a general commitment to economic development and political stability and tended to look to the state for allies and opportunities, but they advocated a more efficient, clean, regularized administration.

For a while, this sort of "semi-opposition" was basically tolerated—unlike challenges from the left, from the Soekarnoist current, or, eventually, from the Islamic right, which were suppressed. However, even this moderately critical space progressively diminished. Disillusioned with the repeat of trends they had opposed under the prior regime, students organized demonstrations in the early 1970s (described in more detail below) against economic mismanagement and corruption, neglect of the poor, the arbitrary power of the state, the role of the military in government, and restrictions on elections. In 1973 and early 1974 in particular, they held significant protests in several cities. These events culminated in January 1974's "Malari affair," a riot surrounding the Japanese prime minister's visit to Jakarta in which eight youths were killed and eight hundred detained. Another round of student-organized protests occurred in 1977–1978 in various Javanese cities against the military, Soeharto, and business relations between senior bureaucrats, Chinese capitalists, and foreign companies. In January 1978, hundreds of students were arrested, troops occupied campuses, and student councils and critical student publications were suspended. Much as had happened on Malaysian campuses several years previously, new policies were promulgated the following year (sparking further protests) to centralize bureaucratic control over student bodies and forbid students to engage in political activities on campus, even in officially recognized groups. The space for student and other organizations was then further whittled away by 1985's Social Organizations Law (Undang-undang Organisasi Kemasyarakatan, ORMAS). This enactment required all associations to have the *Pancasila* as their sole ideological basis (*asas tunggal*). Groups that complied, including some of the largest student organizations, were widely discredited. These restrictions made outreach difficult and left campus activism at its lowest level since before 1965.

More institutionalized political space was curtailed at the same time. In 1973, to curb political competition and dissent on government policies, the existing ten political parties were consolidated into three, and new parties were prohibited. Four Muslim parties were merged into the Partai Persatuan Pembangunan (United Development Party, PPP), and two Christian parties were joined in the secular-nationalist Partai Demokrasi Indonesia (Indonesian Democratic Party, PDI). The only other "party" sanctioned by the government was Golongan Karya (Functional Groups, Golkar), which was basically a vehicle for Soeharto. The restriction of political party competition forced many party members, among them former student activists, to find new avenues for engagement, including NGOs. Secular community-development organizations had begun to emerge by the late 1960s, together with environmental groups and other associations linked with the urban middle class. These groups could be divided into those focused on economic development, which were often willing to work with the government to help fulfill its development objectives, and advocacy organizations dealing with such issues as human rights and political participation. ORMAS and other restrictions constrained not only students but NGOs, as well. Like so many other laws, though, this one could be sidestepped. "Social organizations" were never clearly defined, and many organizations evaded the ruling by eschewing formal membership rolls or by adopting a *yayasan* (foundation) structure, which required only a vague statement of objectives (Eldridge 1996). Regardless, the space for political NGOs, like that for opposition parties, was clearly more narrow in New Order Indonesia than in contemporaneous Malaysia, and the military-linked Indonesian government was more harsh in asserting control.

Activism in the 1980s developed amid a debate in the broader society about the *keterbukaan* policy, democratization, and presidential succession, reflecting frictions within the political elite. Opposition sentiments spread to a broader base after 1989. Social inequalities had increased under economic growth, feeding leftist, nationalist, and populist ideologies. Rooted in the critique of developmentalism and militarism of students and NGOs in the 1970s, this new left retained a niche in the student movement but developed a stronger, more diversified organizational base in the 1990s. NGOs built by former student activists and other dissidents to replace the student councils, critical press, and so on that were closed in the 1970s were particularly important. Most of these NGOs focused on alternative development models to reduce poverty and avoided confrontation or even worked with the state. Others did attack the government; most were at least ambivalent toward it. Students, too, took up a range of causes in the 1990s, from supporting freedom of the press to successfully opposing a national lottery.[4] This sort of opposition remained largely a middle-class phenomenon and was still subject to repression, particularly if activists involved the lower classes, posed an ideological challenge to the *Pancasila*, were too aggressive, or touched on certain controversial issues. However, the era also saw a marked increase in highly visible conflict involving the lower classes, often mobilized by students or small, advocacy-oriented NGOs, including disputes over land, strikes, and illegal organizing by workers (Aspinall 1996).

The situation heated up in the mid-1990s. The government's sloppy attempt to control the PDI, including by ousting its popular chair, Megawati Soekarnoputri,[5] sparked violent protests in mid-1996 and called into question the legitimacy of a government that needed to take such drastic measures to quell opposition.[6] While thousands demonstrated on the streets of Jakarta in support of Megawati, thirty critical, mostly left-wing NGOs, together with labor and student activists and representatives of the small, leftist-intellectual Partai Rakyat Demokrasi (PRD, People's

Democratic Party), united in the Majelis Rakyat Indonesia (Indonesian People's Council, MARI). MARI opposed the government's interference in the PDI, protested against corruption and collusion, and pressed for reform of laws on political activity. Over a dozen activists from MARI (especially from the PRD, which was accused of masterminding riots) were charged with subversion and other political offenses and were sentenced to long prison terms. Other activists were frightened into silence or forced either underground or inside less tightly controlled university campuses. This suppression of dissent broke up an attempt to forge a reformist coalition and paved the way to a smoother general election in 1997 (Eklöf 1999).

These spontaneous or organized protests, and the government's aggressively violent response to them, both indicated the extent of social and economic unrest that was brewing, especially among the young urban poor, and tarnished the New Order's already shaky democratic credentials. Around the same time—late 1996 through early 1997—riots also wracked other parts of Java (Situbondo, Tasikmalaya, Surabaya) as well as West Kalimantan. Ethnic and religious tensions were apparent in these incidents, some of which resulted in serious casualties and costly damage. However, socioeconomic cleavages and political rivalries were also involved, giving rise to prolific political conspiracy theories (Eklöf 1999; Budiman, Hatley, and Kingsbury 1999).

The subsequent elections of May 1997, touted as a *Pesta Demokrasi* (Festival of Democracy), did little to restore the government's legitimacy or credibility. The campaign proved the most violent of the New Order period, and the contest was far from fair. Golkar went so far as to paint government buildings and even trees its signature yellow in a *kuningisasi* (yellowization) campaign; Megawati was barred from contesting; restrictions on campaign activities stalled momentum and mobilization; and while the three main parties were allowed televised debates, they could not criticize the government or its policies. The *Mega-Bintang* (Megastar or Superstar) coalition formed, apparently spontaneously, between supporters of Megawati and the PPP (the symbol of which is a star). Though the coalition helped give some direction to protest activity, including a call (eventually rescinded) to boycott the polls, it was banned by the government. In the end, Soeharto's Golkar declared its best result ever: a highly improbable 75 percent of the vote. Disputed final figures for each party, allegations of election rigging and manipulation by Golkar-linked local-level bureaucrats and military officials, and growing political awareness among the populace put the validity of the results in doubt. Nonetheless, Soeharto was reelected president by the Majelis Permusyawaratan Rakyat (People's Consultative Assembly, MPR) in March 1998, backed by the technocrat B. J. Habibie as vice president and by a rather unimpressive cabinet of loyalists.

Decline and Fall of the New Order

The ill health of both the economy and Soeharto himself caused cracks in the government to become ever more visible in the latter half of 1997 and early 1998. The economic crisis hit Indonesia severely, given contagion effects from the devaluation of the Thai baht as well as doubts about the commitment of Soeharto and his government to deregulation, cutting government spending, and allowing reforms to affect his family and cronies. The government sought help from the International Monetary Fund (IMF) in October; Indonesia's rescue package was the fund's biggest ever. However, despite some reforms, the protection afforded Soeharto's inner circle, in addition to the implications for national sovereignty of having the IMF so closely dictating economic policy,[7] fed mounting political unrest without restoring investors' confidence in the economy. By the end of 1997, the rupiah was disastrously weak; business closures, inflation, unemployment, and poverty were rising; and an El Niño–caused drought, compounded by a crippling haze from fires on plantations in Sumatra and Kalimantan, aggravated matters. Then, in the midst of the turmoil, Soeharto announced that he was taking a ten-day rest in December 1997, sparking fears about a possible succession crisis should anything happen to him. The economic situation and related social and political unrest only grew worse through 1998, particularly in light of the government's unrealistic budgets and still tenuous implementation of reforms.

Following the presentation of one such budget, in January 1998, the modernist Islamic leader Amien Rais proposed an alliance among Megawati, traditionalist Islamic leader Abdurrahman Wahid, and himself for political reform. Megawati agreed, but Abdurrahman, while supportive of the need for reform, was suspicious of Amien and hence reluctant to join.[8] At the same time, students continued to hold referenda calling for political reform and Soeharto's resignation, and intellectuals and other activists also sharply criticized the government.[9] Students, artists, journalists, and activists joined forces under an umbrella organization called Solidaritas Indonesia untuk Amien dan Mega (SIAGA, Indonesian Solidarity for Amien and Mega). SIAGA and other groups demonstrated in early 1998 for economic and political reform and a change of leadership. Overall, this anti-Soeharto Reformasi movement remained relatively small, weak, and uncoordinated, lacking a coherent strategy or real unity. Still, despite a scapegoating campaign directed at Indonesian Chinese and related initiatives to divert negative attention from the government, dissent persisted, often taking more violent forms.

Riots began over surging food prices in East Java in January 1998 and then spread elsewhere. Though inflation and unemployment were the most critical instigants, the incidents frequently assumed a religious or ethnic character as well. The military was unwilling or unable to do much to quell the violence, though a number of student, labor, and pro-democracy activists were kidnapped by security forces in this period. Then, as the MPR prepared for its March 1998 sitting, the number and the scale of protests increased, especially in Jakarta and other cities and particularly at universities, where demonstrations were generally tolerated as long as they were contained on campus. Taking a more conciliatory approach, the appointed ABRI faction in the MPR agreed to a meeting with a delegation of students. The students presented a list of demands for political, judicial, and economic reforms and a change of leadership. Following this symbolic achievement, student protests only gained strength. The military tried both repression and official efforts at reconciliation, such as proposing a national-level dialogue with students,[10] to restore calm.

Students gained moral support from prominent government critics like Amien Rais and student activists from previous generations, and they also profited from information exchanged via the Internet and other media. While the movement lacked national coordination and centralized leadership, groups of students from different universities formed small groups as well as umbrella organizations. These varied in ideology and strategy from radical to accommodationist.[11] Deep divisions within the student movement—particularly between politicized Islamist and more secular factions—weakened it and made unity tenuous (Winters 2001). Regardless, by the end of April 1998, with the support of academic staff, university management, and alumni organizations, students were staging protests at nearly every campus (with those in Jakarta and Yogyakarta particularly volatile) and calling for the election of a new slate of leaders, albeit within the existing constitutional framework. Much of the middle class, especially educated urbanites, supported these protests. However, when students attempted to take to the streets, security forces cracked down violently. These demonstrations not only kept critical perspectives and demands for reform at the forefront but also revealed and deepened cracks in the government, especially between more conciliatory military leaders (such as Armed Forces Commander and Minister for Defense and

Security Wiranto) and the less responsive Soeharto, whom students came to see ever more clearly as the chief obstacle to reform.

In May 1998, urban socioeconomic crisis and elite politicking fed a wave of violence that resulted in over a thousand deaths and devastating property damage (Eklöf 1999: 175). IMF-endorsed cuts to fuel and electricity subsidies early in the month had riled up the masses, sparking enormous, often violent protests. Agents provocateurs, thought to be linked with the military, were suspected to be at work in a number of these demonstrations, often rendering them racially charged (anti-Chinese) riots and encouraging massive Chinese flight—only intensified by a spate of brutal rapes, mostly of Chinese women (Heryanto 1999).[12] The fatal shooting of four students by government troops at Jakarta's Trisakti University on May 12 was particularly momentous. This incident brought wide media coverage and sharp criticism as well as a huge memorial service that degenerated into rioting. While university students were the main force in most of the demonstrations, high school students, labor activists, workers (including unemployed ones), academics, administrators, and alumni figures also lent support. Even rural villagers followed developments sympathetically, thanks to wide media coverage (Cohen 1998a: 21).

On May 14, Soeharto said he was prepared to resign, and rumors spread that the first family had fled the country. By that time, calls were coming even from within the government for the MPR to choose a new executive. With support for Soeharto clearly sparse, Amien Rais tried again to establish a coalition for reform. He announced the formation of the Majelis Amanat Rakyat (MAR, Council of the People's Mandate), which brought together Islamic activists, former cabinet ministers, representatives of social organizations and NGOs, and others (though not Megawati or Abdurrahman) to create an alternative, modern political platform. The MAR eventually evolved into Partai Amanat Nasional (National Mandate Party, PAN) (Budiman 1999: 17–18).

On May 18, with logistical support from NGOs, thousands of students converged on the MPR building. Troops allowed them inside. At the same time, Amien was calling for massive demonstrations on May 20, Hari Kebangkitan Nasional (Day of National Resurgence), the day commemorating the start of the nationalist struggle against the Dutch. Bowing to pressure, Soeharto announced on May 19 that he would appoint a *Kabinet Reformasi,* to be supported by nongovernmental figures, that would oversee the revision of electoral and other political laws and the reduction of corruption. He would then call new elections in which he would not stand. At Soeharto's announcement, students thronged the

MPR until, "with thousands of students swarming the parliament building, climbing on its roof and staging all sorts of political demonstrations
and free-speech forums, the students' occupation of the parliament became a prime symbol of people power in Indonesia" (Eklöf 1999: 209).

On the morning of May 21, Soeharto read a speech of resignation on
national television and named Habibie his successor. Wiranto pledged the
military's support for the new government as well as for the safety of
Soeharto and his family. Though happy with Soeharto's resignation,
many students were less satisfied with the transfer of power to Habibie.
Disappointed with the limited extent of change, they felt that they had
been mere pawns in intraelite machinations. Regardless, with their chief
common target—Soeharto's ouster—achieved, students withdrew from
the forefront, both because of the desire to renew their energies and
strategize anew and because of rifts between factions. In fact, the ascen-
sion of Habibie, the former leader of the Ikatan Cendekiawan Muslim
Indonesia (Indonesian Association of Muslim Intellectuals, ICMI), as
Soeharto's successor proved crippling to the movement. Secular-oriented
students opposed him, but "the more Islamic branch of the student movement—which was perfectly able to reject and attack Soeharto, view him
as an enemy, and join together in solidarity with the rest of the student
movement against the New Order—was utterly unable to perceive
Habibie as part of the same Soeharto regime" (Winters 2001: n.p.; see
also Hadiz 1999: 109–10). Consequently, Soeharto's departure brought
both euphoria and disorientation, stalling protesters' momentum (Aspinall 1999: 225).[13]

Of course, genuine liberalization required more than just Soeharto's
resignation. Sporadic protests continued, particularly as the November
1998 MPR session drew near. At that time, students and thousands of urban poor rallied, targeting government buildings, military bases, and radio and television stations. They demanded Habibie's resignation and the
formation of a provisional government, rejected the MPR, and called for
an immediate end to *dwifungsi,* the military's dual role in defense and
government (Lane 1999). The military and government still saw such
mass action as a serious threat and cracked down harshly. Moreover,
hired paramilitary thugs (*Pam Swakarsa*) clashed with students and other
protesters. Their involvement was part of a larger pattern of using hooli-
gans and former criminals to stir up trouble or for vigilante justice
(Young 1999b; Bourchier 1999). Fourteen people were killed on November 13–14, triggering even more frenzied and militant mobilization
around the country. Overall, though, the November riots just "revealed
the difficulties of pressing an agenda on a New Order political elite more
or less united against radical political change" (Hadiz 1999: 111).

Indeed, as Ken Young explains (199b: 70), by the end of 1998, while "the cause was far from hopeless," substantial change was far from assured, since

the reform movement had thus far failed adequately to engage the participation of the broader citizenry. The regime was in crisis, but the opposition was also weak in leadership, organisation and mass participation. It was lacking in influence over the sources of legitimate force, and command of technical, administrative and economic expertise.

Reformers still lacked a coherent program or leadership. Efforts to form an opposition "people's committee" in mid-1998 had never got off the ground, largely because of squabbling between groups (Hadiz 1999: 109). Undaunted, students and elites again attempted to reach a consensus on what to do next. Although students remained divided in their tolerance for Habibie's government, by late 1998 they had settled upon a platform demanding that Soeharto be put on trial and that *dwifungsi* be immediately abolished.

Student "brokers" identified five leaders they thought could best represent the people in a transitional government: Megawati, Abdurrahman Wahid, Amien Rais, Governor Sultan Hamengkubuwono X of Yogyakarta, and Bishop Carlos Belo of East Timor. At the urging of the students, all but Belo (who was supportive but could not attend) met on November 10, 1998, at Ciganjur, south of Jakarta, to formulate a common platform for reform.[14] The "Ciganjur Four" were essentially moderate in their positions. Their eight-point declaration said they did not favor establishing a transitional government, preferring instead to work toward a fair election as a way out of the nation's political and economic crises. Also, they preferred to phase out the military's political role and presence in Parliament over six years rather than immediately. The declaration supported popular sovereignty, decentralization of government, and fairer sharing of funds between the center and the regions, though it still affirmed the ideal of "unity in diversity" (*bhinneka tunggal ika*) and a unitary state. Condemning corruption, the statement included a commitment to investigate Soeharto's wealth, though his fate was otherwise left unsettled. However disappointing to students who had hoped for a more radical statement, the Ciganjur declaration was significant as a point of reference for the movement and helped establish a common agenda (Mohammad Fajrul 1999: 209–10; Cohen 1998b; Young 1999b).

Despite the disorganization of the Reformasi movement, the latter half of 1998 saw some progress toward change, largely pressed by Habibie and his government in response to popular demands. These reforms included legislation ensuring freedom of the press; regarding human rights,

TABLE 4

1999 Indonesian Election Results

Party	Votes (%)	Seats
PDI-P	34	154
Golkar	22	120
PKB	13	51
PPP*	11	59
PAN	7	35
14 others		43
Total		462

SOURCE: Panitia Pengawas Pemilihan Umum/General Election Monitoring Committee, "Hasil Pemilu 1999," http://www.panwaspemilu.org/d_hasil99.php (accessed April 16, 2005).
*PPP gained 19 seats from an alliance of eight Islamic parties that pooled their votes.

parties, elections, and parliament; curtailing executive powers; and setting terms limits for the president and the vice president. Habibie also recognized the need for increased political and economic autonomy in the regions. The more radical students and democracy activists were impatient, but the reforms did entail "real concessions to democratic forces, and did not deserve to be dismissed out of hand" (Young 1999b: 87).

The next big step was the general election of June 7, 1999. The election was generally judged by domestic and foreign monitors and observers to be fair, transparent, and nonviolent, despite some irregularities (see Blackburn 1999b). Forty-eight parties contested for 462 seats in the Dewan Perwakilan Rakyat (DPR, Parliament). The 700-seat MPR also included 238 appointed representatives (a decrease from 575 out of a previous 1,000): 38 from the military, 135 for regional representatives,[15] and 65 for "functional group" representatives.[16] Megawati's PDI-Perjuangan (the "Struggle" faction of the PDI, or PDI-P) won a plurality of the elected seats, with Golkar running second. Abdurrahman's PKB and the PPP trailed significantly, and Amien Rais's PAN made a particularly poor showing (see Table 4 for results). However, the lack of strict party discipline (and even of clear differentiation among parties) and the contest among key personalities left the results ambiguous, especially in terms of determining who would be president.

Despite the fervor of Reformasi and significant efforts at educating voters and raising awareness, the campaign lacked depth. Ken Young (1999a: 4) critiques it thus: "The winner herself [Megawati] traveled on a surge of popular enthusiasm which called for very little scrutiny or debate about the meaning of *reformasi* (or . . . the other slogans and symbols of PDI-P), and not much exposition of policy initiatives designed to meet Indonesia's multiple crises." Only PAN, he suggests, "offered the electorate some policy substance," but it did poorly in the polls except among educated, urban elites. Interestingly, Vedi Hadiz (1999: 121) attributes much of the PAN platform to NGO activists and intellectuals.[17] Still, Young identifies three themes that were fought out in the polls: the contest between the status quo and reform, secular nationalism versus more political Islam, and issues of regional autonomy.

Parties for reform (loosely defined) did better than those for the status quo, especially when the advantages of incumbency are taken into account. Golkar controlled bureaucratic resources, funds, and entrenched stores of popular loyalty and fear. The far from universal scope of Reformasi was suggested by the clear contrast in election outcomes between Java/Bali and the "outer islands." Golkar did much better in the latter, especially in rural areas, than in the former. Voters in different regions saw different parties as representing their specific concerns, regardless of how effective these parties would really be at advancing regional interests. Thus Golkar was strong in Sulawesi, since Habibie is from there; PDI-P was stronger in East Timor, as the only alternative to the hated Golkar; and the PPP was stronger in Aceh, since it promised to propose a referendum on regional autonomy (van Klinken 1999: 230; Young 1999a: 5).[18] However, as van Klinken explains (1999: 26), "Golkar can no longer be a party of hegemony in the periphery if it has lost control of the centre, which it has." In terms of Islam, while parties such as PKB and PAN drew on Islamic constituencies for their success, both ran on broad, inclusive platforms (though only Muslims may join PKB). The only truly Islamist party to do well was the PPP. The results seem to indicate that political Islam had yet really to take root, though this trend is still developing. Even in 2004, most Islamist parties campaigned more on general issues like corruption and the economy than on Islam per se—and yet it was still only Partai Keadilan Sejahtera (PKS) that did particularly well (Guerin 2004). Islamist parties earned a total of around 40 percent of the parliamentary vote but remained "too fissured to combine into a single bloc" for the presidential polls (Mackie 2004).

While the mere holding of free elections met some key Reformasi demands, the reform process remained in flux, and the various actors in the movement were far from fully satisfied. With Reformasi, however, it seems that a culture of protest was institutionalized. Demonstrations continued beyond the polls, and yet, because they were by then more common and less risky than before, they tended to have less impact.[19] This general but ineffective garrulousness is probably nowhere better represented than in popular responses to Abdurrahman Wahid's government.

Though chosen through established constitutional processes, Abdurrahman was roundly castigated for his autocratic or simply flighty tendencies and his inability to restore stability or prosperity. Calls for his impeachment or resignation came from everyone, from students to parliamentarians. He showed remarkable impunity in sidestepping challenges but was ultimately forced out of office in mid-2001, largely by legislative action. Moreover, the looming specter of territorial disintegration (East Timor voted itself out of Indonesia in October 1999), the inability of the military to prevent violent displays of religious zealotry (and its alleged role in fomenting violence in East Timor, Aceh, and elsewhere), the continued political influence of the military (and the implied suggestion that, as in 1965, they might see fit to take over to set things right), and the continued reticence of foreign and domestic investors kept longer-term, more ideological strategizing on hold and left Reformasi an incomplete project.

"Plus ça change . . . "

Once the dust settled after the 1999 elections, much had changed in Indonesia, but echoes of the New Order persisted. Significant reforms had been made: the press was liberated and lively (perhaps to the point of excess), people felt free to assemble and express themselves, organizational life could flourish unfettered, the elections had been meaningful, the political role of the military had been checked to some extent, accountability and transparency were at least on the agenda, and, of course, Soeharto was out of office. Still, despite the new configurations of parties and leaders, many principal elite actors (not to mention lower-level bureaucrats) traced their roots to New Order structures. Also, while its political role had been curtailed under the new constitution, the military—especially particular prominent generals and factions—remained a critical political force. Its role was enhanced by the imperative of curbing separatist or ethnoreligious violence in certain regions. Indeed, cleavages that were significant or menacing in the past remained or even grew deeper. Overall, as a substantial multiyear "democratic audit" concludes (DEMOS 2004: 3), "The pro-democratic forces . . . have failed to unify the pro-*reformasi* forces and to become politically significant," and while a democracy movement persists, it "has not only been marginalised by the mainstream elitist politics of democratisation . . . [but] also continues to reflect Soeharto's 'floating mass' politics by being fragmented, poorly organised and rather isolated from ordinary people" and has sustained an "anti-statist" focus rather than working more assiduously to change power relations.

A 2002 overhaul of Indonesia's constitution helped further democratic transition, though not yet consolidation, shifting power from the MPR to the voting public in a more balanced presidential system. As of the 2004 elections, Indonesia had an institutionalized system of checks and balances, with separation of powers among the legislative, executive, and judicial branches of government; an elected president; a fully elected legislature, including the new Dewan Perwakilan Daerah (Regional Representative Assembly) and provincial and district-level assemblies; stiffer requirements for passage of constitutional amendments; and a constitutional court (Ellis 2002). Unlike the initial impetus for reform, these changes grew largely out of contained negotiations among formal political actors.

As in Malaysia, Indonesia's Reformasi movement peaked when political opportunity structures were most conducive to radical change, but it had its roots in longer-term processes of sociopolitical transformation. The major players in the movement—students, political parties, NGOs and other mass-based organizations, labor unions, and key personalities—had developed their resources and positions over a period of years or even decades. As Aspinall (1996) describes it, social and political opposition to Soeharto's government gradually developed largely as an externality of economic growth, including industrialization and changes to the urban class structure. The social base of opposition circles expanded over time, ultimately extending well beyond the urban middle class, while the institutional base of opposition took shape as NGOs developed through the 1980s and 1990s. By 1989, "*keterbukaan* and *demokratisasi* . . . emerged not simply as the slogans of a narrow and marginalised alegal opposition, but (admittedly with fluctuations) as key themes of public debate, discussed and promoted by the media, academics, a wide range of 'semi-oppositional' political groups, and elements from within the government itself" (Aspinall 1996: 228). In other words, the issues at the heart of Reformasi had been germinating for quite some time before the confluence of events made them so explosive.

In line with tendencies in Malaysia, Singapore, Thailand, and other Asian states, Indonesia's burgeoning middle class has been far from unequivocal in its support for democratization. In fact, as pressure for reform mounted, many of the new bourgeoisie resisted change, since the structure of the regime left them with strong vested interests in maintaining the status quo. Economic development under Soeharto had rendered much of the upper and middle classes dependent upon state resources. At the same time, the bulk of the population, rural and urban, remained impoverished, leaving the more privileged fearful of explosive "social jealousy," anti-Sinicism (since ethnic Chinese comprised a large proportion of the better-off), and Islamic resurgence, and hence inclined to support a strong state (Aspinall 1996: 225–27). It is hardly surprising, then, that parts of the New Order establishment excluded from government, including the Ciganjur Four, "were just as afraid of mass mobilisations as the regime was" and feared that their coming to power at the hands of a mass movement "would set a precedent which could come back to haunt them at a later date" (Lane 1999: 242, 245). Indeed, the chief leaders of Reformasi, who pursued moderate, contained contention with the Ciganjur declaration, posed much less of a threat to the government than the more volatile, idealistic, and incensed students or *rakyat* (people), who, "because they have never been involved in a participatory and institutionalized way . . . are highly explosive" when they do get involved (Winters 2001: n.p.).

Indeed, although so much of the momentum for change came from below, policymaking after Soeharto's fall remained mostly top-down. Hence, through the latter half of 1998, at least, "the debates about what *reformasi* means and how far it should go were largely conducted among elites, many of whom owed their position, privileges and material well-being to Suharto's system" (Young 1999b: 70; see also Nursyahbani 2000; Boudreau 1999: 14). Hadiz (1999: 113) concurs that Reformasi was largely a middle-class struggle, since the "most politically and economically subordinated elements in Indonesian society . . . lack the organisational muscle and capacity to force their way into the process of contestation and negotiation over the configuration of power after Suharto." Even many middle-class activists, though, were marginalized. For instance, Indonesian NGOs tried to secure for themselves a niche in the *otonomi daerah* (regional autonomy) plans pursued under the new regime. Backed by such agencies as the Ford Foundation, they held up comparable examples, like that of the Philippines, but secured no official NGO role in the decentralization of authority to municipalities.[20] In addition, the politics practiced on the streets remained more about beseeching elites for results than about popular sovereignty, though activists do have much more access to ministers and face less bureaucratic red tape than previously.[21] Indeed, Greg Fealy (2001b: 101–2) suggests that individual leaders dominate Indonesia's political parties now more than they did before the New Order, to such an extent that "Abdurrahman and Megawati in particular have almost cult status and attract unquestioning, often fanatical, loyalty from many of their grassroots supporters." Overall, then, Indonesia emerged from Reformasi with politics still an elite game, albeit one played by a somewhat different set of elites than before.

Moreover, the political parties through which the mass of Indonesians participated in 1999 and even in 2004 were largely the same ones as in the past, even if they had been transformed in significant ways. Aside from New Order stalwarts Golkar, the PDI, and the PPP, the other parties predominant in the era of Reformasi were basically reincarnations or off-shoots of parties of the 1950s and 1960s: the Partai Nahdlatul Ulama (PNU),[22] Masjumi, and so on. Even the more distinctive PAN was led by Amien Rais, who reached prominence during the Soeharto era and had been closely affiliated with the long-standing mass organization Muhammadiyah. Moreover, the configuration of parties still bore a clear resemblance to past patterns. Speculation was rife before the 1999 elections about whether what Clifford Geertz termed the *aliran* (cultural or religious streams) politics of the 1950s would still prevail in the 1990s. The three *aliran* in the 1950s were *abangan* (less strictly observant) Muslims, urban *santri* (pious and highly observant) Muslims, and rural *santri* (generally conservative members of Nahdlatul Ulama, the Renaissance of Islamic Scholars, NU). In 1955, Soekarno's Partai Nasionalis Indonesia (Indonesian Nationalist Party, PNI) and the Partai Komunis Indonesia (Indonesian Communist Party, PKI) received *abangan* votes; Masjumi got the urban *santri* vote, and PNU won the rural *santri* vote.

The context in 1999 was clearly different, with more parties and new issues. *Aliran* politics were still relevant, but the divisions were less clear-cut and deterministic than previously. This shift was less because of activists' or groups' promotion of unifying messages and perspectives than because of demographic and cultural shifts over time. Those parties that garnered substantial votes were associated with particular *aliran*, but the votes of each *aliran* were more divided, and the proportion of the population each represented had changed (Budiman 1999: 12–15; see also Sherlock 2004: 17–20). *Abangan* voters chose PDI-P or Golkar; urban *santri* were divided among PAN (given the Muhammadiyah connection), Golkar (for its links with ICMI), or the PPP; and rural *santri* voted for PKB or the PPP. Over time, the *abangan* vote has increased, while religious votes—urban and rural *santri* as well as Protestant and Catholic[23]—have declined. So, for instance, PDI-P was attacked by some Muslim forces as un-Islamic since it is led by a woman and ran so many Christian candidates, but it still won a plurality of the votes in a population that is about 90 percent Muslim (Budiman 1999: 15). Ken Young, however, insists that the old *aliran* politics could not really manifest itself in the more urban, mobile, educated society of 1999. Contemporary Indonesians are less easily segregated into communal groups based on religious and cultural symbolism, not least because they are no longer so tied to mutually exclusive clusters of civil institutions and patronage networks as in the 1950s. Regardless, he concedes that if only because

Indonesians had a limited repertoire of symbols to deploy after so long a period of depoliticization, patterns of mobilization still tended to emphasize loyalties either to modernist Islam or to a traditionalist-nationalist alliance (Young 1999b: 80–81; see also Azyumardi 2000; Sherlock 2004).

The political clout of the military represented another point of continuity with the past. First, as of 1999, *dwifungsi* had not been abolished, although the military's parliamentary seats had been reduced and the armed forces had officially taken a back seat to civilian leaders—not least because their legitimacy had plummeted as the extent of their human rights violations under the New Order came to light. The military, now called Tentara Nasional Indonesia (TNI, Indonesian National Forces) instead of ABRI, was still granted about 5 percent of the seats in the MPR (phased out by 2004), along with whatever seats ex-generals and other TNI sympathizers gained by standing for election. Wiranto remained strong after Soeharto's fall—he was even Golkar's candidate for president in 2004.

Second, factionalism in the military could still have dramatic political repercussions. Such disputes were significant both to the fall of Soeharto and to the configuration of forces left in his wake. Soeharto and elements of the military had been in conflict over corruption, the professionalism of the military, and the armed forces' role in political processes. To counter the influence of ABRI and especially of particular leaders, Soeharto courted the Islamic community from the late 1980s on, but ABRI found ways of striking back to assert its influence.[24] Crucially, while the pro-Soeharto "green" faction of the military opposed the protests against the government that began with the economic crisis, the nationalist *merah-putih* (red and white) group led by Wiranto was far more lenient. The latter group remained strong as Soeharto's position crumbled.

Even with the 2002 constitutional amendments, the military may retain a decisive role. Fears of such an eventuality mounted with Abdurrahman Wahid's ouster and the unpracticed and comparatively pro-military Megawati's coming to power. The ongoing violent outbreaks in several regions may be used to validate a continued strong military presence if a civilian regime cannot maintain support or restore calm. This role is stated explicitly by Wiranto himself, who claims to support democracy but still sees a role for the military: "Reformasi can be lost. It can lead to national disintegration. Then reformasi would bring nothing to this country but disaster and national demise. In this case, the military has a constitutional duty to avoid this" (quoted in Kafil 2003). The military drew legitimacy in the past from its role in nationalist struggles and in upholding the unity and territorial integrity of the nation. Reports

since the Reformasi era have accused the military of stirring up trouble—
implicating the TNI in everything from bomb blasts in Jakarta to the
killing of UN aid workers in East Timor to the failure to establish a stable peace agreement in Aceh to self-proclaimed jihad vigilante groups.
Such shenanigans were purportedly intended to embarrass the government, stir rivalries within the armed forces, and ensure the continued
need for a strong security presence.[25] A particularly blatant display came
when military tanks aimed their cannon at the presidential palace. It was
then that Abdurrahman Wahid, already impeached by the MPR, knew he
really was obliged to step down (Budiman 2001). Previously, he had tried
and failed to get his security minister and armed forces chief to declare a
state of emergency. When they refused, Abdurrahman, as the commander
in chief, called a state of emergency anyway—but the military, reportedly
distressed at the president's attempts to reform the armed forces, turned
on him. The military could thus take some credit for installing Megawati,
even though the legislature actually appointed her (McGirk 2001). In
other words, then, while curbing *dwifungsi* was a central demand among
reformist students, the TNI still carries enormous political potency, even
with a sharply curtailed institutional role.

Compounding these elements of institutional stickiness as Indonesia
emerged from the New Order was the continuing difficulty of forging
popular consensus for reform, either from the top down or from the
ground up. Not only did the cleavages that rived the opposition in 1998
remain problematic, but mass political attitudes and behavior did not immediately assume a more democratic orientation. The media personality
Wimar Witoelar, for instance, lamented in 2000 that, while popular perceptions of politics had changed since Soeharto's fall, largely because of
the changing bias of the media and the "critical faculties of public institutions," public behavior had been slower to shift. In the same vein,
"stated objectives" and "expressed values" had altered, but programs
and institutional behavior had not kept pace, perhaps because only top
leaders (particularly elected ones), and not the bulk of the bureaucracy,
had changed. Overall, he suggested, "the system has not changed, and
where it has, there are not enough people to drive reform through the
new systems." Wimar pessimistically concluded that with so little real reform achieved, and with the economy still in such poor shape, Indonesia
might be "better off formally" in a political sense but that its political
culture was on the wane (Wimar 2000: 2). Dewi Fortuna Anwar (2001:
15) was somewhat more optimistic, implying that development of a more
democratic political culture may come with experience; in the short term,
"to both the political elites and their followers political freedom to some
extent is translated as the freedom to mobilize masses and intimidate op-

ponents," even if with a personalistic or unusually apocryphal bent. An amusing example of the persistence of less than democratic tendencies is offered in one woman's response when she was asked her views on Wiranto's record of human rights abuses and misuse of funds. (The general has had some success over the past few years in a side career as a recording artist.) She replied: "I do not know about those kinds of things. What I do know is that he is a general and he can sing very well. He had a good voice and I like his singing" (quoted in Kafil 2003). However, these tendencies can change over time, and the constitutional revisions of 2002 aim to escalate a shift toward genuinely popular sovereignty and democratic political culture.

In fact, political culture—especially as embodied in relative endowments of coalitional capital—was probably at the root of Indonesia's failure to progress more rapidly with more constructive elements of Reformasi. A key factor distinguishing Indonesia's experience from Malaysia's was the much higher level of suspicion and relative lack of cooperative effort across sectors of civil society (students, NGOs, labor, and so on) over the years, due largely to the more repressive policies and record of brutality of the Indonesian state. For instance, the New Order regime implemented corporatist measures to organize society into functional groups (students, workers, peasants, and so on) and then to create or coopt the chief institutions for articulation of these groups' interests (Eklöf 1999: 7–8). Echoes of these efforts could be found in the segregation of constituencies active in the Reformasi movement. Boudreau (1999: 11) suggests that a striking feature of the protests in Indonesia through early 1998 was "their isolation from one another" and attributes this fragmentation to "long-standing New Order prohibitions on political dissent and organization . . . for aggrieved populations had little political connection with one another that might help coordinate their activity." Moreover, historical experience has given rise to some elements of Indonesian civil society that are anything but civil and "have little or no place at all in any serious democratization project" (Hadiz 2000). Hadiz cites in particular paramilitary groups, which are often linked with political parties and mass organizations and represent the latest manifestation of New Order–era systems of power and patronage.

Hence, whereas Malaysian CSAs and political parties were comparatively well poised to establish a sturdy, encompassing coalition by the late 1990s and saw electoral contestation as a clear and reasonable option, their Indonesian counterparts were more fragmented at the level of ideas as well as at the level of approaches. In Indonesia, parties and activists alike were hard pressed to find common ground, in terms of preferred strategies or objectives, sufficient for them really to work in concert.

Coalitional possibilities—designed to include CSAs as well as political parties—were broached especially from CSAs, whether these possibilities were embodied in Amien Rais's attempts to unite factions or in students' bringing together the Ciganjur Four to enunciate a common program and electoral strategy. However, these initiatives failed to generate real consensus or to produce a truly functional opposition alliance. Student protesters could highlight the irrationalities and pathologies of authoritarian rule, but they could not alone undercut its legacy enough to entrench more liberal attitudes and approaches, even if their protests were dramatically effective in speeding Soeharto out of office. In the meantime, the continued potency of the very sort of institutions against which Reformasi agitators struggled made real reform slow and generally top-down rather than driven by grassroots priorities—even if, by now, significant reform has clearly taken place at both the institutional and the cultural level.

The Challenge of Building a Coalition for Reform

The fragmentation and weak organization of Indonesian student groups, opposition parties, and other sorts of associations under electoral authoritarianism were at the heart of why *reformasi total* did not occur upon Soeharto's fall (Hadiz 1999). Well in advance of the dramatic events of the Reformasi era, Heryanto posited that only extreme government repression could unite the opposition, even if the situation were otherwise generally conducive to liberalization. He argued, "Not only have religious, gender, or ethnic differences been obstacles to the formation of a political alliance, but tensions between passionate student activists and NGOs, and rivalries among fellow activists, have impeded attempts towards a more collaborative oppositional effort" (Heryanto 1996: 249).

Preeminent among the difficulties of forging a common consensus on the aims and strategies of Reformasi among Indonesian activists—beyond the specter of Soeharto as a common foe—was the diversity of organizational types and actors involved with the fast-breaking movement, particularly given the previous proscription on open, broad-based collective action. Students were concerned to maintain their "purity," elites competed for dominance, and regions or groups organized around non-negotiable demands. These elements could unite on the streets to demonstrate for specific goals, but they had a much harder time articulating a larger picture or assembling a coherent replacement for the New Order they so vehemently toppled. In Malaysia, a reasonably firm reformist coalition formed and agreed upon an agenda before the 1999 elections.

In contrast, such programmatic cross-party alliances remained fuzzy in Indonesia, at least until some time after the polls. This persistent ambiguity was largely due to the structure of the New Order regime, which complicated the development of coalitional capital. Unlike in Malaysia, Indonesia's electoral system was in flux throughout the election period, parties had to organize in haste and campaign almost immediately, and many of the groups involved lacked recent experience in coalition building. As a result, the outcome of the elections could not have been predicted, and what alliances did form tended to be more overtly opportunistic or strategic rather than ideological and formed for the long term.

Too Many Factions, Not Enough Time

Indonesia's *gerakan Reformasi* encompassed students, NGOs, mass Islamic organizations, critical political parties, labor unions, factions of the military, prominent individuals, and more, but it never really evolved into a workable coalition. Over the years, influence and assets—human and financial resources, access to policymakers, and popular legitimacy—have shifted among these sectors. The links among sectors have also shifted, with students, for instance, sometimes working in isolation and at other times collaborating variously with NGOs, mass organizations, labor, opposition parties, the military, the middle class, and the urban poor. However, the New Order regime discouraged linkages across sectors. For example, the government allowed students to be politically engaged only on campuses and attempted to restrict workers' activism to one state-sanctioned labor federation rather than allowing access to an NGO-supported alternative. Mutual suspicion simmered in such a climate. Students accused middle-class NGOs of complicity with the government, NGOs accused students of naïveté and inflexibility, prominent activists charged one another with self-aggrandizement, and so on. The Reformasi period and the years preceding it saw several attempts to build coalitions uniting portions of civil society as well as reformist parties, but these efforts never really took root.

Under the New Order, different sections of Indonesian civil society developed the habit of being cautious about working in concert. Negotiating ways to collaborate for Reformasi was thus tricky—and time was scarce. Part of the difficulty of coalition building in Indonesia was the speed with which events unfolded. For instance, in the Philippines an underground movement against the regime developed over decades, and then activists spent several years above ground networking and settling ideological decisions. In other words, the various groups involved had a chance to sort out whether they could work together, what tactics were acceptable, and whether to use violence. In Indonesia, by contrast, students never wanted to be too closely linked with labor (which was relatively weak and divided anyway); the rest of civil society was fractured among elitist urban NGOs, New Order institutions, professional associations, and mass Islamic organizations (which in turn did little to forge links with each other), and there just was not enough time for careful strategizing.[26]

Students' Fear of Entangling Alliances

At the crux of the problem of building a coalition were students. For them, joining forces with NGOs, the urban poor, labor, the middle class, or any other group carried ideological as well as strategic implications. As described earlier, students have historically been a pivotal force in Indonesian protest politics, being at the heart of movements against the Dutch, Soekarno, and Soeharto.[27] While far from monolithic in organization or ideology, student activists share a common conception of themselves as morally uncorrupt and as carrying on a tradition of student protest developed inside and outside Indonesia.[28] However, in the Reformasi period, aside from significant disagreements over the aims of agitation, students (and other activists) never seemed to surmount their initial problem of being "better at shouting slogans than articulating clear-cut plans for reform" (Cohen 1998a: 22). The student movement therefore played a more destructive than proactively constructive role in reform.

Though consistently politically engaged to at least some extent, the student movement has intermittently allied with the government or other social groups. From 1950 to 1965, students' political life was dominated by large, polarized national student organizations linked with political parties representing nationalist, communist, pro-military, and religious factions. After the assault on the left in 1965, the influential Kesatuan Aksi Mahasiswa Indonesia (KAMI, Indonesian Students' Action Union) formed on the initiative of the education minister. Active especially in Jakarta and Bandung and protected by military allies, KAMI helped lead a student movement against communism and leftism (especially the PKI and Soekarno). The body held influential public seminars, produced publications, and organized mass street protests of high school and university students in late 1965 and 1966. The students involved dubbed themselves the *Angkatan '66* (Generation of '66) and claimed a central role in championing the poor and creating the New Order. At this stage in the movement, though, "themes of modernisation, development and stability were emphasised more than concepts of democracy or popular participation," and the students' collaboration with the military helped legitimate ABRI's interference in politics (Aspinall 1993: 5).

Students of the 1970s were influenced by the example of Angkatan '66, sharing with their predecessors both an emphasis on issues such as corruption and better administration and a sense of religious and moral character. They demanded regularization and reform but did not present a comprehensive alternative. Thanks to this legacy, students were somewhat constrained in their criticism of the government. They felt that it had gone off course but had not been not ill conceived from the outset. However, while in 1973 students had collaborated to some extent with discontented groups within the political elite, by 1977 few wanted to seek elite support, stressing instead that student activism was "pure" and a *kekuatan moral* (moral force). Students also emphasized their anticommunism, including arguments against mobilization of the poor, and were somewhat ambivalent toward the military. By the late 1970s, students had turned firmly against the regime, adopting more confrontational tactics and sharper, structural critiques (Aspinall 1993: 8).

Faced with limitations on campus activism, many students sought out alternative political channels in the 1980s, including study groups (*kelompok studi*) and off-campus NGOs focused on such issues as human rights and the environment. These NGOs were oriented increasingly toward mobilization rather than toward development. Student groups also formed to work on projects in poor communities, fostering ties with the broader community and leading more students to involve themselves with protests over such issues as land disputes and poverty. Students in Jakarta and Yogyakarta met with NGOs and accepted funds from them,[29] but many were disillusioned with the increasing bureaucratization of NGOs and their gradualist, moderate, nonconfrontational approach. As a result, a section of the student movement was opposed to cooperation with NGOs and other middle-class opposition groups.

Subsequently, the most visible venues for student criticism were *kelompok studi* and *kelompok diskusi* (discussion groups) (Muridan et al. 1999). These really took off around 1982 and 1983 on campuses in Jakarta, Yogyakarta, Bandung, and Salatiga. Most involved fewer than twenty students, some of whom were involved with more than one group. The students studied social, economic, and political thinkers and ideas as well as the experiences of democratic forces in Latin America, China, and the Philippines. The groups were generally informal and transient but linked students across campuses to host discussion forums, publish books, and more. Moreover, student activists in Yogyakarta, at least, many of whom were from *pesantren* (Islamic schools), brought some radical changes and discourses to the massive Islamic NU. PKB, which grew out of the NU, benefited from these progressive currents and from the participation of young intellectuals keen to find a new paradigm for politics.[30]

Students in study groups were generally insular in their approach, focusing on "information action" and on raising awareness rather than on mass action. The groups roundly criticized their predecessors, especially former activists who had joined the government. By 1993–1994, some activists, including other students, had begun to critique the intellectualism and "involution" of study groups and their lack of progress, organization, and clear ideology. The groups did invite some outside input, however. Former study group leader Muridan Widjojo, for instance, invited Kwik Kian Gie, Laksamana Sukardi, and other influential figures to meet with students, and some groups became involved in social and political action or NGO-style community development. Still, their main contribution was in developing a radical critique of Indonesian politics, society, and economy that figured prominently in later protests.[31]

At the same time, after a period of relative quiet, more aggressive student activism reemerged in the late 1980s, with nearly daily demonstrations in much of 1989 and 1990. Some students at that time saw the aim of political activity as raising awareness, while others saw it as struggle or resistance. For the most part, though, student protest in the 1980s was radical in orientation (sometimes belittling any strategies other than mass action, even if less confrontational tactics were tried); hostile to the military, capitalism, and elites; and convinced of the need for structural change. While there were some students amenable to cooperation with at least discontented government elites, most strongly rejected it, especially given the failure of the government to respond to student demands. All the same, as Aspinall posits (1993: 17), "it is clear that elite rivalry and an atmosphere of somewhat greater openness created a political space in which student activists could operate and express discontent." In fact, some military and government officials were somewhat encouraging of students' protests and even helped them by not enforcing regulations too strictly.

The dominant theme of student protest in the decade was concern for the rakyat, shown in criticism of development strategies that neglected the poor as well as in hostility toward the rich and (especially capitalist) elite. Students collaborated directly with the rural and urban poor in social and political action in the 1980s—for instance, by escorting community members to and from demonstrations. Such cooperation had not happened in any sustained, systematic way in the 1960s or 1970s. Increased middle-class prosperity by the 1980s had put persistent poverty in sharper relief, encouraging a sense of social responsibility and the need to promote social justice among parts of the middle class, including students. Journalists, artists, lawyers, academics, and NGO activists—much of the urban middle class—were involved in these initiatives as well.

Still, students and their fellow activists were divided in their attitudes toward the poor. Some students (especially those linked with NGOs) tended to see the poor as objects of sympathy, in need of guidance and inspiration, rather than as equals. Winters (2001, n.p.) asserts bluntly, "Students never wanted to involve the *rakyat* in their movement. The group that considers itself, by definition, by character, and by outlook, to be closest to the *rakyat* actually fears the people, or views them as 'stupid' or 'uneducated.'" Hence the bulk of students lacked any strong ties with the people for whom they claimed to speak. Others, however— especially students influenced by lessons from the Philippines and South Korea—saw the *rakyat* as an independent, potentially decisive force for change. Regardless of the genesis of support, "peasants in remote areas and urban workers in poverty-stricken neighbourhoods [were] increasingly aware of the importance of support, however imperfect, from urban middle-class activists in its various forms: journalistic and human rights reports, nongovernmental training, litigation in court, academic seminars, and artistic works" (Heryanto 1996: 263–64). Still, these links were not systematic or well-coordinated but were "*ad hoc,* fragmented, short-lived, and clandestine," constrained by state surveillance and intimidation, "mutually suspicious," and oriented more toward pursuing short-term political and economic interests than toward forging new alliances (Heryanto 1996: 264).

Other themes also colored student discourse during this period. Among these was a strong nationalist current, expressed, for instance, in criticism of the role of foreign capital in the economy, or in portrayals of the movement as part of a historical tradition of student protest that had begun in the colonial era. Islamic as well as Christian[32] themes played a role, too, though religion (particularly Islam) was less central than in the 1960s or 1970s. Also, as had been the case previously, much of the movement's discourse maintained a strong moral tone, emphasizing the honesty, integrity, and purity of students. Most protests centered on off-campus issues, such as land disputes, antimilitarism, human rights, democracy, and repression. Others, though, were about such campus issues as mismanagement of universities or repression of activists. Taboo topics, such as human rights violations in East Timor, mysterious killings, and the real genesis of the New Order, were increasingly raised, too. Most of the protests were still in Java, especially in Bandung and Yogyakarta, and were organized by smaller groups than had been active in the 1970s. However, larger and more stable organizational forms had emerged by the end of the 1980s. Aware that they were under military surveillance, students avoided centralized leadership and kept groups small and fluid to avoid being readily quashed, even when they banded together in the Solidaritas Mahasiswa Indonesia untuk Demokrasi (Indonesian Students' Solidarity for Democracy) or traveled between campuses for demonstrations.

By the late 1990s, students were well positioned to play a central role in the Reformasi movement. They were concentrated in key urban areas, not weighed down by employment or family obligations, inclined toward critical thinking, and very much aware of their historical role. By that time, insistence that the movement not repeat its past collusion with the military discouraged students from allowing outside interference with the movement. All along, though, students remained polarized. Among the primary factions in the student movement at the time were leftists (reds), Islamists (greens), and independents, as well as hybrid groups (Bersihar and Mauluddin 1998; Winters 2001). Aspinall, dividing subsets of students by approach, identifies three primary, overlapping classes of student organizations active in 1998. The first was activist groups, which began forming in the late 1980s. Their most militant wing had been based around the PRD since the mid-1990s.[33] The second was student senates, composed largely of previously politically passive moderates. Criticized as co-opted and conservative by more activist students, these officially sanctioned bodies lent legitimacy and organizational resources to the movement once they joined the fray. The third group was Islamic students, some of whom had been won over by the rapprochement between the government and Islam in the early 1990s, and others of whom were among the most energetic campaigners for human rights and democracy. Despite the initial caution of some Islamic groups, they were able eventually to mobilize huge numbers of students, especially through formal or informal Islamic student fronts, some with the NU as linchpin (Aspinall 1999: 218–22).[34]

The debate over whether students should protest outside campuses and join with nonstudent masses during the Reformasi period was representative of students' hesitancy to risk being co-opted or otherwise sidetracked by alliances but also revealed a degree of elitism and internalized disarticulation from other sectors. More radical students felt it crucial to leave campus grounds and even saw value in clashing with security forces, while others advocated a more gradual progression. For instance, in strategizing for the massive demonstrations planned for May 19–20, 1998, the majority of students felt that inviting the urban population to join would lead to rioting. They voted to mobilize only students. A dissenting minority argued that the urban poor would join in anyway and considered rioting less likely if the political direction of protest were clear (Lane 1999: 243). At the same time, some sections of the student movement consistently rejected overtures from nonstudents, including the urban poor and workers, for fear of sullying the "purity" of their cause. This trepidation toward alliance, Hadiz suggests (1999: 111–12), showed how deeply students had internalized the New Order's fear of the mass politics of the poor and uneducated, and it stalled efforts at uniting disgruntled sections of society. Certain student groups, such as the large, loosely organized Forum Kota (City Forum, FORKOT), took special precautions to preserve their integrity, such as by changing leaders every week to avoid key individuals' co-optation or capture, or by shifting the group's command post from one group to another so that no member of the coalition could dominate (Charlé 1998).

Student activists' reluctance to form coalitions or organize more formally was at least partly a reflection of their internalization of Soeharto's "floating mass" policy, which encouraged Indonesians to place unity and development above involvement in the details of politics. The journalist Margot Cohen (1998b: 16, 18) sums up the students' dilemma:

Their numbers might be impressive and their mobilization is rapid, but as a movement Indonesia's students have yet to assume a cohesive form with coherent policy and direction. Students see themselves as foot soldiers of democracy, yet many activists show little taste for the conflicts and compromises inherent in a democratic system. They pride themselves on being a moral force suspended above the self-interest and infighting of politics, but it is precisely that amorphous nature that blunts the movement's effectiveness and threatens the prospects for popular, sweeping reforms. . . . While every movement has its share of tag-alongs, many students seem to revel in political obliviousness as a badge of moral purity.

Convinced of their own potency, students claimed full responsibility for Soeharto's resignation, giving little credit to activist organizations or turncoat elites. By late 1998, however, with Habibie in power, the military still playing a political role, and free elections still dubious, students saw little chance of maintaining a real political role (Cohen 1998b).

Doubts notwithstanding, students did at times ally with other Reformasi forces, if only to ensure their own influence. Indeed, Aspinall (1999: 232) points out that students constituted too small a portion of the population and were too vulnerable to suppression by the still-authoritarian government (as happened in the 1970s) to achieve their political goals alone. Students succeeded in mobilizing other groups in the months before Soeharto's resignation, and they earned widespread middle-class sympathy—not least because of their own primarily middle-class status. For instance, members of the Aliansi Jurnalis Independen (Alliance of Independent Journalists, AJI, many of them students themselves) instructed students in how to publish newsletters and convey ideas to a broader audience, while faculty members and rectors held teach-ins and joined student protests (Charlé 1998). Moreover, informal ties linked student and NGO activists, especially outside Jakarta. For example, local Lembaga Bantuan Hukum (LBH, Legal Aid Institute) offices served as drop-in centers for the casual sharing of ideas among students and other activists.[35] Fundamentally, too, even if many students eschewed formal coalitions, "their street actions drew wider groups into political action and half-enabled, half-forced more cautious opposition groups and leaders to harden their positions" (Aspinall 1999: 233). Such ties, if informal, were not always very friendly, productive, or trusting, though. Compounding the ingrained trepidation, after Soeharto's fall the rift between students and other civilian opposition forces widened as major sociopolitical forces turned to forming and consolidating political parties and preparing for elections while students still favored demonstrations (Aspinall 1999: 224–26).

By the late 1990s, though, Indonesian students had made some clear progress toward coalition building. Cohen (1998a) lists the most fundamental of these developments. First, protest activity brought together activists from across the religious spectrum—particularly important in light of the ethnic and religious animosity exhibited in many riots. Second, students and workers discussed joining forces and actually forged links, at least in Jakarta, Bandung, and Surabaya. Third, over time, students began to function more as a national movement rather than as desperate, disparate forces. For instance, a national student conference in Bogor in April 1998 came out with a common platform of deposing Soeharto and putting him on trial, demanding lower prices, and asserting that real economic reform requires far-reaching political change. These developments were facilitated both by a blossoming campus press and by coverage in mainstream media (partly thanks to many journalists' student activist roots). Moreover, student protest helped to transmit "the corrosive power of mockery" and "derision of the government" to the grassroots (Cohen 1998a: 24). Fourth, the nature of student protest—the fact that students graduate and move on—made a degree of networking virtually inevitable. Some students from study groups joined (and radicalized) NGOs upon graduation. Others became journalists or civil servants supportive of NGOs. Most maintained links with the student movement.[36]

The Contributions of NGOs

Despite the difficulties of forming and sustaining independent organizations under the New Order, Indonesia did have a wide array of NGOs, more commonly called *lembaga-lembaga swadaya masyarakat* (LSM, institutions for community self-reliance) or, for larger groups that nurture smaller ones, *lembaga-lembaga pengembangan swadaya masyarakat* (LPSM, institutions for developing community self-reliance). The term *organisasi non-pemerintah* (the literal translation of NGO) carried an antigovernment connotation and so was generally avoided, though some activists choose to use the term "NGO" to assert their autonomy (Eldridge 1996).[37] As of 1990, Indonesia had 600,000 to 800,000 NGOs, about half of them social welfare organizations, most local and community-based, and many linked with religious organizations. These groups built upon precolonial village institutions and late-colonial-era, upper-class Javanese nationalist and Westernizing organizations. Many were fostered by Muslim and Catholic institutions or overseas funding agencies (Walker 1996: 10–11).

As long as critics did not embarrass the government too much, form an institutionalized opposition, or adopt a verboten perspective (such as communism), they were generally tolerated under the New Order. While NGOs have a long history of community development and education work in Indonesia, as in Malaysia, their relevance to political or social change has come to be seen only more recently (Eldridge 1996). Still, NGO activity in the New Order period was "bound to raise the consciousness of the village population in Indonesia," even if that did not immediately "translate into community empowerment" (Walker 1996: 20). Eldridge (1996), however, cautions against exaggerating the political role and potential of NGOs too much, even if they help shape political debates. They lack the ideology, organization, and resources to function as independent political parties—and if they had those attributes, they would not be NGOs. Nonetheless, most Indonesians (66 percent) belong to some sort of civil societal organization (women's groups, religious groups, and the like) and over twice the proportion of members of organizations as nonmembers engage in political activity beyond voting. These data suggest significant stocks of social capital and strong links between civic engagement and other sorts of political participation in contemporary Indonesia (Asia Foundation 1999a: 112–14).[38] While some of this engagement is undoubtedly a post-transition phenomenon, such a high level of social organization could not develop in so short a time without a legacy of past involvement.

Rights-related NGO activism developed in stages in Indonesia. Kastorius Sinaga (2000) identifies several waves in this evolution. First, legal advocacy groups began to develop in the late 1970s, the most prominent of them the Jakarta-based but many-branched LBH.[39] These groups pursued both rights-based campaigns and litigation in the early 1980s. The second wave was the environmental movement, which gained strength in the mid-1980s both for its specific "green" goals and because the movement challenged a sector supported and protected by the New Order elite. The environmental movement was of particular significance because "during the New Order, when political expression was restricted, environmentalism was seen as an alternative avenue for dissent"; however, with increasing economic growth and zeal for more from the mid-1980s, the movement lost ground even as environmental resources diminished (Sarwono 2000: 206–7). The third wave emerged in the early 1990s and focused on the rights of women and labor, including child and migrant workers. A fourth stage began in the mid-1990s with the documentation and dissemination of information on human rights violations in Indonesia.

Indonesian NGOs gained strength, visibility, and stronger international and domestic connections through the 1990s. Though prohibited from engaging in "political activity," NGOs were at times allowed to participate in community development programs, including, for instance, World Bank–funded, government-run projects (Walker 1996). However, while many NGOs were relatively free from state intervention from the 1980s on, and while their activists had moral authority as well as local, national, and international ties, political parties as well as societal organizations lacked sufficient independence from the state to press in any significant way for democratization. Nonetheless, advocacy NGOs did forge alliances with students and international NGOs and sponsored forums on campuses on political reform, human rights, economic reform, democracy, and more (Syamsuddin 1997). Molyneux (2000) suggests that it was these nationwide coalitions that eventually formed the crux of the anti-Soeharto movement. He cites in particular the efforts of Indonesia Forum for the Environment (WALHI) to forge the Indonesian Work Forum in April 1998, bringing together key leaders such as Abdurrahman, Amien, Megawati, and Emil Salim, along with academics and community and NGO leaders, to develop ideas for political reform, enhance political education, and bridge student-military relationships. Still, as Syamsuddin (1997) concludes, genuine political reform would require both real changes to the political party system and more substantial networks among civil societal organizations and political parties.

Mobilizing against the Regime

Over time, some such networks did develop across the political opposition, but their progress was hindered significantly by government-imposed constraints. Aristides Katoppo (2000: 217–19), himself involved with NGOs since the 1970s, traces the evolution of nascent opposition efforts into more organized forms of protest: in the face of sometimes brutal suppression, minority groups formed *organisasi tanpa bentuk* (OTB, organizations without shape, or "phantom organizations") outside the gaze of the government; such microlevel activities continued on campuses, too, after Soeharto and the military had consolidated their power by the mid-1970s, presenting "networks of solidarity among the powerless" (217) that allowed leadership training and development of communication and management skills. While resistance to the government remained sporadic and fragmented at first, networking gradually increased, bringing a qualitative change in activism. Within the environmental movement, for instance, linkages developed among NGOs, extending also to academics, intellectuals, journalists, and even politicians (at least those out of power). An influx of students and graduates improved the quality of analysis and awareness of larger, structural issues.

Moreover, several pivotal events in the mid-1990s suggested a renaissance of genuine opposition and a decline in the government's hegemonic power. In 1994, for instance, six NGOs (unsuccessfully) filed suit against Soeharto regarding the reallocation of state funding for reforestation, and a private corporation filed a lawsuit against the banning of its news magazine, *TEMPO,* accompanying another suit filed on behalf of hundreds of readers.[40] Also, the government issued its most pro-market economic policy ever in mid-1994, hinting at a desperate political and economic situation and an urgent need of capital to fulfill growth targets, service the huge foreign debt, and cope with massive nonperforming loans.[41] Opposition to these policies came from economists and the business community, including the press. Around the same time, the official history of the 1965 coup was also being challenged, undercutting the government's foundational myth. The regime had built its initial legitimacy on a narrative of having stamped out a communist threat, and it downplayed or concealed its own role in the brutal violence of the period (Heryanto 1996: 253–55).[42]

Labor unrest also mounted in 1994, with hundreds of thousands of workers joining mass rallies against abuse of their rights. The biggest labor demonstrations in the regime's history occurred April 14–16 in and around Medan.[43] Labor disputes, strikes, and enormous rallies had also been held there and in other industrial centers (especially around Jakarta and Surabaya) since the early 1990s.[44] This time, civilian and military leaders said the mass rallies had turned violent and anti-Chinese, and that NGOs had manipulated the masses to demonstrate in PKI-like ways. Over sixty people were arrested and tried, including dozens of workers and key labor and NGO figures. Pressured to give only the official version of events, mass media distorted the issue into one of anti-Chinese sentiments rather than class conflict (Heryanto 1996: 256–57).

However, it was only in the late 1990s, with the relatively new area of election monitoring, that the products of all these prior waves of mobilization really started to come together. The Komite Independen Pemantau Pemilu (Independent Indonesian Election Monitoring Committee, KIPP) was formed in 1997, supplanting 1992's ineffective, corrupt, government-established monitoring body, Panwaslak. KIPP did little monitoring in its first year but helped forge links among NGOs (including between those in Jakarta and at the provincial and district levels), media, student organizations, and public opinion leaders. Kastorius (2000) explains that through KIPP, NGOs directed their efforts at improving the quality of elections and educating people about their political rights. In the process, they worked to improve the foundations of democracy and to enhance the political system overall. He suggests that, in contrast, NGOs' usual public policy advocacy may have proved largely fruitless. As in Malaysia, monitoring initiatives extended beyond the polls. KIPP Parlimen has worked to bring local-level groups together with members of Parliament, sponsored dialogues and radio shows in which politicians answer questions from villagers, and more.[45] A panoply of comparable "watch" groups proliferated after the elections, too, to fight authoritarianism in the bureaucracy, root out corruption, resist violence and militarism, and work for human rights. These groups have drawn in "extraordinary" numbers of "previously uninvolved teachers, workers, and journalists," who "are completely new to political activism . . . [and] have a much better perspective on democracy than those who just focused on Suharto" (Munir 2000: 5).

Also as in Malaysia, women's groups and activists proved particularly adept at organizing cooperation. Female NGO activists gathered with other women, including academics, artists, students, and workers, in May 1998 to plan a demonstration. They formed the Women's Coalition, later renamed the Coalition of Indonesian Women for Democracy and Justice (KPIDK). The coalition began in Jakarta but was quickly replicated elsewhere. Some of the coalition's demands were specifically gender-related, such as pressing for an end to discrimination and violence against women. Others among its calls were more generally pro-democratic, such as for a clean, transparent, fairly elected government; an end to *dwifungsi* and government-led violence; and the trial of Soeharto and his family and cronies. Representatives of the coalition expressed some of these demands at the MPR building itself when they joined students occupying the structure on May 19, 1998. The Women's Coalition also conducted research and voter education, convened forums with political parties, and lobbied for women's agendas in advance of the 1999 elections (Ruth 2001).

In other words, then, students and NGOs alike adjusted their repertoire of actions over the course of the decades preceding Reformasi, to capitalize upon democratic openings and to avoid undue repression, but were stymied in large part by habits and fears cultivated by New Order restrictions. In general, NGOs had not shied away from direct involvement either with the *rakyat* or with other categories of activists. Students had been more hesitant to ally with other sections of society. Hence, even when student groups and NGOs—and perhaps other clusters as well—addressed similar issues at similar times, their efforts were not always in concert. The public, too, did not always rally behind activists against the regime, even if they were sympathetic, not least for fear of aggressive retaliation by the government or paramilitary vigilantes. Also, however progressive their goals, students and NGOs were both at times ambivalent, or at least not confrontational, toward the government. The same was true of mass Islamic associations, public intellectuals, and other sorts of politically engaged actors and groups. These CSAs' different tactics and opportunities, in addition to a degree of mutual mistrust fostered by New Order policies—in other words, inadequate coalitional capital for coordination, plus coercive restraints upon the mobilization of what social capital was available—kept civil society and the rest of the opposition arena significantly splintered (see Hikam 1999).

Further Impediments to Coalition Building

Forging a united reformist coalition has never been an easy task in Indonesia, and lack of coalitional capital diminished the will to find a way around collective action dilemmas. Most obvious among these hurdles were and are ethnic, religious, and elite-level cleavages as well as the residue of New Order institutional arrangements. These factors continue to constrain the pace and scope of change. As the relative persistence of *aliran* voting suggests, societal cleavages run strong and deep through the country. Among the most salient are religious differences separating groups of Muslims, and separating Muslims from non-Muslims; ethnic differences, especially those marking the ethnic Chinese as "other"; and the distinction between Java/Bali and the "outer islands." Each of these constituencies presses distinctive claims. Many of the most significant of these demands are basically non-negotiable—for instance, demands for regional autonomy or secession, complete assimilation of non-Melayu ethnic groups, or a more Islamist polity.

As is the case in Malaysia, reform-minded Indonesians have shown a predilection for avoiding ethnic separatism. Ethnically charged riots in various parts of Indonesia have confirmed the real danger of chauvinistic tendencies,[46] but racial parties have yet to take root, and regional parties are precluded by electoral guidelines; parties must have support across most provinces to contest. As Jamie Mackie (1999) explains, Indonesia has always been wary of communal parties, given their implications for national unity. For instance, some contemporary Chinese Indonesians sought to establish their own party, comparable to the Partai Tionghua Indonesia (PTI, Chinese Indonesian Party) of the 1930s and 1940s. However, the attempt was disparaged by other ethnic Chinese as both retrograde and fruitless, since their community is too small to wield much influence if it pursues a policy of ethnic separateness. Also, while "assimilationist" versus "integrationist" arguments largely died out after the mid-1960s, Indonesian Chinese have been substantially integrated since then, with most having Indonesian citizenship, primary fluency in the Indonesian language, and so on. Still, some ethnic Chinese have advocated formation of a pressure group to lobby for Chinese rights and rally support from the transnational Chinese community (Heryanto 2001).

The political implications of Islamic revival since the 1970s could, as in Malaysia, ultimately intensify ethnic cleavages, at the same time deepening the rifts between sections of the Muslim community. Mobilized through Islamic associations, Muslims—especially young, middle-class *dakwah* activists—are seeing Islamic governance as a more viable political alternative than in the past, when Islam was promoted more as a cultural than a political force. For instance, the Islamic parties active in the 1950s and 1960s could not garner much support for an Islamic state (Jamhari 1999). By the late 1980s, however, Zifirdaus Adnan could identify a section of Indonesian society advocating a "formal link between Islamic ideology and the state," though this constituency was challenged not only by Christians and other non-Muslims but also by *abangan* and *santri* Muslims who prioritized the peace and unity of the nation and acknowledged no explicit Quranic injunction to establish an Islamic state. Regardless, his conclusion that "the struggle for a formal link between Islamic ideology and the state in Indonesia has come to an end with the legalisation of the *Pancasila* as a sole basis of the state [and of] political parties as well as [of] all socio-religious organisations" (Zifirdaus Adnan 1990: 466) was clearly premature.

The idea of an Islamic state was mooted at the time of independence with the Jakarta Charter, a brief statement in the draft constitution introducing *syariah* law for Muslims. Although the idea was defeated then, it has recently been resuscitated. Through the New Order period, as has happened under undemocratic regimes in other Muslim societies, "precisely because Islam was not merely a political movement, it was able to maintain its coherence and potential as a political force. And so, by the late 1970s, it appeared that Islam was developing as the most vocal and resilient voice of opposition" (Aspinall 1996: 221). With the growth of an educated Islamic middle class and the government's efforts to expand its base of support, Soeharto spearheaded a remarkable rapprochement with part of the Islamist community in the 1980s, shown in increasing appointments of orthodox Muslim officials and military officers, legal and administrative reforms, and the formation of ICMI in 1990 (Aspinall 1996: 235–36). Even so, very few parties today publicly advocate establishment of an Islamic state; most would be satisfied with an Islamic society and values (Arskal 1999). While Islamist discourse does seem to be gaining steam, as Amien Rais asserts, "the Islamic state has been put behind them by 95 percent of Muslim leaders and also the rank and file. . . . The concept of an Islamic state in Indonesia has not been an issue at all since Soeharto's downfall" (Amien 1999: 201). The 2002 constitutional amendments make reintroduction of the Jakarta Charter even less likely, given new requirements for amending the constitution—and parties who raised the issue in 2002 withdrew it before the motion came to a vote (Ellis 2002; Schuman 2003).

Young and educated Muslims now fear sectarian politics based on religion less than their predecessors did. Indeed, surveying the progress of political Islam thus far, Greg Fealy (2001a) proposes that moderate Islamic parties stand a good chance of success in future elections. In contrast to 1955, however, parties advocating Islamic statehood enjoy only limited support. An August 2003 survey found that, of the one-half of Muslim respondents who labeled themselves "devout," 51 percent would support "secular, nationalist-oriented parties" and only 21 percent would vote for parties advocating implementation of *syariah*. Among self-identified "secular" Muslims, support for Islamist parties was even lower (Kurniawan 2003).

The possibility remains that political Islam could develop further, leaving political consensus ever more elusive—even Islamic parties have found cooperation difficult among themselves, let alone with secular counterparts (Fealy 2001a). When Habibie ended the three-party system, permitting the proliferation of new parties, he also abolished the requirement that all organizations be premised upon the nonsectarian *Pancasila*. There were 40 Islamic parties among the 141 registered ahead of the June 1999 elections; several adopted Islam rather than the *Pancasila* as their ideological basis. Still, three decades of authoritarian rule suppressed demands for *syariah* law, and mass Islamic organizations like the NU and

Muhammadiyah have promoted more moderate, pluralist thinking and have stressed that democracy and Islam are compatible and that an Islamic state is not necessary (Kurniawan 2003). Also, competition for power among Muslim leaders, as Azyumardi Azra suggests, will keep the Islamic camp fragmented, with each section of the movement trying to promote its own interests. He concludes, cynically, "In short, the agenda of Islamic parties in the post-Soeharto era appears to be centred, not on Islamic ideology, but on power politics" (Azyumardi 2000: 314).

The threat of extremist Islamist violence since then—especially as linked with Jemaah Islamiah (JI) and embodied in the bombings in Bali in October 2002 and in Jakarta in August 2003 and September 2004—has also spurred Megawati's government to crack down on more radical groups. Most important, Islamist groups now have the option of working within democratic processes, which generally has a moderating effect, as exemplified most clearly by Amien Rais and PAN. As Amien himself asserts, "Political parties based on religion don't have a promising future [in Indonesia]. There is a difference between piety and politics" (quoted in Schuman 2003). He instead advocates a philosophy of pluralism and centrism among Indonesia's range of Islamist and secular factions. Even a representative of Partai Keadilan (Justice Party, PK), the Indonesian party most similar to Malaysia's PAS, explains of the adoption of Islamic law: "These things are very traumatic to most Indonesians. [An Islamic state] is very, very far away" (quoted in Schuman 2003).

Islam also had an impact on the negotiation of gender roles in the context of Reformasi in both Malaysia and Indonesia. To some extent, these debates were more about specific leaders than about broader principles. The question of whether a woman could lead a Muslim-majority state became critical with the rise of Megawati in Indonesia and Wan Azizah in Malaysia.[47] Ironically, though, neither of these women styled herself as any sort of feminist leader or gave much attention to women's issues—to the distress of activist women in Indonesia (Blackburn 1999a: 87). In Indonesia, the NU and PKB were relatively flexible regarding women (although the sentiments of the NU's mass base were hard to gauge), perhaps reflecting Abdurrahman's friendly relationship with Megawati.[48] Parties from the modernist stream, such as PAN, Partai Bulan Bintang (Moon and Star Party, PBB), and PK, expressed doubts about Megawati's leadership capabilities and PDI-P's commitment to reform. Megawati faced theological objections to her Islamic credentials and leadership as well. The Kongres Umat Islam Indonesia (Congress of the Indonesian Islamic Community, KUII) ruled in 1998 that the president and vice president should be Muslim men. Islamists argued that the leader of a Muslim state leads both nation and religion, and Muslim women cannot be religious leaders. Others added that, according to Islam, women have weaknesses that prevent their being more than "companions" of men. The women's wings of both the NU and Muhammadiyah voiced their support of allowing capable and qualified women to serve as national leaders, but without specific reference to Megawati.[49] In other words, there were two approaches to this debate: a contextual discussion of theological sources, and a "pragmatic and interest-driven approach, using the sources to achieve political goals" (Platzdasch 2000: 338). However, the debate itself suggests the greater accessibility of politicized Islam in Indonesia post-Reformasi, even if its appeal is partly personalistic or instrumental.

As of the 1999 elections, however, the efforts of Islamic parties to form a coalition indicated that cleavages among Islamic parties and groups remained about as salient as between Islamic and non-Islamic groups. Amid negotiations to select a president, eight Muslim parties[50] did overcome their differences to organize a *poros tengah* (central axis). The coalition, initiated by Amien Rais, nominated Abdurrahman Wahid as its candidate for president. Creation of this bloc shifted the balance of power enough to keep Megawati out of the presidency (and had she become president then, Megawati would have been indebted to the coalition). However, the *poros tengah* grew less active once Abdurrahman came to power, and eventually Megawati succeeded him anyway (Azyumardi 2000: 316–17; Young 1999a: 7).

Divisions among elites have also been especially salient in Indonesia. The key leaders of the Reformasi movement did not all get along, which hindered coalition building. At the same time, cracks in the ruling elite provided an important catalyst for the movement by signaling an opportunity for change. Openings created by increasing factionalism in the government advantaged reformists; thus students could count on the support of anti-Soeharto sections of ABRI, for instance, and feel less threatened by the military. All the same, the new alliances were basically opportunistic. For example, while factional disputes in the military and the engagement with reformists of powerful individuals like Wiranto were critical, activists did not quite trust the military, and so they remained hesitant to rely upon or work with them too closely. In the same vein, personality clashes and power struggles seriously impaired attempts to build a coalition among Reformasi elites. Most notably, Abdurrahman Wahid and Amien Rais had a history of not getting along, and both were more than willing to be in charge. Thus it was hardly surprising that forging an alliance between their factions was difficult or, for that matter, that Amien was quick to call for Abdurrahman's ouster and to offer to step in as vice president in a Megawati administration ("Top Indonesian Legislator" 2000).

At the same time, characteristics of the state and the economy frustrate real liberalization. Certainly, the armed forces have lost much political legitimacy since the late 1990s. ABRI's reputation reached its nadir when security forces fired on students demonstrating at the MPR in November 1998, killing several. Soldiers grew ever more demoralized and confused about their role. It was various NGOs that did most of the work in bringing military human rights abuses to light and publicizing them, forcing the government to take these issues seriously and to investigate further. The relaxation of restrictions on the mass media unleashed a torrent of criticism of ABRI's past abuses (Crouch 1999; Bourchier 1999). Aside from personal attacks on specific military leaders, the press discussed evidence of the military's role in "disappearances," rapes, and summary executions; in brutal acts in places like Irian Jaya, Aceh, and East Timor; and possibly in stirring up recent riots.

Besieged, the armed forces promised to limit their political role. Wiranto announced a "new paradigm" for ABRI in July 1998 under which the armed forces would no longer be so much in the forefront, would wield less direct influence, and would be ready to share political influence with other sectors (Crouch 1999). However, progress toward implementing this paradigm proved slow, not least because many officers' interests were tied to the old system. Moreover, even with the military's seats eliminated from the MPR as of 2004, the military retains a foothold. Retired ABRI officers are involved not just with Golkar but also with PDI-P, PAN, and the PPP, and so they may find their way into the legislature regardless. Moreover, large numbers of military officers have long staffed the bureaucracy and positions of civilian authority, and military appointments continued to be made even after the transition (Crouch 1999). Indeed, as Bourchier elaborates (1999: 166), "the continuing influence of the military in political life is evident in the language its leaders use. Reforms are depicted as 'concessions', while new freedoms of expression and organisation are often presented as examples of the military's 'tolerance.'" In other words, while significantly and increasingly disempowered, the military still holds a degree of political sway.

Much the same can be said of the bureaucracy, which has been slow to change in personnel or organization since the New Order. While renewal is inevitable over time, bureaucratic reforms have been difficult and slow. Moreover, since the bureaucracy is largely a holdover from Golkar's glory days and still wields enormous clout, especially outside urban areas, it will continue to distort electoral outcomes and impede popular conscientization for some time. Golkar's surprisingly strong showing in the 1999 elections may be attributed to its retaining not just a nationwide organization and effective political machinery but also to control of the state bureaucracy and to plenty of money for various forms of vote buying. In particular, people outside Java and the big cities were less aware of Reformasi and still feared the Golkar-linked local bureaucracy and military (Budiman 1999: 15–17).[51]

The extent and persistence of Indonesia's economic problems and territorial instability, too, may have an disabling impact on political reform. Economic recession helped get the Reformasi movement going by highlighting the inadequacies of Soeharto's government. However, the overwhelming urgency of economic needs, not to mention the fierce primacy of separatist demands (which are linked with economic concerns in the resource-rich areas of Aceh and Irian Jaya), leave the new regime similarly vulnerable. Defense Minister Juwono Sudarsono put this point bluntly, insisting that only 10 percent of Indonesians "can afford to be involved in democracy," while the rest "are involved in the day-to-day grind of trying to find the next plate of food" ("Indonesian Defense Minister" 2000). Indonesia's economy has been maintaining macroeconomic stability and modest growth—slightly under 4 percent in 2002 and 2003—but "fiscal and corporate debt, unemployment, security and corruption, and a lack of government will to do anything about them," have limited foreign investment and consumer confidence and continue to confound the country's future prospects (Guerin 2003). Continuing political uncertainty, especially given sporadic incidents of extremist violence, is a major factor in the lack of further investment and growth. A lack of growth in turn feeds back into political uncertainty, since economic demands could leave political reforms unstable. Furthermore, despite these reforms, Indonesia still ranks as one of the world's most corrupt nations, with an investment climate comparable to that of "poorer African countries" (Guerin 2003).

Fundamentally, too, while a more pro-democratic—or at least antiautocratic—political culture seems to be spreading and should be furthered with the augmentation of direct elections in 2004, it is hard to gauge the internalization of such norms at the grassroots, especially outside urban areas. For instance, Hans Antlöv[52] suggests that the new political parties found it hard to grow roots downward or spread into villages. He proposes that after so long a period of depoliticization, people remained less politicized and partisan post-Reformasi than in the 1950s. This tendency was hardly challenged by the reluctance of most parties (except perhaps PAN) to focus on issues during the 1999 election campaign or to significantly revise their structure, ideology, or policies. The same phenomenon marked the 2004 parliamentary and presidential polls (see, for instance, Sherlock 2004). These trends point to the possibility of only shallow democratization, with limited change in terms of style or political orientation either at the mass or at the elite level.

Public opinion data support the idea that Indonesia faced an uphill battle to consolidate democracy after Soeharto's fall. A nationwide survey carried out between December 1998 and January 1999 found that most Indonesians, especially from among more advantaged groups of citizens, were optimistic about the future, were interested in fair elections, and planned to vote. Nonetheless, many were "unfamiliar with many of the basic tenets of democracy," from not knowing how to vote to being unsure about whether the 1999 elections would actually be any more meaningful or fair than those of the past (Asia Foundation 1999b: 5–8). Even after the elections, while most Indonesians (more than in the prior survey) felt that the country was heading in the right direction, that the elections had been free and fair, and that things were improving, most still did not feel that they could influence government decisions. It is important to note as well that although more respondents than before saw some possible impact for democracy on their personal lives, the general level of interest in or discussion about politics remained relatively low, probably as a legacy of long-term depoliticization under authoritarian rule (Asia Foundation 1999a).

The Role of Civil Society Agents in Indonesian Reform Processes

What is new about the NGOs that have been active in Indonesia and Malaysia since the 1970s is that they are "self-consciously non-governmental, connoting specifically a choice to organize, and to insist upon the legitimacy of organizing, outside the safe circle of public authority. Their very existence raises an argument against the assumption that the state alone is properly responsible for all political and social action" (Lev 1990: 151). This challenge in particular informed dissent in Indonesia and encouraged civil society associations to extend their aims and audience ever further. It also validated the efforts of extralegal parties, such as the PRD and PDI-P, to organize outside the space granted by the New Order state. However, the primary focus and venue of politics in Indonesia remains the formal structures of electoral politics: political parties (especially now that restrictions on them have been relaxed), the institutions of the state, and positions of leadership. While CSAs played a pivotal role in opposing the ancien régime, they have retained little institutionalized clout since then except as monitors and petitioners. They have been overridden by parties when the aims of both are not in accord, and they still resort mainly to the same sort of transgressive tactics— demonstrations, petitions, and the like—as previously.[53]

Post-transition, Indonesia's leading political parties continue to behave much as parties did under the New Order. They remain strongly personalized and centralized, with limited internal democracy. The parties held over from the New Order have done relatively little to change their image, nor have they ever been more than basically moderate with regard to reform, at least compared with the consensus position among students. Moreover, the results of the June 1999 popular vote were hardly reflected in the resultant slate of leaders. Despite having won a plurality of votes, PDI-P initially failed to secure the presidency or more than a token (and, it turned out, ephemeral) number of cabinet positions, although Megawati did eventually succeed Abdurrahman as head of state.[54] In consequence, disillusionment and frustration with the political parties on offer, and with institutions of government more broadly, continued after the polls.[55] Furthermore, the sixty-five social group seats in the MPR were not readily suited to the institutionalization of influence for social activists and their issues. Not only did those seats retain a reputation of being more to enforce government-led corporatism than to empower independent voices, many activists also remained wary of "dirtying" themselves in politics. Indeed, when political parties desperate for good candidates did their best to recruit NGO activists and academics to stand for office in 1999, not all that many joined.[56]

In Indonesia as in Malaysia, it is in public education, awareness raising, and discourse that CSAs may have a particularly strong impact on reform processes. Thus, for instance, elements from civil society will likely continue to play a role alongside parties as a conduit for the transnational spread of reform-supporting ideas into the local context. Demonstration effects from elsewhere, such as mass uprisings or student activism, especially in South Korea, the Philippines, China, and Burma, have caused a reaction in Indonesia. These examples have spread both the notion that change is possible and specific lessons—and not just liberal ideas from the west (Uhlin 1997: 239–41). Anders Uhlin traces these effects to links among "like-minded activists and organizations abroad" that cooperate with different sectors of the Indonesian pro-democracy movement, supported by the latest in communications technology. Also of help is the expansion of mass media, to allow activists to see what is going on elsewhere and to draw comparisons and lessons appropriate to the Indonesian context (Uhlin 1997: 244–45). There is no reason to expect this process to stop, especially now that Indonesia is more open than before and has become the object of so much attention from foreign agencies eager to offer suggestions for speeding democratic consolidation.

Moreover, diffusion of these sorts of ideas will be much smoother now that the Indonesian media are so much more free than previously. During the Reformasi period—as in Malaysia's Reformasi movement, Thailand's May 1992 uprising, and the Philippines' 2001 anti-Estrada unrest—media and tools that could spread information quickly, broadly, and without state control, including cellular telephones, faxes, the Internet, tabloids, and leaflets, were critical in facilitating networking, disseminating critical perspectives on the regime, and putting the military and Golkar on the defensive. As early as 1996, journalists negotiated censorship and lent support to the pro-democracy movement by, for instance, exaggerating the number of people at demonstrations in their accounts.[57] With the media in Indonesia now quite free and the Internet eroding even the possibility of tight censorship, the media will likely continue to perform significant monitoring and awareness-raising roles.

Domestic commentators, such as media personalities and prominent persons, as well as foreign and local academics, will also likely retain a role. During the Reformasi era, public intellectuals were highly influential in the media and in setting public opinion, but their role in stirring up events was not really clear.[58] They probably functioned primarily as resource people, contributing to the momentum of reformist discourse and offering guidance, rather than as masterminds. Still, while most student protests seemed genuinely nonpartisan and student activists generally denied significant links to particular parties (let alone to military or other political forces), nonparty political activists did coach students to some extent—for instance, by encouraging them to take a broadly inclusive approach.[59]

Some of these individuals entered politics, playing similar roles to those of social activists who have joined electoral politics in Malaysia. For instance, faced with a public relations disaster, Abdurrahman named the popular commentator Wimar Witoelar his official spokesperson. Other academics and activists assumed positions of authority, too, including Abdurrahman Wahid himself and Amien Rais (both representatives of mass Islamic organizations) as well as Muhammad Hikam (an academic and minister of state for research and technology), Erna Witoelar (a consumer advocate and minister for housing and regional infrastructure), Laksamana Sukardi (an intellectual, lawyer, and anticorruption activist who became a leader in PDI-P and a cabinet minister), and Nurcholish Majid (an academic who came to play a mediating role with government). As in Malaysia, these individuals' presence may lend credibility and legitimacy to political parties and the government. They bring to politics their reputation as social activists, purportedly concerned with aptitude and cleanliness rather than with the spoils of office. However, also as in Malaysia, and as the human rights lawyer Munir laments (2000: 5), the entry of these NGO activists and intellectuals into formal politics "represents the loss of an enormous non-partisan resource that used to be available to push for change"; he adds, "What we have seen the past year does not make them look like a strong force for change from within either. Outside forces are still more effective."

Arrayed on the side of liberalizing reforms are not just domestic CSAs and political parties but also international agencies. These bodies have clearly influenced the progress of democratization in Indonesia. Organizations such as the Ford Foundation, the Asia Foundation, and a range of government-funded aid bodies (Dutch, American, Japanese, and others) have long been active in the country. Before, during, and after the 1999 Indonesian elections, international donors supported particular NGOs, trained and provided election monitors, sponsored civic education programs, and more (Clear 2000).[60] Longer-term policies, such as the World Bank's requiring the involvement of NGOs in the implementation of development plans, likewise help legitimate and entrench nonstate political actors and embed both state and civil society in international contexts and partnerships. As aid programs are ongoing and even growing, this entrenchment of civil society's legitimacy and role, as well as of the salience of foreign agendas, will likely persist.

Malaysia and Indonesia Compared

While Malaysian and Indonesian events bear some similarities, especially in the importance of the attribution of opportunity and threat in stimulating activism, these cases are in fact very different in scale, scope, and processes involved; in the nature of the incumbent regime; in the incentives and resources available for contained versus transgressive contention; and in the availability of social capital and coalitional capital. In both countries, forces from civil as well as political society were critical to the Reformasi movement. In both, CSAs were more active and influential in the early stages, and then political parties took the initiative as elections approached in 1999. However, lower levels of coalitional capital as well as more disparate ideologies and key issues—both artifacts of the more restrictive incumbent regime—made consensus and a unified reform coalition harder to achieve in Indonesia, even if change has since proceeded farther there, given the new regime in place. In other words, this comparison suggests how much of the Malaysian experience of interaction between CSAs and political society can or cannot be extrapolated to contexts marked by different regime types and societal cleavages.

First, the participation of various groups does not necessarily mean that they are working—or even could or would work—in concert. Malaysian CSAs have had far fewer qualms about cooperating than have their Indonesian counterparts. This facility at networking across the institutional bases of opposition represents coalitional capital. Indonesian

CSAs have initiated a range of coalitions, from student coordinating networks to MARI and SIAGA to ad hoc groups involved with particular campaigns. NGOs include former student and party activists, and so they may be able to draw on those connections in forging coalitions. Students also have some ties with political parties, whether directly, as with the PRD or indirectly, as by influencing the NU and, through it, PKB. Islamists and students have cooperated, too, when their aims have converged. All the same, encouraged by Soeharto's "floating mass" policy, each of these sectors has seen its role and perspective as quite distinct. Students see themselves as "angelic," NGOs espouse largely middle-class interests, and Islamic organizations represent distinct subsets of Muslims and have had a stake in party politics from the outset. Moreover, Indonesia's only recently revised three-party system can hardly be compared with Malaysia's. Throughout the New Order, political parties may have maintained links with particular sorts of organizations, but these were limited, especially since contained contention via parties was so dubious a route to reform. Even now, while PDI-P may court students' support or PKB may draw on its NU base, Indonesian parties have formed nothing to compare with the civil society–supported BA in Malaysia. Overall, then, extrapolation from the Malaysian case is limited by the specific nature and long-term stability of illiberal democracy there, since oppositional organizations have had time to accumulate coalitional capital over the years, and since playing by the rules—relying at least in part on contained contention—holds out the promise of efficacy.

The relative availability of coalitional capital within sectors of the opposition may offer a hint of what goals reformers will advocate. If, for instance, Islamist forces coalesced but secular NGOs could not work out their differences, the dominant reformist discourse in either Indonesia or Malaysia might have been (or may yet become) far more Islamist and perhaps less pro-democratic. In other words, whatever the common ground that unites the groups pooling their efforts, it is likely to emerge as the dominant position, even if it is not necessarily representative of society at large. What may be key to broadly popular and acceptable reform, then, is "bridging" coalitional capital so that all sorts of groups see sufficient advantage in circumventing obstacles to participate in a coalition.

The case of Indonesia suggests that a focus on civil society can easily be overstated. Malaysia's unique structural, cultural, and historical configuration has given CSAs a more critical role in opposition coalition building than in many otherwise comparable states. Even so, at some point the formal political sphere takes center stage, at which time CSAs may be driven back into the wings if they have not already secured a firm foothold—for instance, by the entry of a coterie of social activists into political parties. This shift was significantly more stark in Indonesia: CSAs (especially students) played a reactive, destructive role, but then more moderate political parties took over the process of reform. Moreover, state institutions other than political parties, most notably the military and the bureaucracy, may significantly help or hinder reform processes and determine how far social activists can press their demands. This factor, too, played out clearly in Indonesia—making attribution of threat at least as significant as attribution of opportunity for activists—whereas the military in Malaysia has been consistently relegated to the background in political affairs. Hence the balance of power and responsibility between elements from civil and political society depends on the stage of the process and the specific circumstances of the case.

These differences notwithstanding, the congruence of catalysts across the two cases suggests the importance of changes in prevailing opportunities and threats, from economic crises to elite factionalism to the availability of charismatic leaders, to bring long-simmering dissent to a boil as government opponents reframe and reorient their activism. The contrast between the countries, though, implies the significance of the precise nature of those triggers. In both countries, political unrest was spurred by economic crisis. However, the far more severe economic crash in Indonesia and the greater involvement of the IMF meant that Indonesian protesters had less to lose and remained more desperate than in Malaysia. In Malaysia, economic issues were less fundamental to protests, aside from diatribes against high-level cronyism and bailouts or articulation of relatively minor grievances.[61] Protests could therefore be more readily presented within an enduring frame of democratization and social justice, resonating with collective memory of past grievances and movements. Also, Malaysia had Anwar and a cast of generally cooperating supporting characters, while Indonesia had Megawati, Amien Rais, Abdurrahman Wahid, and various other leaders. These reformist elites played both symbolic and substantive roles in both countries, but their failure to cooperate so tidily in Indonesia presaged the difficulties of forging a common consensus across the reformist spectrum. What the Malaysian case suggests, then, about the eruption of long-term gripes, given the right set of circumstances or political opportunities, is borne out by the comparison across cases, but the resolution of those grievances depends on the context.

In sum, the contrast between these two cases helps to highlight the complex, interlacing dynamics of political reform. Any interpretation of reform trajectories and processes requires a balance of attention between institutional and cultural, formal and informal, and materially rational and ideational structures and processes. Clearly, the nature of the incumbent regime matters in terms of activists' choice of strategies and their legacy of engagement with the state, society, and each other. Also, the contrast between these cases points out the usefulness of having adequate social as well as coalitional capital to facilitate popular mobilization and preclude atomized CSAs and parties' struggling independently of, and possibly at cross-purposes with, each other. Such collaboration may further reforms that are supported across a broad swath of society and elites, that are reasonably well thought out, and that are likely to be stable and enduring. The implications, applications, and limitations of this framework for reform are explored in the final chapter.

Conclusion: Insights, Implications, and Extensions

The evolution of opposition politics in Malaysia from the 1920s through the late 1990s yields important insights about politics in Malaysia and in illiberal democracies more generally. The contrast between Malaysia and Indonesia indicates the significance of specific state structures and political conditions to the type of coalitions and agendas that may take shape. A complex understanding of the relative input of CSAs into reform processes, particularly coalition building, has both empirical and theoretical value. It places segments of civil society, opposition parties, individual voters, and the state in context, describing a transformation that is both cultural and institutional. Regardless of how far the complete framework developed here may travel, an abstracted version of its major tenets clearly resonates with the experiences of other illiberal democracies, particularly those with a configuration of forces at least loosely resembling Malaysia's. It helps us to grasp what sort of links form to unite opposition actors and why, what the relative contributions are of activists from civil and political society in propelling a state toward a new political paradigm, and what the balance is between contained and transgressive forms of contention. Careful attention to context, history, and process thus enables useful theoretical understandings of the roles of CSAs and parties in political reform and of the relative comparability of such roles across states.

Progress toward political reform in Malaysia has proceeded on two tracks, one cultural and one institutional. The former involves a change in political norms and behavior, which makes reform more durable and legitimate. Malaysian political culture has consistently included noncommunal possibilities, premised primarily on class or on religion. These norms have gained prominence and legitimacy through issue-advocacy work in civil society since the 1970s and the selection of noncommunal issues as the common denominator to unite opposition parties sporadically since the 1950s, and more concertedly in the 1990s. To have an impact, this normative shift must be institutionalized in government structures and policies. Recognizing the receptiveness of the public to a new message and the opportunity for change, and building on the experience and example of cross-racial civil societal campaigns, party-based reformers have been stimulated to find new ways of cooperating for shared ends. Serendipitous catalysts, most notably the regime's inability to avoid economic crisis and the availability of charismatic reformist leaders, have added a sense of urgency and opportunity. Looming always in the background, though, has been the state. The nature of the regime plays a major role in determining the nature of protest, especially the relative significance of contained and transgressive strategies. As the opposition mobilizes, the government retains the ability to quash reformers (at the risk of losing legitimacy), cede power to them (or at least take the risk of doing so by engaging at the polls), or undercut them by implementing at least some of the reforms demanded. Malaysia's political opposition has thus been pressed not only to find creative ways to avoid suppression and convince the public that the omnipresent government is fallible but also to strike an optimal balance among strategies of protest, both inside and outside the system.

Reformasi in either Malaysia or Indonesia is best regarded not as a one-time cataclysmic movement but as a stage in a historical process. How civil society and political society have developed and interacted over time largely determines what sort of institutions may emerge to support a reform effort. By the time of Malaysia's 1999 elections, the opposition—political parties and other forces—had taken its prior experience of coalition building one step further. The major opposition parties had united in a single coalition and reached a reasonably stable consensus on a set of immediate priorities, policy preferences, and leaders. Political opportunities had shifted by the time of the 2004 elections. Mahathir had exited the scene and been replaced by a leader who promised to work with CSAs and reform the party and government. Moreover, the economy was picking up, Islamism had lost some popular appeal (at least as presented by PAS), and the Anwar issue had faded. It is hardly surprising, then, that opposition unity was harder to achieve and that the incumbent government was able to reconsolidate control. Indonesia has followed a different trajectory. There, a history of regime repression and lack of trust across sections of the opposition meant that what alliances formed and what priorities were set were fragmented and continually contested. As of 1999, Indonesia had no counterpart to Malaysia's BA, and, indeed, coalitional possibilities remained shaky in 2004. However, if only because the ancien régime had lost its leader and been firmly discredited, new political institutions and norms had kept percolating, albeit with uneven participation, and with, at best, uncertain consensus from the forces most critical to the collapse of the New Order.

The 2004 Elections

Both Malaysia and Indonesia held elections in 2004. The results in both places indicate continuing popular engagement with some of the same issues as in 1999, even if different parties were seen as best able to tackle those concerns. Malaysian reformists seem to have retreated to contained contention, including the pursuit of top-down reforms. While discontent with the regime remains, it is insufficiently galvanizing (and current alternatives are insufficiently convincing) to spur strong efforts at systemic change. Indonesia, by contrast, could be drifting more toward a Malaysian-style illiberal democracy: institutions for participation are in place, but politics remains elitist, cliquish, and driven more by pragmatism or opportunism than by coherent aims or lofty ideals.

Malaysia

Malaysia's eleventh general elections, held March 21, 2004, seemed superficially to signal the demise of reformism.[1] Posting its best result since 1955, the BN won around 90 percent of parliamentary seats, regained Terengganu's state government, and nearly recaptured Kelantan. While the DAP fared slightly better than before, winning twelve seats (compared with ten in 1999), PAS lost nineteen of its twenty-six seats, and Keadilan (including PRM) lost all but one of its five (albeit still garnering 9 percent of the vote). One independent from Sabah also won a seat. All told, though, the BN won only 56 percent of the vote in the Malay heartland and 64 percent nationwide, while support for PAS slipped by less than 1 percent (to 15 percent overall). Three key factors must temper judgment of the polls and their import.

First, election monitors declared the polls "the most disorganized" in Malaysian history. Problems ranged from allegations of phantom voters to sudden transfer of voters to incorrect ballot papers to last-minute extensions of polling center hours. The Elections Commission blamed some hassles on the record-breaking brevity of the campaign—eight days— which left little time to prepare. The elections were unusually suspenseful, too, because of the number of seats that were decided after recounts and on whisker-thin margins. Both PAS and Keadilan rejected the results and called for new polls, and even the BN complained of malfeasance.

The mainstream media, too, sustained their bias in news coverage and advertisements; the "three Ms" mattered as much as ever. The BN benefited enormously from majoritarian electoral rules and disproportionality in electoral districts—though the DAP gained, too, in majority-Chinese areas.

Second, part of the reason why the BN—especially UMNO—fared so well was its own adoption of core Reformasi demands. In turn, a major cause of PAS's decline in 2004 appears to have been its greater emphasis on Islamic statehood than on such issues as economic growth, jobs, crime, social problems, and education (which polls had shown to be core concerns for most voters, regardless of ethnicity), not least because Abdullah Badawi had already seized more middle ground in decrying corruption and promoting moderate, progressive Islam (packaged afresh as *Islam Hadhari*) himself (Ibrahim 2004: 4–8). Also, PAS's fielding of women in ten seats (unsuccessfully) could only go so far to counter UMNO's diligent efforts to woo Malay women. In addition, many CSAs and ex-UMNO members seemed willing to give Abdullah Badawi and his cabinet lineup—touted as both younger and cleaner than before (despite prior charges against several ministers)—a chance, especially in the absence of the Anwar factor or other galvanizing issues. The incumbent government could count on a "feel good" factor, with the results thus perhaps to be read more as a green light to Abdullah Badawi to pursue reforms than as a rejection of the opposition.

Third, that the main opposition parties failed to articulate a unified, relevant platform though the BA issued a joint manifesto pledging stronger civil liberties, reinstatement of local council elections, reservation of 30 percent of top government posts for women, cuts in road tolls and car prices, and more (Barisan Alternatif 2004)—says less about voter preferences than about the parties themselves. Keadilan, for instance, was basically trapped between PAS and the DAP, and it was plagued by a weak organizational network and an excess of inexperienced, young idealists. PAS, meanwhile, seemed to be suffering from overconfidence, internal division, and disorganization, especially since the death of Fadzil Noor (Ibrahim 2004). One columnist offered the following harsh critique: "In a space of five years, Pas and Keadilan lost it all. . . . They alienated the non-Muslims; they alienated business; they alienated foreign investors; and without even realizing it, they had alienated their own constituency, the Muslims" (Kalimullah 2004). The media's playing up of acrimonious negotiations between PAS and the other parties did not help—but neither did Nik Aziz's much publicized insistence that PAS supporters would go to heaven, whereas "those who support[ed] un-Islamic parties [would] logically go to hell," for they "like gambling and condone adultery and rape" (Ng 2004; "Pak Lah Steps" 2004). Simply failing to develop a coalition hurt the opposition overall, too: at least a few seats were lost in three-cornered fights.

Thus the 2004 elections represent a setback to opposition-based reformists, but not necessarily the end either of reform or of gradual coalition building. James Wong (2004b) sums the situation up in referring to Keadilan: "Whatever its actual strength on the ground, it has been playing a critical but not widely and fairly acknowledged role of reducing racialist sentiment and propaganda in Malaysian politics in the last five years because of its multiracial approach to democratic mobilisation." Indeed, mass mobilization as well as contained initiatives for top-down change are key; the 2004 elections demonstrated clearly that the electoral system so strongly favors the incumbent that a straightforward electoral approach, leaving reform just to opposition parties, cannot hope to succeed.

Indonesia

The 2004 Indonesian parliamentary and presidential elections likewise represented a change from 1999. Parliamentary elections were held on March 8. The initial round of the first-ever direct presidential elections was held on July 5; the runoff (since no candidate won a majority of the popular vote plus at least 20 percent in at least half the provinces) was on September 20. Partly to preclude another Soeharto, partly to ensure adequate representation for the outer islands, and partly because the leading parties set the rules to their own advantage, the system favors large, established parties—for instance, by tying eligibility for the presidential contest to parties' performance in the parliamentary polls.[2] As one observer describes it, the current system "essentially formalises the entrenched interests of existing major parties, the shifting balance between nationalist-secularist and Islamist strains and the money politics that go with the decentralization of corruption."[3] The ranks of parties and candidates signal persistence of old patterns as well as elements of change.

Perhaps the clearest sign of continuity as opposed to significant reform in Indonesia is the continued popularity of Golkar, and especially of its presidential candidate, General Wiranto (who supplanted the corruption-tainted Akbar Tanjung). Golkar won the largest share of parliamentary votes (21.6 percent), and Wiranto came in a close third in the presidential race. Golkar has retained support largely on account of its record in local administration, especially in rural areas, but also partly out of popular disappointment with democracy and nostalgia for the strong leadership of the past (DEMOS 2004: 3). PDI-P, on the other hand, lost substantial support between 1999 and 2004; its vote total declined from around 33.3 percent to 18.5 percent of the electorate. (The remainder of the vote was split among twenty-two smaller parties.) Megawati paid for her support of business and military interests and her failure to restore socioeconomic stability or eradicate corruption (S. Weiss 2003; Lane 2004; Mackie 2004). Apart from the decline of PDI-P, the results were largely similar to those of 1999.

However, two new parties touting better governance and clean leadership did noticeably well, garnering around 7 percent of the parliamentary vote each: Partai Demokrat (PD) and the more Islamist PKS (Lane 2004). PD leader Susilo Bambang Yudhoyono then went on to win the presidency. This development seems to signal a shift away from New Order politics. All the same, it was "SBY" (as he is popularly known), a former general and coordinating minister for political and security affairs, who oversaw the military crackdown in Aceh. His party's policies are "similar to the platform of the military itself" (Guerin 2004). Indeed, even if the support of PD and PKS, especially in Jakarta—where political change tends to occur first—represents the rejection of old political elites, neither party has really distinguished itself as progressive or otherwise atypical (Lane 2004).

What is perhaps most striking about the conduct of the 2004 campaigns in Indonesia, especially given the rhetoric of Reformasi, is the relative paucity of issues and idealism in party platforms (Sherlock 2004: 15–16) and especially in selection of running mates. As the analyst Dewi Fortuna Anwar scoffs, Indonesian politics is marked by "a great deal of promiscuity. . . . Anyone can get married to anybody" (quoted in Guerin 2004). For instance, Megawati beat out Wiranto to secure NU leader Hasyim Muzadi as her running mate, not to signal an attachment to Islamist policies but just to boost her chances at the polls (Mackie 2004). Wiranto settled for Solahuddin Wahid, Abdurrahman's brother, in a bid for the same NU votes—even though, as deputy chair of the National Human Rights Commission, Solahuddin has investigated Wiranto for alleged abuses (Muninggar 2004). Even the ascendance of PD was tempered by the reality of its need to forge an alliance for the executive ticket. Bambang nominated former Golkar member and cabinet member (under Megawati) Yusuf Kalla as his running mate, hoping to attract Islamists, Golkar members, and voters from Sulawesi. Such strategies for leverage reinforce the leader-focused and factional nature of party politics and foster "ramshackle and ill-functioning" coalitions (Sherlock 2004: 11–12). More broadly, the major parties "have made very little progress in developing coherent policy platforms and . . . their political identity derives almost entirely from symbolic gestures and rhetoric designed to appeal to the divisions that have historically marked Indonesian society [even though] . . . they have very little to show those communities in terms of targeted policies" (Sherlock 2004: 4). There were attempts at forging less opportunistic coalitions, but these failed. A National Coalition of left/democratic parties formed in mid-2003, but then two linchpin parties opted to go it alone. Also, the PRD attempted to develop the Party of the United Popular Opposition (POPOR) with local worker, peasant, and pro-democracy organizations, but it was slow to take off, had a weak base, and was undercut by student groups' advocating an electoral boycott (Lane 2004).

Overall, as in Malaysia, the lack of a clear enemy and the decline of critical awareness, along with a diminution in the sense of crisis, changed electoral dynamics. Despite democratic institutions, remnants of the New Order elite may be even more dominant now than before, having gained control of local and national elected positions as well as of political parties. Democracy in Indonesia is more delegative than representative; although rights and freedoms are in place, with such elite-dominated parties in control, the mass of people lack the institutional and other means to exercise them (DEMOS 2004: 10–11, 21–22). Much as suggested by this comparison with Malaysia, the researchers at DEMOS recommend "drastic changes to power relations by way of social movements and mass organising before rights and institutions may be deemed to carry any meaning"; repoliticization of civil society is a necessary precursor to altering power relations to enable real democratization, "based upon improved links between civic and political action" (DEMOS 2004: 3).

Understanding Opposition

Opposition coalition building is thus an evolutionary process, requiring not just appropriate political opportunities, so that the rewards of mobilization seem likely to outweigh the costs, but also normative agreement and a legacy of trust linking constituencies. However important contingent factors, such as regime failure, may be to catalyzing protest by altering perceptions of opportunity and threat, the array of possible reform-supportive initiatives depends upon the stock and quality of social and coalitional capital available in the polity at a particular point in time, as well as on the relative incentives attached to different strategies of engagement.

Malaysia is an illiberal democracy; New Order Indonesia was a hegemonic electoral authoritarian regime. The contrast between the two cases suggests that the greater the regime's tendency toward democracy, the easier it is for opposition actors to develop the ideological and strategic resources over time to coordinate. As a result, the reform that occurs in a more autocratic regime might be expected to be haphazardly organized and more reactive and destructive than proactive and constructive. Indonesia's facade of democracy under the New Order was too thin to give NGOs, students, party activists, and others the space to develop coalitional capital, including mutual trust and an understanding of their shared aspirations, even if social capital was at work in the formation of various associations. Moreover, party-based opposition in Indonesia had been hobbled even more by government regulations than had less institutionalized arenas. While these controls had been relaxed by the time of Indonesia's 1999 elections, the various sectors of the opposition had not yet had enough time to sort out their respective new niches or to forge a common agenda and strategy. As Boudreau describes the situation (1999: 13), "Given the divisions in the Indonesian opposition movement, the decisive elements in the transition did not involve mobilization of a single but socially diverse opposition movement, but a gathering of more dispersed discontent, unrest and violence." Even now, most democracy activists remain "marginalised by the mainstream elitist politics of democratisation," and so they focus on civil societal activism rather than on the political or legal systems, thus enhancing the public sphere without necessarily institutionalizing critical rights and procedures (DEMOS 2004: 3,13–14). Hence the two-track process that allowed CSAs to prime voters for reformism, and then parties to work toward institutionalizing those preferences in Malaysia, proved elusive in Indonesia.

To summarize, the different comparative advantages of formal and informal opposition actors complement each other in circumventing the constraints of an illiberal democratic regime. A broad-based coalition premised on some degree of ideological and programmatic consensus stands a greater chance not only of making use of all available political space but also of pressuring the regime forcefully enough to unseat it or induce top-down reforms and of commanding the mass support to make a reformed order stable. It is not just social capital that sparks concerted mobilization for reform; coalitional capital is also necessary to coordinate protest among groups. Charismatic leaders or obvious moments of regime failure help aggravate the public's awareness of their grievances, but the situation must be bad enough for average citizens to be willing to take a risk. Furthermore, voters will be easier to motivate if they have been exposed to independent media that allow party and nonparty activists to attribute increased opportunity and reduced threat to current circumstances, explain themselves, counter the government's messages, and propagandize. An essential part of these messages is a validation of protest. That is, issues-based activism in civil society promotes a new conception of popular participation in politics and of CSAs' role in the polity. Such activism feeds into opposition parties' rubric that challenging the government in power is within their rights and not antinational or ungrateful. Finally, international demonstration effects may provide fresh ideas and motivation to further coalition building and reform. Political change may occur even if not all these factors are present—witness Indonesia's democratic transition. However, their availability facilitates popular mobilization as well as the institutionalization of an alternative to the regime that reflects and furthers new political norms.

This study questions several common empirical generalizations. First, while it is true that communalism remains important in Malaysian politics, its centrality needs to be reconceptualized. Ethnicity is no longer so defining a political trait as previously. Moreover, its importance was exaggerated in the past by the suppression of subaltern histories and non-communal political alternatives, and by the blurring of race and class. Still, the waning of one set of cleavages may push others to the forefront. In contemporary Malaysia, religious categories may be usurping the prominence of communal ones dividing voters. Counterbalancing this development is a shared concern for particular issues that unite voters across ascriptive cleavages. The salience of those particular issues may eventually diminish, but inclusive, issues-based activism will no doubt persist and may again provide a kernel for a shared effort at systemic change.

Second, and more broadly, the analytical or practical separation of the spheres of civil society and political society is dubious. As Malaysian experience suggests, even if individuals or organizations from one sphere are ascendant at a given point in time, contributions from both are necessary and significant in an at least superficially democratic polity. Furthermore, civil society and political society share not only overlapping constituencies but also activists. An ideological reluctance to "dirty" themselves in party politics may hobble social activists, particularly if, as in Indonesia, even those operating in different sectors of civil society lack mutual trust or a basis for cooperation. At the same time, although opposition parties may push through reforms, their interest is more in the mechanics of securing and deploying power than in socialization at the grassroots. Parties' reach, efficacy, innovativeness, and expertise may be significantly improved if they are willing to acknowledge and work with CSAs, and such collaboration maximizes available political space.

Third, no single level of analysis can explain the progress of coalition building and reform. For instance, a focus on individuals obscures questions of collaboration across organizations. Even if ample social capital, ideological predilections (perhaps developed through civic education by

CSAs), and rational calculations favoring engagement encourage individuals to join organizations, those organizations may work at cross-purposes or find themselves unable to muster broad enough support to effect or maintain control over desired changes. Hence, while a focus on individual mind-sets and behavior is vital to any discussion of political reform, the average citizen is a very small cog in a large, complex apparatus. Traversing the individual, cultural, and institutional levels helps show how all the pieces of that mechanism work in concert to produce coalitions and ultimately, perhaps, political reform.

That said, the centrality of the individual (but pliability of preferences) suggests a twist on rational choice theories of social dilemmas and collective action. The pursuit of reform requires not just that people act to optimize their preferences, often through innovative strategies, but also that they first change their priorities and perhaps compromise in order to maximize collective utility. In the case of Malaysia, then, reform begins with getting individuals to adopt less communal or patronage-based norms, and then it shifts to finding ways to maximize these new, non-communal interests. CSAs enhance voters' trust in reformers and expectations of reciprocity, particularly through creative framing strategies (for instance, through speaking in terms of *keadilan* rather than Islam). Changes in popular attitudes and behavior, as well as prevailing conditions, in turn motivate political parties to explore new coalitional possibilities to meet voters' altered demands, capitalize on opportunities for change, and institutionalize reforms.

This conceptualization of opposition politics helps rectify the paucity of theoretically inclined research on Malaysia (and most of Southeast Asia), particularly with regard to very recent reformist initiatives. The discussion here suggests that the nature of protest and the process of reform have qualitatively changed since the evolution of the current generation of pro-democracy and (at least in Malaysia) *dakwah* organizations. These shifts have implications for the relative success or vulnerability of reform movements, but the larger historical and institutional context remains salient as well.

Civil Society and Political Transformation

This approach suggests that CSAs play a more complex role in political transformation than is sometimes presumed. Within the framework of an illiberal democracy, CSAs magnify their impact more through interaction with other sectors of the opposition, including the use of whatever established institutional channels are available, than through independent or baldly antisystemic action. For instance, as partners to political parties,

CSAs play vital roles in facilitating coalition building, mediating among parties and perspectives, and mobilizing the public to support those parties. Indeed, CSAs not only pressure the state for liberalization or other reforms but also target the public and the rest of the opposition to prioritize reformist norms and policies. As a tactical measure, by taking advantage of democratic channels, however constrained, CSAs may intimidate the public and government less, making both popular endorsement and regime forbearance (or even top-down reforms) more likely. In other words, CSAs may vacillate strategically between contained and transgressive contention to take full advantage of resources and opportunities. Thus the broader conceptualization presented here—of reformism over time, and across sectors of the polity—puts CSAs' efforts at various stages in context.

In return for their contribution to reform processes, CSAs may enjoy significant clout. While during "normal politics" in an illiberal democracy the average NGO can hope for little more than marginal involvement in policymaking, at watershed moments CSAs may help determine the shape and direction of the regime as a whole. Moreover, particularly if they establish and maintain ties with successful party-based challengers, CSAs may enjoy regularized input into policymaking processes under a new government. This influence may come as a reward for CSAs' assistance in elections—and opposition parties may feel deeply beholden to CSAs for their vote-getting power—or in recognition of their expertise. For instance, Malaysian opposition parties seem to be more willing now than previously to accommodate CSAs in crafting budgets and policy statements or in *ceramah* and other forums, acknowledging their equal legitimacy as political actors. Such a niche, though, represents an intensification of CSAs' interdependence with the (would-be) state.

This dependency may be problematic if a continued role for CSAs in policy processes relies upon perpetuation of the dominance of one coalition or party. The enhanced regard that Malaysian opposition parties today show for NGOs is no doubt linked with the fact that activists seem not to disdain or avoid party politics as much as before. With so many CSAs now actually in or backing opposition parties, they clearly have a vested interest in those parties' success. Moreover, just by dint of sharing norms and policy goals, CSAs and the rest of the (former) opposition will have a mutual stake in a new order. Under such conditions, at least some portions of civil society may find it difficult to play effective monitoring roles. CSAs may be hard pressed to critique a reformist coalition for which they helped secure power as it implements (or fails to implement) strategies and objectives that those CSAs helped to formulate.

The pattern of development of opposition politics that this perspective reveals suggests that Malaysian political norms will continue to shift toward support of a less explicitly communal order. With issue-oriented CSAs involved, and not just parties, this evolution will probably proceed less fitfully, at least on the cultural level, than if it is chiefly synchronized to electoral cycles. At the same time, the study suggests that Malaysian CSAs will see an incentive to continue developing partnerships with political parties. Government repression or strategic concessions could slow this process, but the prevalence of hard-to-control new media, together with mounting evidence of liberalization in other states, will limit the deterrent impact of crackdowns and the sufficiency of marginal concessions more than in previous instances. In addition, coalitional capital, along with the increasing skill and sophistication of reformist leaders in both civil society and political society, facilitates further activism. Finally, more issues-oriented, noncommunal political discourse will probably progress—whether touted by the BN, the opposition, or both—as voters' norms and priorities continue their gradual shift away from the racialized, patronage-dependent status quo. As Loh (2003) concludes, these changes do not point to the end of the BN, but probably to an end to its assured dominance.

Larger Significance

The question remains of whether the processes described here are uniquely Malaysian, are (Southeast) Asian, or are more broadly relevant. In fact, while the precise trajectory of events in Malaysia may not be repeated anywhere else, an extrapolation of key processes carries explanatory and even predictive value elsewhere. Drawing out some of the implications of this framework for Malaysia and other cases contributes to our understanding of liberalization or democratization—for example, by raising the question of whether an illiberal democracy can ever be truly stable (Case 2001), or how much political openness is needed to make a difference in strategies of popular engagement, or whether reforms are likely to hit a ceiling beyond which liberalization is unlikely to be pressed or to succeed, or whether the processes that get reforms under way are replicated over time or transform significantly as reform proceeds.

The empirical validity of problem-driven theory inhibits the aim of universality promoted by theory-driven research. The problem in this instance is how a reformist coalition can solidify and succeed in Malaysia. Observation of the process of coalition building in Malaysian history yields the framework described here. That empirically derived framework suggests intriguing theoretical insights but cannot be expected to fit other contexts so neatly. The theoretical insights may apply—that CSAs should be explored as a portion of the opposition, or that both norms and institutions need to shift for reforms to stick—but context-specific factors will determine how closely the model approximates reality. These findings are worthwhile, though, inasmuch as they encourage students of reform to conceptualize differently the actors and processes involved.

As comparison with Indonesia suggests, this framework is highly qualified. Its basic tenets regarding the role of CSAs in facilitating the adoption of a consistent reform agenda by CSAs and parties may travel well. However, the cases in which the process described can actually be played out, so that CSAs have a chance to fulfill this potential role, are limited. The model applies specifically to illiberal democracies, and possibly only to those marked by significant social pluralism, or in which all major groups are represented in civil society. Moreover, contingent factors—such as political opportunities that catalyze mobilization, the amount of time allowed for coalition building, the legacy of past cooperation, and the response of the state to the challenge posed by reformers—may affect the process. Competing explanations, such as the notion that modernization may do at least as much as CSAs' consciousness raising to erode social cleavages, are also plausible in some cases. These limitations do not undermine the theoretical validity of the framework, but they do highlight how much of an idealization it may be.

Narrowly bounded as it is, this study does not touch on whether new coalitions actually implement promised changes if elected into office, nor does it touch on the predictors or conditions for follow-through. At stake are both the will to change the polity and reformers' ability to implement changes amid constraints. It is important to note that, should a reformist government come to power, it would still likely face some of the same challenges that precipitated the failure of its predecessor. Even if, for instance, problematic social cleavages were less of an issue under a reformed regime than previously, economic or other limitations cannot be socialized away. Indonesia is a good example. Abdurrahman Wahid may have had the best of intentions, but his regime could do only so much for social welfare, given IMF mandates and the dismal state of the economy.

Therefore, future research might explore the circumstances under which reformers follow through with changes as promised, if they win, or successfully pressure the incumbent government to reform, if they lose; examine how reformers modify their rhetoric, tactics, and coalitions over time; or evaluate whether voters' preferences and parties' or CSAs' strategies necessarily shift in tandem. Also meriting further study is how CSAs gauge the extent to which cooperation with political parties of the opposition or government is safe, or whether certain attributes help groups withstand co-optation by opposition or government parties. As Dryzek

(1996) suggests, excessive collaboration may be ultimately disempowering for civil society. Political parties' strategic decisions as to whether to share the stage with nonparty actors, work in coalition with other parties, or try to go it alone likewise bear examination. Far from the final word, then, this study represents a stepping-off point for enriching and expanding our knowledge of political protest and reform.

Review and Implications

The framework presented here of how political reform proceeds in an illiberal democracy is revealing for Malaysia and relevant to other, comparable polities, even if the specific cleavages, constraints, and sequence of events vary with time and place. Against a range of state-imposed regulations, activists and organizations from civil society and political society have contributed to fostering reformist norms, facilitating political engagement, and enabling political liberalization through contained and transgressive means, altering their strategies and collective action frames as necessary to take advantage of changing political opportunities and threats. Moreover, as implied by the contrast between Malaysia and Indonesia, the more democratic the regime, the easier coalition building becomes, since a broader range of proponents of reform are able to discuss more freely their preferences, expectations, and ideas and develop a sense over time of why, how, and on what grounds to collaborate.

In Malaysia, popular awareness of the fallibility of the BN regime and growing acceptance of pro-democratic norms, plus the sturdiness of noncommunal norms in the opposition over decades, suggest that reform will continue, whether pressed from above or from below. After decades of gradual change, complemented by demographic and environmental shifts, political culture has come to assume a new timbre. At the same time, citizens have more options for how to participate in the polity, and increasing numbers have come to accept the legitimacy and value of political engagement. These trends will almost certainly continue in Malaysia and be replayed—albeit with variations—in other states. In Malaysia as elsewhere, then, forces from civil society and political society—both the government and the opposition—will likely continue to innovate strategically and ideologically as state and society gradually change.

REFERENCE MATTER

NOTES

Chapter 1

1. I use the terms "race" and "ethnicity" here as they are commonly used in Malaysia: as interchangeable terms to refer to ascriptive categories (that is, Malay, Chinese, Indian). "Communalism" is the organization or pursuit of interests along racial lines. So, for instance, a party representing Malays is deemed a race-based or communal party.

2. Consider, for example, parent-teacher associations (PTAs) in private schools in the United States, by comparison with their counterparts in Chinese schools in Malaysia. PTA members in the United States may give up some leisure time, spend a bit of money, and get frustrated if they fail to secure policy changes. PTA members in Chinese schools in Malaysia run all these risks but may also be thrown in jail for their pains; in fact, a substantial proportion of those detained in a major crackdown in 1987 were proponents of Chinese-medium education whose activism was portrayed as sowing ethnic discord.

3. I use "civil society agents" rather than just "civil society" to stress the heterogeneous, fragmentary nature of civil society, coalitional capital notwithstanding.

4. Chan cogently validates, as a form of political participation, the "rumour-mongering" encountered at coffee shops, in bars, and at dinner parties in Singapore. Malaysians, too, may feel cause "to look over their shoulders before they spout their political viewpoints" (Chan 1997: 299), but, as in Singapore, it is in such casual settings that much political discussion and debate takes place.

5. These roles are suggested in large part by the coalition-building processes that Elinor Ostrom (1998) describes in developing a behavioral approach to the rational choice theory of collective action. While the analysis presented here is not based on a rational choice perspective, Ostrom's framework turns a useful lens on the nature of the interactions that allow individuals to perceive their common interests and feel confident about acting collectively.

6. That is, "government by elite cartel designed to turn a democracy with a fragmented political culture into a stable democracy" (Lijphart 1969: 216); see chap. 2, this volume.

7. For instance, both PAS and the leader of the purportedly secular Keadilan raised the hackles of the DAP and precipitated a crisis in the BA by suggesting in mid-2001 that the idea of an Islamic state was still on the table. See the daily coverage in *Malaysiakini* beginning June 29, 2001. This issue proved the coalition's Achilles' heel: the DAP withdrew from the BA that September, in large part because of continuing disagreement over Islamization.

Chapter 2

1. But see Alagappa 2004.

2. Far from taking offense at Gellner's hardly concealed disdain for such societies, Malaysia's Anwar Ibrahim gushes, "Sociologist Ernest Gellner recently put forth a concept of 'High Islam' or Islam that is rational, prioritizes scientific knowledge . . . and is based on an urban culture as the foundation for the Muslim community to create a modern, successful society" (Anwar 1997: 8). (This and subsequent translations from Malay are my own.)

3. Chandra Muzaffar, interview with the author, July 9, 1998, Kuala Lumpur.

4. See MINDS 1997 and the contributions therein, especially the chapter by Syed Muhammad Naquib Al-Attas, for a more thorough explication of the concept and its roots. This volume offers the proceedings of a 1996 conference on *masyarakat madani* that included most of the leading proponents and students of the concept. For the concept placed in a broader context, see also Verma (2002: 5–7).

5. The cultivation and study of *masyarakat madani* was associated in the mid-1990s with the Anwar-linked think tank Institut Kajian Dasar (Institute for Policy Studies) and with several of Anwar's strong followers, such as the intellectual and longtime social activist Chandra Muzaffar. The idea never really took root in popular consciousness, though, and even academic discussion of the concept virtually ceased after Anwar's departure from office.

6. For instance, see Hefner 2000 on the variations in predilections for democracy among subsets of Indonesian Muslims.

7. Klandermans and Tarrow (1988) identify the four most important NSMs of Western democratic capitalist countries as the student movement of the 1960s, the environmental and women's rights movements that developed by the end of the 1960s, and the peace and antinuclear movement that developed by the early 1980s.

8. Makmor (1998: 62) states that use of the term *NGO* in academic work, journalism, and other fields has become popular only since the 1980s. Prior to that time, terms such as *social welfare bodies* were used for apolitical groups, with *NGO* coming into vogue only as more political groups, comparable to interest groups in the West, developed.

9. A brief glance at virtually any recent United Nations Development Programme or World Bank document demonstrates this perspective. See, for instance, United Nations Development Programme (2003: 140–43).

10. See Alatas 1977. Including individuals alongside associations in civil soci-

ety is unconventional, but these public intellectuals tend to perform about the same role as many organizations. Moreover, some of the most politically engaged associations in Malaysia at least began, really, as vehicles for one or more outspoken activists.

11. But see Schedler (2002: 43) for why such a characterization is useful. He deems "illiberal democracy" an oxymoron.

12. See, for instance, Case 2001; Crouch 1993.

13. In recent years, this disparity has also come to benefit the opposition Parti Islam SeMalaysia (PAS).

14. The Federal Constitution defines a Malay as someone who habitually practices Malay culture, speaks the Malay language, and is Muslim. As Funston (1980: 3) suggests, "for Malays the concept of being Malay is not ethnic," since anyone who adheres to these three criteria is considered Malay.

15. See, for instance, Alvarez (1990) and Mainwaring and Viola (1984). Increasing attention to the political potential of Islam is adding an important dimension to this literature (see, for example, Wickham 2002; Hefner 2000).

16. The Malaysian state has never been entirely secular. All but Muslims have freedom of religion, but state policies specifically privilege Islam (Abdul Aziz 2001).

17. Political or other social norms present the playing field on which substantive contests over resources, power, or other goods are waged. Stable and resistant to change (and backed by internal and external sanctions), norms represent underlying notions of what sort of behavior is acceptable, what ends are to be valued, and how interpersonal interactions ought to be structured. Norms are ideals, even if not necessarily fully realized at all times (Elster 1989; Legro 1997). Norms provide the backdrop to political behavior; as March and Olsen (1984: 743–44) assert, political action is "often based more on determining normatively appropriate behavior than on calculating the return expected from alternative choices."

18. Bermeo (1992) finds that "political learning" takes place in small, free spaces of civil society (including professional or other associations, churches, media, or even, among dissidents, prison or exile), spaces that even the strongest regimes cannot entirely obliterate. Moreover, authoritarian regimes may breed pro-democratic ideas rather than authoritarian attitudes, since actors determine what has worked or failed in the old regime and set their normative goals accordingly. Once critical elites are exposed to such ideas and change their assessment of the relative efficacy of democratic institutions for achieving goals, they will press for and continue to support democratization.

19. Conversely, beleaguered elites, in deciding when to crack down and when to proceed with liberalization, also calculate the costs of repression versus toleration (Bermeo 1997).

20. Where the policymaking apparatus and bureaucracy are particularly strong and efficient, only "insiders" may have real influence. Former People's Action Party (PAP) member of Parliament Seet Ai Mee of Singapore explained, for instance, that she had accomplished more for disabled people's rights in three

years in Parliament, where she could "shift the pyramid" to achieve change, than she could have done in twice as long as a lobbyist (Seet Ai Mee, interview with the author, Aug. 17, 1996, Singapore).

21. Similarly, Sonia Alvarez finds that pro-democracy women's groups in Brazil need to accept some degree of co-optation or containment if they are to succeed. They may gain policy influence by cooperating with state institutions or opposition parties, but they are then likely left working under patriarchal or male-dominated structures, perhaps fragmenting along partisan lines. Hence post-transition, more radical elements in women's groups become increasingly marginalized while more moderate elements are absorbed into the mainstream or locked into "female political ghettos" (Alvarez 1990: 268).

22. Dryzek (1996: 480) identifies environmentalists as best able to link their core demands with an emerging state imperative: environmental conservation; overall, though, the Mexican state's "longevity and stability can be attributed to its brilliantly successful incorporation of successive waves of potential trouble-makers" (478).

23. Dryzek's definition is helpful: "Legitimation is secured when subordinate classes and categories with the capacity to destabilize the political economy instead support or accept that structure" (Dryzek 1996: 479).

Chapter 3

1. Malaya did not become Malaysia until the eleven peninsular states merged with Singapore and the Borneo states of Sabah and Sarawak, in 1963. Singapore left the federation in 1965.

2. Indeed, Sumit Mandal (2004) stresses that racial categories in Malaysia are actually less stable than often presumed, and that transethnic cultural politics has always been significant, albeit neglected in mainstream accounts.

3. The following discussion draws heavily on Roff (1994: 91–125).

4. This classification was based not so much on the immigrant/nonimmigrant dichotomy, since Indonesian immigrants were immediately given legal status as "Malay," as on the criteria of economic function, ethnic origin, and cultural (dis)similarity.

5. See, for instance, Shamsul 1996a; Tan 1988.

6. The situation in northern Malaya was different. Thailand regained the states of Kelantan, Terengganu, Kedah, and Perlis (lost to the British in 1909) through an agreement with Japan. The British fought back through a guerilla war waged by Patani (southeastern Thai) Malays (see Christie 1996: 177–79).

7. Debate periodically resurfaces on whether the language should be termed *Bahasa Melayu* or *Bahasa Malaysia*—that is, on the extent to which the language should be identified with a race rather than with a nation-state.

8. The Straits Chinese, also called *peranakan* or *baba*, had lived in Malaya, often for generations, and been acculturated to Malay culture to a greater extent than was true of the more recently arrived Chinese. The acculturation of the Straits Chinese included their speaking Malay as their mother tongue instead of a Chinese dialect.

9. Political poetry has retained a particular appeal. Even now, humorous and serious poems, or *sajak*, are avidly circulated in print and electronic form. In the same vein, some of the most beloved theater in Malaysia is political satire.

10. This debate was especially significant, as manifested in the Melayu Raya or Indonesia Raya (Greater Malaysia or Greater Indonesia) concept, which linked ethnic Malays in the two colonial entities. This movement spurred the participation of Malay nationalists in the Indonesian revolt against Dutch rule and involved overseas student activism, newsletters, and other political initiatives (Firdaus 1985).

11. Firdaus (1985) further subdivides the latter group—the "radical nationalists"—into Islamic-educated and generally vernacular-educated, left-wing teachers and writers. The former advocated an Islamic nation through the Pan-Malayan Islamic Party (PMIP, now Parti Islam SeMalaysia, or PAS) and the latter formed the Angkatan Pemuda Insaf (API, Movement of Aware Youth, banned in 1948) and Parti Kebangsaan Melayu Malaya (PKMM, Malay Nationalist Party, disbanded in 1950), then Parti Rakyat Malaysia (PRM, Malaysian People's Party, formed in 1955; formerly Parti Sosialis Rakyat Malaysia, or Malaysian Socialist People's Party, PSRM). See also Shamsul 1996b; Y. Mansoor 1976.

12. Exceptions included local branches of foreign organizations or groups founded and supported by the wives of British administrators, such as the Women's Service League (1946) (Manderson 1980).

13. For instance, Lee (1985) explains that secret societies were not "consciously political" and denied being so when the British sought to proscribe them. The societies declared that their intention was to maintain law and order, and they pointed out that they did not urge Chinese to cut off their queues, which would have been an anti-Manchu—and hence clearly political—act. However, the societies did sound and act political, especially when xenophobic feelings spilled over from China, or when Malayan Chinese felt economically or otherwise threatened by the British. See Tan 1983; Tan 1997; Heng 1996.

14. Chinese-medium schools remain significant. As of the late 1980s, close to 90 percent of Chinese parents still sent their children to Chinese-medium primary schools, and even without state financing at the secondary level, sixty privately funded schools were in operation (Heng 1996: 514). Chinese schools now also cater to a growing number of non-Chinese students.

15. This section relies heavily on Stenson 1980 and Dass 1991.

16. The basic demands of the GLU as of October 1945 were abolition of contract employment; an eight-hour day and a six-day week; equal pay for men and women and between ethnic groups (since Chinese workers were often paid more than Indians); and social insurance and compensation (Dass 1991: 38).

17. For the three decades preceding the Japanese occupation, Indians made up 67 to 80 percent of estate workers, though this proportion steadily declined after the war, to less than 50 percent by the early 1990s (Jomo and Todd 1994: 16).

18. On Indian labor activism, see Jomo and Todd 1994; Institute for Social Analysis 1989; and Dass 1991, from all of which this section draws significantly.

19. The Pan-Malayan Chinese Rubber Workers Union, intended to be multiracial, despite its name, was denied registration in the mid-1950s despite its

10,000-strong membership. The Malayan Estate Workers' Union, formed in the late 1950s by disgruntled Chinese and Indian ex-NUPW members, was registered in 1961 but deregistered a year later. The United Malayan Estate Workers' Union (UMEWU), registered in 1963 and boasting 15,000 members by 1964, was more successful, but planters preferred to negotiate only with the more compliant NUPW. Activists from the Labour Party (LPM) and PRM tried to help the UMEWU from 1965 on, but after a 1967 strike, the union was deregistered, and several UMEWU and LPM representatives were detained (Dass 1991).

20. Fifty years later, plantation workers (especially Indians) are still fighting for a monthly living wage.

21. Whether or not Singapore would join Malaya was contentious, given its heavily Chinese population.

22. For details, see Stenson 1980; Ampalavanar 1981; Khong 1987.

23. The term *Persekutuan Tanah Melayu* (literally, Federation of Malay Lands) was retained in Malay and "perpetuated the duality of two incompatible modes of thought," since only the Malay-language term is race-specific (Tan 1988: 18).

24. Discussing these provisions, Funston (1980: 4–11) disputes the conventional wisdom that Malays benefited much at all from their privileged position before more substantial preferential policies were introduced in 1970. He argues that it was only in their constitutional position and control of national symbols that Malays initially were "decisively on top." Moreover, Shamsul (1999) points out that the easy availability of government rural development funds benefited both Malays and Chinese, since UMNO politicians won contracts and then subcontracted the work to Chinese.

25. So alarmed were Penang's Straits Chinese elites at the inclusion of Penang and Malacca, but not Singapore, with the rest of the peninsula that they took the unprecedented step of forming the Penang Secession Committee in December 1948. The "perceived dangers of being cut loose from their traditional ties with Singapore and Britain, and swallowed up by an ethnic-Malay dominated nation," led the committee to demand exclusion from the Malayan Federation, asking instead that Penang be allowed to remain in the British Straits Settlements; though the campaign came to naught, "the fears for the future that it embodied were substantially justified in the years after independence" (Christie 1996: 28–29).

26. Most of the information in this section is drawn from Vasil 1971, probably the most comprehensive account available of Malayan noncommunal parties and the early years of Malaysia.

27. Terms such as *dato, datuk, tunku, tun, seri,* and *tan sri* are honorifics, bestowed either upon or by the hereditary aristocracy. Specific titles vary by state as well as by rank or degree of relationship to the *raja*.

28. It was only in May 2001 that UMNO decided to admit Chinese members, and then only in Sabah (where non-Malay *bumiputera* had already been accepted into the party). As one local news headline trumpeted then, "Onn Jaafar vindicated" (*New Straits Times*, May 20, 2001).

29. In contrast, independence from the British was not even mentioned in the

initial UMNO charter. *Merdeka* (Freedom) replaced *Hidup Melayu* (Long Live the Malays) as UMNO's slogan only in March 1951 (Vasil 1971: 39–40).

30. Ampalavanar (1981) suggests that the British fostered the IMP and, to a lesser extent, other moderate noncommunal parties in order to counter the appeal of the MCP.

31. So, for instance, UMNO and the MCA did not think of cooperating in the Georgetown, Penang, municipal elections in December 1951. The MCA fielded no candidates, and UMNO managed to win only one of the nine seats. Noncommunal parties took the rest: the local Radical Party won six seats, and the LPM won one (Vasil 1971: 80).

32. Held in Kuala Lumpur, this conference included representatives from the All Malaya Muslim Association, the Ceylon Federation of Malaya, the Eurasian Association of Malaya, the Federation of Indian Associations, the IMP, the Malayan Indian Association, the MIC, the Malayan Pakistani Association, the Malayan Sikh Association, and the Malayan Sinhalese Association. No Malay or Chinese associations participated. UMNO, the MCA, and the Pan Malayan Labour Party boycotted the conference, although some government leaders and other prominent individuals attended. While a working committee was formed to make representations, and a follow-up conference was held that September, these efforts were but "pathetic attempts by Dato Onn bin Jaafar, the father of Malay nationalism, to re-establish himself as the leader of the mainstream of Malayan nationalism. . . . Thus failed the attempt to establish a national coalition of all political organizations in the country" (Vasil 1971: 76–78).

33. Vasil explains that in the MCA (not the MIC), politicians first gathered strength in the Alliance government and then used patronage to build support in the party. This mechanism allowed the Alliance, at least under Tunku Abdul Rahman, "to impose a certain leadership on the MCA" (Vasil 1971: 35).

34. See Vasil 1971; Tham 1977; Ampalavanar 1981.

35. David Brown (1994) offers a compelling case for the significance of this nexus. He explains that so-called communal parties really represent "ethno-class fractions." The relative strength of PAS or UMNO, for instance, depends upon the class characteristics of a particular region, while changes within UMNO are traceable to the rise of nonaristocratic, bureaucratic leaders.

36. Long before then, however, active unions had already taken shape. The first trade union in Malaya was the Kelab Kapitan-kapitan dan Injinir-injinir (Captains' and Engineers' Club), established among Malay seamen in 1894, followed in 1908 by the Pineapple Cutters' Association. It was only in the 1920s, though, that "genuine," more effective labor unions developed (Dass 1991). However, the effect of early trade unions was limited by employers' hostility, contract-based and plentiful labor, the geographical isolation of most plantation and mine workers, and "the difficulties of class organisation in a multi-racial society" (Morgan 1977: 152). For detailed analyses of the waves of unionization and strikes both independent of and organized by the MCP and its affiliates, see also Stenson 1970; Stenson 1980; Cheah 1987.

37. See Cheah 1987; Heng 1996. See also Anderson (1998: 325).

38. See Khong 1987; Heng 1996; Cheah 1987; Hack 1999.

39. For more on Malay radical organizations, parties, and leaders, see Khoo 1991; Firdaus 1985; Zawawi 1989.

Chapter 4

1. The salience of subnational state divisions to political identity faded over this period, as did subcommunal divisions based on place of ancestral origin (Banjarese, Minang, and so on). Political outcomes are still at times attributed to states' exceptionalism, however: PAS's strength in Kelantan or Terengganu, or UMNO's in Johor, is often explained in terms of the unique character of those states and their people. Also, states' rights have remained key to the politics of Sabah and Sarawak and have surfaced in peninsular states as well when these have been under opposition rule. This study shares an unfortunate bias of much work on Malaysia: it concentrates almost exclusively on peninsular politics. Political contests and priorities differ in the East Malaysian states of Sabah and Sarawak, given demographic and developmental distinctions.

2. See National Operations Council 1969; Das and Suaram 1989; Snider 1968.

3. See, among others, Funston (1980: chap. 8); Gomez and Jomo 1997; Yong 1974.

4. The *tunku* is rather apologetic about his tendency to find "a communist behind every bush" yet seems sincerely to believe that the riots in both 1967 and 1969 could be pinned largely on ambitious Maoist insurgents. Later governments, such as Mahathir's in the wake of a 1987 crackdown, also dredged up supposed communist plots but were more prone to blame foreign meddlers than the dregs of the long-defunct MCP. Attacking PAS for its "misuse" of Islam remains as popular now as in the *tunku's* time, however.

5. For discussion of the various parties' campaign appeals, see Enloe 1970; Abdul Rahman 1969; National Operations Council 1969.

6. Today's BN includes fourteen parties: UMNO, the MCA, the MIC, Gerakan, the People's Progressive Party (PPP), the Liberal Democratic Party (LDP), the United Pasokmomogun Kadazan Organisation (UPKO), Parti Bersatu Rakyat Sabah (PBRS), the Sabah Progressive Party (SAPP), Parti Pesaka Bumiputra Bersatu (PBB), the SUPP, Parti Bansa Dayak Sabah (PBDS), Parti Bersatu Sabah (PBS), and the Sarawak Progressive Democratic Party (SPDP).

7. Demographic trends suggest that the Chinese proportion of the population may comprise as little as 13 percent by 2100 (Milne and Mauzy 1999: 90).

8. See, for instance, Rachagan 1984; Case 2001; Ong 2002.

9. Rabushka and Shepsle discuss the lead-up to this legislation. After having further augmented the relative clout of rural voters in 1962, the national government suspended most local councils and elections in 1964–65 in order to curb socialist influence, and on grounds of corruption and malpractice. At the time, Chinese- and Indian-based parties controlled the municipal councils of Georgetown, Malacca, Seremban, and Ipoh. The authors suggest a vendetta

against Chinese politicians: "The coincidence between charges of city council malpractice and the growth of urban Chinese political power cannot be overlooked" (Rabushka and Shepsle 1972: 127).

10. See, for instance, Gomez and Jomo 1997; Yong 1974; Tan 1990; Khoo 1995; Chandra 1979; Abdul Rahman 1996; Heng 1996; Stafford 1997.

11. In the early 1950s, 1.2 million rural Chinese suspected of communist sympathies were forcibly resettled, about half of them in New Villages, in an effort to cut supply lines to the insurgent MCP. There are still 1.5 million Chinese residing in 452 of these mostly Chinese, generally poor, usually opposition-supporting villages (Loh 1988: 167); see also Chinese Organisations 1999.

12. A few representatives of minority subgroups (Punjabi, Sikh, Christian, and so on) hold positions of power in the MIC, more often by appointment than by election, but Tamils have controlled the party leadership since the 1950s (Daniel 1992: chap. 7).

13. The Iban (commonly subsumed under the Dayak category) are the largest ethnic group in Sarawak (30 percent of the population), while the Kadazan (Dusun) are the largest in Sabah (28 percent). Politically, the primary groupings are Muslim *bumiputera*, non-Muslim *bumiputera*, and Chinese, with religious cleavages sometimes as salient as racial ones.

14. For an overview of politics in Sabah and Sarawak, see Loh 1997, especially the contributions by Loh and Goldman. On parties and elections, see Searle 1983; J. Chin 1996; Jawan 1993. See Reid 1997 on identity politics; for the larger context, see Milne and Mauzy 1999; Muhammad Ikmal 1996.

15. The community formally articulated its political demands for the first time in a 1982 memorandum (Means 1985–86: 650–52). See also Zawawi 1996; Dentan et al. 1997.

16. Barraclough (1985a) documents other initiatives of the 1950s to the 1980s, such as 1957's Malay Congress, 1963's United Opposition, and 1975's Barisan Rakyat, but these either failed really to get off the ground or stayed at the level of electoral pacts.

17. The British fostered the formation of the MTUC in 1950 as a central consultative body to represent less radical unions and counter the influence of the PMFTU. English-speaking Indians dominated the MTUC, although, interestingly, its first vice president was a Malay woman. The MTUC retains its role as an umbrella organization over labor unions today. While it cannot engage in collective bargaining, the MTUC coordinates the activities of unions and liaises with the government, still generally preferring compromise or compliance over a more confrontational stance, and eschewing political issues or working-class conscientization. A proposed alternative Congress of Industrial Unions was denied registration (see Dass 1991: chap. 5).

18. The ascendance of the Chinese-educated in the LPM coincided with the break in Singapore between procommunist, Chinese-educated and moderate, English-educated members in the PAP and the formation of the extremist, Chinese-chauvinist Barisan Sosialis (Socialist Front) there in September 1961. The LPM immediately established strong links with this front (Vasil 1971).

19. In fact, when Chinese unionists distrustful of the LPM's English-educated leadership tried to join the smaller PRM in 1958, PRM would not take too many, for fear of upsetting its racial balance.

20. On the Socialist Front, see Snider 1977; Vasil 1971; Enloe 1970; Heng 1996; Sanusi and Ang 1998; Jomo 1996; Barraclough 1985a.

21. Other ex-MCA members joined either the PPP or the United Democratic Party (UDP). The latter was formed in 1962 and was headed first by Lim Chong Eu and then by a prominent Malay, Zainal Abidin bin Haji Abas. The rank and file of the officially noncommunal UDP remained more committed to pro-Chinese policies than did the more moderate leadership. The UDP cooperated with the Socialist Front to a limited extent in the early 1960s, to avoid splitting the opposition vote, until a falling out in 1964, ostensibly over the allocation of seats. Lim then wanted to link his party with the PAP but was rebuffed. The party did poorly in the 1964 polls and disbanded soon after. Lim moved on to help form Gerakan (Vasil 1971).

22. Aziz, formerly a key player in both UMNO and the IMP, launched the NCP in 1963 with the support of poor Malays, especially peasants and fishermen. He tried to forge a united coalition against the Alliance for the 1964 general elections. Then, over the protests of PRM, the NCP joined the Socialist Front, though none of its candidates won in 1964. Aziz and other party leaders were detained for alleged pro-Indonesian activities in 1965 and were barred from political activity upon their release in 1967, dooming the personalistic NCP (Vasil 1971).

23. See Lee 1965a; Lee 1965b; Lee 1998, esp. 602–44; Vasil 1966; Barraclough 1985a: 37.

24. Having dropped the slogan after the 1970s, the DAP resuscitated it in 1998.

25. A critical deciding factor was the DAP's loss of an earlier by-election (in Serdang) because Gerakan played a spoiler role.

26. See also Kua 1996; Enloe 1970; Lee 1987; Jomo 1996.

27. Syed Husin Ali, interview with the author, March 2, 1999, Petaling Jaya; Sivarasah Rasiah, interview with the author, Feb. 13, 1999, Petaling Jaya; Sanusi Osman, interview with the author, Apr. 15, 1999, Petaling Jaya. See also Sanusi and Ang 1998; Jomo 1996.

28. A 1957 declaration by PAS founding father Burhannudin Al-Helmy is illustrative: "The Malays should not be asked to pay for the mistakes of the imperialists in bringing non-Malays into the country. This does not mean that we must push non-Malays out, but there must be a distinction between the aliens and the masters" (quoted in Vasil 1966: 55).

29. See, for instance, Zainah 1987; Chandra 1987; Sloane 1996.

30. In light of riots and demonstrations sparked by a heated leadership struggle in PAS but directed against ethnic Chinese, the federal government declared a state of emergency in the state in November 1977, detaining three PAS members under the ISA for inciting violence (see Alias 1991). The move was widely seen as part of a BN plan to retake control of the PAS-led Kelantan.

31. One of the most notable such incidents concerned Ibrahim Mahmud

(a.k.a. Ibrahim Libya). Allegedly supported by PAS, Ibrahim established a community in Memali, Kedah, that acquired arms and provoked disturbances in 1985. When troops stormed his house as part of a rather poorly planned response, Ibrahim led a violent struggle that resulted in the deaths of fourteen civilians (himself included) and four policemen (see Milne and Mauzy 1999: 87).

32. See Y. Mansoor 1976; Alias 1994; Enloe 1970; Jesudason 1996; Milne and Mauzy 1999; Jomo 1996; Muhammad Ikmal 1996; Weiss 2004a.

33. UMNO was ordered deregistered after a suit to have the party election results thrown out on grounds that delegates from illegal UMNO branches had voted. High Court Justice Harun Hashim decided that the existence of the illegal branches rendered the party itself illegal under the terms of the Societies Act. Since Mahathir was then also home minister, he could arrange to be the first to lay claim to the UMNO name once the original party had been deregistered. With the party's enormous assets at stake, lawsuits continued for some time.

34. For instance, PAS and three smaller parties—PRM, the Socialist Democratic Party, and the Malay Nationalist Party (Parti Nasionalis Malaysia)—had joined in the Harakah Keadilan Rakyat (referred to in English as the United Opposition Front) for the 1986 elections. See Khong 1991a.

35. BERJASA broke away in 1977–1978 to join the BN in opposing the Mohamad Asri–led PAS. HAMIM was established by Mohamad Asri upon his ouster from PAS in 1982.

36. A sizable faction from the MIC formed the IPF in mid-1990. The party quickly attracted a large number of especially working-class Indians. The IPF later joined the BN, over objections from the MIC (Jomo 1996; Syed Arabi and Mazni 1995).

37. Despite the PBS's snap decision to withdraw from the BN and support the opposition coalition, James Chin (1996) argues, Gagasan and the two-coalition ideal carried less resonance outside the peninsula. The PBS's decision to join was based on the central government's intruding upon states' rights and Kadazan interests.

38. See Khoo 1995; Khong 1991b; Case 1993; Jesudason 1996.

39. Gomez 1996; Syed Arabi and Mazni 1995; Jesudason 1996.

40. Many Malaysian NGOs rely on foreign funds when they can get them, but such aid is limited and dwindling. Foreign NGOs contribute a relatively minuscule sum to autonomous NGOs, by comparison with the amount disbursed to state-sponsored NGOs and other state agencies (Tan and Bishan 1994: 10–11). Some NGOs are reluctant to take such aid, even when it is available, to preclude charges of foreign manipulation or meddling. The Malaysian government funds certain NGO projects, such as consumer protection or anti–domestic violence programs. However, these funds are limited and raise fears for some NGOs of compromising their independence (see M. Weiss 2003).

41. For example, in the late 1980s and early 1990s, Malaysia's three most vocal, active, and well-known environmental groups claimed a total of only about 150 formal members (Nair 1999: 96).

42. Among these gripes are a compulsory Malay-language examination, the neglect of Chinese temples and burial grounds, and the government's refusal to

recognize the Unified Examination Certificate granted by Malaysian Chinese secondary schools.

43. See the discussion of the Malaysian Chinese Organisations' Election Appeals Committee (Suqiu) in the next chapter.

44. Chinese and Indian associations, asked to provide feedback to the government ten years after this policy's implementation, presented memoranda urging a more egalitarian approach encouraging of diversity. They stressed particular concerns, such as language and education (especially the Chinese memorandum) and religious freedom (especially the Indian memorandum). For details, see Kua 1985.

45. Yong 1974: 9–10; Kua 1985. See also Milne and Mauzy (1999: 89–93).

46. ABIM boasts of 60,000 members, a 1,000-strong staff, a corporate arm (Koperasi Belia Islam, Islamic Youth Cooperative), an extensive system of Islamic schools, substantial property and other holdings, and a network of state and district branches, stretching down to the grassroots nationwide (Shaharuddin Badaruddin, interview with the author, Apr. 7, 1999, Wangsa Maju).

47. ABIM prohibits its officers from simultaneously holding office in any political party.

48. In 1946, 27 percent of working Malays were employees, compared with 56 percent of Chinese and 90 percent of Indians. By 1980, 55 percent of Malays, 64 percent of Chinese, and 84 percent of Indians worked as employees (Jomo and Todd 1994: 16–17). Jomo and Todd caution, however, that different government agencies supply contradictory labor-force data. Across all the principal officer positions in peninsular Malaysian unions in 1986, 63 percent of officers were Malay, 20 percent were Chinese, and 17 percent were Indian (Grace 1990: 44–45).

49. For example, electronics workers are defined by the registrar as producing electronics components. Therefore, they may not join the national union for electrical workers, who are defined as producing finished electronic products.

50. The MTUC was long aligned with the opposition, although not with any specific party. Now the organization is less politicized and confrontational than previously (Francis Xavier, interview with the author, July 1, 1997, Penang).

51. Regardless, the number of unionized workers in the public sector had actually surpassed that of the larger private sector by 1984.

52. However, workers of other races, not women, are generally used to break strikes.

53. Despite the significant increase in women's participation in the labor force, their proportion of union membership has hovered at around 25 percent since the 1950s, not least because their "double burden" leaves women with little time for union activities (Grace 1990; Rohana 1988).

54. See Grace 1990; Rohana 1988; Rohana 1997; Lai 2003.

55. For instance, the labor-related Catholic groups Young Christian Workers and Urban Rural Mission were implicated in the 1987 ISA crackdown (Selvaraja, interview with the author, June 25, 1997, Penang).

56. On student activism in the 1960s and 1970s, see Fan 1988; Hassan and Siti Nor 1984. On communal tendencies among students, see Chandra 1984;

Abraham 1999. On Islam and social justice activism, see Zainah 1987. For a historical overview, see Weiss 2004b.

57. FOMCA, the umbrella consumers' organization, has the most extensive relations with the government of all Malaysian NGOs, representing consumers in a number of councils and ministries (Tan and Bishan 1994: 18).

58. Zaitun Kasim, interview with the author, Aug. 1, 1997, Petaling Jaya. Irene Xavier concurs that the government will not consult NGOs with which it has fundamental differences, or it may call those NGOs in to inform rather than consult with them (Irene Xavier, interview with the author, Aug. 7, 1997, Petaling Jaya). See also Lim 1995; Tan and Singh 1994; M. Weiss 2003.

59. Except those covered by other legislation, such as trade unions, companies, and cooperatives.

60. Even a permit for publication may not be enough. For example, in late 1999, NGO Aliran charged that it could not find a printer willing to print its monthly magazine because of alleged governmental pressure tactics directed at potential printers (see "We Apologise" 1999).

61. Aliran 1981; Tan and Singh 1994; Ahmad Fauzi 2000; Kua 1998b.

62. In fact, lawyer and activist T. Rajamoorthy suggests that the proliferation of NGOs in Malaysia actually reflects the depoliticization of society. Citizens now have the option of critiquing the government via NGOs rather than more directly, through radical parties or even student groups, and may become myopic by focusing on small problems without heeding the larger context (T. Rajamoorthy, interview with the author, July 11, 1997, Penang).

63. Zaitun Kasim, interview with the author, Aug. 1, 1997, Petaling Jaya.

64. The NGOs were Aliran, the Consumers' Association of Penang (CAP), the Environmental Protection Society Malaysia (EPSM), the Selangor Graduates Society (SGS), and the Bar Council. The parties were the DAP and PAS.

65. The detainees included politicians from the DAP, the MCA, Gerakan, PAS, and UMNO Youth as well as Chinese educationists, NGO figures, university lecturers, Muslim and Christian activists, and environmentalists.

66. For details, see Committee Against Repression in the Pacific and Asia 1988; Das and Suaram 1989; Nair 1995; Khoo 1995.

67. The cases in question, all decided between 1986 and 1988, were the release on account of procedural errors of oppositionist Karpal Singh, held under the ISA; a challenge to actions taken by the government against the *Asian Wall Street Journal* and two affiliated journalists; an injunction granted against a Japanese firm for releasing radioactive waste in Perak; an injunction, granted on grounds of corrupt practices to DAP leader Lim Kit Siang, that stalled construction of the North-South Highway; the decision (an appeal against Minister of Home Affairs Mahathir) that the *Aliran Monthly* could be published in Malay as well as in English; and the forced dissolution of UMNO.

68. Judicial review had been codified as article 4 (1) of the federal constitution as well as being one of the five pillars of the *Rukunegara*, the national ideology. The 1988 Federal Constitution (Amendment) Act left the courts' powers conferred by Parliament instead of enshrined in the constitution; the High Courts stripped of the power of judicial review; and the attorney general able to instruct

the judiciary on which cases to hear, in what courts, and with which judges. For the former lord president's personal and highly indignant take on events, see Salleh and Das 1989; Fan 1990; Khoo 1995; Milne and Mauzy 1999.

69. For example, only about 15 percent of the approximately two hundred members of Women's Crisis Centre (WCC, since renamed Women's Centre for Change), a Penang NGO, constitute its active core, although about seventy more occasionally lend support (Rohana Arifin, interview with the author, June 27 1997, Penang).

70. "Money politics" refers to the intertwining of political power and business interests. See Gomez 1991; Gomez and Jomo 1997.

Chapter 5

1. For instance, a group of non-Islamic opposition and NGO activists met with Anwar within about a week of his dismissal, surprising even Anwar with their supportive response (Rustam Sani, interview with the author, Apr. 15, 1999, Kuala Lumpur).

2. A prominent example is the report "Justice in Jeopardy: Malaysia in 2000," drafted by a commission composed of representatives of the International Bar Association, the Centre for the Independence of Judges and Lawyers of the International Commission of Jurists, the Commonwealth Lawyers' Association, and the International Lawyers Union (International Bar Association et al. 2000). In September 2004, a panel of judges quashed Anwar's sodomy conviction and set him free.

3. While support for PAS was highest along the east coast, and local opposition *ceramah* (public lectures) were well attended, few if any demonstrations were held there. Endorsement of the opposition and the need for change seemed to be taken for granted rather than shouted in the streets in Kelantan and Terengganu.

4. Rumor had it that Abu Hassan had been involved in a long-running affair with his sister-in-law, possibly fathering her child. He denied these allegations, claiming that a Chinese Muslim, also named Abu Hassan, was the real father. Interestingly, it was Indonesia's *Jawa Pos*, rather than the Malaysian media, that broke the story ("Menteri Besar Selangor" 2000; Wan Hamid 2000).

5. He settled on a political newcomer, Mohamad Khir Toyo.

6. Rumors also circulated (without any proof) that this story had actually been concocted by the government to justify a strong state and discredit reformers.

7. Such charges had been levied previously but dismissed without redress. However, in a landmark decision in June 2001, a High Court judge in Sabah ordered a BN state assemblyman to vacate his seat on the grounds that the electoral roll for his constituency had been padded by the improper registration of noncitizens. Justice Muhammad Kamil Awang also complained in his judgment that he had been ordered by a superior to drop the case ("Former Sabah CM" 2001).

8. See Chan 1999; Khoo 1999; Liebhold 1999. Also James Wong, interview with the author, March 27, 1999, Petaling Jaya.

9. Administered by Universiti Kebangsaan Malaysia undergraduates, this sur-

vey had serious flaws and is far from fully reliable. However, the results may at least be used in a "confirm or deny" sense to gauge whether generally held ideas about political attitudes and behavior seemed to be borne out by respondents' answers.

10. These profiles (and much of the rest of the empirical information in the chapter) are based on observation of Reformasi events and analysis of movement-related media.

11. The translation from Chinese to English was hotly debated. Younger activists wanted to use the term *demands*, while their elders favored the less aggressive *appeals* (Liew Chin Tong, personal communication, July 5, 2001, Canberra).

12. Text available at <http://bosses.faithweb.com> (accessed Apr. 2, 2005). See also Oon 1999.

13. The remaining demands were as follows: curbing corruption; promulgating a fair and equitable economic policy; reviewing the privatization policy; developing an enlightened, liberal, and progressive education policy; protecting the Malaysian environment; ensuring housing for all; allowing a fair media; restoring confidence in the police force; upgrading social services; respecting the rights of workers; and providing for Malaysia's indigenous peoples (Chinese Organisations 1999). See also Oon 1999; Lim 1999a; Loh 2000.

14. The list reached the National Economic Consultative Council (NECC), the body appointed to draw up Malaysia's next ten-year plan, the New Vision Policy. Possibly in response, the NECC considered curbing affirmative action, although NECC Vice Chairman David Chua's presentation of the case for rethinking affirmative action (Gilley 2000) drew immediate flak.

15. These included Barisan Bertindak Mahasiswa Negara (National Students' Action Front), the Inter-Varsity Council, Gabungan Mahasiswa Islam Semenanjung (Peninsular Islamic Students' Association), and Gerakan Demokratik Belia dan Pelajar Malaysia (Malaysian Youth and Students Democratic Movement). Another ten youth groups lambasted the local media for twisting the facts to heighten tensions.

16. See, for instance, "Hapus Hak Istimewa" 2000; Kabilan 2000; Kua 2000; " 'Special Rights' " 2000; Syed Husin 2000.

17. James Chin (2001) explains that the MCA and Gerakan (others say just the latter) privately urged Suqiu to put aside any "sensitive" demands.

18. When women did stage a demonstration in October 1998, protesting outside Istana Negara (the national palace), the government claimed that among them were prostitutes who had been paid to participate ("NGOs 'Hired Prostitutes' " 1998).

19. Further information on the WCI can be found at <http:www.candidate. freeservers.com> (accessed Apr. 2, 2005). On both the WAC and WCI, see Martinez 2003; Tan and Ng 2003. Wan Azizah was not closely connected with either effort. While she acknowledged that her gender earned her sympathy, Wan Azizah characterized herself more as "a symbol of motherhood, being a wife, endurance" than as a champion for women, which was why she felt Islamists so readily tolerated her leadership (Wan Azizah Wan Ismail, interview with the author, Jan. 7, 1999, Kuala Lumpur).

20. In fact, the government threatened to take children away from parents who brought them to demonstrations, on grounds of their showing insufficient regard for their children's well-being.

21. In September 2003, EC chief Abdul Rashid Abdul Rahman announced that he was lifting the ban on outdoor rallies for the 2004 elections. Government officials, including Mahathir himself, said it was up to the police to do so, since questions of national security were involved. Abdul Rashid countered by citing the recently amended Election Offences Act, which allows outdoor public campaign rallies ("Aliran: Don't Use National Security" 2003; Arfa'eza 2003a; Arfa'eza 2003b; "Najib: Without Public Rallies" 2003).

22. The BN also holds *ceramah* but is less dependent upon them, given its recourse to the media, access to selective incentives (such as patronage) to lure voters, and excellent party organization. UMNO and its partners can also afford, for example, to transport voters to their polling stations, thus reinforcing a sense of obligation and offering voters last-minute reminders about how to cast their votes.

23. *Ceramah*, Nov. 25, 1999, Selandar, Malacca.

24. While the Universities and University Colleges Act (UUCA; see chap. 4, this volume) deterred many students from participating openly or at all, significant numbers of secondary and tertiary students played a role in Reformasi protests. In fact, opposition to the UUCA itself was a key factor in students' agitation. Mohd. Azizuddin 1999; Weiss 2004b.

25. The inspiration for Pemantau was not only regional election monitoring bodies such as the Asian Network for Free Elections (ANFREL), based in the Philippines, and the offer of seed money and training from groups like the American National Democratic Institute for International Affairs (NDI), but also a previous, smaller-scale monitoring effort in Malaysia: 1990's Election Watch, consisting of six prominent individuals. See especially Netto 1990; "Election Watch" 1990.

26. Wan Azizah Wan Ismail, interview with the author, Jan. 7, 1999, Kuala Lumpur; Sivarasa Rasiah, interview with the author, Feb. 13, 1999, Petaling Jaya.

27. Alison Wee, personal communication, Sept. 19, 1999.

28. In Sarawak, the DAP, Keadilan, and the State Reform Party (STAR) worked together. Sabah's PBS cooperated, too, contesting only in Sabah so as not to split the peninsular opposition vote. In 1995, the PBS had contested fruitlessly in Penang, Sarawak, Labuan, and Johor as well as in Sabah.

29. Anwar's close ally Kamarudin Jafar, for instance, joined PAS in July 1999 upon being ousted from UMNO for "helping the opposition." He justified his choice to join PAS rather than Keadilan as strategic, saying he hoped to "further strengthen the cooperation and understanding between the parties" and to bolster the BA in its fight against UMNO (quoted in "Switching Teams" 1999: 11).

30. Other NGO activists who contested included the human rights lawyer and activist Sivarasa Rasiah; Zainur Zakaria, former president of the Bar Council; Jeyakumar Devaraj, a physician and activist; and the human rights and peace activist Fan Yew Teng, who had previously served under the DAP. A number of candidates from ABIM, JIM, and other Islamic organizations also con-

tested. The reform-minded novelist Shahnon Ahmad of PAS, who raised an uproar with his scatological 1999 political satire *Shit*, also made his political debut, winning a parliamentary seat.

31. Campaigning is permitted only between nomination day and election day, both of which are declared by the incumbent government. Malaysian campaign periods have been shrinking over the years, but nine days is unusually brief. For a more thorough review and analysis of the elections, see Loh and Saravanamuttu 2003; Kamarudin 2000; Funston 2000; Weiss 2000a.

32. The BA won about 43 percent of the vote in peninsular Malaysia, but in East Malaysia, the BA and the PBS only received about 15 percent each. Johor presents something of an anomaly, perhaps because UMNO's machinery is particularly strong there—Johor is the birthplace of the party—and because Anwar had never cultivated much of a base in that state.

33. Chandra Muzaffar (1990: 3) opined after the 1990 elections that UMNO's "fear tactic" had had little impact in Kelantan because Malays there comprise over 90 percent of the population and so "feel politically and psychologically secure." The locals' very strong ties to Malay culture and Islam paved the way for PAS to counter UMNO's claim to indispensability as the champion of Malay rights and interests. Moreover, Kelantanese, like Sabahans, may resent their neglect by and lack of clout with the federal government. These arguments no doubt still carry weight, especially given Kelantan's distinct culture and dialect.

34. Thanks to these electoral arrangements, the BN had won 71 percent of parliamentary seats with 52 percent of the popular vote in 1990 and 84 percent of seats with 65 percent of the vote in 1995. Loh (2002a) explains how April 2002 amendments to the election laws have skewed the system even more in the BN's favor than before.

35. In terms of votes and seats, the party did not do quite as well as its closest counterpart, the now-defunct S'46, did in 1990 or 1995, but it did seem to have more of a nationwide impact.

36. Four UMNO cabinet ministers and five deputy ministers lost their seats. Others, including Mahathir, won with sharply reduced margins.

37. Surveys, including some purported Special Branch reports leaked by civil servants in the months after Anwar's sacking, suggest that a clear majority of civil servants, Malay voters overall, and UMNO members did not support Mahathir. For instance, Hiebert and Jayasankaran (1998) cite an UMNO survey finding that 70 percent of Malays were unhappy with the way Anwar had been ousted, and Hari (2000) offers the estimate of at least six out of ten UMNO members' not agreeing to Anwar's expulsion from the party. Several of my informants offered similar or higher statistics, with 80 percent being the most common figure. One senior UMNO member and founding member of ABIM was more specific, stating that 80 percent of civil servants and 60 percent of students did not support Mahathir, while *kampung* dwellers were about evenly split between support for Anwar and for Mahathir (interview with the author, Jan. 20, 1999, Kg. Gajah).

38. After the DAP's somewhat disappointing performance in 1990, party

leader Lim Kit Siang explained that the party had made a choice to work in coalition, even at the cost of some seats. Having fared even worse on its own (more or less) in 1995, the DAP again took the gamble of linking up with its fellow opposition parties in 1999, only to be marginalized and attacked. See Lim 1999b for his justification of the DAP's participation in the BA.

39. See, for instance, Kamar Ainiah 1999; Raja Petra 1999; Marina Yusoff 1999.

40. Cynicism and apathy usually deter many from voting, especially non-Malays (see, for instance, Martinez 1999). Even a number of NGO activists had never registered to vote.

41. Indeed, one provision in the BA's proposed budget—the eradication of television user license fees—was promptly incorporated into the BN's own budget and was announced before the government remembered to revise its revenue estimates.

42. Lim's wife, Betty Chew, like Wan Azizah, was also elected on a *keadilan* platform, but hers was a safe seat for the DAP (Liew Chin Tong, personal communication, June 13, 2001, Canberra).

43. Although some seats with narrow margins had particularly high levels of spoiled ballots, no clear pattern is evident. Fanning the assumptions of foul play were charges on election day that, for instance, the box to check for the opposition candidate had been waxed to prevent its being easily marked on some ballots, or that there was a preprinted stroke in one party's box (Mahathir said it was in PAS's box, and Keadilan said it was in the BN's), and so a vote for the other would spoil the ballot. See Raja Petra 1999; Marina Yusoff 1999.

44. The legal limits are RM30,000 per state seat and RM50,000 per federal seat. In 2004, too, PAS (a comparatively well-resourced opposition party) is thought to have spent less than 10 percent of what UMNO spent per seat (Ibrahim 2004: 2).

45. The DAP has been beset for some time by internal dissent and opposition to longtime leader Lim Kit Siang (see, for instance, Kua 1998a). The leaders of one anti-Lim initiative went on to form the MDP. Also, the DAP took umbrage in early June 1999 and again in February 2001 when Keadilan admitted two anti-Lim DAP members and ex-leaders. The DAP's chief rival in Penang, Gerakan, faces leadership struggles, too, which led to the resignation of two Gerakan state assembly members in December 1999. To Gerakan's irritation, the two were subsequently admitted into the MCA, giving the latter more state seats than Gerakan.

46. Zaitun Kasim, interview with the author, Nov. 23, 1999, Selayang.

47. Keadilan deputy president Chandra Muzaffar prevaricated in an April 4, 1999, press conference in Kuala Lumpur. He said that the constitution leaves the office open to any citizen but that the prime minister is "often" from the "majority community."

48. The same speaker also insisted that although any Muslim, regardless of race, can enter PAS, and although the difference between the BA and the BN is that only the former is for *perpaduan* (unity) among races, the BA does not ignore Malay or indigenous peoples' special rights, and the DAP agrees in the joint man-

ifesto with the implementation of Islamic law—a rather misleading statement, since the document skirts such details (PAS-organized *ceramah*, Nov. 23, 1999, Selayang).

49. This quite detailed (*too* detailed, many complained) platform of action first describes the causes of popular frustration with the regime—from cronyism and corruption to human rights abuses to rising income inequality—and then presents proposals for improving the economy, transparency and accountability, social services, national unity, the quality of democracy, and Malaysia's international image (Barisan Alternatif 1999).

50. PAS's less compromising stance had confounded coalition-building efforts for the 1986 elections (Alias 1994). On the 1990 elections, see especially "Can the Opposition" 1990; "A Change in Emphasis" 1990; "An Islamic State" 1990; and "Towards a Two-Coalition System?" 1990. With collaboration less an issue in 1995, PAS asserted its religious character more strongly, alienating non-Muslims.

51. One PAS leader explained that a *negara Islam* is about justice, unity, brotherhood, transparency, public accountability, and freedom—all of which both PAS and the DAP want—and that the problem is therefore terminological: once PAS labels such a state Islamic, the DAP refuses to cooperate (Husam Musa, interview with the author, Feb. 23, 1999, Kota Bharu). The issue resurfaced in mid-2001, when PAS (particularly its less compromising older leaders) refused to sign a BA statement saying that the coalition would not implement an Islamic state if it came to power (Abdul Aziz 2001; Loone 2001a; Loone 2001b).

52. Wan Azizah and PRM's Syed Husin Ali reaffirmed in 2003, "We are of the opinion that the usage of the term Islamic state continues to raise misunderstanding and unnecessary fears among certain sections of society, especially among non-Muslims" ("Keadilan Raps PAS" 2003).

53. Mahfuz Omar, interview with the author, Apr. 13, 1999, Petaling Jaya.

54. However, PAS had appointed female senators. Dewan Muslimat, the women's wing of PAS, insisted that the protective ban against campaigning was only a provisional measure until the circumstances of campaigns changed (Jamilah Ibrahim and Arniwati Sabirin, interview with the author, Feb. 24, 1999, Kota Bharu). As an indication of the pressure for change, at the PAS *muktamar* (national convention), in June 2000, two Muslimat leaders openly challenged the degree of gender segregation among party leadership (Tan 2000).

55. However, his political secretary stated that PAS could at least endorse Wan Azizah if she ran under another party (Husam Musa, interview with the author, Feb. 23, 1999, Kota Bharu).

56. This sort of Islamist outbidding by the government may further legitimate the opposition's Islamist discourse; see, for instance, Al-Sayyid (1995: 292); Norton 1996.

57. Whereas most accounts of the DAP's departure from the BA stress the Islamic state issue, Khoo (2002: 6) argues that the "BA came to grief over issues of power." With PAS having won 27 parliamentary seats, the DAP 10, and Keadilan only 5, power was highly unbalanced in the BA after the elections.

58. Terengganu controls about 64 percent of Malaysia's proved oil reserves

and 40 percent of its gas reserves. Under a 1974 agreement, the state government received a royalty of 5 percent on oil produced, in addition to revenues from the gas and petrochemical industries (see Shameen 1999). Royalties for 2000 were anticipated to be about RM810 million, just over half of which had been paid out in February. Terming the royalties a "goodwill payment," Mahathir channeled further payments into a special fund to be managed by the federal government rather than the PAS state government, purportedly as a way of precluding misappropriation (Ng and Loone 2000).

59. In Kelantan, for example, the BN promised construction of a third bridge (worth $43.7 million) over the Kelantan River and a $394.7 million flood-mitigation project in the river basin.

60. See Zaharom 1998 on the current structure of the Malaysian media, and Mustafa 1998 on the historical evolution of media regulation and the media's role in elections of the 1950s and 1990s.

61. The MCA sparked a rift within and an uproar outside the party in mid-May 2001 with its hasty decision to purchase two Chinese dailies. Critics of the deal charged that the party hoped to make those newspapers more quiescent and to ensure favorable coverage of the MCA in the next elections (Loh 2001). As for the *Star* and the *Sun*, the former has become Malaysia's most widely read English newspaper but quite tame, and the latter is nearly defunct.

62. The English-language section generally included more secular articles, such as statements from other parties' leaders and opinion pieces on justice, to appeal to a wide spectrum of readers and underplay the strength of PAS's Islamic ideology. The Malay-language section retained much the same Islamic focus as before.

63. This reluctance did not prevent a January 2003 raid on *Malaysiakini* ("Police Raid" 2003).

64. The term *kafir* has particular political salience in Malaysia. Used not only to refer (disparagingly) to non-Muslims, it has also featured in PAS-UMNO fights. At a *ceramah* in Terengganu in 1981, Hadi Awang of PAS reportedly first issued a dictum branding UMNO a party of infidels (see Wan Hamidi 2001).

65. Sisters in Islam began with eight members and has grown only slightly since then. Nevertheless, it offers incisive, controversial, nonpartisan critiques of Islamic practice and dogma in Malaysia (Zainah Anwar, interview with the author, Apr. 7, 1999, Kuala Lumpur).

66. These attacks were carried a step further with a January 2002 memorandum from the Persatuan Ulama Malaysia (Malaysian Muslim Scholars' Association)—also signed by a number of Muslim organizations, though not by ABIM or PAS—to the Conference of Rulers (the sultans). The document requested punitive action against six writers, among them activists, academics, a lawyer, and a journalist, for denigrating Islam and the Persatuan Ulama Malaysia (Nash 2002; Yap 2002).

67. Liew Chin Tong, personal communication, July 5, 2001, Canberra.

68. Mahfuz Omar, interview with the author, Apr. 13, 1999, Kuala Lumpur.

Chapter 6

1. *Dakwah* groups in Malaysia seem at least partly to fill a niche similar to that of comparable groups elsewhere. Norton (1999: 33) suggests that Islamic movements in the Middle East act as vehicles for political and economic demands because by "cloaking themselves in the symbols of their faith" they are better able to resist government restrictions than other sorts of groups. A less cynical explanation lies in Greg Barton's observation (2001: 249) that in Indonesia, as urban professionals grow more devout, they become not just more observant but "also more knowledgeable about [Islam] in a way that encourages them towards tolerance and open-mindedness." Many of the same sorts of educated professionals are involved with *dakwah* groups in Malaysia, so the same logic may apply.

2. See contributions to Loh and Saravanamuttu 2003 for evidence, especially the chapters by the editors, Maznah, and Tan and Ng.

3. Rustam Sani, interview with the author, Apr. 15, 1999, Kuala Lumpur.

4. For instance, Universiti Bangsar Utama, named for a neighborhood near Universiti Malaya, has a membership of over one hundred undergraduates and presses for change in society through study groups, forums, and creative means, such as stage dramas (Kabilan 2001; Hishamuddin Rais, interview with the author, Dec. 18, 2003, Kuala Lumpur).

5. See Weiss 2004b for details.

6. Loh (2002b: x) defines "the discourse and practice of participatory democracy" promoted by NGOs as "not only the institutional checks and balances associated with free and fair elections and procedural democracy . . . [but also] the creation of an autonomous public sphere that allows for alternative views of development and democratic participation to be aired."

7. For instance, while 95 percent of the respondents acknowledged the value of elections as a means to express voters' needs and demands, non-Malays were more critical than Malays regarding how just the electoral system is (Saravanamuttu 1992: 56–57). He is reluctant, though, to give too much weight to his findings, since they could either indicate a strong orientation toward democratic norms and repudiation of communalism or simply reflect that respondents were less than honest. In a later article, he cites commensurate survey data suggesting that "although Malaysians are essentially ethnic political actors, they are at the same time also democratic political actors" (Saravanamuttu 1997: 8), with crosscutting affiliations in other sorts of civic groups superimposed over ethnic associations and goals.

8. Much the same can be said for neighboring Singapore, where, contrary to social scientific predictions, Singapore's middle class has largely failed to demand political liberalization (Jones and Brown 1994). Mahathir and others use the Malay idiom *kacang melupakan kulit* (peanuts that forget their shells) to berate those who do not act duly grateful.

9. In the same vein, Sloane (1996: 80–81) finds also that, despite attempts since the 1970s to integrate urban areas, Kuala Lumpur and outlying Petaling Jaya still consist mostly of segregated pockets with "very little social interaction across ethnic lines," even in areas that appear well integrated. In particular, sym-

bols of food and alcohol and norms of behavior demarcate Malay and non-Malay public space.

10. See also Syed Husin 1984; Khoo 1997; Jesudason 1996.

11. Challenging this characterization is the MCA's 2001 takeover of Nanyang Press Holdings, which controls two major Chinese newspapers, creating "a virtual BN monopoly of the electronic media as well as of the major presses" (Loh 2003: 279; see also Loh 2001).

12. James Wong Wing On, interview with the author, March 27 1999, Petaling Jaya. See also Ng 2003; Loh (2003: 261–63).

13. Wan Azizah Wan Ismail, interview with the author, Jan. 7, 1999, Kuala Lumpur.

14. Details drawn from the following sources: Elizabeth Wong, interview with the author, Oct. 1, 1998, Petaling Jaya; Saliha Hassan, interview with the author, Oct. 28, 1998, Petaling Jaya; Sivarasa Rasiah, interview with the author, Feb. 13, 1999, Petaling Jaya; Syed Husin Ali, interview with the author, March 2, 1999, Petaling Jaya; Mahfuz Omar, interview with the author, Apr. 13, 1999, Petaling Jaya; Sanusi Osman, interview with the author, Apr. 15, 1999, Petaling Jaya; Rustam Sani, interview with the author, Apr. 15, 1999, Kuala Lumpur; Keadilan, *Majlis Pelancaran* (official launch), Apr. 4 1999, Kuala Lumpur; Wan Azizah Wan Ismail, *ceramah*, Apr. 7 1999, Kuala Lumpur.

15. Barraclough (1984: 460) unwittingly offers an operational definition of coalitional capital in explaining the significance of the cross-communal campaign against the 1981 amendments to the Societies Act: "Should there emerge in the future a general issue touching upon basic political rights, or a specific issue relatively free of communal overtones, the example of the campaign . . . might well enable diverse communal groups once again to cooperate in a bid to modify official policy."

16. A colorful example: after the March 1999 Sabah state elections (in which the opposition PBS faced the same weakness), one defeated PBS candidate both derided the BN's lavish gift giving and bemoaned the fact that he himself had had only a small amount of cash to distribute to voters (personal communication, March 13, 1999, Kota Kinabalu).

17. Discussions at NDI/ANFREL election monitoring training, Kuala Lumpur, July 1999.

18. Oorjitham refers specifically to Suqiu, the Women's Agenda for Change, and the Group of Concerned Citizens, an Indian organization focusing on plantation workers' wages and Tamil-medium education. These groups are among a long list of independent groups that Saravanamuttu (2003a: 12–14) identifies as voicing concerns to the BN and BA.

19. Khairy Jamaluddin, interview with the author, Aug. 26, 2003, Putrajaya.

20. Conversely, the credibility of the party was challenged when the most prominent such individual, Chandra Muzaffar, left, especially since this change seemed to usher in a retreat to "old UMNO culture" (Khairy Jamaluddin, interview with the author, Aug. 26, 2003, Putrajaya).

21. The desire to control information and monitor historical readings also helps explain why discussion of such tumultuous and controversial events as the 1969 riots is so tightly controlled. Any suggestion that the government may in

any way have encouraged the outbreak is deemed seditious and is chargeable in court. In fact, Marina Yusoff, formerly of Keadilan (and, before that, of UMNO and S'46), was found guilty in February 2001 of sedition for her allusions to 1969 in a campaign *ceramah*.

22. During the Reformasi movement, Malaysia had about 480,000 Internet subscribers among a population of 22 million. As of mid-1999, the country's largest Internet service provider, TMNet, reported about 14,000 new subscribers per month since September 1998, compared with about 9,000 per month before that. Also, Malaysians had more than 900,000 Hotmail accounts, the largest number in Asia (Pereira 1999). A June 13, 1999, post to ADIL-Net noted that 2,836,837 newsgroup postings per day came from domains ending with .*my* (Malaysia) and that 3,471 pro-Reformasi Web sites were experiencing a total of about 1.7 million transactions per day. Attention to Internet-based information has proved durable. Now a subscription-based news service, *Malaysiakini* still claims over 100,000 Malaysian readers. Over half the site's subscribers are under forty-five, and—interestingly—the overwhelming majority are male ("Traffic & Demographics" n.d.).

23. For instance, in an Internet-based survey, Rozhan Othman found that of 170 respondents (the sample overwhelmingly urban and Malay), 70 percent claimed to read *Harakah,* the PAS newsletter, more than double the number reading the runner-up, the mainstream *Star.* Moreover, among the most common reasons respondents gave for why people "on the fence" were not ready to support "alternative" parties was that they did not get information from alternative media. Results and conclusions were circulated on ADIL-Net, ISLAH-Net, and ALAMIN-Net on Aug. 11, 1999.

24. For a highly critical perspective, see Har and Hutnyk 1999.

25. See Ostrom 1998 for a more technical discussion of when and why face-to-face communication is more efficacious than computer-based signaling of intentions (which could be seen as comparable to signaling via the identity-obscuring Internet).

26. With this by-election, the BN lost its two-thirds majority in the legislature of Mahathir's home state, Kedah. Netto credits a "decisive swing among the ethnic Chinese [one-third of voters] towards the opposition" for this win; Malays (43 percent in the constituency) "remain deeply divided," and Indians "remained fairly solidly behind the ruling coalition" (Netto 2000: 4–5).

27. For instance, within two weeks of taking office, Abdullah launched initiatives to cut red tape in government departments and reduce corruption, soliciting public feedback as well as increasing spot-checks (*Malaysiakini,* Nov. 14, 2003). Also Abdullah 2003; Khairy Jamaluddin, interview with the author, Aug. 26, 2003, Putrajaya.

28. One of the reasons the Lunas by-election of November 2000 was deemed such a watershed was that it was the first time those voters who had been left off the electoral rolls in 1999 were included. Keadilan won the seat by 530 votes after having lost it by 4,700 votes one year previously (Netto 2000: 4).

29. The NVP (2001–2010) reduces the emphasis on numerical quotas but maintains the distinction between *bumiputera* and others.

30. The distinction between race and religion among Muslims was first made

by Malay nationalists in the colonial era, to exclude non-Malay Muslims—who were generally wealthier than indigenous Malays—from the *bangsa Melayu* (Tan 1988). Even today, non-Malay Muslims "are often not perceived to be 'genuine Muslims' . . . Privately, such marginal Muslims are often the object of scorn and distrust" (Sloane 1996: 78).

31. For instance, Chandra Muzaffar's International Movement for a Just World.

32. While the framework I develop is not based upon a rational choice approach, I borrow these informative and more broadly applicable concepts from Ostrom's work.

33. Saravanamuttu (2003b) pleads for additional placements of NGO leaders in electoral contests.

34. James Wong Wing On, personal communication, May 28, 1999.

35. In the meantime, it is perhaps an artifact of the cogency of communalism that the bulk of Chinese civil society organizations, especially those with mostly Chinese-educated members, ally primarily with one another, albeit for basically noncommunal aims and with the blessing of non-Chinese counterparts.

36. In the same interview, he explained that, before becoming an officer of Keadilan, "because I had anticipated these illogical and jittery sentiments [unhappiness that a Christian leader was entering opposition politics] on the part of some in the Christian leadership, for me to have the freedom to exercise my personal Christian conscience, I took care to (voluntarily) disentangle and distance myself from all the Christian organisations I used to serve in." The interview, originally published in the Graduates Christian Fellowship newsletter, *Communique*, was posted with permission to the sangkancil discussion list on June 28, 1999.

Chapter 7

1. Soeharto's reshuffling of ABRI in the early 1990s decreased the influence of the "red and white" (nationalist) faction associated with Benny Murdani and promoted "green" (Islamist) officers sympathetic to Vice President Habibie and himself (Eklöf 1999: esp. chap. 1).

2. The tenets of *Pancasila* are belief in one supreme god, humanism, nationalism, popular sovereignty, and social justice. First articulated by Soekarno in 1945, *Pancasila* was more deeply entrenched by Soeharto to derail potential challenges through the 1970s and 1980s.

3. The following discussion draws heavily on Aspinall 1996 and Eklöf 1999.

4. The latter was particularly significant, sparking two waves of student-led demonstrations—the largest since 1978—in 1991 and 1993. Senior Muslim leaders also played a key role in these demonstrations, foregrounding moral and religious issues. Heryanto (1996: 258–59) contrasts these demonstrations with a legal dispute over a state-proposed lottery in the Philippines in 1994 and concludes that, unlike in the Philippines, "real politics in Indonesia takes place primarily outside the confines of formal institutions."

5. The daughter of *Bapak Indonesia* (Father of Indonesia) Soekarno, Mega-

wati was popular largely on account of her name and "the notion among her supporters that she represented the ideas and charisma of her late father" (Eklöf 1999: 25). Megawati herself was not all that confrontational or even active in the party or the government, at least not at that stage, and even afterward was castigated for remaining aloof or insufficiently vocal.

6. The government had also intervened with the PDI in 1993, trying unsuccessfully to get its own nominee installed as head instead of Megawati. Megawati's supporters formed an *arus bawah* (undercurrent), standing fast despite intimidation (Heryanto 1996: 258).

7. Particularly damning was a January 1998 televised ceremony in which IMF director Michel Camdessus stood behind Soeharto, arms crossed, while the latter signed an agreement for an emergency aid operation.

8. Abdurrahman, popularly called Gus Dur, also suffered a stroke that month, which curbed his political activism for a time.

9. A key event was a February 1998 petition by nineteen individuals from the influential Lembaga Ilmu Pengetahuan Indonesia (Indonesian Institute of Sciences), demanding Soeharto's resignation.

10. Students' demands to meet with Soeharto himself were denied, but a national dialogue was held on April 18 with representatives from the government, the military, and social organizations as well as intellectuals and students and rectors from thirty-nine institutions of higher education. The meeting reaped more media attention than it did concrete results, but it highlighted for the students just how beleaguered and internally divided the government felt.

11. Among the most radical was Jakarta's Komunitas Mahasiswa Se-Jabotabek, more commonly known as Forum Kota (FORKOT, Greater Jakarta Student Community or City Forum), which spanned over forty campuses. See Lane 1999; Cohen 1998b.

12. An estimated 30,000 to 40,000 Sino-Indonesians (who number about 6 to 8 million in all, or 3–4 percent of Indonesia's population), together with enormous amounts of money, left Indonesia after May 1998. Their migration followed that of many others who had left after the economic chaos intensified, in January 1998 (Mackie 1999: 189–90).

13. Interestingly, just as the Reformasi movement began to subside in urban areas after Soeharto's resignation, it took off in the countryside. The same tactics that had been used in the cities (calls for good governance, demands for resignations, turning against the police, and the like) were directed largely against local-level functionaries. The protests were supplemented by more direct action, such as poor villagers' occupying land that companies or individuals were presumed to have acquired illegally. See Loekman 1999.

14. The students were following a historical precedent: youths abducted Soekarno and Hatta in 1945, on the eve of independence, to force them into making a more bold proclamation.

15. The five representatives per region are supposed to reflect the popular vote in that province, though the specific mechanisms for allocating seats among parties remained murky even beyond the elections (Young 1999a: 6).

16. Of these 65 appointed representatives, there were 20 for religious groups,

9 for economic groups, 9 for artists, intellectuals, and journalists, 5 for military veterans, 5 for women's groups, 5 for NGOs and students, 5 for civil servants, 5 for ethnic minorities, and 2 for disabled people (Young 1999a: 6).

17. The party opposes *dwifungsi*, endorses regional independence and federalism, and advocates constitutional reform. Headed by Amien Rais of the modernist Islamic Muhammadiyah movement, PAN's leadership includes Islamists, Christians, Chinese, and other secularists as well as young academics. Amien was known as a staunchly sectarian Islamic leader until he turned against Soeharto, became a prominent critic, and promised to work closely with other communities. While PAN could have done very well if it had drawn in both modernist Islamic and non-Islamic votes, it was pegged as a traitor by Muslims and as untrustworthy by non-Muslims (Budiman 1999).

18. Overly regional orientations were deterred by the rule that only parties with offices in at least half of Indonesia's twenty-seven provinces could participate in the polls. Of the major parties, only PAN supported the independence of Irian Jaya and East Timor.

19. Reports (for instance, Brancaccio 2000) on "rent a mob" schemes also delegitimized demonstrations, to some extent, as a pressure tactic.

20. Hans Antlöv, interview with the author, Apr. 25, 2000, Jakarta. Critics suggest that this resurgence of attention to local politics in light of regionalization plans is basically just "moneygrubbing" among forces hoping to have a hand in spending funds allocated to the regions.

21. Margot Cohen, interview with the author, Apr. 26, 2000, Jakarta.

22. Established in 1926, the NU is Indonesia's largest Islamic organization, with at least 35 million members. The political party it formed was the third largest party in the 1955 elections and was second only to Golkar in 1971. However, the votes of NU members were split among at least five parties in 1999, among them the PPP and PKB. Of these parties, only PKB espoused a nationalistic, pluralistic agenda and was linked with the central board of the NU. The others were more exclusivist in their approach to Islam and represented factions in the NU. See Kadir 2000; Mietzner 1999.

23. In 1999, Partai Kristen Nasional (Protestant) and Partai Katolik Demokrat (Catholic) gained only a small proportion of their predecessors' share of the vote.

24. One such challenge was ABRI's nominating General Try Sutrisno as its candidate for the vice presidency in 1993.

25. For instance, Kusnanto 2000; Chew 2000. There was also a flurry of articles in the domestic and foreign media in October and November 2000.

26. David Timberman, interview with the author, Apr. 25, 2000, Jakarta; Boudreau 1999.

27. Much of the information here is drawn from Aspinall 1993.

28. Charlé 1998 notes that Indonesian students, in addition to drawing on their own predecessors' legacy, borrowed slogans, tactics, and even cultural trappings (fashion, music, and so on) from French and American leftists of the 1960s and 1970s, Thai students of the 1970s, and recent protests in Korea.

29. Muridan Widjojo, interview with the author, Apr. 26, 2000, Jakarta.

30. Ibid.

31. Ibid.

32. Latin American liberation theologists were popular, especially in study groups, and not just among Christians.

33. Most New Order socialist-oriented civil societal organizations were linked with the self-identified Marxist PRD. However, the PRD was influential in only a handful of cities, and its strategies were not accepted by all student groups. The party had wings for labor, artists, students, and farmers. Its political ideas and programs directly and explicitly opposed the New Order's foundations. The PRD attacked *dwifungsi*, adopted international language concerning human rights and democracy, and so forth. However, the PRD's intervention may have been more incidental and less intense than the government thought. Moreover, once the government cracked down on the PRD, after 1996, its network was hard to reconnect, though portions were resurrected underground (Muridan Widjojo, interview with the author, Apr. 26, 2000, Jakarta). Post-Soeharto, the PRD tried to unite the various alliances it had made. It formed the anti-Golkar, anti-TNI National Assembly Campaign (KRN) with seventy-five mass organizations, including student groups, trade unions, supporters of Abdurrahman Wahid, and elements of the liberal bourgeoisie (Lane 2001; see also Goenawan 2001).

34. The NU's role among Islamist students echoed that of the PRD. The NU, in turn, fed into PKB (Robin Bush, interview with the author, Apr. 25, 2000, Jakarta).

35. Margot Cohen, interview with the author, Apr. 26, 2000, Jakarta.

36. Muridan Widjojo, interview with the author, Apr. 26, 2000, Jakarta.

37. Other groups used terms such as *kelompok diskusi* (discussion group) to emphasize their vagueness and informality.

38. The Asia Foundation's 1999 national voter education follow-up survey is available along with the original survey; see Asia Foundation 1999a and 1999b.

39. A major source of critical opinion and influence in sociolegal issues, the LBH proved difficult for the government to get rid of and served as a model for other legal aid organizations and reform-oriented NGOs (Lev 1990).

40. Heryanto (1996) analyzes the revocation of the licenses of the major Jakarta-based weeklies *DëTIK*, *TEMPO*, and *Editor*. This ban—presumably because of the publications' coverage of conflicts within the government over the purchase of warships, but also clearly because certain conglomerates coveted the publications' press licenses and market share—showed the government's paranoia and discouraged much-needed foreign investment by raising the specter of social unrest. The dubious legality of this action provoked a long series of protests across Indonesia—the first such occurrence of widespread urban middle-class protest in New Order Indonesia. The protests cut across religious, ethnic, gender, professional, ideological, and geographical lines. They involved student and NGO activists, academics, lawyers, religious leaders, artists, union leaders, women's groups, and hundreds of journalists, supplemented by criticism from members of Parliament, the National Committee on Human Rights, mass organizations, legal aid groups, and the PDI as well as from individual government

and military officials. In the end, the government offered to renew the publishers' licenses.

41. A $650 million nonperforming bank loan was revealed in May 1994, and the revelation resulted in the trial and conviction of a Chinese-Indonesian business leader and several top executives of the government's Indonesian Development Bank. Several former state ministers were also implicated and, under pressure from the media and students, were summoned to testify. While this probably was not Indonesia's worst credit scandal—the banking system had been causing concern among analysts for some time—the case's notoriety and political implications seriously rattled political and economic institutions (Heryanto 1996: 255–56).

42. The Gerakan 30 September (30 September Movement, G30S) was officially an abortive coup by the PKI that provoked the quick ascendancy of the military-dominated New Order regime. Critical new perspectives have suggested that Soeharto may have masterminded the whole thing, using the PKI as a scapegoat (Heryanto 1996: 259–60; see also Anderson and McVey 1971).

43. Some 30,000 workers demanded an increase in the daily minimum wage; the repeal of a decree recognizing only the Serikat Pekerja Seluruh Indonesia (SPSI) as a union, and recognition of the alternative Serikat Buruh Sejahtera Indonesia (SBSI); investigation into the death of a worker; and reinstatement of 400 workers who had recently been sacked after a strike.

44. The death of the twenty-five-year-old labor activist Marsinah in May 1993 near Surabaya—portrayed as a heroic sacrifice for the cause—was a prime catalyst.

45. Margot Cohen, interview with the author, Apr. 26, 2000, Jakarta.

46. The causes of these outbreaks were not so clear-cut. The outbreaks may have been stirred up by forces linked with the military or by other troublemakers rather than sparked by ethnic rivalries.

47. Interestingly, relatively few women were nominated as candidates in Indonesia (less than 13 percent), with even fewer placed close enough to the top of their parties' lists to stand a realistic chance of getting into office. No leaders of women's organizations stood for office, though they lobbied from outside for attention to such issues as violence against women and women's economic situation, and some demanded quotas within parties or for parliamentary seats (Blackburn 1999a).

48. Still, Abdurrahman vacillated, saying a woman could theoretically become president, but that most Indonesians, as Muslims, would not accept a woman leader—and that he would have to support the will of the democratic majority. After the elections, Abdurrahman joined Amien Rais (who had said that in Islam a woman could govern only in the absence of any man capable of doing so) and others in opposing women's leadership (Blackburn 1999a: 88).

49. Women leaders outside Islamic organizations were more strongly positive regarding women's right and ability to lead. Though slow to take a firm stand, women's organizations issued a joint communiqué in June 1999 upholding the right of a woman to be president according to both Quranic and democratic prin-

ciples (Platzdasch 2000; Blackburn 1999a). Likewise, pre- and postelection surveys indicated that a clear majority of Indonesians felt that women should be as active as men in political leadership(Asia Foundation 1999a; Asia Foundation 1999b).

50. The PAN, the PPP, the PBB, the PK, Partai Ummat Islam, Partai Kebangkitan Ummat (Community Resurgence Party), Masyumi, Partai Syarikat Islam Indonesia (Indonesian Muslim United Party), and Partai Nahdlatul Ummat (Party of Islamic Community Awakening).

51. Moreover, Budiman suggests, regions exporting agricultural products were doing very well economically, crisis notwithstanding, and may thus have been grateful to Golkar. The party could also capitalize on regional sentiments in certain areas.

52. Hans Antlöv, interview with the author, Apr. 25, 2000, Jakarta.

53. The government, though—acceding to requests of NGOs in the Coalition for Participatory Policies in a bid to boost support for its policies—has moved to increase public access to legislative deliberations (Kurniawan 2004).

54. Abdurrahman's "National Unity Cabinet" evolved into one consisting only of people close to him and the PKB (Budiman 2001: 147–48).

55. Hans Antlöv, interview with the author, Apr. 25, 2000, Jakarta. See also, for example, Tesoro 2000.

56. David Timberman, interview with the author, Apr. 25, 2000, Jakarta. There was some controversy over these seats, too; for instance, representatives of the NU could enter that way, even though the group had virtually its own party already.

57. Muridan Widjojo, interview with the author, Apr. 26, 2000, Jakarta.

58. Fealy explains that many intellectuals have avoided joining parties in the post-Soeharto era, participating instead through NGOs or independent think tanks or as academic commentators. He cites a 1999 regulation prohibiting civil servants (including academics at public universities and government researchers) from becoming party members or executives as partly responsible for this trend, but he suggests that many intellectuals also just hold parties in low regard (Fealy 2001b: 103).

59. Robin Bush, interview with the author, Apr. 25, 2000, Jakarta; Hans Antlöv, interview with the author, Apr. 25, 2000, Jakarta; Margot Cohen, interview with the author, Apr. 26, 2000, Jakarta.

60. As cited by Molyneux (2000), *The New York Times* reported on May 20, 1998, that since 1995 the U.S. Agency for International Development had spent over $26 million to help Soeharto's opponents. This report led Indonesian members of Parliament to write to President Clinton, saying that while they appreciated these contributions, they were inappropriate and had possibly been used by NGOs to destabilize the country.

61. In fact, Marina Mahathir, the prime minister's daughter, castigated Malaysian protesters for trivializing Indonesia's desperate economic, political, and social situation by co-opting the term *Reformasi* (Marina Mahathir 1999).

Chapter 8

1. Information in this section is drawn from Aliran 2004; Cheong 2004; Hardev and Pereira 2004; Lian 2004.

2. Only parties that win at least 5 percent of the parliamentary vote may field presidential candidates, and only parties that hold at least 2 percent of seats in the incumbent Parliament, or that have offices in two-thirds of all provinces (and in two-thirds of the districts in each), may field DPR candidates. These rules prevent the rise of region-specific parties but augment the centralized tendencies of the system and push separatist groups toward secessionism (Sherlock 2004: 6).

3. "Juwono Sudarsono: Elections and Efficacy?" (posted to I-Discussion e-mail list, Oct. 26, 2003).

BIBLIOGRAPHY

Abdul Aziz Bari. 2001. "The Federal Constitution's Alleged Secular Nature." *Malaysiakini,* July 4.

Abdul Rahman Embong. 1996. "Social Transformation, the State and the Middle Class in Post-Independence Malaysia." *Tonan Ajia Kenkyu* [Southeast Asian Studies] 34(3): 524–47.

———. 1999. "Malaysian Middle Class Studies: A Critical Review." In K. S. Jomo, ed., *Rethinking Malaysia.* Hong Kong: Asia 2000/Malaysian Social Science Association.

Abdul Rahman Putra Al-Haj. 1969. *May 13: Before and After.* Kuala Lumpur: Utusan Melayu Press.

Abdullah bin Haji Ahmad Badawi. 2003. "Tabling a Motion of Thanks to the Member of Parliament for Kubang Pasu, Tun Dr Mahathir Mohamad." Mar. 11. <http://www.pmo.gov.my/WebNotesApp/PMMain.nsf/o/fc77edbac3bac 74048256ddao0046e19?OpenDocument> (accessed Apr. 28, 2005).

Abraham, Collin E. R. 1997. *Divide and Rule: The Roots of Race Relations in Malaysia.* Kuala Lumpur: Institute for Social Analysis.

Abraham, Sheela J. 1999. "National Identity and Ethnicity: Malaysian Perspectives." Paper read at 2d International Malaysian Studies Conference, Kuala Lumpur, Aug. 2–4.

Ackerman, Susan E. 1986. "Ethnicity and Trade Unionism in Malaysia: A Case Study of a Shoe Workers' Union." In R. Lee, ed., *Ethnicity and Ethnic Relations in Malaysia.* DeKalb: Center for Southeast Asian Studies, Northern Illinois University.

———, and Raymond L. M. Lee. 1988. *Heaven in Transition: Non-Muslim Religious Innovation and Ethnic Identity in Malaysia.* Honolulu: University of Hawaii Press.

Adi Suryadi Culla. 1999. *Masyarakat Madani: Pemikiran, Teori, dan Relevansinya dengan Cita-cita Reformasi.* Jakarta: PT RajaGrafindo Persada.

Ahmad Baso. 2000. "Islam dan 'Civil Society' di Indonesia: Dari Konservatisme menuju Kritik." *Tashwirul Afkar* 7: 4–19.

Ahmad Fauzi Abdul Hamid. 2000. "Political Dimensions of Religious Conflict in

Malaysia: State Response to an Islamic Movement." *Indonesia and the Malay World* 28(80): 32–65.

Alagappa, Muthiah, ed. 2004. *Civil Society and Political Change in Asia: Expanding and Contracting Democratic Space*, Stanford, CA: Stanford University Press.

Alatas, Syed Hussein. 1977. *Intellectuals in Developing Societies*. London: Frank Cass.

Alias Mohamed. 1991. *Malaysia's Islamic Opposition: Past, Present and Future*. Kuala Lumpur: Gateway.

———. 1994. *PAS' Platform: Development and Change, 1951–1986*. Petaling Jaya, Selangor: Gateway.

Aliran. 1981. *Aliran Speaks*. Penang: Aliran Kesedaran Negara.

———. 2004. *A Brave New World? Understanding the 2004 Election*. Special issue on the 2004 general election. *Aliran Monthly* 24(3).

"Aliran: Don't Use National Security Excuse to Curb Rallies." 2003. *Malaysiakini*, Sept. 23.

Al-Sayyid, Mustapha K. 1995. "A Civil Society in Egypt?" In A. R. Norton, ed., *Civil Society in the Middle East*. New York: E. J. Brill.

Alvarez, Sonia. 1990. *Engendering Democracy in Brazil: Women's Movements in Transition Politics*. Princeton, NJ: Princeton University Press.

Amien Rais. 1999. "Islam and Politics in Contemporary Indonesia." In G. Forrester, ed., *Post-Soeharto Indonesia: Renewal or Chaos?* Singapore: Institute of Southeast Asian Studies.

Ampalavanar, Rajeswary. 1981. *The Indian Minority and Political Change in Malaya, 1945–1957*. Kuala Lumpur: Oxford University Press.

Andaya, Barbara Watson, and Leonard Y. Andaya. 1982. *A History of Malaysia*. London: Macmillan.

Anderson, Benedict. 1983. *Imagined Communities: Reflections on the Origin and Spread of Nationalism*. London: Verso.

———. 1998. *The Spectre of Comparisons: Nationalism, Southeast Asia and the World*. New York: Verso.

———, and Ruth McVey. 1971. *A Preliminary Analysis of the October 1, 1965, Coup in Indonesia*. Ithaca, NY: Cornell University Press.

Anwar Ibrahim. 1997. "Islam dan Pembentukan Masyarakat Madani." In MINDS, ed., *Masyarakat Madani: Satu Tinjauan Awal*. Ampang, Selangor: Malaysian Institute of Development Strategies.

"Anwar's Party Votes to Merge with Malaysian Opposition Ally." 2001. Agence France-Presse newswire, June 25.

Arfa'eza A. Aziz. 2003a. "Election Commission to Lift Ban on Public Rallies." *Malaysiakini*, Sept. 10.

———. 2003b. "EC Chief Defends Decision on Outdoor Rallies." *Malaysiakini*, Sept. 18.

———. 2003c. "No Tyranny under Islamic State: PAS." *Malaysiakini*, Nov. 12.

Aristides Katoppo. 2000. "The Role of Community Groups in the Environment Movement." In C. Manning and P. v. Diermen, eds., *Indonesia in Transition:*

Social Aspects of Reformasi and Crisis. Singapore: Institute of Southeast Asian Studies.

Arskal Salim. 1999. *Partai Islam dan Relasi Agama-Negara*. Jakarta: Pusat Penelitian IAIN.

Asia Foundation. 1999a. *Indonesia National Voter Education Follow-Up Survey*. < http://www.asiafoundation.org/pdf/indo_voter-ed99fu.pdf> (accessed Apr. 26, 2005).

——. 1999b. *Indonesia National Voter Education Survey*. <http://www.asi-afoundation.org/pdf/indo_voter-ed99.pdf > (accessed Apr. 26, 2005).

Aspinall, Edward. 1993. "Student Dissent in Indonesia in the 1980s." Working paper no. 79. Clayton, Victoria: Centre of Southeast Asian Studies, Monash University.

——. 1996. "The Broadening Base of Political Opposition in Indonesia." In G. Rodan, ed., *Political Oppositions in Industrialising Asia*. London: Routledge.

——. 1999. "The Indonesian Student Uprising of 1998." In A. Budiman, B. Hatley and D. Kingsbury, eds., *Reformasi: Crisis and Change in Indonesia*. Clayton, Victoria: Monash Asia Institute.

Azyumardi Azra. 2000. "The Islamic Factor in Post-Soeharto Indonesia." In C. Manning and P. v. Diermen, eds., *Indonesia in Transition: Social Aspects of Reformasi and Crisis*. Singapore: Institute of Southeast Asian Studies.

Banton, Michael, and Mansor Mohd. Noor. 1992. "The Study of Ethnic Alignment: A New Technique and an Application in Malaysia." *Ethnic and Racial Studies* 15: 599–614.

Barisan Alternatif. 1999. *Ke Arah Malaysia Yang Adil*. Pamphlet.

——. 2004. *Bersama Malasyia Baru: Kesejahteraan untuk Semua*. Pamphlet.

Barraclough, Simon. 1984. "Political Participation and Its Regulation in Malaysia: Opposition to the Societies (Amendment) Act 1981." *Pacific Affairs* 57(3): 450–61.

——. 1985a. "*Barisan Nasional* Dominance and Opposition Fragmentation: The Failure of Attempts to Create Opposition Cooperation in the Malaysian Party System." *Asian Profile* 13(1): 33–43.

——. 1985b. "The Dynamics of Coercion in the Malaysian Political Process." *Modern Asian Studies* 19(4): 797–822.

Barton, Greg. 2001. "The Prospects for Islam." In G. Lloyd and S. Smith, eds., *Indonesia Today: Challenges of History*. Singapore: Institute of Southeast Asian Studies.

Bell, Daniel A., and Kanishka Jayasuriya. 1995. "Understanding Illiberal Democracy: A Framework." In D. Bell et al., eds., *Towards Illiberal Democracy in Pacific Asia*. New York: St. Martin's.

Berman, Sheri. 1997. "Civil Society and Political Institutionalization." *American Behavioral Scientist* 40(5): 562–75.

Bermeo, Nancy. 1992. "Democracy and the Lessons of Dictatorship." *Comparative Politics* 24(3): 273–91.

——. 1997. "Myths of Moderation: Confrontation and Conflict during Democratic Transitions." *Comparative Politics* 29(3): 305–22.

Bersihar Lubis, and Mauluddin Anwar. 1998. "Potret Gerakan Berwarna-warni." *Gatra,* Apr. 11, 66–67.

Blackburn, Susan. 1999a. "The 1999 Elections in Indonesia: Where Were the Women?" In S. Blackburn, ed., *Pemilu: The 1999 Indonesian Election.* Clayton, Victoria: Monash Asia Institute.

———, ed. 1999b. *Pemilu: The 1999 Indonesian Election.* Clayton, Victoria: Monash Asia Institute.

Blythe, Wilfred. 1969. *The Impact of Chinese Secret Societies in Malaya: A Historical Study.* Kuala Lumpur: Oxford University Press.

Boudreau, Vincent. 1999. "Diffusing Democracy? People Power in Indonesia and the Philippines." *Bulletin of Concerned Asian Scholars* 31(4): 3–18.

———. 2001. *Grass Roots and Cadre in the Protest Movement.* Manila: Ateneo de Manila University Press.

Bourchier, David. 1999. "Skeletons, Vigilantes and the Armed Forces' Fall from Grace." In A. Budiman, B. Hatley, and D. Kingsbury, eds., *Reformasi: Crisis and Change in Indonesia.* Victoria: Monash Asia Institute.

Brancaccio, David. 2000. "Indonesia's Poor Economy Results in Persons Hiring Themselves Out as Protesters." *Marketplace,* National Public Radio, Nov. 1. Transcript.

Bratton, Michael. 1989. "Beyond the State: Civil Society and Associational Life in Africa." *World Politics* 41(3): 407–30.

———, and Nicolas van de Walle. 1992. "Popular Protest and Political Reform in Africa." *Comparative Politics* 24(4): 419–42.

Brockett, Charles D. 1991. "The Structure of Political Opportunities and Peasant Mobilization in Central America." *Comparative Politics* 23(3): 253–74.

Brown, David. 1994. *The State and Ethnic Politics in Southeast Asia.* London: Routledge.

Budiman, Arief. 1999. "The 1999 Indonesian Election: Impressions and Reflections." In S. Blackburn, ed., *Pemilu: The 1999 Indonesian Election.* Clayton, Victoria: Monash Asia Institute.

———. 2001. "Indonesia: The Trials of President Wahid." In Institute of Southeast Asian Studies, ed., *Southeast Asian Affairs 2001.* Singapore: Institute of Southeast Asian Studies.

———, Barbara Hatley, and Damien Kingsbury, eds. 1999. *Reformasi: Crisis and Change in Indonesia.* Clayton, Victoria: Monash Asia Institute.

"Can the Opposition Work Together?" 1990. *Aliran Monthly* 10(4): 2–3.

Carothers, Thomas. 1999–2000. "Civil Society." *Foreign Policy* 117: 18–29.

Case, William. 1993. "Semi-democracy in Malaysia: Withstanding the Pressures for Regime Change." *Pacific Affairs* 66: 183–205.

———. 2001. "Malaysia's Resilient Pseudodemocracy." *Journal of Democracy* 12(1): 43–57.

———. 2004. "Testing Malaysia's Pseudo-democracy." In E. T. Gomez, ed., *The State of Malaysia: Ethnicity, Equity and Reform.* New York: RoutledgeCurzon.

Chan Chee Khoon. 1999. " 'Japanese' Encephalitis: A Re-emergent Nightmare?" *Aliran Monthly* 19(3): 7–8.

Chan Heng Chee. 1997. "Politics in an Administrative State: Where Has the Politics Gone?" In Ong J. H. et al., eds., *Understanding Singapore Society*, rev. ed. Singapore: Times Academic Press.

Chandra Muzaffar. 1979. *Protector? An Analysis of the Concept and Practice of Loyalty in Leader-led Relationships within Malay Society.* Penang: Aliran.

———. 1984. "Has the Communal Situation Worsened over the Last Decade? Some Preliminary Thoughts." In S. Husin Ali, ed., *Kaum Kelas dan Pembangunan Malaysia/Ethnicity, Class and Development Malaysia.* Kuala Lumpur: Persatuan Sains Sosial Malaysia.

———. 1987. *Islamic Resurgence in Malaysia.* Petaling Jaya: Penerbit Fajar Bakti.

———. 1990. "How the Barisan Retained Its Two-thirds Majority." *Aliran Monthly* 10(10): 2–4.

———. 1997. "Pembinaan Masyarakat Madani: Model Malaysia." In MINDS, ed., *Masyarakat Madani: Satu Tinjauan Awal.* Ampang, Selangor: Malaysian Institute of Development Strategies.

"A Change in Emphasis." 1990. *Aliran Monthly* 10(7): 3–4.

Charlé, Suzanne. 1998. "Banning is Banned!" *The Nation*, Oct. 5: 15–19.

Chazan, Naomi. 1992. "Africa's Democratic Challenge." *World Policy Journal* 9(2): 279–307.

Cheah Boon Kheng. 1987. *Red Star Over Malaya: Resistance and Social Conflict During and After the Japanese Occupation of Malaya, 1941–1946.* 2d ed. Singapore: Singapore University Press.

Cheong Suk-Wai. 2004. "Now to Walk the Talk." *Straits Times*, Mar. 22.

Chew, Amy. 2000. "Aceh Peace Deal Faces Threat of Vandalism." Reuters newswire, May 12.

Chin, James. 1996. "PBDS and Ethnicity in Sarawak Politics." *Journal of Contemporary Asia* 26(4): 512–26.

———. 2001. "Malaysian Chinese Politics in the 21st Century: Fear, Service, and Marginalisation." Paper read at 5th ASEAN Interuniversity Seminar on Social Development, Singapore, May 23–25.

Chin Ung-Ho. 1996. *Chinese Politics in Sarawak: A Study of the Sarawak United People's Party.* Kuala Lumpur: Oxford University Press.

Chinese Guilds. 1985. *Joint Declaration by the Chinese Guilds and Associations of Malaysia.* Pamphlet.

Chinese Organisations. 1999. "Seventeen-Point Election Demands of Chinese Organisations." *Aliran Monthly* 19(8): 9–12.

Christie, Clive J. 1996. *A Modern History of Southeast Asia: Decolonization, Nationalism, and Separatism.* Singapore: Institute of Southeast Asian Studies.

Clear, Annette. 2000. "The International Dimension of Democratization: Foreign Aid for the 1999 Indonesian Elections." Paper read at annual meeting of the American Political Science Association, Washington, DC, Aug. 31–Sept. 3.

Cohen, Jean L. 1985. "Strategy or Identity: New Theoretical Paradigms and Contemporary Social Movements." *Social Research* 52(4): 663–716.

Cohen, Margot. 1998a. "To the Barricades." *Far Eastern Economic Review*, May 14: 21–22, 24.

————. 1998b. "Unguided Missiles." *Far Eastern Economic Review,* Nov. 26: 16, 18.

Committee Against Repression in the Pacific and Asia. 1988. *Tangled Web: Dissent, Deterrence and the 27th October 1987 Crackdown.* Haymarket, NSW: Committee Against Repression in the Pacific and Asia.

Consumers' Association of Penang. 1993. *Wasted Lives: Radioactive Poisoning in Bukit Merah.* Penang: Consumers' Association of Penang.

Crouch, Harold. 1993. "Malaysia: Neither Authoritarian nor Democratic." In K. Hewison, R. Robison, and G. Rodan, eds., *Southeast Asia in the 1990s: Authoritarian Democracy and Capitalism.* St. Leonards, NSW: Allen & Unwin.

————. 1999. "Wiranto and Habibie: Military-Civilian Relations since May 1998." In A. Budiman, B. Hatley, and D. Kingsbury, eds., *Reformasi: Crisis and Change in Indonesia.* Clayton, Victoria: Monash Asia Institute.

Daniel, J. Rabindra. 1992. *Indian Christians in Peninsular Malaysia.* Kuala Lumpur: Tamil Annual Conference, Methodist Church, Malaysia.

Democratic Action Party. 1991. *25 Years of Struggle: Milestones in DAP History.* Petaling Jaya: Democratic Action Party.

————. 1998. Whither Justice? New Crisis of Confidence in the System of Justice. *The Rocket,* May/June.

Das, K. , and Suaram, eds. 1989. *The White Paper on the October Affair and the 'Why?' Papers.* Kelana Jaya, Selangor: Suaram Komunikasi.

Dass, Arokia. 1991. *Not Beyond Repair: Reflections of a Malaysian Trade Unionist.* Hong Kong: Asia Monitor Resource Center.

DEMOS. 2004. *1st-Round Study of the Problems and Options of Indonesian Democratisation.* Jakarta: Indonesian Center for Democracy and Human Rights Studies. Executive report.

Dentan, Robert Knox, et al. 1997. *Malaysia and the Original People: A Case Study of the Impact of Development on Indigenous Peoples.* Boston: Allyn and Bacon.

Dewi Fortuna Anwar. 2001. "Indonesia's Transition to Democracy: Challenges and Prospects." In D. Kingsbury and A. Budiman, eds., *Indonesia: The Uncertain Transition.* Adelaide: Crawford House.

Diamond, Larry. 2002. "Thinking about Hybrid Regimes." *Journal of Democracy* 13(2): 21–35.

Diani, Mario. 1992. "The Concept of Social Movement." *The Sociological Review* 40(1): 1–25.

Doherty, Ivan. 2001. "Democracy Out of Balance: Civil Society Can't Replace Political Parties." *Policy Review* 106: 25–35.

Dryzek, John S. 1996. "Political Inclusion and the Dynamics of Democratization." *American Political Science Review* 90(1): 475–87.

Ekiert, Grzegorz, and Jan Kubik. 1998. "Contentious Politics in New Democracies: East Germany, Hungary, Poland, and Slovakia, 1989–93." *World Politics* 50: 547–81.

Eklöf, Stefan. 1999. *Indonesian Politics in Crisis: The Long Fall of Suharto, 1996–98.* Copenhagen: Nordic Institute of Asian Studies.

Eldridge, Philip. 1996. "Development, Democracy and Non-government Organisations in Indonesia." *Asian Journal of Political Science* 4(1): 17–35.

"Election a 'Wake-up Call' for Malaysia's Ruling Party: Minister." 1999. Agence France-Presse newswire, Dec. 5.

"Election Watch—Dr M's Target." 1990. *Aliran Monthly* 10(7): 9–11.

Elliott, Dorinda. 1999. "Who Can Say 'Reformasi'? The Battle to Define a New National Identity." *Newsweek*, Apr. 12 (international edition).

Ellis, Andrew. 2002. *Constitutional Reform and the 2004 Election Cycle*. Report on briefing to the United States–Indonesia Society (USINDO). <http://www.usindo.org/Briefs/Andrew%20Ellis.htm> (accessed Apr. 3, 2005).

Elster, Jon. 1989. "Social Norms and Economic Theory." *Journal of Economic Perspectives* 3(4): 99–117.

Enloe, Cynthia H. 1970. *Multiethnic Politics: The Case of Malaysia*. Berkeley: Center for South and Southeast Asia Studies, University of California.

Entelis, John P. 1999. "State-Society Relations: Algeria as a Case Study." In M. Tessler, ed., *Area Studies and Social Science: Strategies for Understanding Middle East Politics*. Bloomington: Indiana University Press.

"Fadzil: An Islamic State is Our Objective." 1999. *New Straits Times*, Apr. 11.

Fan Yew Teng. 1988. *Oppressors and Apologists*, rev. ed. Kuala Lumpur: Egret.

———. 1990. *The Rape of the Law*. Kuala Lumpur: Egret.

Farish A. Noor. 1999a. "Looking for *Reformasi*: The Discursive Dynamics of the Reformasi Movement and Its Prospects as a Political Project." *Indonesia and the Malay World* 27(77): 5–18.

———. 1999b. *Malaysian Elections 1999: A Shift in the Political Terrain*. Special report, AsiaSource. <http://www.asiasource.org/news/at_mp_02.cfm?newsid=6541> (accessed Apr. 3, 2005).

Fealy, Greg. 2001a. "Islamic Politics: A Rising or Declining Force?" In D. Kingsbury and A. Budiman, eds., *Indonesia: The Uncertain Transition*. Adelaide: Crawford House.

———. 2001b. "Parties and Parliament: Serving Whose Interests?" In G. Lloyd and S. Smith, eds., *Indonesia Today: Challenges of History*. Singapore: Institute of Southeast Asian Studies.

Firdaus Haji Abdullah. 1985. *Radical Malay Politics: Its Origins and Early Development*. Petaling Jaya: Pelanduk Publications.

Foley, Michael W., and Bob Edwards. 1996. "The Paradox of Civil Society." *Journal of Democracy* 7(3): 38–52.

———. 1997. "Escape from Politics? Social Theory and the Social Capital Debate." *American Behavioral Scientist* 40(5): 550–61.

"Former Sabah CM Loses Seat Over 'Phantom Voters.'" 2001. *Malaysiakini*, June 8.

Funston, John. 1980. *Malay Politics in Malaysia: A Study of UMNO and PAS*. Kuala Lumpur: Heinemann Educational Books.

———. 1985. "The Politics of Islamic Reassertion: Malaysia." In Ahmad Ibrahim, S. Siddique and Yasmin Hussain, eds., *Readings on Islam in Southeast Asia*. Singapore: Institute of Southeast Asian Studies.

————. 1988. "Challenge and Response in Malaysia: The UMNO Crisis and the Mahathir Style." *The Pacific Review* 1(4): 363–73.

————. 1999. "Malaysia: A Fateful September." In D. Singh and J. Funston, eds., *Southeast Asian Affairs 1999*. Singapore: Institute of Southeast Asian Studies.

————. 2000. "Malaysia's Tenth Elections: Status Quo, Reformasi or Islamization?" *Contemporary Southeast Asia* 22(1): 23–59.

Galston, William A. 2000. "Civil Society and the 'Art of Association.'" *Journal of Democracy* 11(1): 64–70.

Garner, Roberta, and Mayer N. Zald. 1985. "The Political Economy of Social Movement Sectors." In G. D. Suttles and M. N. Zald, eds., *The Challenge of Social Control: Citizenship and Institution Building in Modern Society: Essays in Honor of Morris Janowitz*. Norwood, NJ: Ablex.

Gellner, Ernest. 1994. *Conditions of Liberty: Civil Society and Its Rivals*. London: Penguin.

Gilley, Bruce. 2000. "Affirmative Reaction." *Far Eastern Economic Review*, Aug. 10: 26–27.

Goenawan Mohamad. 2001. "Remembering the Left." In G. Lloyd and S. Smith, eds., *Indonesia Today: Challenges of History*. Singapore: Institute of Southeast Asian Studies.

Goldstone, Jack A. 2003. "Introduction: Bridging Institutionalized and Noninstitutionalized Politics." In J. A. Goldstone, ed., *States, Parties, and Social Movements*. New York: Cambridge University Press.

Gomez, Edmund Terence. 1991. *Money Politics in the Barisan Nasional*. Kuala Lumpur: Forum.

————. 1996. *The 1995 Malaysian General Elections: A Report and Commentary*. Singapore: Institute of Southeast Asian Studies.

————, and Jomo K.S. 1997. *Malaysia's Political Economy: Politics, Patronage and Profits*. Cambridge: Cambridge University Press.

"Got a Complaint? Now You Can E-mail the PM." 2003. *Malaysiakini*, Nov. 14.

Government of Malaya. 1959. *The Communist Threat to the Federation of Malaya*. Kuala Lumpur: Government Press.

Government of Malaysia. 1971. *The Resurgence of Armed Communism in West Malaysia*. Kuala Lumpur: Jabatan Chetak Kerajaan.

————. n.d. "Message from the Registrar of Societies, Haji Kaswuri Bin Keman." <http://www.jppmros.gov.my/speech01.htm> (accessed Apr. 3, 2005).

Grace, Elizabeth. 1990. *Shortcircuiting Labour: Unionising Electronic Workers in Malaysia*. Kuala Lumpur: Institute of Social Analysis.

Guerin, Bill. 2003. "Indonesia's Economy: Everything but Money." *Asia Times*, Oct. 16.

————. 2004. "Promiscuity and Untidy Alliances in Indonesia." *Asia Times*, May 11.

Gurmit Singh K. S. 1984. *Malaysian Societies: Friendly or Political?* Petaling Jaya: Environmental Protection Society Malaysia/Selangor Graduates Society.

————, ed. 1987. *No to Secrecy: The Campaign against 1986's Amendments to the OSA*. Kuala Lumpur: Aliran et al.

————. 1990. *A Thorn in the Flesh*. Petaling Jaya: Gurmit Singh K. S.

Habermas, Jürgen. 1981. "New Social Movements." *Telos* 49: 33–37.

Hack, Karl. 1999. " 'Iron Claws on Malaya': The Historiography of the Malayan Emergency." *Journal of Southeast Asian Studies* 30(1): 99–125.

Hadiz, Vedi R. 1999. "Contesting Political Change after Suharto." In A. Budiman, B. Hatley, and D. Kingsbury, eds., *Reformasi: Crisis and Change in Indonesia*. Clayton, Victoria: Monash Asia Institute.

———. 2000. "Paramilitaries: Civil Society Gets Ugly." *Jakarta Post*, May 24.

Hall, John A. 1995. "In Search of Civil Society." In J. A. Hall, ed., *Civil Society: Theory, History, Comparison*. Cambridge: Polity Press.

"Hapus Hak Istimewa Melayu." 2000. *Utusan Malaysia*, Aug. 14.

Har, Anna, and John Hutnyk. 1999. "Languid, Tropical, Monsoonal Time?: Net-Activism and Hype in the Context of South East Asian Politics." *Saksi* 6.

Hardev Kaur and Pereira, Brendan. 2004. "Landslide for BN." *New Straits Times*, Mar. 22.

Hari Singh. 2000. "The 1999 Malaysian General Election." Unpublished manuscript.

Hassan Karim, and Siti Nor Hamid, eds. 1984. *With the People! The Malaysian Student Movement, 1967–74*. Petaling Jaya: Institute for Social Analysis.

Haynes, Jeff. 1997. *Democracy and Civil Society in the Third World: Politics and New Political Movements*. Cambridge: Polity Press.

Hefner, Robert W. 1999. "Southeast Asian Pluralisms: Social Resources for Civility and Participation." Paper read at Research Workshop on Southeast Asian Pluralisms: Social Resources for Civility and Participation in Malaysia, Singapore and Indonesia, Petaling Jaya, Aug. 5–6.

———. 2000. *Civil Islam: Muslims and Democratization in Indonesia*. Princeton, NJ: Princeton University Press.

Hellman, Judith Adler. 1994. "Mexican Popular Movements and the Process of Democratization." *Latin American Perspectives* 81(21/22): 124–43.

Heng Pek Koon. 1996. "Chinese Responses to Malay Hegemony in Peninsular Malaysia, 1957–96." *Tonan Ajia Kenkyu* [Southeast Asian Studies] 34(3): 32–55.

———. 2004. "The Mahathir Generation and Nation-Building in Malaysia: Political, Economic and Socio-Cultural Dynamics." In B. Welsh, ed., *Reflections: The Mahathir Years*. Washington, DC: Southeast Asia Studies, Johns Hopkins University–SAIS.

Heryanto, Ariel. 1996. "Indonesian Middle-Class Opposition in the 1990s." In G. Rodan, ed., *Political Oppositions in Industrialising Asia*. London: Routledge.

———. 1999. "Rape, Race, and Reporting." In A. Budiman, B. Hatley, and D. Kingsbury, eds., *Reformasi: Crisis and Change in Indonesia*. Clayton, Victoria: Monash Asia Institute.

———. 2001. "Remembering and Dismembering Indonesia." *Latitudes* 1: 10–15.

Hicks, George, ed. 1996. *Chinese Organisations in Southeast Asia in the 1930s*. Singapore: Select Books.

Hiebert, Murray, and S. Jayasankaran. 1998. "A Single Spark." *Far Eastern Economic Review*, Oct. 29: 12–14.

Hikam, Muhammad A. S. 1999. "The Role of NGOs in the Empowerment of

Indonesian Civil Society: A Political Perspective." Paper read at 12th INFID Conference, Bali, Sept. 14–17.

———. 2000. " 'Civil Society' sebagai Proyek Pencerahan." *Tashwirul Afkar* 7: 83–87.

Ibrahim Suffian. 2004. "Negotiating the Uneven Electoral Landscape: A Superficial Examination of PAS and Its Performance in the 2004 General Elections." Paper read at 4th Malaysian Studies International Conference, Bangi, Malaysia, Aug. 3–5.

"Indonesian Defense Minister: Country Can't Afford Democracy." 2000. Associated Press newswire, Apr. 11.

Institute of Social Analysis. 1989. *Sucked Oranges: The Indian Poor in Malaysia.* Kuala Lumpur: Institute of Social Analysis.

International Bar Association et al. 2000. *Justice in Jeopardy: Malaysia 2000.* <http://www.ibanet.org/images/downloads/malaysia.pdf> (accessed Apr. 26, 2005).

"An Islamic State—If the Opposition Wins?" 1990. *Aliran Monthly* 10(4): 4.

Jamhari. 1999. "Islamic Political Parties: Threats or Prospects?" In G. Forrester, ed., *Post-Soeharto Indonesia: Renewal or Chaos?* Singapore: Institute of Southeast Asian Studies.

Jasper, James M. 1997. *The Art of Moral Protest: Culture, Biography, and Creativity in Social Movements.* Chicago: University of Chicago Press.

Jawan, Jayum A. 1993. *The Iban Factor in Sarawak Politics.* Serdang: Penerbit Universiti Pertanian Malaysia.

Jayasooriya, Denison. 2004. "Indian Voters and the General Election." *Malaysiakini*, March 18.

Jesudason, James V. 1995. "Statist Democracy and the Limits to Civil Society in Malaysia." *Journal of Commonwealth and Comparative Politics* 33: 335–56.

———. 1996. "The Syncretic State and the Structuring of Oppositional Politics in Malaysia." In G. Rodan, ed., *Political Oppositions in Industrialising Asia.* London: Routledge.

Jomo Kwame Sundaram. 1988. *A Question of Class: Capital, the State, and Uneven Development in Malaya.* New York: Monthly Review Press.

———. 1996. "Deepening Malaysian Democracy with More Checks and Balances." In Muhammad Ikmal Said and Zahid Emby, eds., *Malaysia: Critical Perspectives: Essays in Honour of Syed Husin Ali.* Petaling Jaya: Persatuan Sains Sosial Malaysia.

———, and Ahmad Shabery Cheek. 1992. "Malaysia's Islamic Movements." In J. S. Kahn and F. Loh K. W., eds., *Fragmented Vision: Culture and Politics in Contemporary Malaysia.* North Sydney: Asian Studies Association of Australia/Allen and Unwin.

———, and Patricia Todd. 1994. *Trade Unions and the State in Peninsular Malaysia.* Kuala Lumpur: Oxford University Press.

Jones, David Martin, and David Brown. 1994. "Singapore and the Myth of the Liberalizing Middle Class." *Pacific Review* 7(1): 79–87.

———, et al. 1995. "Towards a Model of Illiberal Democracy." In D. Bell et al., *Towards Illiberal Democracy in Pacific Asia.* New York: St. Martin's.

Kabilan, K. 2000. "Umno Youth Protests Outside Chinese Assembly Hall." *Malaysiakini*, Aug. 18.

———. 2001. "Rumble in the Varsities." *Malaysiakini*, July 7.

Kadir, Suzaina. 2000. "Contested Visions of State and Society in Indonesian Islam: The Nahdlatul Ulama in Perspective." In *Indonesia in Transition: Social Aspects of Reformasi and Crisis*, edited by C. Manning and P. v. Diermen. Singapore: Institute of Southeast Asian Studies.

Kafil Yamin. 2003. "Indonesia's Wiranto: Reform as a Military Duty." *Asia Times*, Aug. 30.

Kahn, Joel S. 1996. "The Middle Class as a Field of Ethnological Study." In Muhammad Ikmal Said and Zahid Emby, eds., *Malaysia: Critical Perspectives: Essays in Honour of Syed Husin Ali*. Petaling Jaya: Persatuan Sains Sosial Malaysia.

Kalimullah Hassan. 2004. "Malaysians Come Through for Pak Lah." *New Straits Times*, Mar. 22.

Kamar Ainiah Kamaruzaman. 1999. *Memorandum to the Election Commission*, Oct. 27. <http://members.lycos.co.uk/grinner/MEMOSPR2.htm> (accessed Apr. 26, 2005).

Kamarudin Jaffar. 2000. *Pilihanraya 1999 dan Masa Depan Politik Malaysia*. Kuala Lumpur: IKDAS.

Kastorius Sinaga. 2000. "NGOs as Part of the Civil Society Movement in the 1999 Elections in Indonesia." Paper read at annual meeting of the Association for Asian Studies, March 9–12, San Diego.

"Keadilan Raps PAS over Islamic State Memo." 2003. *Malaysiakini*, Nov. 12.

Kessler, Clive S. 2000. "UMNO's Malay Dilemma." Paper read at seminar at the Australian National University, Canberra, Sept. 14.

Khadijah Md. Khalid. n.d. "Continuity and Change in Women's Political Participation in West Malaysia." Unpublished paper.

Khalid Jafri. 1998. *50 Dalil Mengapa Anwar Tidak Boleh Jadi PM*. Ampang, Selangor: Media Pulau Lagenda.

Khong Kim Hoong. 1987. "The Early Political Movements before Independence." In Zakaria Haji Ahmad, ed., *Government and Politics of Malaysia*. Singapore: Oxford University Press.

———. 1991a. "How the Opposition Faired [sic] in the 1986 Malaysian Elections." In Muhammad Ikmal Said and Johan Saravanamuttu, eds., *Images of Malaysia*. Kuala Lumpur: Persatuan Sains Sosial Malaysia.

———. 1991b. *Malaysia's General Election 1990: Continuity, Change, and Ethnic Politics*. Singapore: Institute of Southeast Asian Studies.

Khoo Boo Teik. 1995. *Paradoxes of Mahathirism: An Intellectual Biography of Mahathir Mohamad*. Kuala Lumpur: Oxford University Press.

———. 1997. Democracy and Authoritarianism in Malaysia since 1957: Class, Ethnicity and Changing Capitalism. In Anek Laothamatas, ed. *Democratization in Southeast and East Asia*, Singapore: Institute of Southeast Asian Studies.

———. 1999. "Beyond Pigs and Lotteries." *Aliran Monthly* 19(3):2, 4–6.

———. 2000. "Conjuncture for Coalition: A Conjecture on the Significance of the Barisan Alternatif." Paper read at workshop on the general election of November 1999, Universiti Sains Malaysia, Penang, Apr. 1–2 .

———. 2002. "Can There Be Reforms Beyond BA?" *Aliran Monthly* 22(1): 2, 4–7.

Khoo Kay Kim. 1991. *Malay Society: Transformation and Democratisation.* Petaling Jaya, Selangor: Pelanduk Publications.

Klandermans, Bert. 1989. "Introduction: Social Movement Organizations and the Study of Social Movements." In *International Social Movement Research* 2. Greenwich, CT: JAI Press.

Klandermans, Bert, and Sidney Tarrow. 1988. "Mobilization into Social Movements: Synthesizing European and American Approaches." In *International Social Movement Research* 1. Greenwich, CT: JAI Press.

Kua Kia Soong. 2000. "A Demonstration of Bigotry." *Malaysiakini*, Aug. 21.

———. 1996. *Inside the DAP, 1990–95.* Kuala Lumpur: Oriengroup.

———. 1998a. "DAP's Latest Purge." *Aliran Monthly* 18(6): 33–34, 40.

———. 1998b. "The Struggle for Human Rights In Malaysia." Paper read at Asia-Pacific People's Assembly Human Rights Forum, Kuala Lumpur, Nov. 9.

———, ed. 1985. *National Culture and Democracy.* Petaling Jaya: Kersani Penerbit/Selangor Chinese Assembly Hall.

Kurniawan Hari. 2004. "Lawmaking to be More Open." *Jakarta Post*, May 18.

Kurniawan, Moch. N. 2003. "Survey Finds Muslim Voters Favor Pluralism." *Jakarta Post*, Nov. 19.

Kusnanto Anggoro. 2000. "Gus Dur Struggles to Control TNI." *Jakarta Post*, Sept. 28.

Lai Seck Ling. 1997. "Corak Pengundian di Kalangan Pengundi Cina di Kawasan Dewan Undangan Negeri (DUN) Seri Kembangan: Di antara Straight-ticket Voting dan Split-ticket Voting." Academic exercise, Jabatan Sains Politik, Fakulti Sains Kemasyarakatan dan Kemanusiaan, Universiti Kebangsaan Malaysia, Bangi.

Lai Suat Yan. 2003. "The Women's Movement in Peninsular Malaysia from 1900–99: A Historical Analysis." In M. L. Weiss and Saliha Hassan, eds., *Social Movements in Malaysia: From Moral Communities to NGOs.* London: RoutledgeCurzon.

Lane, Max. 1999. "Mass Politics and Political Change in Indonesia." In A. Budiman, B. Hatley, and D. Kingsbury, eds., *Reformasi: Crisis and Change in Indonesia.* Clayton, Victoria: Monash Asia Institute.

———. 2001. "Indonesia: Golkar and Army Preparing for Comeback." *Green Left Weekly*, Jan. 17: 24.

———. 2004. "Indonesia: Rejecting the Old 'Elit Politik.'" *Green Left Weekly*, Apr. 21: 20.

Lee Kam Hing. 1987. "Three Approaches in Peninsular Malaysian Chinese Politics: The MCA, the DAP and the Gerakan." In Zakaria Haji Ahmad, ed., *Government and Politics of Malaysia.* Singapore: Oxford University Press.

Lee Kuan Yew. 1965a. *The Battle for a Malaysian Malaysia.* Singapore: Ministry of Culture.

———. 1965b. *Towards a Malaysian Malaysia.* Singapore: Ministry of Culture.

Bibliography 299

———. 1998. *The Singapore Story: Memoirs of Lee Kuan Yew*. Singapore: Times Editions/Straits Times Press.

Lee Poh Ping. 1985. "World-view of Social Belonging among the Chinese in Malaysia and Singapore: The Case of Secret Societies, Clans and Dialect-Group Associations." In Mohd. Taib Osman, ed., *Malaysian World-view*. Singapore: Institute of Southeast Asian Studies.

Legro, Jeffrey W. 1997. "Which Norms Matter? Revisiting the 'Failure' of Internationalism." *International Organization* 51(1): 31–63.

Lev, Daniel S. 1990. "Human Rights NGOs in Indonesia and Malaysia." In J. Claude E. Welch and V. A. Leary, eds., *Asian Perspectives on Human Rights*. Boulder, CO: Westview Press.

Levi, Margaret. 1996. "Social and Unsocial Capital: A Review Essay of Robert Putnam's *Making Democracy Work*." *Politics and Society* 24(1): 45–55.

Levitsky, Steven, and Lucan A. Way. 2002. "The Rise of Competitive Authoritarianism." *Journal of Democracy* 13(2): 51–65.

Lian, Benjamin. 2004. "NGOs Tell Candidates What They Expect from Them." *Malaysiakini*, Mar. 12.

Liebhold, David. 1999. "Hog Hell." *Time* (Asia), Apr. 5 <http://www.time.com/time/asia/asia/magazine/1999/990405/pigs1.html> (accessed Apr. 26, 2005).

Lijphart, Arend. 1969. "Consociational Democracy." *World Politics* 21(2): 207–25.

Lim Kit Siang. 1999a. "Demands—No Threat but Popular Will." Press statement, Sept. 16. <http://malaysia.net/dap/sg1899.htm> (accessed Apr. 26, 2005).

———. 1999b. "1999 GE: Uncertain and Perilous Future for Malaysia." Press statement, Nov. 30. <http://malaysia.net/dap/sg2132.htm> (accessed Apr. 26, 2005).

Lim Teck Ghee. 1995. "Nongovernmental Organizations in Malaysia and Regional Networking." In T. Yamamoto, ed., *Emerging Civil Society in the Asia Pacific Communit*. Singapore: Institute of Southeast Asian Studies/Japan Center for International Exchange.

Lipset, Seymour Martin. 2000. "The Indispensability of Political Parties." *Journal of Democracy* 11(1): 48–55.

Loekman Soetrisno. 1999. "Current Social and Political Conditions of Rural Indonesia." In G. Forrester, ed., *Post-Soeharto Indonesia: Renewal or Chaos?* Singapore: Institute of Southeast Asian Studies.

Loh, Francis Kok Wah. 1988. "Chinese New Villagers and Political Identity in Malaysia." In J. Cushman and Wang Gungwu, eds., *Changing Identities of the Southeast Asian Chinese Since World War II*. Hong Kong: Hong Kong University Press.

——— (ed.). 1997. *Sabah and Sarawak: The Politics of Development and Federalism*. Special issue. *Kajian Malaysia* 15 (1&2).

———. 1999a. "The Sabah State Elections 1999." *Aliran Monthly* 19(3): 33–37, 39–40.

———. 1999b. "Where Has (Ethnic) Politics Gone? The Case of the Barisan Nasional Non-Malay Politicians and Political Parties." Paper read at Research

Workshop on Southeast Asian Pluralisms: Social Resources for Civility and Participation in Malaysia, Singapore and Indonesia, Petaling Jaya, Aug. 5–6.

———. 2000. "A Crisis of Malay Rights or an UMNO Crisis?" *Aliran Monthly* 20(7): 2, 4–7.

———. 2001. "The Nanyang Takeover Crisis: Representing or Opposing Community Interests?" *Aliran Monthly* 21(5): 2, 4–8.

———. 2002a. "New Threats to the Electoral System." *Aliran Monthly* 22(3): 4–8.

———. 2002b. "NGOs and Non-electoral Politics." *Aliran Monthly* 22(11): 2–9.

———. 2003. "Towards a New Politics of Fragmentation and Contestation." In F. Loh K. W. and J. Saravanamuttu, eds., *New Politics in Malaysia*. Singapore: Institute of Southeast Asian Studies.

———, and Saravanamuttu, Johan, eds. 2003. *New Politics in Malaysia*. Singapore: Institute of Southeast Asian Studies.

Loone, Susan. 2001a. "PAS Refuses to Sign BA Joint Statement on Islamic State." *Malaysiakini*, July 10.

———. 2001b. " 'I Never Said Islamic State Plan Deferred': Fadzil." *Malaysiakini*, July 12.

Lumumba-Kasongo, Tukumbi. 1995. "Social Movements and the Quest for Democracy in Liberia: MOJA and Its Transformation into a Political Party." In M. Mamdani and E. Wamba-dia-Wamba, eds., *African Studies in Social Movements and Democracy*. Dakar: Codesria.

Lustick, Ian. 1979. "Stability in Deeply Divided Societies: Consociationalism versus Control." *World Politics* 31(3): 325–44.

Lyon, M. L. 1979. "The Dakwah Movement in Malaysia." *Review of Indonesian and Malayan Affairs* 13(2): 34–45.

Mackie, Jamie. 1999. "Tackling the Chinese Problem." In G. Forrester, ed., *Post-Soeharto Indonesia: Renewal or Chaos?* Singapore: Institute of Southeast Asian Studies.

———. 2004. "Jigsaw of Jakarta's Presidential Race." *The Australian*, May 13.

Mahathir Mohamad. 1970. *The Malay Dilemma*. Singapore: Times Books International.

———. 1991. *Vision 2020*. Kuala Lumpur: Institute of Strategic and International Studies/Malaysian Business Council.

Mainwaring, Scott, and Eduardo Viola. 1984. "New Social Movements, Political Culture, and Democracy: Brazil and Argentina in the 1980s." *Telos* 61: 17–52.

Mak Lau Fong. 1981. *The Sociology of Secret Societies: A Study of Chinese Secret Societies in Singapore and Peninsular Malaysia*. Kuala Lumpur: Oxford University Press.

Makmor Tumin. 1998. "NGO Dalam Sistem Demokrasi Malaysia." *Massa*, May 16: 62–63.

Malaysian NGOs. 1999. *Malaysian Charter on Human Rights*. Petaling Jaya: ERA Consumer.

Malaysian Students. 1999. "Manifesto Mahasiswa Malaysia." *HarakahDaily*, Nov. 21.

Mandal, Sumit. 2004. "Transethnic Solidarities, Racialisation and Social Equality." In E. T. Gomez, ed., *The State of Malaysia: Ethnicity, Equity and Reform*. New York: RoutledgeCurzon.

Manderson, Lenore. 1980. *Women, Politics, and Change: The Kaum Ibu UMNO, Malaysia 1945–1972*. Kuala Lumpur: Oxford University Press.

Manirajan, R. and Zarina Tahir. 1999. "Alternative Front Fails to Deny Two-thirds Majority." *Sun*, Dec. 1.

March, James G., and Johan P. Olsen. 1984. "The New Institutionalism: Organizational Factors in Political Life." *American Political Science Review* 78: 734–49.

Marina Mahathir. 1999. "The Claim for Reformation." *The Star*, Sept. 23.

Marina Yusoff. 1999. "Bukti Kukuh Tentang Penipuan Pilihanraya," Dec. 10. <http://pemantau.tripod.com/artikel/11Dec1999bukti.html> (accessed Apr. 28, 2005).

Martinez, Patricia. 1999. "More than Meets the Eye: More Complex Factors to Explain Election Outcome." *Aliran Monthly* 19(10): 10–11.

———. 2003. "Complex Configurations: The Women's Agenda for Change and the Women's Candidacy Initiative." In M. L. Weiss and Saliha Hassan, eds., *Social Movements in Malaysia: From Moral Communities to NGOs*. London: RoutledgeCurzon.

Maznah Mohamad. 2002. "Puteri UMNO: Sound and Fury Signifying Nothing New." *Aliran Monthly* 22(8): 2, 4–6.

———. 2003. "The Contest for Malay Votes in 1999: UMNO's Most Historic Challenge?" In F. Loh K. W. and J. Saravanamuttu, eds., *New Politics in Malaysia*. Singapore: Institute of Southeast Asian Studies.

McAdam, Doug, Sidney Tarrow, and Charles Tilly. 1997. "Toward an Integrated Perspective on Social Movements and Revolution." In M. I. Lichbach and A. S. Zuckerman, eds., *Comparative Politics: Rationality, Culture, and Structure*. Cambridge: Cambridge University Press.

———. 2001. *Dynamics of Contention*. New York: Cambridge University Press.

McGirk, Tim. 2001. "The Torch Passes." *Time* (Asia), Aug. 6.

Means, Gordon P. 1985–86. "The Orang Asli: Aboriginal Policies in Malaysia." *Pacific Affairs* 58(4): 637–52.

———. 1991. *Malaysian Politics: The Second Generation*. Singapore: Oxford University Press.

———. 1996. "Soft Authoritarianism in Malaysia and Singapore." *Journal of Democracy* 7(4): 103–17.

"Menteri Besar Selangor Bantah Skandal Seks." 2000. *Jawa Pos*, July 7.

Mietzner, Marcus. 1999. "Nahdlatul Ulama and the 1999 General Election in Indonesia." In S. Blackburn, ed., *Pemilu: The 1999 Indonesian Election*. Clayton, Victoria: Monash Asia Institute.

Milne, R. S., and Diane K. Mauzy. 1999. *Malaysian Politics under Mahathir*. New York: Routledge.

Milner, A. C. 1991. "Inventing Politics: The Case of Malaysia." *Past and Present: A Journal of Historical Studies* 132: 104–29.

MINDS, ed. 1997. *Masyarakat Madani: Satu Tinjauan Awal*. Ampang, Selangor: Malaysian Institute of Development Strategies.

Mohammad Fajrul Falaakh. 1999. "Islam and the Current Transition to Democracy in Indonesia." In A. Budiman, B. Hatley, and D. Kingsbury, eds., *Reformasi: Crisis and Change in Indonesia*. Clayton, Victoria: Monash Asia Institute.

Mohd. Azizuddin Mohd. Sani. 1999. "Mahasiswa Pasca Krisis." Unpublished paper.

Molyneux, Joseph I. 2000. "Years of Living Dangerously: NGOs and the Development of Democracy in Indonesia." Paper read at 41st annual convention of the International Studies Association, Los Angeles, March 14–18.

Morgan, Michael. 1977. "The Rise and Fall of Malayan Trade Unionism, 1945–50." In Mohamed Amin and M. Caldwell, eds., *Malaya: The Making of a Neo-colony*. Nottingham: Spokesman Books.

Muhammad Ikmal Said. 1992. "Ethnic Perspectives of the Left in Malaysia." In J. S. Kahn and F. Loh K. W., eds., *Fragmented Vision: Culture and Politics in Contemporary Malaysia*. North Sydney: Asian Studies Association of Australia/Allen and Unwin.

———. 1996. "Malay Nationalism and National Identity." In Muhammad Ikmal Said and Zahid Emby, eds., *Malaysia: Critical Perspectives: Essays in Honour of Syed Husin Ali*. Petaling Jaya: Persatuan Sains Sosial Malaysia.

Muninggar Sri Saraswati. 2004. "Solahuddin's Nomination No Problem Komnas Chief." *Jakarta Post*, May 8.

Munir. 2000. "The Slow Birth of Democracy." *Inside Indonesia* 63: 4–5.

Muridan S. Widjojo, et al. 1999. *Penakluk Rezim Orde Baru: Gerakan Mahasiswa '98*. Jakarta: Pustaka Sinar Harapan.

Musolf, Lloyd, and J. Fred Springer. 1977. "Legislatures and Divided Societies: The Malaysian Parliament and Multi-Ethnicity." *Legislative Studies Quarterly* II(2): 113–36.

Mustafa K. Anuar. 1998. "Defining Democratic Discourses: The Mainstream Malaysian Press." Paper read at REPUSM-GESEAS Project on Discourses and Practices of Democracy in Malaysia Work-in-Progress Meeting, Penang, July 18–19.

———. 2003. "The Role of Malaysia's Mainstream Press in the 1999 General Election." In F. Loh K. W. and J. Saravanamuttu, eds., *New Politics in Malaysia*. Singapore: Institute of Southeast Asian Studies.

Muzaffar Tate. 2003. "New Politics and a New Party." *Aliran Monthly* 23 (7): 2–5.

Nair, Sheila. 1995. "States, Societies and Societal Movements: Power and Resistance in Malaysia and Singapore." Ph.D. diss., University of Minnesota.

———. 1999. "Constructing Civil Society in Malaysia: Nationalism, Hegemony and Resistance." In Jomo K. S., ed., *Rethinking Malaysia*. Hong Kong: Asia 2000/Malaysian Social Science Association.

"Najib: Without Public Rallies, M'sia is Also Democratic." 2003. *Malaysiakini*, Sept. 20.

Nash Rahman. 2002. "Abim Should Mediate between PUM and Writers." *Malaysiakini*, Mar. 2.

National Operations Council. 1969. *The May 13 Tragedy: A Report*. Kuala Lumpur: National Operations Council.

Netto, Anil. 1990. "Don't Panic Dr M!" *Aliran Monthly* 10(3): 2–3.

———. 1994. "A Clean Sweep?" *Aliran Monthly* 14(11): 3–7.

———. 2000. "Lunas: A New Era Begins." *Aliran Monthly* 20(9): 2, 4–6.

———. 2001. "Student Activism Crosses Ethnic Lines." *Malaysiakini*, July 12.

Ng Boon Hooi. 2000. " 'Tudung' Issue May Affect PAS' Chance in Serdang." *Malaysiakini*, Mar. 23.

———, and Loone, Susan. 2000. "Payment to Terengganu is an 'Oil Royalty.' "*Malaysiakini*, Nov. 20.

Ng, Eileen. 2004. "Nik Aziz Warns of 'Fires of Hell.' " *Malaysiakini*, Mar. 15.

Ng Tien Eng. 2003. "The Contest for Chinese Votes: Politics of Negotiation or Politics of Pressure." In F. Loh K. W. and J. Saravanamuttu, eds., *New Politics in Malaysia*. Singapore: Institute of Southeast Asian Studies.

"NGOs 'Hired Prostitutes to Join Rally.' " 1998. *Straits Times*, Oct. 14.

Nicholas, Colin. 2000. *The Orang Asli and the Contest for Resources: Indigenous Politics, Development and Identity in Peninsular Malaysia*. Copenhagen: International Work Group for Indigenous Affairs.

Norton, Augustus Richard. 1996. "Introduction." In A. R. Norton, ed., *Civil Society in the Middle East*. New York: E. J. Brill.

———. 1999. "Associational Life: Civil Society in Authoritarian Political Systems." In M. Tessler, ed., *Area Studies and Social Science: Strategies for Understanding Middle East Politics*. Bloomington: Indiana University Press.

Nursyahbani Katyasungkana. 2000. "Exchanging Power or Changing Power? The Problem of Creating Democratic Institutions." In C. Manning and P. v. Diermen, eds., *Indonesia in Transition: Social Aspects of Reformasi and Crisis*. Singapore: Institute of Southeast Asian Studies.

Offe, Claus. 1985. "New Social Movements: Challenging the Boundaries of Institutional Politics." *Social Research* 52(4): 816–68.

Ong, K. 2002. "The 2002 Delimitation Exercise." *Aliran Monthly* 22(8): 33–35, 40.

Oon, Yeoh. 1999. "Divided Malay Electorate Gives Minorities Clout." *Nikkei Weekly*, Sept. 13.

Oorjitham, Santha. 2000. "A New Type of Activism: The Post-Anwar Era Gives Rise to Lobby Groups." *Asiaweek*, Nov. 3: 32.

Ostrom, Elinor. 1998. "A Behavioral Approach to the Rational Choice Theory of Collective Action." *American Political Science Review* 92(1): 1–22.

Oxhorn, Philip. 1994. "Where Did All the Protesters Go? Popular Mobilization and the Transition to Democracy in Chile." *Latin American Perspectives* 82(21): 49–68.

"Pak Lah Steps into Heaven-for-Votes Row." 2004. *Malaysiakini*, Mar. 9.

Pereira, Brendan. 1999. "Umno Battles PAS for Malay Hearts." *Straits Times*, June 29.

————. 2003. "Mainstream Newspaper Sales Go Up." *Straits Times*, Feb. 19.

Platzdasch, Bernhard. 2000. "Islamic Reaction to a Female President." In C. Manning and P. v. Diermen, eds., *Indonesia in Transition: Social Aspects of Reformasi and Crisis*. Singapore: Institute of Southeast Asian Studies.

"Police Raid Malaysiakini." 2003. *Malaysiakini*, Jan. 20.

PuruShotam, Nirmala. 1998. "Between Compliance and Resistance: Women and the Middle-Class Way of Life in Singapore." In K. Sen and M. Stivens, eds., *Gender and Power in Affluent Asia*. New York: Routledge.

Putnam, Robert. 1993. *Making Democracy Work: Civic Traditions in Modern Italy*. Princeton, NJ: Princeton University Press.

————. 2000. *Bowling Alone: The Collapse and Revival of American Community*. New York: Simon and Schuster.

Rabushka, Alvin, and Kenneth A. Shepsle. 1972. *Politics in Plural Societies: A Theory of Democratic Instability*. Columbus, OH: Charles E. Merrill.

Rachagan, Sothi. 1984. "Ethnic Representation and the Electoral System." In S. Husin Ali, ed., *Kaum Kelas dan Pembangunan Malaysia/Ethnicity, Class and Development Malaysia*. Kuala Lumpur: Persatuan Sains Sosial Malaysia.

Raja Petra Kamarudin. 1999. "Open Letter to the Electorate: Was It Really the People's Choice?" *Aliran Monthly* 19(10): 14–5.

Rajoo, R. 1985. "World-view of the Indians with Regard to Their Social Identity and Belonging in Malaysia." In Mohd. Taib Osman, ed., *Malaysian Worldview*. Singapore: Institute of Southeast Asian Studies.

Ramasamy, P. 1984. "Malaysian Indians: Ethnic and Class Loyalties." In S. Husin Ali, ed., *Kaum Kelas dan Pembangunan Malaysia/Ethnicity, Class and Development Malaysia*. Kuala Lumpur: Persatuan Sains Sosial Malaysia.

Reid, Anthony. 1997. "Endangered Identity: Kadazan or Dusun in Sabah (East Malaysia)." *Journal of Southeast Asian Studies* 28(1): 120–36.

Rodan, Garry, ed. 1996. *Political Oppositions in Industrialising Asia*. London: Routledge.

————. 1997. "Civil Society and Other Political Possibilities in Southeast Asia." *Journal of Contemporary Asia* 27(2): 156–78.

Roff, Margaret. 1969. The Rise and Demise of Kadazan Nationalism. *Journal of Southeast Asian History* 10 (2):326-43

Roff, William R. 1994. *The Origins of Malay Nationalism*. 2d ed. Kuala Lumpur: Oxford University Press.

Rohana Ariffin. 1997. *Women and Trade Unions in Peninsular Malaysia with Special Reference to MTUC and CUEPACS*. Penang: Universiti Sains Malaysia.

————. 1988. "Malaysian Women's Participation in Trade Unions." In N. Heyzer, ed., *Daughters in Industry: Work Skills and Consciousness of Women Workers in Asia*. Kuala Lumpur: Asian and Pacific Development Centre.

Rueschemeyer, Dietrich. 1997. "The Self-Organization of Society and Democratic Rule: Specifying the Relationship." Paper read at annual meeting of the American Political Science Association, Washington, DC, Aug. 28–31.

Rustam A. Sani. 1999. "Malaysia's Economic and Political Crisis Since September 1998." Paper read at 2d International Malaysian Studies Conference, Kuala Lumpur, Aug. 2–4.

Ruth Indiah Rahayu. 2001. "The Women's Movement in Reformasi Indonesia." In D. Kingsbury and A. Budiman, eds., *Indonesia: The Uncertain Transition*. Adelaide: Crawford House.

Saliha Hassan. 1997. "Islamic Revivalism and State Response to Islamic-Oriented Non-Governmental Organisations in Malaysia." Paper read at workshop on Islamic Revivalism and State Response: The Experiences of Malaysia, Indonesia and Brunei, Institute of Southeast Asian Studies, Singapore, June 2–3.

―――. 1998. "Non-governmental Organisations and Political Participation in Malaysia." Paper read at meeting on Discourses and Practices of Democracy in Malaysia, Universiti Sains Malaysia, Penang, July 18–19.

―――. 2003. "Islamic Non-governmental Organisations." In M. L. Weiss and Saliha Hassan, eds., *Social Movements in Malaysia: From Moral Communities to NGOs*. London: RoutledgeCurzon.

―――, and Meredith L. Weiss. 1999. "KeADILan: Another 'Parti Nyamuk'?" *Saksi 6*.

Salleh Abas and K. Das. 1989. *May Day for Justice: The Lord President's Version*. Kuala Lumpur: Magnus Books.

Santiago, Charles, and M. Nadarajah. 1999. "The Anwar Debacle and the Potential for Democratic Reforms in Malaysia." In K. Gaerlen, ed., *Transition to Democracy: Case Studies on the Philippines, Thailand, South Korea, Indonesia and Malaysia*. Quezon City, Philippines: Institute for Popular Democracy.

Sanusi Osman. 1989. *Ikatan Etnik dan Kelas di Malaysia*. Bangi: Universiti Kebangsaan Malaysia.

Sanusi Osman, and Ang Hiok Gai. 1998. *Masyarakat Adil: Asas-asas Perjuangan PRM*. Kuala Lumpur: Parti Rakyat Malaysia.

Saravanamuttu, Johan. 1992. "The State, Ethnicity and the Middle-Class Factor: Addressing Nonviolent Democratic Change in Malaysia." In K. Rupesinghe, ed., *Internal Conflict and Governance*. New York: St. Martin's Press.

―――. 1997. "Transforming Civil Societies in ASEAN Countries (with special focus on Malaysia and Singapore)." CIS Working Paper 1997–98. Toronto: Centre for International Studies, University of Toronto.

―――. 2000. "Act of Betrayal: The Snuffing Out of Local Democracy in Malaysia." *Aliran Monthly* 20(4): 23–25.

―――. 2003a. "The Eve of the 1999 General Election: From NEP to *Reformasi*." In F. Loh K. W. and J. Saravanamuttu, eds., *New Politics in Malaysia*. Singapore: Institute of Southeast Asian Studies.

―――. 2003b. "NGO Candidates for the Election?" *Aliran Monthly* 23(6): 14–16.

Sarwono Kusumaatmadja. 2000. "Through the Crisis and Beyond: The Evolution of the Environment Movement." In C. Manning and P. v. Diermen, eds., *Indonesia in Transition: Social Aspects of Reformasi and Crisis*. Singapore: Institute of Southeast Asian Studies.

Schedler, Andreas. 2002. "The Menu of Manipulation." *Journal of Democracy* 13(2): 36–50.

Schmitter, Philippe C. 1992. "The Consolidation of Democracy and the Representation of Social Groups." *American Behavioral Scientist* 35(4/5): 422–49.

Schuman, Michael. 2003. "The Politics of Islam." *Time* (Asia), Mar. 10 <http://www. time.com/time/asia/covers/501030310/politics.html> (accessed Apr. 26, 2005).

Scott, James C. 1968. *Political Ideology in Malaysia: Reality and the Beliefs of an Elite.* New Haven, CT: Yale University Press.

Searle, Peter. 1983. *Politics in Sarawak, 1970–1976: The Iban Perspective.* Singapore: Oxford University Press.

Shameen, Assif. 1999. "Malaysia's Pandora's Box State." *Asiaweek* (online edition), Dec. 7 <http://www.asiaweek.com/asiaweek/business/9912/08/index. html> (accessed Apr. 26, 2005).

"A Shameful Episode." 1998. *Aliran Monthly* 18(8): 40.

Shamsul A. B. 1996a. "The Construction and Transformation of a Social Identity: Malayness and Bumiputeraness Re-examined." *Journal of Asian and African Studies* 52: 15–33.

————. 1996b. "Nations-of-Intent in Malaysia." In S. Tonnesson and H. Antlöv, eds., *Asian Forms of the Nation.* London: Curzon Press.

————. 1999. "From *Orang Kaya Baru* to *Melayu Baru*: Cultural Construction of the Malay 'New Rich.'" In M. Pinches, ed., *Culture and Privilege in Capitalist Asia.* London: Routledge.

Sherlock, Stephen. 2004. *The 2004 Indonesian Elections: How the System Works and What the Parties Stand For.* Canberra: Centre for Democratic Institutions.

Sloane, Patricia. 1996. "Good Works and Networks: Islam, Modernity, and Entrepreneurship among the Malays." Ph.D. diss., St. Anthony's College, Oxford University.

Snider, Nancy L. 1968. "What Happened in Penang?" *Asian Survey* 8(12): 960–75.

————. 1977. "Malaysian Noncommunal Political Parties." In J. A. Lent, ed., *Cultural Pluralism in Malaysia: Polity, Military, Mass Media, Education, Religion.* DeKalb: Center for Southeast Asian Studies, Nothern Illinois University.

Social Owl. 1999. *'Islamic State': What Are We Afraid Of?* Petaling Jaya: Gerakbudaya Enterprise.

"'Special Rights': No Such Thing in Islam – Nik Aziz." 2000. *Harakah Daily*, Aug. 18.

Stafford, D. Geoffrey. 1997. "Malaysia's New Economic Policy and the Global Economy: The Evolution of Ethnic Accommodation." *The Pacific Review* 10(4): 556–80.

Stenson, Michael. 1970. *Industrial Conflict in Malaya: Prelude to the Communist Revolt of 1948.* London: Oxford University Press.

————. 1980. *Class, Race, and Colonialism in West Malaysia: The Indian Case.* St. Lucia: University of Queensland Press.

Stepan, Alfred. 1988. *Rethinking Military Politics: Brazil and the Southern Cone.* Princeton, NJ: Princeton University Press.

Stewart, Ian. 2000. "Ruling in Islamic State Silences Women." *South China Morning Post,* July 31.

Suaram. 1999. "Sabah State Elections 1999 Monitor's Report." Unpublished report.

"Switching Teams." 1999. *Asiaweek,* Aug. 6: 11.

Syamsuddin Haris. 1997. "Pembinaan Politik, Demokratisasi dan Pembentukan 'Civil Society': Problematik Kerpartaian Indonesia di bawah Order Baru." *Jurnal Ilmu Politik* 17: 58–68.

Syamsurizal Panggabean. 2000. " 'Civil Society' Sebagai Kawasan Kebebasan." *Tashwirul Afkar* 7: 88–95.

Syed Arabi Idid and Mazni Hj. Buyong. 1995. *Malaysia's GE 1995: People Issues and Media Use.* Bangi: Jabatan Komunikasi, Universiti Kebangsaan Malaysia.

Syed Husin Ali. 1984. "Social Relations: The Ethnic and Class Factors." In S. Husin Ali, ed., *Kaum Kelas dan Pembangunan Malaysia/Ethnicity, Class and Development Malaysia.* Kuala Lumpur: Persatuan Sains Sosial Malaysia.

———. 2000. "Special Position of Malays." *Aliran Monthly* 20(7): 8–9.

Tan Beng Hui and Cecilia Ng. 2003. "Embracing the Challenge of Representation: The Women's Movement and Electoral Politics in Malaysia." In F. Loh K. W. and J. Saravanamuttu, eds., *New Politics in Malaysia.* Singapore: Institute of Southeast Asian Studies.

Tan Boon Kean and Bishan Singh. 1994. *Uneasy Relations: The State and NGOs in Malaysia.* Kuala Lumpur: Gender and Development Programme, Asian and Pacific Development Centre.

Tan, Joceline. 2000. "PAS Women Seek Active Role." *New Straits Times,* June 11.

Tan Liok Ee. 1988. *The Rhetoric of Bangsa and Minzu: Community and Nation in Tension, the Malay Peninsula, 1900–1955.* Clayton, Victoria: Centre of Southeast Asian Studies, Monash University.

———. 1997. *The Politics of Chinese Education in Malaya, 1945–1961.* Kuala Lumpur: Oxford University Press.

Tan, Simon. 1990. "The Rise of State Authoritarianism in Malaysia." *Bulletin of Concerned Asian Scholars* 22(3): 32–42.

Tan, Thomas Tsu-Wee. 1983. "Singapore Modernization: A Study of Traditional Chinese Voluntary Associations in Social Change." Ph.D. diss., University of Virginia.

Tarrow, Sidney. 1996. "Making Social Science Work across Space and Time: A Critical Reflection on Robert Putnam's *Making Democracy Work.*" *American Political Science Review* 90(2): 389–97.

Tesoro, Jose Manuel. 2000. "The Parties' Democracy." *Asiaweek,* May 26 <http://www.asiaweek.com/asiaweek/magazine/2000/0526/nat.indon1.html> (accessed Apr. 26, 2005).

Tham Seong Chee. 1977. *The Role and Impact of Formal Associations on the Development of Malaysia.* Bangkok: Friedrich-Ebert-Stiftung.

"Top Indonesian Legislator Ready to be Vice President under Megawati." 2000. Agence France-Presse newswire, Nov. 11.

Törnquist, Olle. 1993. "Democratic 'Empowerment' and Democratisation of Politics: Radical Popular Movements and the May 1992 Philippine Elections." *Third World Quarterly* 14(3): 485–515.

"Towards a Two-party Coalition System?" 1990. *Aliran Monthly* 10(7): 2–3.

"Traffic & Demographics," *Malaysiakini*. <http://www.malaysiakini.com/info/ads.php?t=ia> (accessed Apr. 26, 2005).

Uhlin, Anders. 1997. *Indonesia and the "Third Wave of Democratization": The Indonesian Pro-Democracy Movement in a Changing World*. Richmond and Surrey: Curzon Press.

"Unanswered Questions on BN's Failure in Kelantan." 1999. Bernama newswire, Nov. 30.

United Nations Development Programme. 2003. *Human Development Report 2003*. New York: Oxford University Press.

van Klinken, Gerry. 1999. "Democracy, the Regions and Indonesia's Future." In S. Blackburn, ed., *Pemilu: The 1999 Indonesian Election*. Clayton, Victoria: Monash Asia Institute.

Varshney, Ashutosh. 2002. *Ethnic Conflict and Civic Life: Hindus and Muslims in India*. New Haven, CT: Yale University Press.

Vasil, R. K. 1966. "Why Malaysia Failed." *Quest* 49: 51–59.

———. 1971. *Politics in a Plural Society: A Study of Non-communal Political Parties in West Malaysia*. Kuala Lumpur: Oxford University Press.

Verma, Vidhu. 2002. *Malaysia: State and Civil Society in Transition*. Boulder, CO: Lynne Rienner.

von Vorys, Karl. 1975. *Democracy without Consensus: Communalism and Political Stability in Malaysia*. Princeton, NJ: Princeton University Press.

Wan Hamidi Hamid. 2000. "Former Selangor MB's Friend Lying Low." *Straits Times*, Aug. 13.

———. 2001. "PAS, Umno Members Use Mosques as Battlegrounds." *Straits Times*, Apr. 13.

Women's Agenda for Change. 1999. *Women's Agenda for Change*. Kajang, Selangor: Women's Agenda for Change.

Walker, Millidge. 1996. *NGO Participation in a Corporatist State: The Example of Indonesia*. Berkeley: Institute of Urban and Regional Development, University of California.

"We Apologise." 1999. *Aliran Monthly* 19(8): 39.

Weiss, Meredith L. 1999. "What Will Become of *Reformasi*? Ethnicity and Changing Political Norms in Malaysia," *Contemporary Southeast Asia* 21(3): 424–50.

———. 2000a. "The 1999 Malaysian General Elections: Issues, Insults, and Irregularities." *Asian Survey* 40(3): 413–35.

———. 2000b. "Political Participation in Malaysia." Unpublished paper.

———. 2003. "Malaysian NGOs: History, Legal Framework, and Characteristics." In M. L. Weiss and Saliha Hassan, eds., *Social Movements in Malaysia: From Moral Communities to NGOs*. London: RoutledgeCurzon.

———. 2004a. "The Changing Shape of Islamic Politics in Malaysia." *Journal of East Asian Studies* 4(1): 139–73.

———. 2004b. "With the People? The Checkered Path of Student Activism in Malaysia." Paper read at 4th Malasyian Studies International Conference, Bangi, Malaysia, Aug. 3–5.

Weiss, Stanley A. 2003. "An Early Guide to Indonesia's Next President." *Asia Times,* Sept. 4.

Welsh, Bridget. 1996. "Attitudes toward Democracy in Malaysia: Challenges to the Regime?" *Asian Survey* 36(9): 882–903.

Wickham, Carrie Rosefsky. 2002. *Mobilizing Islam: Religion, Activism, and Political Change in Egypt.* New York: Columbia University Press.

Wimar Witoelar. 2000. "Horizontal Conflict and the Ordinary People of Post-Suharto Indonesia." Paper read at conference on Religion and Culture in Asia Pacific: Violence or Healing, Melbourne, Oct. 22–25.

Winters, Jeffrey. 2001. "Leadership in Indonesian Politics." Paper read at Indonesia Next conference, Jakarta, May.

Wong, James Wing On. 2001. "Is the 'Islamic State' a Real Issue?" *Malaysiakini,* July 4.

———. 2004a. "Five Reasons Why the Opposition Got Mauled." *Malaysiakini,* March 22.

———. 2004b. "The Tasks Ahead for PAS, Keadilan." *Malaysiakini,* March 25.

Xavier, Irene, and Maria Chin Abdullah. 1999. "Launching the Women's Agenda for Change." *Aliran Monthly* 19(6): 33–35, 40.

Y. Mansoor Marican. 1976. "Malay Nationalism and the Islamic Party of Malaysia." *Islamic Studies* 16(1): 291–301.

Yamamoto, Tadashi, ed. 1995a. *Emerging Civil Society in the Asia Pacific Community: Nongovernmental Underpinnings of the Emerging Asia Pacific Regional Community.* Singapore: Institute of Southeast Asian Studies.

———. 1995b. "Integrative Report." In T. Yamamoto, ed., *Emerging Civil Society in the Asia Pacific Community: Nongovernmental Underpinnings of the Emerging Asia Pacific Regional Community.* Singapore: Institute of Southeast Asian Studies.

Yap Mun Ching. 2002. "Muslim Groups Seek Royal Help to Curb 'Abusers' of Islam." *Malaysiakini,* Feb. 4.

Yeoh, Michael Oon Kheng. 1988. "The Chinese Political Dilemma." In Ling Liong Sik et al., eds., *The Future of Malaysian Chinese.* Kuala Lumpur: Malaysian Chinese Association.

Yong Mun Cheong. 1974. "Malaysia in 1973: The Search for a New Political and Economic Order." In Yong M. C., ed., *Trends in Malaysia II.* Singapore: Singapore University Press/Institute of Southeast Asian Studies.

Young, Iris Marion. 1999. "State, Civil Society, and Social Justice." In I. Shapiro and C. Hacker-Cordón, eds., *Democracy's Value.* New York: Cambridge University Press.

Young, Ken. 1999a. "The National Picture—A Victory for Reform?" In S. Blackburn, ed., *Pemilu: The 1999 Indonesian Election.* Clayton, Victoria: Monash Asia Institute.

————. 1999b. "Post-Suharto: A Change of Regime?" In A. Budiman, B. Hatley, and D. Kingsbury, eds., *Reformasi: Crisis and Change in Indonesia.* Clayton, Victoria: Monash Asia Institute.

Zaharom Nain. 1998. "Commercialisation, Concentration and Control: The Structure of the Malaysian Media Industry and Its Implications for Democracy." Paper read at REPUSM-GESEAS Project on Discourses and Practices of Democracy in Malaysia Work-in-Progress Meeting, Penang, July 18–19.

Zainah Anwar. 1987. *Islamic Revivalism in Malaysia: Dakwah among the Students.* Petaling Jaya: Pelanduk Publications.

Zakaria, Haji Ahmad. 1989. "Malaysia: Quasi Democracy in a Divided Society." In L. Diamond, J. J. Linz, and S. M. Lipset, eds., *Democracy in Developing Countries,* vol 3: *Asia.* Boulder, CO: Lynne Rienner.

Zawawi Ibrahim. 1989. "Ethnicity in Malaysia." In D. Kumar and S. Kadirgamar, eds., *Ethnicity: Identity, Conflict and Crisis.* Hong Kong: ARENA Press.

————. 1996. "The Making of a Subaltern Discourse in the Malaysian Nation-State: New Subjectivities and the Poetics of Orang Asli Dispossession and Identity." *Tonan Ajia Kenkyu* [Southeast Asian Studies] 34(3): 568–99.

Zifirdaus Adnan. 1990. "Islamic Religion: Yes, Islamic (Political) Ideology: No! Islam and the State in Indonesia." In A. Budiman, ed., *State and Civil Society in Indonesia.* Clayton, Victoria: Centre of Southeast Asian Studies, Monash University.

INDEX

In this index an "f" after a number indicates a separate reference on the next page, and an "ff" indicates separate references on the next two pages. A continuous discussion over two or more pages is indicated by a span of page numbers, e.g., "57–59."

National Justice Party, *see* Parti Keadilan Nasional
National Mandate Party (PAN), 201, 204f, 209, 229, 231f, 282nn17, 18, 285n50
National Muslim Students' Association (PKPIM), 111, 114
National Operations Council (NOC), 85
National Party, 76
National Students' Action Front (BBMN), 165, 271n15
National Union of Plantation Workers (NUPW), 69
NCP, *see* National Convention Party
NDP, *see* National Development Policy
Nehru, Jawaharlal, 68
NEP, *see* New Economic Policy
Neurocratic tendencies, 40
New Awakening Party (PKB), 204f, 209, 216–17, 237, 282n22
New Economic Policy (NEP), 86–87, 104, 111, 115, 120, 165, 180, 182
New Hope Society, 60
New Order Indonesia, 43–44, 45–46, 193, 202, 206, 208f, 210ff, 213ff, 222f, 237, 246, 283–84nn33, 40, 42; fall of, 194, 242; opposition to, 195–99; student activism, 218, 220; Muslims and, 227–28
New social movements (NSMs), 28–29, 258n7
Newspapers, 61, 156, 283–84n40
New UMNO, 91
New Villages, 88, 98
New Vision Policy (NVP), 182, 271n14, 279n29
NGLU, *see* Nanyang (South Seas) General Labour Union
NGOs, *see* Nongovernmental organizations
Nik Aziz Nik Mat, 148, 154, 243–44
Nipah virus, 132
NOC, *see* National Operations Council
Nongovernmental organizations (NGOs), 1, 7f, 9ff, 14–15, 24, 44, 48, 109f, 112–13 (table), 117f, 122, 125, 156, 179, 185, 189, 197, 237, 258n8, 267n40, 269nn57, 58, 62, 64, 270n1, 272–73n30, 277n6, 283n39, 285n58; religious issues, 17–18; defining, 27–28; Malaysian, 29–30; Islamist, 42, 111, 114, 129; political, 103, 120–21; government opposition to, 123–24; Reformasi movement and, 135, 141,

171; Indonesia, 207, 214, 216, 221–23, 231, 235–36; labor movement and, 224–25
NSMs, *see* New social movements
NU, *see* Nahdlatul Ulama
NUPW, *see* National Union of Plantation Workers
Nurcholish Majid, 235
NVP, *see* New Vision Policy

Official Secrets Act, 122
"One Heart, One Vision" campaign, 88
Onn bin Jaafar, 74, 76, 80, 179, 263n32
Operation Lalang, 119, 124
Opinion (journal), 123
Opposition Front, 125
Orang Asli, 79, 90–91, 96
Orde Baru, *see* New Order Indonesia
Organisasi tanpa bentuk (OTB), 224
Organizations, 122; ideological and political maneuvering, 5–6; Malay, 59–62; women's, 62–63; Chinese, 63–67; Indian, 67–70
ORMAS, *see* Social Organizations Law
OTB, *see* Organisasi tanpa bentuk

Pam Swakarsa, 202
PAN, *see* Partai Amanat Nasional
Pancasila ideology, 195ff, 227f, 280n2
Pan-Malayan Federation of Trade Unions (PMFTU), 66–67, 69, 71, 265n17
Pan-Malayan Labour Party (PMLP), 93
Pan-Malayan/Malaysian Islamic Party (PMIP; PAS), 78, 92, 94, 97f, 106, 114, 125, 129, 150, 157, 159, 181, 258n7, 259n13, 261n11, 263n35, 264n1, 266–67nn31, 34, 269nn64, 65, 275nn51, 54, 55, 276n64; and UMNO, 103–4; Islamicism of, 104–5, 107f, 151–55; and Reformasi movement, 139, 160, 170, 172; elections, 145, 147f, 242, 243–44. *See also* Parti Islam SeMalaysia
Panwaslak, 225
PAP, *see* People's Action Party
Partai Amanat Nasional (PAN), 201, 204f, 209, 229, 231f, 282nn17, 18, 285n50
Partai Bulan Bintang (PBB), 229, 285n50
Partai Demokrasi Indonesia (PDI), 196, 197–98, 209, 281n6
Partai Demokrat (PD), 245
Partai Keadilan (PK), 229
Partai Keadilan Sejahtera (PKS), 205, 245

EAST-WEST CENTER SERIES
ON CONTEMPORARY ISSUES
IN ASIA AND THE PACIFIC